The Wheel of Things

A biography of L.M. Montgomery
author of *Anne of Green Gables*

Mollie Gillen

Goodread Biographies

CANADIAN CATALOGUING IN PUBLICATION DATA

Gillen, Mollie.
  The wheel of things
Bibliography: p.
Includes index.
ISBN 0-88780-109-9

1. Montgomery, L. M. (Lucy Maud), 1874-1942 —
Biography.   2. Novelists, Canadian (English) — 20th
century — Biography.*   I. Title.
PS8526.045Z63 1983   C813'.52   C83-098340-6
PR9199.3.M6Z63 1983

First published in 1975 by Fitzhenry & Whiteside Limited
Published in paperback 1983 by Goodread Biographies
Canadian Lives series publisher: James Lorimer

Photo Credits
Mrs. Ruth Campbell: Hugh John Montgomery, Alexander Macneill, Lucy
Macneill; *Public Archives of Canada:* Senator Donald Montgomery,
Maud at 16, Maud at 19, Maud with veil; *Dr. Stuart Macdonald:*
Old Macneill homestead, Maud at 28, Maud at 11, Maud at 33, Ewan at 40,
Glasgow 1911, Stuart (at 3) and Chester (at 6); *Confederation Centre,
Charlottetown:* Anne ms. page 1; *Wilfrid Eggleston:* Ephraim Weber; *George
McMillan:* George MacMillan, Ewan and George; *Public Archives of PEI:*
Maud with amateur company, Cavendish cemetery; *Mrs. M. Laird:* Stuart as
national junior gymnastics champion, 1924 trip; *Mrs. D. St. John:* Chester at 3,
Stuart at 4.

Goodread Biographies is the paperback imprint of
Formac Publishing Company Limited
333 - 1657 Barrington Street
Halifax, Nova Scotia
B3J 2A1

Printed and bound in Canada

Where, then, is the River? My dream told me to find it . . . . By it one attains freedom from the Wheel of Things . . . .

—Rudyard Kipling
(*Kim*)

Contents

Preface and Acknowledgements

Maud Montgomery had many close friends, men and women both, but with two men she corresponded for forty-odd of her sixty-seven years. One of them, Ephraim Weber, a Canadian, she met briefly three times—in 1928, 1930 and 1935. The second, George Boyd MacMillan, a Scot, she met once only, when he and a friend accompanied her and her husband on a ten-day trip during her honeymoon visit to Scotland in 1911.

The letters she wrote to Weber were handed after his death to his former student and long-time friend Professor Wilfrid Eggleston and lodged in the Public Archives in Ottawa. When work on this book began, no one had tried to discover if her letters to George MacMillan had survived.

My attempt to locate them began with a letter to the Clackmannan County Librarian in Alloa, where I knew Mr MacMillan had lived. From there, through the kindness of many people, through a variety of searches—to find a will (and the name of a possible executor), to find a colleague (Mr. John Gardner, a fellow-reporter), and to find possible descendants or relatives—I was led to Mr George McMillan, son of George Boyd MacMillan's brother John, who lives with his sister Margaretha in Clackmannan.

And the miracle happened—the sort of miracle all biographers hope to experience. The letters had indeed survived, carefully fastened in folders in chronological order, and preserved in his uncle's trunk—the classic location for such undiscovered treasure—by Mr MacMillan's nephew (he has changed the spelling of his name, by local custom, to avoid confusion).

This collection (some eighty long letters, with postcards, clippings and briefer notes) will now find a home in Ottawa, available for future scholars who want to find out more about L. M. Montgomery. It has revealed much about her, although of course for this book much rich material has had to be reluctantly omitted. One fact of incidental but special interest emerges and is worth emphasizing: she wished to be known either as L. M. Montgomery or Maud Montgomery. "I was never in my life called 'Lucy Maud,'" she wrote. "My friends called me 'Maud' and nothing else." And she won her battle to have *Anne* published under the name L. M. Montgomery and not "Lucy Maud Montgomery which I loathe."

On her Island in summer, tourists drive the red roads through a landscape of field and sea and sky to visit Green Gables in its beautiful setting not far from where Maud Montgomery grew up "eleven miles from a railway and twenty-four miles from a town, but only half a mile from one of the finest sea-beaches in the world."

One of her monuments on Prince Edward Island is the National Park at Cavendish, its eighteen-hole golf course embracing the farms and fields, the lanes and woods she had loved so well. The other is the body of her work, especially *Anne of Green Gables,* still selling millions of copies in dozens of languages around the world. Mention Anne to any woman in English-speaking countries, and the reply, more often than not, will be, "I was brought up on her."

A plaque on the lawn of the Manse at Leaskdale erected by the Ontario Historic Sites Board in July 1965 commemorates Maud's residence there. In Charlottetown, Montgomery Hall was opened at Prince of Wales College in 1961 as a women's residence and student centre. In 1969 the Canadian National Railway renamed its 100-car ferry plying between New Brunswick and the Island the *Lucy Maud Montgomery.*

The old home of Maud's grandparents where she spent those magic years of growing up has been for a long time a heap of rubble, but the federal government has sponsored the restoration of a house of the period, opened in August 1973, "approximately 100 years old and an almost exact duplicate of the MacNeill home" to serve as the present Cavendish post office, with Mary Lowther, granddaughter of Maud's Uncle John as its first postmaster. It is unfortunate that the brochure about the post office spelt Macneill with a capital N, and wrongly identified a portrait of Aunt Mary Lawson as that of Grandmother Macneill.

Maud's birthplace, the little frame house at Clifton (New London) looking out over the incredibly blue water, has become an L. M. Montgomery museum. It has her wedding dress and shoes, and other souvenirs: in one of her scrapbooks this "relic hunter of the most aggravated description," as she once described herself, preserved a piece of fur from Daffy the cat. At Park Corner, by Anne's Lake of Shining Waters, home of Maud's Uncle John and Aunt Annie Campbell and her cousins, Stella, Frederica and George, can be seen the great wooden bed with its patchwork quilt where she slept in the upstairs bedroom; the parlour downstairs in which she was married, the organ that played for her wedding; first editions of her books; literary scrapbooks, photographs of her family, samples of her handmade lace and other treasures. On the stair landing, the small iron screw against which Maud measured her growth sticks out from the wall: just on a level with her nose "in the dawn of memory," level with her knees when she was grown up. The house, now the home of Ruth Campbell, widow of Uncle John Campbell's grandson James Townsend Campbell, is open to visitors, another L. M. Montgomery museum.

Prince Edward Island is honoured as the home of Canadian Confederation, the location of the conference held in Charlottetown in 1864 out of which came, eventually, the Canadian nation. But it would be hard to say whether this historic event has done more to bring fame to "the only Island there is" than the writing of L. M. Montgomery.

My debt to so many people who have helped me with information and reminiscences cannot be properly repaid. It is invidious to single out those who could give me more from those who, with less to contribute, nevertheless were unfailingly kind in providing what they could. Without any one of them, I could not have produced a work that I hope shows some insight and understanding, and contains as few as possible of the gaps and misinterpretations almost inevitable in any biography. The author must intrude in any work. I can only hope I have done justice to a complex and fascinating personality, with less to work from than I could have wished.

My heartfelt thanks, therefore, to all the following people and institutions for kind and willing assistance:

Chatelaine and its editor, Doris Anderson, for permission to use some sections of my article on L. M. Montgomery, and information collected in the course of research for it.

Archivists in Charlottetown, the Presbyterian Church of Canada, the Free Church of Scotland College, the United Church of Canada.

Dr F. W. P. Bolger, Chairman, Department of History, University of Prince Edward Island, for his encouraging interest in my work and his kind permission to quote from some of Miss Montgomery's youthful letters in *The Years Before "Anne."*

Mrs Ruth Campbell, of Park Corner, P.E.I., who received me privately in her home, now a museum in memory of L. M. Montgomery, where visitors may see the room in which she was married and some of the intimate souvenirs of her life. Mrs Campbell also gave kind permission to use several photographs in her possession.

John Gardner, formerly a reporter with the *Alloa Journal* and friend of George Boyd MacMillan, who brought Miss Montgomery's letters from Scotland for my use, and to whose wholehearted cooperation I owe much.

Professor Wilfrid Eggleston, who directed me to the unpublished correspondence with Ephraim Weber, and whose book *The Green Gables Letters* was an invaluable source.

Mrs Heber Jones (Charlottetown) who drove me to Cavendish; Mrs Murray Laird (Norval); and Miss Anita Webb (Toronto): three sisters whose childhood home was the house now known as Green Gables, and who, as relatives of Miss Montgomery, gave me many reminiscences and photographs.

Dr Stuart Macdonald, Toronto, L. M. Montgomery's son, who received me kindly, gave me information and documents about his famous mother, and his permission to quote from her letters.

George McMillan and his sister Margaretha, of Alloa, Scotland, to whom George Boyd MacMillan left his letters from L. M. Montgomery, and who gave me the unrestricted use of them, together with photographs and other information.

Miss Isobel Macneill, daughter of Maud Montgomery's cousin Murray, who provided family history and a family photograph.

James Kennedy Macneill of Boston, Maud's first cousin, whose childhood recollections have added much to this narrative, and whose friendship I value.

W. M'K. Murray, County Librarian of Clackmannan, whose initial response to my inquiry led to the discovery of the MacMillan letters.

Mrs. J. Goliath, librarian at Prince Albert, for information about that city.

Residents of Leaskdale and Norval, Ontario, whose reminiscences added much detail.

Mrs Donald St John, Uxbridge, Ontario, president of the Uxbridge Historical Society, who gathered together much information and many photographs, and made me familiar with the Leaskdale neighbourhood.

The Reverend and Mrs H. D. Smith who showed me the Norval Manse and Church.

Dr Moncrieff Williamson, director of the Confederation Art Gallery & Museum, Charlottetown, who holds the original manuscript of *Anne of Green Gables*, and who checked other information for me.

Public Archives of Canada and the National Library, Ottawa, whose staff was unfailingly obliging: especially Barbara Wilson (Manuscript Division) and Laura Adams (Newspaper Library).

Mollie Gillen

Toronto, Canada, and London, England, 1975

THE WHEEL OF THINGS

CHAPTER ONE

Beginnings

Wherever chance had brought this child to birth, she would have exulted in what her eyes beheld, made its beauties and eccentricities her own personal possessions, illumined her spirit with a passionate response to every experience, made every stick and stone, rock and tree, ditch and hillock in her environment part of an enchanted country to dwell in. "I had, in my imagination, a passport to fairyland," she wrote.

Had she been a waif in the Sahara Desert, the world would not have known Anne's Lake of Shining Waters, her Haunted Wood, her Green Gables, her Dryad's Bubble; would not have wandered the green corners and sun-steeped ferns of Emily's Land of Uprightness or seen the Wind Woman sweep over the hillside; would never have heard of Pat's Mince Pie Field or the Field of Farewell Summers. But a Maud Montgomery born by chance in the sandy wastes of Africa would still have been a child of secret delights, treasuring her Oasis of Rustling Palms, her Well of Echoes, her Shadowed Sandhills and the Caravans of Ancient Araby.

"The only Island there is," she would say, was her birth-place. In Clifton, a tiny community of green fields and rust-coloured roads on the Atlantic coast of Canada's smallest province, where the northern shore curves away to east and west, Hugh John Montgomery, a country merchant, and his young wife Clara became the parents of a daughter born on 30 November 1874—a date she would later remark with interest as the birth-date of another child, Winston Churchill. The little village of Clifton can't be found on today's maps of the Island. You must look instead for New London. Even then it won't be easy to find, its population little more than the few dozen families who lived in Clifton in 1874.

Hugh was nearly thirty-three, his bride not quite twenty-one when they had married the previous March. She had been Clara Woolner Macneill, daughter of Alexander and Lucy Woolner Macneill of Cavendish. The baby, named Lucy for her grandmother and Maud for herself, inherited a long line of Island ancestors from both father and mother, and some intriguing family legends of which she would make good use in later years. The Macneills and the Montgomerys had arrived in Prince Edward Island about the same time, and both families had produced figures of note in the community. Montgomerys, Macneills, Woolners, Townsends, Simpsons and Campbells still form a network of relationships across the Island, and this newest member of the clan carried some of the blood of all of them.

From Scotland came the first Montgomery in 1769, the first Macneill in 1770 or 1772: from England in 1775 the first Townsend, the first Woolner—comparative newcomer—in 1836. Family tradition says the first Montgomery—another Hugh John—had not intended to settle in Prince Edward Island. He had been heading for Quebec with his wife and family and two brothers. But when the ship anchored off the Island for water after the long Atlantic crossing, Hugh John's wife Mary MacShannon, who had been intolerably seasick, went ashore with the boat for a temporary escape, and made it permanent. Once on dry land, she firmly announced that nothing would ever make her embark again. All Hugh John's protests were in vain. He landed there, perforce, and established the family line in the New World. His grandson Donald, grandfather of the little Maud, was one of seventeen children: known as Big Donald to distinguish him from his cousin, Little Donald. Both became members of the Island Legislature: Big Donald, president of the Legislative Council from 1862, had been appointed to the Canadian Senate a year before this latest grandchild's birth, and served altogether fifty-four years as a legislator, twenty of them in the Senate.

The first Island Macneill, John, came from Campbelltown on the Kintyre Peninsula in the county of Argyll, bringing with him a romantic family history going back to the little island of Colonsay in the Inner Hebrides. Coming unmarried, he settled in Charlottetown, capital of the province. Legend (again) has it that his log cabin was built where the present Legislative Building now stands, and that once, ordered by the governor to stop felling trees without permission, he felled the messenger as well and continued with his work. His marriage around 1780 brought Simpson blood into the family, and with his young wife Margaret he settled in Cavendish in 1791. Their eldest son William, born in Charlottetown in 1781 and great-grandfather of the young Maud Montgomery, had been a member of the Legislature from 1814 to 1834 and comes down in the family story as "Old Speaker Macneill." William was a man of substance: he owned the first four-wheeled carriage in Cavendish. He had been law clerk in Halifax, Nova Scotia, and shipbuilder at French River on the Island before he married, in 1806, Eliza Townsend, daughter of his partner and granddaughter of "a gentleman from England who had received from George Third . . . a grant of land for his services in the British Army." The Townsend tract was named Park Corner, from the name of the family estate in the land they had left. The gentleman's wife Elizabeth, so tradition has it, was so homesick that she stalked the floor of her new home for weeks still wearing her bonnet, refusing to remove it and demanding to return to England. Had she *slept* in it too, all that time, the little Maud used to wonder? There were forceful women in her family tree.

The small frame house in which Hugh and Clara Montgomery lived still stands, today painted white with green trim, but the store on the corner next door where Hugh John operated his business is now a gas station. The young man, possessed of an enterprising energy that would get him into a certain amount of trouble in later years, ambitiously traded with the West Indies and several American ports to further his interests in commerce and navigation. In 1875 he was appointed chairman of a commission to value lands mediating between the tenants and the government of Prince Edward Island, for which he was paid five dollars a day, but this work was completed a year later and his appointment terminated. Already he had started putting fingers in many pies.

This year—1876—brought sadness and a change in his life.

His young wife died from tuberculosis on September 14 in her parents' home at Cavendish when Maud was just over twenty-one months old.

Though she was a precocious child with a prodigious memory, and learned to read and write at an early age through a process of osmosis she could not understand or recall ("I might as well have been born with a capacity for reading"), it is hard to believe that so young a child could really remember seeing her mother lying dead in her coffin, as she later insisted. More likely the scene was conjured up in her vividly imaginative mind by the recollections of her elders. But she has given us a picture of the little girl in her embroidered white muslin dress, held in her weeping father's arms in the room where leaf-shadows danced on the floor, looking down on the fair hair, long lashes and thin face of her mother, so pretty and so still. After this, Maud lived in the old Macneill home in Cavendish with her maternal grandparents, Alexander and Lucy Macneill, and Hugh Montgomery took a variety of different occupations, including, it seems, connection with a firm shipping produce across the country.

It is possible that these widespread business dealings and his father's senatorial experience in a world beyond the small Island province awakened Hugh Montgomery's interest in the developing Canadian West. He also had friends who now lived in that part of Canada known as Saskatchewan, N.W.T. Until 1881, when his daughter was seven, it does not appear that he left Prince Edward Island for any extended period. For a couple of years prior to 1884 he spent summers in Prince Albert as agent for the Saskatchewan Forks Colonization Company, and worked in a real estate office, returning to the Island for the winters. Though she did not live with her father, Maud in these early years was not totally deprived of his presence. Indeed, many of her early recollections include her father's companionship and comments.

"I spent my childhood and girlhood in an old-fashioned Cavendish farmhouse, surrounded by apple orchards," she wrote. No place could have offered more to appease her insatiable appetite for beauty. Everything she has written is shot through with the memories of the child who ran free in the

4

woods and meadows and sandhills of "the old north shore." Shafts of sunlight, shifting shadows, "the rich red of the winding roads . . . the dark dappling of spruce and fir . . . the bracing tang of the salt air"—these were to become her refuge and her inspiration. "Everything was invested with a kind of fairy grace and charm, emanating from my own fancy, the trees that whispered nightly around the old house where I slept, the woodsy nooks I explored, the homestead fields, each individualized by some oddity or fence or shape, the sea whose murmur was never out of my ears—all were radiant with 'the glory and the dream' . . . amid all the commonplaces of life, I was very near to a kingdom of ideal beauty. Between it and me hung only a thin veil. I could never draw it quite aside, but sometimes a wind fluttered it and I caught a glimpse of the enchanting realm beyond—only a glimpse—but those glimpses have always made life worth while."

This would be the "flash" that pulled Emily of New Moon into ecstasy. This instant response to beauty would stay with Maud Montgomery throughout her sixty-seven years of life— the shiver of sudden recognition, the soul-healing touch of splendour. In her mid-fifties she wrote to a friend: "Coming home from a sick call I saw something that suddenly rested me—the pines on the western hill dark against a sunset sky. Oh, there was the way, the truth, the light—sheer ecstasy above the world possessed me—re-youthed me. . . ."

Always, the richness of her inner life—the joys she found in nature, in words, in friendships—would support her through the buffetings of fortune. But there was a core of steel in Maud Montgomery that went beyond even this: the sense of duty. It would delay her marriage until she was thirty-six while she stayed to help an aging grandmother, hold her rigidly in the role of minister's wife as she saw it, and strengthen her in a continuing struggle with her husband's melancholia. It also did much to cancel out the gift for happiness with which she had been born: at one and the same time making disappointments easier to cope with and harder to bear.

It is said that she was a solitary child, though she was surrounded by relatives, uncles, aunts, cousins living not too far away. Her grandfather Montgomery was one of seventeen children, her grandfather Macneill one of eleven, her father one of eleven, her mother one of six. Grandfather Macneill, as well as farmer, was also the Cavendish postmaster, which meant many people coming and going from the house. Moreover, the school was just across the road, with children straggling in and out and shouting in the playground. It was less loneliness than delicious fantasy that provided the little girl with two companions to chatter to, looking-glass figures who came to shadowy life in the oval glass doors of the bookcase used as a china cabinet. In the left-hand door was Katie Maurice, a child of Maud's own age, with whom she shared endless confidences. Behind the right-hand door lived Lucy Gray, a grown-up widowed lady who entrusted Maud with sad tales of past tragedies. Katie Maurice and Lucy Gray did not like each other, and Maud favoured Katie, but she was polite to Lucy Gray and conscientious about including both in her friendship and attention.

If solitary, Maud was never truly a lonely child, except perhaps in her very earliest years; not with the intense, passionate inner life she lived, with her eager curiosity and effortless imagination. Trees—particularly trees—leaves, shadows, flowers, clouds, kittens—especially kittens—sea-shells and sea-spray, moonlight and sunshine, all were the breath of life to the young Maud.

CHAPTER TWO

Passport to fairyland

Though her treasured memories were not etched with the singular clarity of nostalgia until after infancy—"the first six years of my life are hazy in recollection"—isolated memories rear up, monoliths of terror, of fascination, of humiliation, of new understandings. At four, she was comforted by discovering "the exact location of Heaven": not remote and unattainable beyond the farthest star, but in the attic of the Clifton Presbyterian Church. Heaven could be reached through a square hole in the ceiling—Maud's unmarried Aunt Emily herself had pointed upward silently in response to a whispered query. Why, then, did they not sometimes go up to visit Mother, wondered Maud?

She was nine years old before she first learned the reality of sorrow and mental suffering, watching her kitten Pussy-willow dying from poison. But four years earlier, on a visit to Grandfather Montgomery's farm at Park Corner, she had gained firsthand knowledge of physical pain. She learned the hard way, by picking up the wrong end of a red-hot poker. Though she spent a miserable night of real suffering, her arm up to the elbow in a pail of ice-water, one corner of her mind enjoyed the ensuing commotion. "For the time being, I was splendidly, satisfyingly important." She became more important over the next few days, when the violent headache that developed was diagnosed as typhoid fever. Excitement caused by the arrival of Grandmother Macneill, summoned in a hurry, raised the small patient's temperature so alarmingly that her worried father hastily informed her that Grandma had gone home again. Believing his attempt to soothe her, the child refused to recognize her grandmother during subsequent days of delirium, insisting that she must be an unpopular Mrs Murphy "who was tall and thin, like Grandmother." When recognition returned, she could hardly bear to be out of her grandmother's arms in case she disappeared again.

At five, too, Maud knew with awful certainty that the world would end next Sunday, having overhead an item read aloud from the newspaper. It *must* be true—"it had been *printed*." In an agony of wretchedness she awaited the Last Trump and the Day of Judgment, unable to comprehend the casual and unheeding routine activities of her elders under threat of such enormous doom. Until that interminable Sunday ended and "the beautiful green world of blossom and sunshine" proved to be still intact, she cowered in mortal terror. Two chapters in *The Story Girl* would recreate that terror for the children in Maud's 1910 novel.

Visits to Uncle John and Aunt Annie Campbell, and to Grandfather Montgomery, both at Park Corner—their farms almost facing one another across the road—were infrequent but cherished occasions. The drive to get there was "such a pretty one, those winding thirteen miles through hill and wood, and by river and shore." But two of the rivers had to be crossed by "drawbridges," and Maud was afraid of them. It was a fear that persisted throughout her life. Did that all-too-vivid imagination picture the bridge rising up and depositing them, carriage, horses and all, in a heap on the road below?

Uncle John Campbell's house was "a big white one, smothered in orchards," standing above the Lake of Shining Waters, with a pantry full of goodies to be raided in later days with three boisterous cousins. Grandfather Montgomery's home was a charming old frame house "full of cupboards and nooks, and little, unexpected flights of stairs." Maud dearly loved the pair of white, green-spotted china dogs that stood on the sitting room mantel and which, her father told her with great solemnity, leaped down to the hearth and barked when they heard the strokes of midnight. She was never allowed to satisfy her ardent longing to stay up late enough to catch them at this magic; and insult was added to injury when it was revealed that the story was not, in fact, true. Father had actually *lied* to her. But he saved his reputation by explaining that the dogs had to *hear* the clock strike. And of course, china dogs could not hear.

If visits to Park Corner were infrequent, visits to town were even more rare. Five-year-old Maud's first taste of this heady excitement brought a small adventure. Town was a place of exotic delights—shop-window displays, an abundance of nuts and candies and oranges, and streets full of glamorous strangers. Never afraid to venture (except in the face of ghoulies and ghosties and other powers of darkness), Maud slipped confidently down a side street, absorbing amazing new experiences while her grandparents chatted on a corner with friends. A woman was shaking rugs *"on the top of a house. I felt dizzy with excitement over such a topsy-turvy sight. We shook rugs in the yard."*

A dim room full of barrels and curly wood-shavings rewarded a daring descent of steps through an open door. And then, on the way back to guardians who had not yet missed her, Maud met a kindred spirit—a black-eyed, black-haired little girl carrying a pitcher. *"We told each other how old we were, and how many dolls we had, and almost everything else there was to tell except our names which neither of us thought about. When we parted, I felt as though I were leaving a life long friend."*

So friendly and outgoing a child would not have failed, when similar chance offered to make contact, however brief and superficial, with any child coming to the post office, or wandering by the farm, or (before her own school days) going to and from school in the "white-washed, low-eaved building on the side of the road just outside our gate" next to a spruce grove that was Maud's idea of fairyland. In the summer of 1881, when she was six, Aunt Emily took her to the school-house, neatly and respectably shod with the buttoned boots she so much resented in the company of barefoot fellow pupils. She felt discrimination in other ways, too. Children from more distant homes could stay for a delightful schoolyard lunch, sitting in sociable groups under playground trees, their bottles of milk cooled from a morning stashed in one of the hidey-

9

holes in the brook that bubbled through the grounds. Deprived Maud, except on a few welcome stormy days, had to go home for a hot midday dinner. Later, mortification and teasing had to be endured with the wearing of "baby" pinafores, detestable long sack-like garments with the sleeves that no other child wore.

School discipline was harsh at times. Maud remembered in furious italics a *whipping* the teacher administered to impress on her the iniquity of using the phrase *by the skin of my teeth*. "He said it was slang. If I had but known then what I know now!!!" she wrote some twenty-five years later, the memory still rankling. "It is in *Job*." But it was her experience of just this kind of incident that would bring her child characters leaping from the page in suppressed fury, smarting over similar injustices.

For gregarious Maud, however, school was not on the whole an unpleasurable experience, and she had the delight, the following summer, of acquiring two young companions, Wellington and David Nelson (Well and Dave), who came to board with the Macneills for school attendance.

Her friendship with these youngsters, and her spontaneous chatter to the small stranger in Charlottetown are a little at variance with some of her later recollections. "I was a lonely child," she would write some twenty-three years after, but by this she meant that in her very earliest years she had few intimate playmates, and in her adolescence she lacked the freedom her contemporaries enjoyed. "I was shut out from all social life, even such as this small country settlement could offer, debarred from the companionship of other children, and in early youth, other young people. I had no companionship except that of books and solitary rambles in wood and fields. This drove me in on myself and early forced me to construct for myself a world of fancy and imagination very different indeed from the world in which I lived." Yet her own account of these pre-teen years, in *The Alpine Path*, published in 1917, is sharp and clear, filled with the childhood joys that ring so true in her books. In retrospect, a natural shyness and reserve and the lack of child companions in her home may have led her to overemphasize her solitary state, interpreting the richness of her inner life at that time as a greater loneliness than she actually experienced. And it is possible that awareness of her father's seeming desertion grew in his daughter's mind into a memory of a childhood more lonely than the reality.

The three children ran riot in field and wood and sand-dunes, Maud with her long hair flying: gathered flowers, picked berries, fished the brooks in the woods for trout (Maud managed—shudderingly—to put her own worm on the hook, and earned the boys' respect by catching a large fish on one memorable occasion); laced together a playhouse from fir boughs in a circle of young spruce trees to the west of the Macneill front orchard; planted little gardens, where the ever-green rock plant *live-forever* overran carrots, lettuces, phlox, sweet peas, and beans that "persisted in coming up with their skins over their heads," promptly (and ruinously) pulled off by the young gardeners; carried eight o'clock breakfasts, mid-day dinners and often suppers to the fishing house on the shore for hungry French-Canadian mackerel fishers who had gone out in Grandfather Macneill's boat at three or four on sum-mer mornings; scrambled among pools and rocks for shells and pebbles and mussels, gathering up the "great, white, empty 'snail' shells, as big as our fists, that had been washed ashore from some distant strand or deep sea haunt"; ate dulse "by the yard," perched on rocks carved in queer shapes by con-stantly crashing Atlantic waves; chased each other, tumbling and shouting, through fragrant fields of new-cut hay; revelled in the trees individually named by Maud—apple trees in both orchards known as Aunt Emily's tree, Uncle Leander's tree, Little Syrup tree, Spotty tree, the Spider tree, the slim White Lady birch in a corner of the front orchard, and the spruce and maple so closely intertwined that they could only be The Lovers.

Both Well and Dave had a store of ghost stories. In summer twilight, companionably perched on the back porch steps, Well told tales that curdled young blood with delicious, half-believed terror, conjuring up a grandfather whose wraith had been seen tending the cows while his real body lay sleeping on the sofa; envisioning a terrible, headless "lamb of fire" pursu-ing unwary evil-doers in the dark; and so realistically peopling the Haunted Wood with "white things" fluttering in the small hours that an all-too-real "white thing" flapping one evening under the juniper tree sent the three children shrieking from their field-play for the house. Grandmother, who should have been quietly sewing in her room, wasn't. The three tore off for aid and comfort to a neighbour's, where derision greeted their horrified burblings. But no, they stammered, it wasn't the white calf they had tried at first to tell themselves it was. No, it wasn't queer Mag Laird, wandering vacantly along the lanes. It was a ghost, dreadfully advancing to punish sinful children. Sceptical servants equipped with pail of oats and pitchfork, returned to report no calf, no spectral visitor ("This did not surprise us. Of course [it] would vanish when it had fulfilled its mission"). Only Grandfather, disgustedly calling to collect the trembling trio, was able to reassure them. The "white thing" had been a tablecloth, set out on the grass to bleach in the sun, and dropped by Grandmother, who had sallied forth, knitting in hand, to retrieve it; and, bending down to pick up a ball of wool fallen into the dyke, was not visible to the children.

CHAPTER THREE

Young writer

Aunt Mary Lawson, a beloved great-aunt, youngest of Speaker Macneill's eleven children, to whose vivid story-telling about her own youth, her ancestors, and the activities of pioneer days Maud would owe many of the anecdotes in her books, wrote some years later to a nephew about their forebears. "[They] filled a large space in the moral, intellectual, and religious development of the country, and . . . were strongly impressed with the idea that they were above the common herd." Island records are full of family names among the magistrates, teachers, ministers and legistators of the province. With that heritage, Maud grew up with a strong and well-justified pride of family.

Her grandfather, Alexander Macneill, she described as "a man of strong and pure literary tastes, with a considerable knack of prose composition." Lucy Woolner, his wife, born at Dunwich in Suffolk and educated in England before coming to Canada at the age of twelve, was accounted a remarkable woman by all who knew her. A much younger grandchild, the youngest son of Maud's Uncle Leander by his third wife, who spent pre-teen summers in Cavendish in the last ten years of Lucy Macneill's almost eighty-seven-year life, still speaks of her with love and admiration. "Grandmother was one of the most lovable, thoughtful, competent, and unselfish women I ever had the privilege of knowing. To her last days in 1911 she ran the home, the post office, our own family on our visits each summer, and she utterly spoiled me with her attentions and kindnesses. She was surely an unforgettable lady and strong too, as I recall seeing her walking back from the well with two buckets of water when well into her eighties."

It is possible that the youthful Ken Macneill, some twenty-five years younger than his famous cousin, saw a softer, more outgoing grandmother than Maud did during her growing years, at a time when religious practices and principles were even narrower and stricter, and social attitudes still more restrictive. The total responsibility for rearing and training a child does not always allow the "spoiling" indulged in when the child's training is known to be in other, and competent, hands. The child Maud dearly loved many aspects of her grandmother; but there are hints in letters from the adult Maud that resentment and rebellion against a rigidity in her upbringing went deep, and left a residue of bitterness. "In material respects [my grandparents] were good and kind to me and I am sincerely grateful to them, but in many respects they were unwise in their treatment of me."

Aspects of Lucy Woolner Macneill come to life in Anne's guardian Marilla Cuthbert and Emily's Aunt Elizabeth Murray, strong women endowed with human character weaknesses they may recognize and deplore but be powerless to change; women stern but just, governed by a sense of duty, slightly tyrannical, not dour but not outgoing, capable of more affection than they can allow themselves to show, seldom uncertain of the principles by which they lived.

Maud's heroines often suffer under the same kind of humiliations and frustrations as she resented, and reflect her own feelings of outrage when forced into similar situations by well-meaning adults. She writes of her "anger, humiliation and disgust" when, after discovery of some childish naughtiness, she was forced by her grandmother to kneel on the floor and pray to God to be forgiven for being such a bad girl. Grandmother "meant well," but could never have pictured the impotent anger and "queer sense of degradation" the child was feeling at what was an invasion of personal privacy and dignity. Certainly she could never have realized the hatred and disgust for prayer and religion—"what *she* called prayer and religion"—Maud would carry into her adult life.

"Something inside me was outraged. . . . To force a human

14

soul to utter words of prayer and contrition when not in a fit state to do so—when stormy rebellion and bitterness filled it!"

The result was a hangover of humiliation that "manifests itself in a *feeling* which lurks under all the beliefs and conclusions of my reason—that religion and all connected with it was something which—like sex—it is necessary to have but made one feel ashamed for all that."

This rebellion against religion as it was manifest to the imaginative little girl growing up in a strict Presbyterian home was fostered by a twice-a-year visit from a Bible Society traveller, a thin, pale man with a straggly beard and squeaky voice. Hunched over a fire on a frosty night, he suddenly asked: "Little girl, isn't it nice to be a Christian?" He would have been appalled if he had been a mind-reader. If *he* was, *she* certainly didn't want to be. Remembering his "shivery, bony form, pinched blue face, purple hands," Maud was never able totally to separate the two ideas "so incongruously wedded at that fatal moment." How difficult this would make her future role as minister's wife she has intimated in later letters to friends.

Two events when she was seven shook her world. In the winter of 1881-82 her Aunt Emily was married to John Montgomery in a whirl of pre-wedding baking, cake-frosting, visiting relatives, and a night of gala supper, dancing and games after the seven o'clock ceremony. For the first time, Maud was allowed to stay up past midnight—probably for lack of a room not occupied with festivities. When departure time came, the bridegroom who was carrying off her beloved Aunt Emily found himself assaulted verbally and physically by a small fury weeping with weariness and sick enough from over-indulgence in the goodies to be laid up for a week afterwards.

And in the spring, her father went off to Saskatchewan on probably the first of the trips that ended with his permanent residence there. Maud's various child heroines were often given the same fatherless status. Emily of New Moon, in particular, is shown as having had a close relationship with the father she lost to death, and clearly was bereft by the loss. Maud, living in another house and therefore not as close to him in everyday living, probably did not miss her father as much as she might have done: nevertheless, his absence from her life for increasingly long periods seems to have left a gap.

For all its quiet, backwater atmosphere, the Macneill home was a cultured and literate environment. Not many books stood on the shelves, but the child devoured them all. Hans Andersen's *Tales* led to an entracing dream-world. A two-volume *History of the World*, full of coloured pictures, covered time from Adam and Eve to Queen Victoria. There were poets—Tennyson, Whittier, Scott, Longfellow, Byron, Milton, Burns. A few novels—*Rob Roy, The Pickwick Papers* and Lord Lytton's *Zanoni*: these, though, with the poets, were banned Sunday reading. For Sundays, allowable books were one about Pacific Islands missionaries "in which I revelled because it was full of pictures of cannibal chiefs with the most extraordinary hair arrangements"; *The Pilgrim's Progress*—"read and re-read with never-failing delight": and Talmage's *Sermons*, not so much for its religion—"though at that age I liked the Talmage brand much"—but for its anecdotes and lively word-pictures. "His sermons were as interesting as fiction." In later years, Maud would shudder away from Talmage.

Top favourite Sunday reading, however, was a small volume entitled *The Memoir of Anzonetta Peters*, the story of a saintly child of ten, who died after five years of agonizing and uncomplaining illness and who talked in Scripture instead of English. Anzonetta was transferred bodily to *Emily of New Moon*, the most autobiographical of Maud Montgomery's books. The child Maud identified with Anzonetta, envying her the very obvious admiration of her biographer and the central position she occupied on her little stage—a position Maud herself always enjoyed holding, both then and later. Besides, tragedy (in fiction anyway) was so emotionally satisfying. After feasting her eyes on glamour in the fashion pages of *Godey's Lady's Book*, to which her grandmother subscribed, Maud wept piteously and happily over the sufferings of the unselfish and peerlessly lovely heroines in the fiction pages.

Until February 1886, when Maud was eleven and the newly

founded Cavendish Literary Society set up an embryo library, her reading material was probably confined to what could be found in home and school. But it was enough. It was only a step from reading stories to writing them: and one can only wish for some Time Machine to whisk into today the biographies of cats and dolls, histories of visits, descriptions of favourite haunts, and critical reviews of books that were produced by the young author in the "stacks of manuscripts, long ago reduced to ashes."

Maud was nine, she says, when she made her first attempt at writing poetry, inspired by "a little black, curly-covered atrociously printed copy" of James Thomson's *The Seasons*. Paper on which to write would have been hard to come by except for the lucky chance of the long red post-office "letter-bills," written on one side only and discarded three times a week by her grandfather the postmaster. On one of these she penned the pretentious, clearly derivative little poem called *Autumn*, beginning:

"Now autumn comes, laden with peach and pear;
The sportsman's horn is heard throughout the land,
And the poor partridge, fluttering, falls dead."

Even from the beginning, Maud could scan. She was able to present this masterpiece to her father, home for a while from the West. It didn't, he remarked, sound much like poetry.

" 'It's blank verse,' I cried.
'Very blank,' said father."

The poetry phase now invaded the classroom, when sums and spelling should have been scribbled on slates. Maud and Alma, a friend with her own flair for poetry, busily scribbled poems instead: first addressed to each other, then developed as a daring series of verses on various teachers. The current teacher, noticing their absorption and quite rightly feeling it could not be inspired by sums, swept the slates out of their hands. The horrified poets, cowering before the expected onslaught, were spared the ordeal of hearing their verses sarcastically read aloud (as Emily of New Moon was not); but the verses were rubbed off with frenzied haste when the slates were returned. Maud would turn such incidents to good account, embroidering them and enlarging their effect, in her books.

At twelve, she had no way of judging the quality of her verse, afraid to hand the poems over to possible laughter and scorn. An opportunity to earn an impartial judgment occurred during the visit of a lady with a reputation as a singer. Had the lady ever heard of a song called *Evening Dreams*, Maud asked, quaking? The lady thought she might know, if she could hear the words. Two verses of Maud's current masterpiece were stammered out by the now petrified poetess: the lady said she did not know them, but that they were "very pretty."

This, her first commendation, sent Maud dancing in ecstasy through the birches. The poem might even be good enough for publication. She copied it carefully that winter and sent it off, first to an American publication whence it speedily returned, and then, after this first rejection had cooled her enthusiasm for a full year, to the Charlottetown *Examiner*, with no better luck. These first rejections dashed her hopes but not her need to write. The stacks of manuscripts grew: more poems and, by now, stories too, usually full of tragedy and tribulation, "in which almost everyone died." The Story Club in *The Story Girl* came from a real-life incident, when she and two school friends wrote a story from the same plot—"a very tragic plot . . . the heroines were all drowned while bathing on Cavendish sandshore." A first-person story followed, entitled *My Graves*: the harrowing journey of a Methodist minister's wife from circuit to circuit across Canada, leaving a child buried at each stop from Newfoundland to Vancouver.

The chrysalis author was struggling toward what she fondly hoped would be butterfly wings.

CHAPTER FOUR

The
Marco Polo

Some of the early disappointments of the young writer in the *Emily* books, whose work failed to win in school competitions, probably mirror fifteen-year-old Maud's firsthand experience when her account of *The Wreck of the Marco Polo* was placed only third for Queens County in the Canada Prize Competition of 1890. That the second place went to another Cavendish school pupil would have added salt to the wound. The account by "Miss Lucy," said the Charlottetown *Patriot* of May 31, "is a very chaste description of a sad event of coast life."

Miss Lucy had been only eight in the summer of 1883 when, at nine o'clock on the morning of Wednesday, July 25, a tremendous sight brought all the residents of Cavendish flying to the shore. They saw the famous old ship "coming straight on before the northern gale with every stitch of canvas set. She grounded about three hundred yards from the shore and as she struck the crew cut the rigging, and the huge masts went over with a crash that was heard for a mile, above the roaring of the storm."

The 1,625-ton, three-decker *Marco Polo* had been famous in her day. Built at Saint John, New Brunswick, in 1851, she had had a distinguished career for ten years as a modified clipper on the Liverpool-Australia run. After an unhappy launching into a spring tide, when she ended up jammed in the mud on the far side of the creek and eventually capsized in the ebbing tide, she was dug out, refloated, and sent to Liverpool with a cargo of timber. Bought for the Black Ball Line of Australian packets, extensively and luxuriously refitted to take passengers, she made a record outward run of sixty-eight days and a record round trip of five months twenty-one days on her maiden voyage under Captain James Nicol ("Bully") Forbes: on her return to the Mersey she was hung with a banner reading THE FASTEST SHIP IN THE WORLD.

Under other captains, she maintained her reputation until 1861, when she hit an iceberg on the homeward run and had to limp to Valparaiso for repairs. By 1867 she had become a tramp, ending up under the Norwegian flag. Her last voyage, under Captain A. P. Bull of Christiania, had started from Quebec on July 19, 1883, with a load of pine deals and ends.

There are divided opinions about the reason for the wreck of the ship (phonetically metamorphosed by one paper into *Mark Apollo*). The first version implied fraud: that the vessel, creaking and now unprofitable, was deliberately wrecked for the insurance. The second—that she was the victim of a gale in the Gulf of St Lawrence and, leaking so badly that the pumps could not cope, was driven on shore to prevent her foundering—had Maud's personal endorsement. In the margin of a volume belonging to one of her relatives—an account of the square-rigged merchant marine of British North America, *Wooden Ships and Iron Men*—she has written firmly, "purposely run on shore to save crew & cargo as she had started an unstoppable leak."

It has been claimed that no bad weather was reported in the gulf at the time of the wreck. However, Maud herself was a witness, and even though she was only eight, a very observant one. Moreover, the report of the wreck in the official government sessional paper states, under the heading of "Statement of Wrecks and Casualties to Sea-going Vessels," that the stranding was "due to thick weather."

The unforgettable sight of the great trapped ship, smothered in Atlantic spray, photographed itself indelibly on the impressionable young mind as the little girl watched spellbound from the red sands of the Cavendish beach; or perhaps, for better viewing, from the red rocks twenty to thirty feet high. It had been rumoured at first that two lady passengers had shared the crew's hazardous adventure, but this was contradicted by the captain, who wrote to the *Patriot* from Rankin House Hotel in Charlottetown. "There were no lady or gentleman passengers on board the ship, therefore no lady or gentlemen passengers were in peril."

The arrival on shore next day of the twenty crew members —a motley, colourful lot, Irish, English, Scots, Spaniards, Swedes, Dutch, German and two Tahitians, who boarded out among Cavendish farmhouses while investigation into the wreck continued—gave even more impact to the event. For weeks the men roared through the quiet countryside in truck-wagons, shouting and singing. The two Tahitians, with "wool-ly heads, thick lips, and gold earrings" not too far removed from the pictures in the missionary book, were an especial joy to Maud. Important people from town, too, came and went, standing on the beach to look at the stranded ship: the Norwegian vice-consul, insurance men, surveyors. On August 1 a Wreck Sale was advertised "For the Benefit of all Concerned." The Hull and Materials of the Barque *Marco Polo*, plus the cargo, would be put up to auction where she lay stranded, at noon on the 8th.

On the day of the sale—a fine, clear day—Cavendish was crowded with buyers—"every town, village and hamlet from Alberton to Georgetown was represented." Others came from as far away as Quebec, Saint John, Sackville, Moncton, Shediac and Kouchibouguac in New Brunswick.

The little girl's darting eyes would have missed no detail of the solemn, important businessmen in city clothes, with gold watch chains, who stared, squint-eyed and appraising, at the rock-fast vessel, nodding their approval or their doubts to each other and oblivious of the *chiel amang them takin' notes*. How many of them turned up later as Lofty John, the Awkward Man, Jarback Priest, Drowned John Pen-hallow, drawn in bold brushstrokes on the pages of Maud's books? And did she think about her great-great-grandfather John Macneill and her great-great-great-grandfather William Simpson, both of whom had arrived on the Island from ship-wrecked vessels?

There was a bustle that day in the Macneill home, where the auctioneer from Charlottetown—another Alexander Mac-neill—brought in a total of about eight thousand dollars. The stores and fittings were sold in small lots, "many being seemingly anxious to own something which belonged to the great packet ship." It is possible that even today there are people in Prince Edward Island who will tell you—as people were telling visitors up to forty years ago—that the great explorer Marco Polo actually landed at Cavendish Capes.

The Norwegian captain boarded at the Macneill home, his excellent but sometimes confused English—"Thank you for your kindness *against* me, little Miss Maud"—delighting the child's quick ear for eccentricities. When the crew was paid off, all the men sitting on the Macneill lawn beneath the parlour window and feeding biscuits to old dog Gyp, the three children saw, goggle-eyed, the table top vanish beneath an unimagined wealth of gold sovereigns.

On a cool summer night some forty-five years later Maud would stand on Cavendish beach and bring to vivid life the story of the wreck for a group of young people gathered around a bonfire on the sand. "She made us see it before our very eyes," one of them has recalled.

The small schoolhouse provided the growing girl with an excellent basic education, extended by her own avid curiosity and her literary and cultural family heritage. The Charlottetown *Patriot* of Friday, July 4, 1890, reported the regular half-yearly examinations held a week earlier at the Cavendish school "in the presence of the trustees and parents of the children. Classes were examined in Reading, English Grammar and Analysis, English History, Geography, Arithmetic and Geometry. The examination extended over three hours and was very thorough and minute in the different branches. The pupils showed good progress and creditable proficiency in all the subjects upon which they were examined."

On the following Monday, an "entertainment" was given by the scholars in Cavendish Hall, consisting of thirty-nine items, in five of which Miss Maud Montgomery was individually named: she could also have been in eight others— those performed by "the choir," or "eight girls," or "school." Her personal contributions consisted of instrumental music —*Swedish Wedding March* and a *Medley*; a "reading speech" entitled *Buckwood's Wedding*, which she performed with Master Garfield Stewart: and two recitations, *Over the Hills to the Poor House* and *The Schoolmaster's Guests*. "The above lengthy and varied programme," said the *Patriot* benevolently, "was rendered with great spirit and success by the scholars. All, from the youngest to the oldest acquitted themselves to the satisfaction and delight of the audience. . . . The unanimous verdict of the audience was that a more enjoyable evening had not been spent for a long time."

Elusive pictures of Maud on this night flash into the mind with each mention of her name in the *Patriot's* columns—the small, intense fifteen-year-old, delicate of feature and graceful in person as she would always be, eyes shining with excitement; with the determination to excel that informed her every act; proud of achievement; her secret heart impatient for the future in which she intended to succeed; and—surely —proud of the satisfaction that she would see in the faces of the grandparents who had brought thus far the child of their dead daughter.

But the shine in Maud's eyes on the night of the "entertainment" covered a greater excitement still—the knowledge that she was about to embark on an almost transcontinental journey. She was going to Prince Albert, Saskatchewan, N.W.T., with Grandfather Senator Montgomery, to stay with her father, who had remarried in April 1887 and could now offer a home to his daughter.

CHAPTER FIVE

A very active and energetic man

Hugh Montgomery, with his keen business sense, had been quick to see Prince Albert's potential. The *Saskatchewan Herald* at Battleford had been publishing articles for some years about the community: in February 1880 a Prince Albert correspondent had glowed with pride over its rapid expansion.

"This settlement is making rapid progress . . . we have had a good steam-mill for some time . . . it is reported . . . that two new grist-mills are to be built here during the coming summer. . . . We are living in the expectation of seeing some more branches of business and trade spring up. . . . We very much want a watchmaker, shoemaker, tanner, soap factory, baker, butcher, tailor, painter, a furrier—who might be a merchant or a tailor at the same time; and a goodly number of common laborers could find constant employment. . . . Our settlement is not nearly filled up yet. We have room for hundreds, yes, thousands of energetic men, women and children, but not one square inch for a dead beat. . . ."

In 1880, travel was still not without difficulties in the area. "Some of our best citizens are contemplating a journey to the capital, to advance the interests of the place. They intend going by the river with dogs. A number of our merchants are making ready to perform the same journey overland. . . ."

In November 1882 (its first number) the Prince Albert *Times* had reported that "Hugh J. Montgomery Esq., of Saskatchewan Forks Colonization Co., who has been engaged during the summer in locating the lands of the Company in the neighborhood of the Forks, has taken up his winter quarters in Prince Albert, after having made a general examination of the Company's tract." The lively development of the area had continued: the paper remarked on the improvement in lighting in the new Presbyterian church by the addition of new chandeliers, on meetings of the Saskatchewan Curling Club, on hopes for a mail service to begin shortly; and asked why some enterprising person didn't build a large hall for concerts and balls, with dressing rooms.

Montgomery seems to have shuttled back and forth between east and west on many occasions and in all seasons. In mid-January it was noted that "Mr Montgomery, who has been a resident of Prince Albert for the last six months, goes east in a few days, as far as Toronto and Ottawa, on a visit to friends. The many friends he has made during his stay here wish him *bon voyage*, and a speedy return to Prince Albert, where he intends to reside for some time to come." He returned on April 10, and on the 18th was advertising from his office at Tait & Co.'s Block, above Ashdown's Store, in two and a half column inches, as a Real Estate Agent, Auctioneer, Etc.; Money invested, Best of Representation given, A number of very desirable town lots and farm lands for sale ("We wish him success," the *Times* editorialized).

By May, reported as having disposed of over two-thousand-dollars-worth of property in the previous week, and adding to his repertoire the provision of patents where required, he was well integrated into the social life of the community. For the Queen's birthday, he was a judge at the programme of sports, amusements and pony races. In July the paper was regretting the severe illness that had caused him to be "confined to his Quarters for the past week," and hoped soon to see him "enjoying his usual good health and spirits." Later that month he moved his office into McLean & Elliott's law chambers.

In August he sold a lot for the construction of a new Methodist church in the fall. Prince Albert, said the *Times*, was now a favourite summer resort: all the hotels were overcrowded, and by October the proprietors were planning a business directory to list the many enterprises that had sprung up in a steadily more prosperous community.

On 1 May 1884, Montgomery was appointed to the Department of the Interior as a forest ranger based at the Crown Timber Office in Prince Albert, with an annual salary of seven hundred dollars plus twenty per cent of dues on timber seized. Having been given the job while he was at Winnipeg, and having had the intention, he said, of returning to Prince Edward Island had he not received it, he protested a departmental veto on reimbursement of his expenses from Winnipeg to Prince Albert. These totalled $87.95, covering hotel at Winnipeg while awaiting instructions, train fare to "Capelle" and overnight hotel bill, stage fare thence to Prince Albert, meals en route (seven days) and cartage and freight on luggage. The claim had been disallowed on the grounds that he was already a resident of the West. His father, the Senator, brought big guns to bear in a July letter to the Acting Minister of the Interior. Hugh John received his money.

A year later he came under fire from his supervisor, the Crown Timber Agent David Waggoner, who strongly objected to his taking private commissions while being paid as a government official. Hugh Montgomery, with his usual ambition and keen eye for opportunities, had been doing some moonlighting and, continuing unrepentant, was soon embroiled in some public bitterness that found him defendant at an official inquiry into his conduct in mid-October 1885. Waggoner, whose distress over his activities had increased, had written to the Deputy Minister of the Interior in September enclosing a published letter of accusation against his forest ranger, which accusation he felt compelled to endorse. Among other things, the writer accused Montgomery—"This horse jobber, land speculator, conveyancer, land agent, would-be town assessor . . . [and] store agent for Hudson's Bay Co's blankets and other goods"—of publicly belittling Waggoner.

Montgomery was suspended, and at the inquiry held before Homestead Inspector R. S. Park, prosecution and defence witnesses were heard. Charges of fraudulent dealings in land and diseased horses were ramblingly presented by one claimant, whose honesty seems to have been pretty well discredited by defence witnesses. This, and private inquiries by Mr Park, led to little more than censure for Montgomery—"a very active and energetic man," wrote Mr Park, "[who] would take hold of any business that came in his way, so it is quite possible, if there was not much to do in the Crown timber office, that Mr Montgomery employed himself in making an addition to his salary . . . [but] he should be severely censured in making remarks against his superior officer calculated to destroy his influence. . . . This disagreement . . . has done a good deal towards augmenting the feelings against government officials."

It was true, said Mr Park, that some citizens probably resented a man on government salary competing with private individuals. However, "I should be sorry to see Mr Montgomery suffer for his indiscretion." Park recommended removal to serve under another officer.

The Dominion Lands Office agreed. "The extreme penalty of dismissal would not be imposed, but . . . he should be severely reprimanded, warned against a repetition of the offence, and reinstated."

His reinstatement took Hugh Montgomery to Battleford, switching places with the ranger already there, and with instructions to work under the agent of Dominion Lands: and—perhaps to keep the idle hands of this volatile civil servant from further mischief—"to assist in the office generally when not engaged upon work connected with timber matters." By March 1886 he was writing, somewhat tongue-in-cheek, to the "Hon. Minister of Interior, Ottawa," suggesting modestly that his good behaviour on forest-ranger duties pushed into overtime by his dutiful daytime attention to Land Agent office work surely deserved some recognition in increased salary.

He may already at this time have been considering the marriage with his second wife, Mary Ann McRae, which would take place a year later. But by October, when he was back in Prince Albert for a while, he fell foul of Waggoner's principles again. Waggoner was after him at once, writing more in sorrow than in anger to the Commissioner in Winnipeg about his conduct.

Irrepressible and canny Hugh was up to his old tricks again. Opportunities in this burgeoning community were too good for him to miss. Montgomery had had the temerity to be first to operate as soon as the issuing of scrip began and "broke the rules in consequence of his over anxiety to make money." Montgomery had in some way defrauded two poor men over the sale of land at the forks of the river. Montgomery had bought up some property no one else bid on ("when supposed to be on Government duty") and sold part of it next day for a healthy profit. People, said Waggoner, were beginning to imagine that the government was to blame when its officers behaved this way.

Three days later, Waggoner met Montgomery driving into the country while he himself was out on government business, and was outraged to discover later that the delinquent had been posting bills for private auctions when he should have been minding the Land Office during the temporary absence of the Government Agent, Mr McTaggart. "I am of the opinion," concluded Waggoner, more than a little pompously and, one suspects, with a soupçon of jealousy, "you will certainly agree . . . that such conduct of an official is lowering the character of the Civil Service. . . . It is unfair to all to allow an official to bring contempt and ridicule and walk around the streets making his boast that he has made independent of his salary since he left Battleford $1,550."

Within a week, Waggoner was dismayed to learn that Montgomery's "expected matrimonial alliance" was with Mr McTaggart's stepdaughter. There went any likelihood of McTaggart's support for his complaint. He was also dismayed to learn that the Commissioner proposed to allow Montgomery, in addition to his salary, a percentage on the collection of dues. Waggoner considered this to be a mistake: agents should be paid a straight salary. It was another nail in the coffin he would like to see prepared for Montgomery.

The Department of the Interior was probably heartily sick of its problem child Montgomery and probably also of gadfly Waggoner. However, another inquiry was ordered. Hugh was not dismissed. He continued with his job as forest ranger at Battleford, still on the books of the department in early 1890. At that time his request for four months' leave of absence was granted, "as this is the time of year at which Mr Montgomery's duties are lightest." He was planning to move his residence to

Prince Albert, his family now consisting of a wife and baby daughter Kate.

Leave of absence he may have had, but the papers are full of the strenuous rushing about he seems to have been doing, visiting as "an employee of the railway company," the tie camps and Duck Lake "to look after the interests of the Government among the tie contractors." In April the Prince Albert *Times* reported that "Mr Montgomery will return here with his wife and family, where he will reside in future."

The Prince Albert to which Maud was coming was a boom town. Officially designated a town five years earlier, in mid-1890 it boasted two bakeries, two hotels, two drugstores, two blacksmiths, two photographers, two jewellers, two breweries; a barber's shop, a millinery establishment, a sash and door factory, three butchers; one gunsmith, one tailor, one taxidermist; two gristmills (one waterpower, one steam-roller process) and three steam sawmills; one brickyard (another about to be established), two printing offices, three purveyors, four painters, five carpenter shops, seven bricklayers and masons; two doctors and a dentist, four law firms and one private bank. "Not a bad showing for a town situated as it has been, three hundred miles from a railway," said the *Times* complacently. The North-West Mounted Police division in the town, too, had recently organized a full brass band (it played at the Dominion Day celebrations attended by a thousand people— "no drunks and not a single arrest"), and sports were flourishing—lawn tennis, cricket, curling, baseball and lacrosse.

CHAPTER SIX

Prince Albert
year

On Friday, August 22, the *Times* announced that "Senator Montgomery of Prince Edward Island arrived here on Monday last. . . . He is accompanied by Miss Maude [*sic*] Montgomery, daughter of our esteemed townsman, H. J. Montgomery."

Three months earlier the travellers would have had to choose one of three routes into the town: by river steamer running between Winnipeg and Edmonton; by trail from Qu'Appelle Station (from which point the Royal Mail stage left every Wednesday); or by the Canadian Pacific Railway to Regina, changing there to the Regina and Prince Albert Railway as far as Saskatoon, "from which point conveyances may be had" for the remaining hundred miles. It was probably by the latter route that Maud reached the town. Nearly fifty years later she would comment that when she saw Saskatoon in 1890 it was "a railway station, a store and post-office and about half a dozen houses." In 1930, when she visited the West again, she found Saskatoon a university city.

The railway to Prince Albert was being pushed ahead so quickly that only three weeks after the arrival of the two Islanders the first through train arrived; and on the afternoon of October 24, Maud's unquenchable interest in significant events would surely have taken her into the crowd outside the newly plastered and painted station building, when the last spike of the Regina and Prince Albert Railway was driven by Lieutenant-Governor Royal.

Hugh Montgomery had added another occupation to his

busy schedule in August, when he was appointed one of several fisheries overseers (but without salary) with the powers of a Justice of the Peace. These additional duties may have kept him at home when his father continued his journey to the west coast, but he went with him nine days later as far as "the end of the track." Maud was left to get acquainted with her new family. The first heady excitement of a new environment would surely have needed a stronger word than the "int'resting" her little heroine Marigold would later use for the entrancing new experiences she was forever encountering. It never needed much to send Maud into raptures. "Oh, Susan, there is no such thing as a common day," her Anne would say in *Anne of Ingleside*. "Every day has something about it no other day has. Haven't you noticed?"

For Maud at this time there was the new young stepmother to size up, already three months pregnant with her second child. There was the little half-sister to love and cuddle—"the dearest sweetest prettiest little angel you can imagine," she wrote to her friend and cousin Penzie Macneill at the end of August. "She has a head covered with silky curls of the palest gold and big dark blue eyes so bright and sparkling." There was Prince Albert itself—had not her grandfather told the press he was "delighted with our town"?—not a flat prairie community, but set in a valley 1,400 feet above sea level, surrounded by forests and lakes and bluffs, and bisected by a satisfactory river where boats plied busily in summer and dog teams sped in winter. There was a new Presbyterian church, St Paul's, to attend, new friendships to make in high school. And there were *Indians*, romantic children of nature she could now see in the flesh—alas, not the brave, proud people she had expected, but a dispirited people walking the streets in poverty and distress.

But despite the novelties assaulting her senses from all sides, inevitable homesickness set in after Grandfather Montgomery had finally gone home after his return from the west coast— he was back in the Island at the end of September "looking hale and hearty," reported the Charlottetown *Patriot*. The recently discovered letters from teen-age Maud to her cousin Penzie complain of tedious baby-sitting chores, of the cranky little half-brother Bruce, born in February 1891 ("the baby is so cross. Oh my! he is a terror. One of us has to have him in our arms the whole time"). There was disagreement, too, with her stepmother, who, only twenty-seven and a bit domineering, was finding some difficulty in coping with a highly sensitive girl on the edge of womanhood, and who seemed to regard her stepdaughter as a substitute for the servant she could not find. In fact, for nearly two months a resentful Maud was kept home to help with domestic chores, missing the education she was so anxious for (even though she wrote of "the dreadful place they call the high school" and wished it were "in Venezuela"). "I am ready to cut my throat in despair," she wrote in letters that ache with homesickness. "Oh I *couldn't* live another year in this place if I were paid a thousand dollars an hour."

Perhaps, too, Maud thought of her stepmother as a usurper. *Magic for Marigold*, written nearly forty years later, is shot through with a little girl's fear that her mother will allow some other man to take the place of her cherished dead father, though that mother was herself a second wife. Marigold, as possessive as Maud herself for her own, resented the replacement for the dead parent too.

It was a busy year for Hugh Montgomery. His multiplicity of jobs kept him on the run, rushing about the countryside ("Monty has very many warm friends here," said the Duck Lake correspondent), buying cattle and horses, land and railway ties, selling Confederation Life insurance policies since his appointment as local agent in the spring, arranging property sales, holding auctions of household goods, farm stock and implements. Toward the end of 1890 he was elected to the town council, and took his seat at the first meeting in January 1891. He was appointed to Finance Assessment, and became chairman of the Board of Works. He was also one of the managers of the Presbyterian church, and a dedicated member of the Saskatchewan Club curling team.

The weather was intermittently bad—"cold and rainy all the time, and the mud"—and "it is dreadful to be among strangers all the time," a heartfelt cry from a girl fresh from the warmth of close family ties. But Maud loved the tobogganning, and became almost swelled-headed from the reception her recitations received at local concerts. And if Maud was homesick, she had a refuge—"I was an indefatigable little scribbler"—and she could always escape into the ever fascinating world of writing, catching that elusive thought, or scene, or experience, in a net of words. In *Emily's Quest* she spoke for herself through her heroine: "A thing—an idea—whether of beauty or ugliness, tortured her until it was 'written out' . . . the comedy and tragedy of life enthralled her and demanded expression through her pen."

In this mood, and now recovered from the three-year setback after rejection, Maud wrote—in thirty-nine four-line verses—the legend of Cape Le Force, and sent it off to the *Patriot* in Charlottetown. Her grandfather Macneill had often told the story of the French sea-captain killed in a duel on the cape that now bore his name: legend of an earlier day, when Prince Edward Island was Ile-St-Jean and under the flag of France. Dividing up the gains ill-gotten from piracy on the high seas, while the ship lay anchored offshore and the men slept in tents on the headland, captain and mate quarrelled. In the duel fought next morning, the sneaky mate fired before the signal, while the ground was being paced off, and shot the captain dead. Assault by the waves on the soft sandstone of the cliffs had long since tumbled the grave into the ocean, but Grandfather could remember that *his* father had actually seen the spot where the captain lay buried.

The unbelievable happened. Father came home one night waving the *Patriot*—and there, on the front page of the issue of November 26, in a full column's worth of print, was Maud's epic, all thirty-nine verses, with her name in large capitals at the bottom. "It was the first sweet bubble on the cup of success and of course it intoxicated me." No matter that "some fearful printer's errors" made her cringe—misplaced apostrophes, omitted inverted commas, an *o* substituted for *e* that produced *repontance*, a *both* that should have been *loth*. No matter: it was *her* poem, and—at last!—in *print*. The idea of being paid for her work never entered the head of the young author. The prestige was enough.

More success was to follow. On June 17, 1891, the Prince

Albert *Times* published "A Western Eden, by Lucy Maud Montgomery," two and a third columns of her views on Saskatchewan in general and Prince Albert in particular.

As usual, what impressed Miss Montgomery were the scenic beauties of the little town "nestling at the foot of the terraced hills . . . and beyond it the vast sweep to the forest primeval . . . the level grassy meadows . . . picturesque bluffs which curve around, every few yards, to enclose a tiny blue lake . . . the magnificent river that rolls its blue tides freighted with the mysteries of former ages, past its poplar-fringed banks, with the busy little town on the one side and the unbroken forests of the northland on the other."

She spelt out her disappointment in the Indians. She had half-expected "to see a dusky warrior, clad in all his ancient panoply of war-paint and feathers, spring from [the] shadows, and ring his war-whoop over the waters of the river." But, alas, "the warrior never does appear . . . he belongs to an extinct species now." Nevertheless, Maud had great hopes for Saskatchewan—"a country where prosperity and freedom are awaiting thousands. . . . Hurrah for Saskatchewan!"

The sixteen-year-old author was further encouraged by seeing her article picked up by Winnipeg papers. The Manitoba *Evening Free Press and Sun* reprinted it as "the following excellent paper by Lucy Ward [*sic*] Montgomery . . . Words from the Pen of a Lady Writer." If the lady writer was not totally happy in Prince Albert, the year 1890-91 proved to be a lucky one for Maud's career. That winter saw publication of other articles and verses, including a prize-winning story in the Montreal *Witness*. She attended high school, made some lifelong friendships, and took her part as usual in church entertainments: before a packed audience in the Town Hall on January 30, Miss M. Montgomery gave a recitation at a special event by which the ladies of the Presbyterian church raised fifty-three dollars toward the new building planned for construction next summer.

It seems evident that Hugh Montgomery intended his eldest daughter to make her permanent home with him, now that he felt able to offer her one, but she was not comfortable in the renewed relationship and the call of the Island was too strong. He took her back to Cavendish in the summer of 1891. Yet gleams of happiness from that time persisted. More than twenty-five years later, when a friend glorying in "the yellowness and mellowness" of an October landscape in Saskatchewan regretted that she had not seen and described it, she replied: "I never left any description of it, I believe, but I saw it—oh, I saw it . . . that year in Prince Albert that I spent with father. Never shall I forget it. I used to soak my soul in it. I believe people call me a cheery person who 'brings a gift of laughter'. If so I think it should be attributed to that self-same western golden-ness which penetrated my being so deeply in that far-off magic month that even amid to-day's middle-aged grayness some stray gleams and embers are visible."

And the grandeur of Saskatchewan storms, though they terrified her at the time, stayed in her memory. "I remember how frightened I was by my first Western thunderstorm when I was a girl of fifteen used only to the much milder storms of the Maritimes. I positively *crouched*. It seemed as if every simultaneous crash and flash must rend the house in pieces."

She gave at least one story a Prince Albert setting—*Tannis of the Flats*, published in *Further Chronicles of Avonlea* in 1920—though it lacks any vivid background of the area.

In early 1891, while Maud was on her western visit, her father ran for the federal parliament as a Liberal. The Prince Albert *Times*, strongly Conservative, supported his opponent, D. H. Macdowall. "People are astonished at an old Conservative like Montgomery turning Grit so suddenly, and want explanations which will have to be very clear before proving satisfactory." Both candidates published addresses to the electors based on a platform in which many of the planks were the same. The point of divergence was the issue of "unrestricted reciprocity between Canada and the United States and the free interchange of products, both natural and manufactured." It was a policy that would divide Canadian thinking for years to come.

The *Times* reported "enthusiastic meetings" and "rousing receptions" for the Conservative candidate. But as for "poor

Monty," there was commiseration. "His reception was decidedly frigid. . . . Four years ago he fed at the Government expense and now they refuse to employ him." (Did Waggoner finally get rid of his bugbear after that second inquiry?) "Let us warn Monty and his ultra grit friends that he cannot consistently stroke the American eagle with one hand and with the other pull the British Lion's tail. We pity Monty, he has been made a tool of."

Nevertheless, "Monty" was a popular local figure, and even the *Times* sugared the pill with some compliments. He was "a man of boyant [sic] spirits, full of hope and a belief in man's honesty, [who] was induced by stuffed telegrams to enter the contest. . . . Mr Montgomery made a strong figure, and, unlike many of his supporters, will take his defeat like a man."

In the eight years that followed before his death, Maud's association with her father can have been little more than an exchange of letters, though perhaps he occasionally came east to visit his native province. For all his energy and enterprise, Hugh Montgomery does not seem to have been highly successful in any of his jack-of-all-trades undertakings. Although in her mid-fifties Maud would stand by his grave in Prince Albert and remember "I loved my father very very deeply. He was the most lovable man I ever met," the ties between them had stretched very thin. The host of fatherless children who rise from her pages treasuring their memories of a lost and idealized parent may reflect a subconscious resentment that her father had been lost to her by his own act: had, in effect, deserted her and denied her the security she clearly wanted and needed by removing himself from her life and handing her into the care of grandparents far removed from her in age and temperament. Security, in fact, she did not lack: but the need of this warm and responsive child to feel close, to be wanted, was rebuffed by her father's departure and may well have been responsible for the wall of reserve she would soon begin to build around her emotions.

Hugh John Montgomery died of pneumonia at Prince Albert on January 16, 1900, at the age of fifty-eight. In the years since his eldest daughter had returned to Prince Edward Island, Hugh Montgomery had continued to play his forceful part in community life. As town councillor he had been defeated after one year in office, but he had continued to find "ample scope," as the Prince Albert *Times* put it, for "his indomitable business enterprise," filling "many positions of trust, municipal and financial, with his characteristic ability and efficiency." Among these was the post of town jailer.

His obituary regretted the loss of "a man of extraordinary energy, enterprising ability and of sterling uprightness and strength of character." Another half-brother and -sister for Maud, Carlyle and Ila, had been added to Kate and Bruce, the two babies she had known. Their mother would die in 1910 at the age of forty-seven.

CHAPTER SEVEN

Schoolteacher

Maud spent the winter of her return to the Island at Park Corner, giving music lessons and writing poems, and more poems, for the *Patriot*. Perhaps it was now, beset by the passionate urgings of adolescence and better able to understand romantic love, that she may have re-read Lytton's *Zanoni*, weaving her daydreams around that intense and masterful figure.

"Zanoni!" she wrote in 1936, half-amused by her youthful passion, half-haunted still by that magic memory. Such a lush, flamboyant allegory, in which the good are noble beyond belief, the bad bestial beyond saving, was well calculated to attract a mind already half in love with mysticism and reaching for a beauty that *must* exist beyond earthly understanding, beyond the fragile veil. Its esoteric Rosicrucian philosophy hinted at secrets of unimaginable splendour attainable only by the pure and the steadfast. The high-sounding, second-person-singular dialogue carried overtones of poetic grandeur, removing its human participants far from any link with reality. Maud, already a seasoned traveller in fairyland, found this new realm only one stage beyond familiar territory.

The writing was authentic Maud-language. "Since his dark eyes have haunted me," cries Viola after meeting the mysterious Zanoni, "I am no longer the same. I long to escape from myself—to glide with the sunbeam over the hill tops—to become something that is not of earth. . . ."

"Thou only, methinks, in all the earth [Zanoni to Viola]

hast the power to wound or delight me!" Rapturous Viola: "Mould me to what thou wilt...."

Attainment of the final power meant standing fast against the dread Haunter of the Threshold: after which, magical powers and "a sense of unearthly delight—of an existence that seemed all spirit"—would reward the transformed soul. Maud recalled being so wildly in love with Zanoni "that local beaus had no chance"—probably, she said, saving her from a lot of silly "calf" affairs. She learned whole chapters of the book by heart, and rewrote some of it herself to make the heroine rise to Zanoni's stature. "I thought her silly, weak and unworthy of him ... I could never forgive her for her desertion of him." Maud would never have deserted him. She wrote herself in as Viola, "but not the Viola of the book.... In my version we were parted, but not through any fault of our own, and at last we escaped the Terror [of the French Revolution] and fled back to our own isle."

At times she was not Viola, nor in love with Zanoni, but a pupil of Mejnour the Master Mystic, one of the immortals. Unlike the Englishman Glyndon, who had succumbed to the delights of temptation, and failed the final test, Maud would be a pupil who passed the Threshold and "attained the great secret—the first woman who ever 'passed the Order.' " Sometimes she added a "codicil," making Mejnour appear suddenly in the last chapter, adopt Zanoni's child, and bring it up to be a second Zanoni. "It always worried me terribly to think of that poor baby alone in the world, especially the world of the Terror."

With this kind of romantic dreaming, despite the stinging disappointment of rejection by the New York *Sun* of a story she had sent some months earlier, she "scribbled" during her year at Park Corner and then returned to school at Cavendish to prepare for the entrance examination to Prince of Wales College in Charlottetown. At the college during a winter of study for a teacher's certificate (she received a Second Class Certificate in 1894), she received the first payment for any of her writing—two subscriptions to an American magazine for her poem *Only A Violet*. Around 1927, she gave a group of

Presbyterian ministers and their wives in Hamilton, Ontario, another version of her first payment—the choice of seeds to the value of fifty cents. This was the version she used for Emily of New Moon's first success. Whichever payment came first for Maud herself, "It is a start," she recorded jubilantly in her journal, "and I mean to keep on. Oh, I wonder if I shall ever be able to do anything worth while in the way of writing. It is my dearest ambition."

But more than yearning is needed to achieve ambition. "When people say to me, as they occasionally do, 'Oh, how I envy you your gift, how I wish I could write as you do,' I am inclined to wonder, with some inward amusement, how much they would have envied me on those dark, cold, winter mornings of my apprenticeship." For dark and cold they were when she was boarding at a Bideford farmhouse during the year of teaching that followed.

Maud Montgomery, uncertain of her talent but determined not to lodge it useless, had courage and tenacity. Finding her creative genius dulled after weary hours of teaching, she would rise at six o'clock, dressing by lamplight. Wrapped in a heavy coat, with feet tucked under her to keep them warm, she would write for an hour with frozen fingers in a frozen house where yesterday's ashes still lay in the grate.

After her year of teaching at Bideford on the Island, she decided to enter Dalhousie College (now Dalhousie University) for a special course in literature under Professor Archibald MacMechan, and spent the following winter in Halifax, Nova Scotia. The course was a delight to her, but perhaps the real highlight of that period was the "Big Week" that occurred during her stay. Monday of Big Week saw the arrival of a cheque for five dollars from *Golden Days* of Philadelphia, for a juvenile story (the magazine failed later, and "I don't know whether my stories killed it or not," she quipped). On Wednesday, she was awarded the Halifax *Evening Mail*'s five-dollar prize for the best letter on "Which has the greater patience—man or woman?" On Saturday, twelve dollars arrived for a poem sent to *Youth's Companion*. No wonder she became known in the college as "the girl who writes stories and poems for the magazines and gets paid for them."

Her prize "letter" had been submitted in the form of verses written at three o'clock in the morning (a room-mate remembers her nocturnal risings to jot down ideas and lines of poems). She took her first five dollars and spent it on lasting remembrances of her triumph: five volumes of poetry—Tennyson, Byron, Milton, Longfellow and Whittier.

She may have been responsible also for two articles appearing in the *Dalhousie Gazette*. The first, *The Bad Boy of Blanktown*, published in the issue of 4 March 1896, and signed L.M.M., is almost certainly her work, an amusing anecdote by someone who has been a teacher, and marked by her happy knack of pungent phrasing. . . . *As for his mouth— you could have cut mouths for a dozen boys from it and still have a good piece left over . . . George's voice . . . was of great compass, was cracked in three distinct places, and regularly fell all to pieces at the end of every sentence, when he was reading.* The second piece, a letter to *Dear Gazette* in the March 20 issue and signed *Maud*, is less recognizably hers, though light-hearted and whimsical.

She received her First Class Licence for teaching on July 23, 1895, four months before her twenty-first birthday. During two more years of teaching, first at Belmont Lot 16 and then at Lower Bedeque, she "grubbed away industriously . . . and ground out stories and verses on days so hot that I feared my very marrow would melt and my gray matter be hopelessly sizzled up. But oh, I love my work! I love spinning stories, and I love to sit by the window of my room and shape some 'airy fairy' fancy into verse."

Many of them were published, and she added more markets to her list of those she had "sold." Her only regret was the necessity of dragging a moral into juvenile stories. "The kind of juvenile story I like best to write—and read, too, for the matter of that—is a good, jolly one, 'art for art's sake', or rather 'fun for fun's sake', with no insidious moral hidden away in it like a pill in a spoonful of jam!"

In March 1898 Grandfather Macneill died at the age of almost seventy-eight. Maud gave up teaching and returned to Cavendish, where her grandmother was now alone. Her Uncle John, who lived on the next lot, ran his own and now also his father's farm; the womenfolk attended to the household chores. When Lucy Macneill was appointed postmistress in her dead husband's place, Maud became her assistant.

Maud remained at Cavendish for the next thirteen years until her grandmother's death in March 1911, except for nearly a year, from the fall of 1901 until June 1902, when she went to Halifax and became "the *Echo* proof-reader and general handy-man!"—the *Daily Echo* being an evening edition of the Halifax *Chronicle*.

"I'm a newspaper woman!" she wrote in her journal.

CHAPTER EIGHT

Newspaperwoman

The *Echo* could hardly have chosen better for its newspaper-woman. She was quick, she was versatile, she was used to la-bouring over words and phrases, she was cheerful, and—as Ephraim Weber, the correspondent whose lifelong friendship with Maud would begin this very year, commented after her death—she would never produce "a single careless or perfunc-tory line."

In the rush of newspaper production, errors could creep in, however much care was taken, "and then there is mischief to pay . . . headlines wildly askew and editorials hopelessly ho-cussed": but few could have done better at the job than Maud, with her care for detail. Proofreading, "although tedious," she actually enjoyed. In Saturday editions she became editor of the society page, sometimes required to fake a social report when an out-of-town correspondent's letter failed to materi-alize. This she disliked, but she had no real trouble in pro-ducing when necessary. She wrote ironically: "Poor Miss Montgomery goes meekly to work, and concocts an introduc-tory paragraph or so about 'autumn leaves' and 'mellow days' and 'October frosts', or any old stuff like that to suit the sea-son. Then I go carefully over the columns of the weekly, clip out all the available personals and news items, about wed-dings, and engagements, and teas, etc., hash them up in episto-lary style, forge the Windsor correspondent's nom de plume —and there's your society letter! I used to include funerals, too, but I found the news editor blue-pencilled them. Evi-dently funerals have no place in society."

On Mondays she was Cynthia, who wrote *Around the Tea*

Table, "a column or so of giddy paragraphs." At Christmas, she was required to visit firms that advertised in the *Echo*, and boil down for a free write-up the impressions gained from interview and inspection. This was another job she disliked, but at least on one occasion it paid off. Promised a new hat if the Bon Marché millinery establishment was well boosted, she was agreeably surprised to find that the promise was not a joke. "Sure enough . . . up came the hat, and a very pretty one it is too."

Not for nothing did Maud call herself the *Echo*'s general handyman. "All the odd jobs that go a-begging in this office are handed to the present scribe." When the ending of a story was lost after half the copy had been set, she was pressed into completing it. In real life she never heard whether the original author saw the superimposed ending. In *Emily's Quest*, she made good use of the incident, creating an eccentric writer who came breathing the fire of outraged authorship and stayed to propose marriage. But she did encounter one aftermath of an assignment to tighten up a draggy serial, "cutting out most of the kisses and embraces, two-thirds of the love-making, and all the descriptions": a month later, a conversation overheard on a streetcar almost convulsed her.

"Two ladies beside me were discussing the serial that had just ended in the *Echo*. 'You know,' said one, 'it was the strangest story I ever read. It wandered on, chapter after chapter, for weeks, and never seemed to get anywhere; and then it just finished up in eight chapters, licketty-split. I can't understand it!' "

Although the paper went to press at two-thirty, routine duties kept Maud in the office until six o'clock to answer phones, accept telegrams, cope with extra proofs; often sitting alone, but with noise all around. "Overhead, in the composing room, they are rolling machines and making a diabolical noise. . . . In the inner office two reporters are having a wrangle."

It was a busy, tiring, grubby year. "This office is really the worst place for getting dirty I ever was in." She found herself too tired at night to do more than darn stockings and sew on buttons. Early rising was no solution: the hours she had to work made the early-to-bed of her schoolma'am days impossible. If she were to write at all, she would have to squeeze odd minutes from a day beset with the noise of machines and loud voices and telephone bells, interrupted by galleys to be proofread, people to be interviewed, writing assignments to be completed. "All my spare time here I write, and not such bad stuff either, since the *Delineator*, the *Smart Set* and *Ainslies'* have taken some of it. I have grown accustomed to stopping in the middle of a paragraph to interview a prowling caller, and to pausing in full career after an elusive rhyme, to read a lot of proof, and snarled-up copy."

She was now about to discover that her precious words were not being loosed on the unresponsive air. Poems published in the national magazines of North America were read and cherished by a network of ardent souls who sought, and often found, a response to their own yearning for beauty in thought and word: many of them, like Maud herself, making their own lonely and often defeated attempts to trap ideas and experiences in elusive rhyme. Among such as these, the need to communicate with others they thought they recognized as kindred spirits often expressed itself in spontaneous letters of appreciation and respect.

Living in Philadelphia and numbered among these literary dabblers, a lady named Miriam Zieber had become an indefatigable collector of pen friends, Maud among them. She belonged to (and may have initiated) a writers' club established for just this purpose—to put in touch by letter people who shared similar cultural interests. In March 1902, a letter came to Cavendish from Ephraim Weber, a bachelor homesteader in Alberta, who for some time past had been attracted by poems from the pen of a person he supposed was *Mr* L. M. Montgomery. His impression corrected by Miss Zieber, he was urged to write to *Miss* Montgomery, who belonged to Cavendish, Prince Edward Island, but who was for the moment living and working in Halifax.

Weber's first letter was bald and brief, without salutation other than name and address at the head of the page. "Miss Zieber says I am to write to you. She tells me she has obtained permission for me to do so, and that she is sure a correspondence between us would give us both much pleasure and literary edification. The idea is altogether hers, and I hope she is right." He told Maud he liked those of her poems he had seen; hoped to see more; had himself had a few small things printed; looked forward to hearing from her.

Weber, thirty-one when the correspondence started, was brought up in Waterloo County, Ontario, Canadian-born into a Pennsylvania German Mennonite farm background. He was twelve years old before he spoke any English. There had been little culture in either his heredity or the farm environment of his youth; he deeply envied Maud her childhood of books and reading. At nineteen he had gone back to school with children little more than half his age and continued through high school to Normal School. Then, after discovering that teaching was an uncongenial occupation, he decided to follow his family to western Canada. His grandfather had founded the town of Didsbury, Alberta, in the early 1890s. Weber took up a homestead tract nearby and found the work healthy and satisfying, except—in his hunger for music and culture—for its isolation. His literary pen-friendships and his literary scribblings were a reaching-out to the wider world of the intellect.

In the first few years, at least until *Anne of Green Gables* soared to totally unexpected heights of fame and Maud's time fell victim to the demands of publisher and public, as many as half a dozen letters a year were exchanged between Maud and Weber. As responsibilities made heavier demands on them both, the exchanges dwindled in frequency, though not in length. Maud's letters turned into journal-like packages running up to thirty-odd pages in her sprawling handwriting, started in a free moment, put aside for days—sometimes weeks —and continued when time permitted.

She had her twenty-seventh birthday in Halifax, and spent a Christmas not as lonely as she had feared, dining at the Halifax Hotel with a friend and attending a performance of Barrie's *Little Minister*. March 30 found her writing up the Easter Sunday parade after a week of fog and rain and neuralgia. She was now selling quite regularly to such markets as the *Sunday School Times,* the *Family Herald, Current Literature, Youth's Companion.* But poetry was always her first love. In her spare time, she continued doggedly to grind out what she called pot-boilers—"various blameless rhymes for a consideration of filthy lucre," but many of them still earned only the prestige of publication. She yearned with a painful and unfulfilled longing for the touch of genius capable of producing the grand power and sweep of words that went to her heart from the pages of Byron, Tennyson, Arnold—knowing full well that this further gift would be forever denied her. Of Emerson's "poet," the *fated man of men whom the ages must obey,* she wrote regretfully, *"I* shall never hear that random word. My ear is not attuned to its lofty thunder."

"Her own efforts were naive," writes her son. But she tried. "I've written one real poem out of my heart," she recorded in a week when pot-boilers were in the majority. But even the poem out of her heart never achieved greatness.

She plodded on with stories, both juvenile and adult, selling chiefly to United States publications because they paid best, but occasionally breaking into the journals of her own country. One of her earliest stories, *Kismet,* was published in *The Canadian Magazine* of July 1899. Slight and sentimental, in which (as a modern critic has commented) she proved herself to be "mistress of the cliché," it was nevertheless a vignette not wholly unworthy, written during her apprenticeship and showing a glimmering of her peculiar ability to take the reader beyond the moment and behind the mask: the ability to picture the before and after of the particular moment on which she was casting her spotlight; to make her reader see more aspects of her characters than those she sets out in the words on her pages. But it is a contrived story—the chance meeting of an estranged husband and wife at a horse race on whose outcome they impulsively place the decision to take up life together again—written for a commercial market by one who, as she freely admitted, expected only to "attain to a recognized position among the everyday workers of my time." She had not yet found her true talent as the authentic recorder of childhood aspirations and anxieties. Much of her writing, especially at this time, was sentimental, romantic, fey, often painfully contrived, sometimes downright silly, with forced humour and farcical situations. In 1906 she commented on a serial being written to order, "It is a very sensational yarn, written to suit the taste of the journal that ordered it and I don't care much for writing such but they offer a good price for it. It deals with a lost ruby, a lunatic, an idiot boy, a mysterious turret chamber and a lot of old standard truck like that." Even when she had matured, her short stories were never very successful, and her books retain much of her sentimentality, but she was honest enough to recognize her limitations, even though—like all true writers—she hoped one day to produce something memorable, even great. Although she never achieved greatness, some of her books became memorable.

"She was the first to admit that her writings were not great literature," writes her son Stuart, "and also that they did not spring to life through any inspiration, but were the result of constant observation, note-taking, phrase-making and hard work. However, I know that her main source of strength was the knowledge that she came up the hard way by her own efforts, with never in her life violating her personal and professional integrity in the most minute way."

CHAPTER NINE

Pen-friendships

In June 1902, Maud returned to Cavendish, to join her grandmother again. Her life during the next eight years, apart from the writing that to her was certainly its most important occupation, was the daily round of necessary chores—housecleaning, painting, sewing ("non-excitably nice"), cooking (which she liked), gardening (which she loved)—that were the lot of almost all countrywomen of the day: in her case, illumined by her private visions and special responses to every scene and every event. Homecoming to orchards in full bloom was like "an exquisite drink" to Maud. "Have you become sober yet from the lily fragrance?" asked Weber.

In her early letters—and indeed threaded through her later ones—are bursts of rare delight in the beauties of nature, in the kernel of laughter at the heart of a trivial incident, in that flash of the spirit—Emily's flash—that so often uplifted her. "It was like being born again to see the drifts go and the catkins bud on the willows. I know exactly what I shall feel like on the resurrection morning! . . . The woods are getting ready to sleep—they are not yet asleep but they are disrobing and are having all sorts of little bed-time conferences and whisperings and good-nights. . . .

" . . . Thermometer 5 below zero. A raging snowstorm to boot. Frost on window panes. Wind wailing in chimney. A box of white Roman hyacinths sending out alien whiffs of old summers.

" . . . Three evenings ago I went to the shore. We had a wild storm of wind and rain the day before but this evening was clear, cold, with an air of marvellous purity. The sunset was lovely beyond words . . . my soul was filled with a nameless exhilaration. . . . The woods are human but the sea is of the company of the archangels. . . ."

The letters were full, too, of the curiosity of a questing mind. *What is your conception of an angel? Are you the owner of a Spanish castle? What do you think of the spelling reform agitation? Have you read* Through Science by Faith *by Norman Smith? . . . Jack London's* Sea Wolf? *. . . Gibbon's* Decline and Fall? *. . . The Law of Psychic Phenomena? . . . Yes, I have read Trench's* Study of Words *. . . Congratulations on discovering—the Bible!*

In mid-1903, Maud was once again the beneficiary of Miriam Zieber's literary ambitions. Another of Miriam's correspondents was a young man who lived in Alloa in the county of Clackmannan, Scotland. George Boyd MacMillan, then aged twenty-two, was an apprentice printer with the *Alloa Advertiser*; a year later, having taught himself shorthand, he joined the *Alloa Journal* as a reporter, where he had a long and respected career. He, too, was an aspiring writer, and at the age of seventeen he had won first prize for Scotland in a national essay competion on "Our Queen," followed by a moderate success in various British journals.

Miss Zieber had by now conceived an optimistic plan: a community of writers, set up for mutual aid. She had already persuaded Weber to move to Philadelphia. "I keep house for myself and board a friend, Mr Weber," she had written to MacMillan on July 10. " . . . Lately I am [having] one tiny success after another, and so is Mr Weber. We are, therefore, much encouraged." She then launched into her pet project, with dubious spelling and grammar. "*Say*, cannot you come over here? . . . There is a darling wish very close to my heart for many a day: that of forming an exclusive circle of writers for entirely unselfish helpfulness towards each member. So far I am sure of the quality of character for this purpose of only you, Mr Weber, a young lady of superior ability living on Prince Edward's Island, and myself. My plan is to take in no one who is not willing to freely give his or her very best help to all the other members. We three have already aided one another finely, for some time past, but we are not organized. There would be no money in the case, only a full understanding and Christian love and kindness. It will be better to keep the circle small. I'll broach the matter to Miss Montgomery, and if she consents I'll give you an introduction to her and you'll find her a most delightful correspondent. She is ahead of us, is working her way, slowly, into some of our best magazines. She is best on verse. Writes sketches and stories too. . . . I wish to restrict the circle to ten or a dozen members, and I will want to claim the right to accept, or reject candidates for admission, as I have studdied human character deeply and feel fully able to choose discreetly. . . . What do you think of the plan?''

Apparently no one thought much of it. Eventually even Weber gave up and returned to Canada. But some time between July and November of 1903, MacMillan wrote to Maud, who replied on December 29 to say she would be "very pleased to carry on a literary correspondence with you and hope we can make it mutually helpful and interesting." For reasons that puzzled her, Miss Zieber had asked her not to mention MacMillan to Weber, and she faithfully did not. But "she did not put any prohibition on my mentioning him to you." Weber, she explained, was also a writer, and "very clever . . . you missed a good thing in not capturing [him] as a correspondent. He is A-1 in that respect and writes most delightful epistles."

MacMillan, too, wrote most delightful epistles to this pen-friend whose name had come to him through the happy chance of Miss Zieber's eccentricities. "I remember well," another Alloa man, Roy Carmichael, wrote to MacMillan in 1951, "when we joined that American writers' club which furnished you with L.M.M. as a correspondent, and me with a Kansas City man of whom after a few years I lost track, and whose name I do not even remember. You were fortunate in that long literary and friendly acquaintance."

Perhaps the vagaries of Carmichael's memory caused him to confuse Weber with the Kansas City man. At any rate, Maud was vastly intrigued to discover in 1905 that Weber had a Scottish journalist on his list. He turned out to be Carmichael, who later became an active press correspondent in Montreal until his death in 1954.

The friendship with both Weber and MacMillan lasted for

forty years, until Maud's death brought it to an end. Miss Zieber, the catalyst, faded away into obscurity within a few years, marrying a Mr Watrous—"an architect or contractor or something of the sort." Though they were always formally addressed as "My dear Mr Weber/MacMillan," though Maud and Weber married other partners, though she met Weber briefly in the flesh only three times, MacMillan only once (but that once a span of a couple of weeks), these two men may have given her the most intense and happy relationships of her life. "What a wonderful thing our friendship has been," she would tell MacMillan thirty years later. " . . . It seems to me something predestined . . . I realize how much would have been lacking in my life had this correspondence never materialized."

Though other needs and other values were satisfied by other relationships, Maud Montgomery's questioning mind and strong literary interests found in her correspondence with both men a richly rewarding experience. To MacMillan she opened out even more than to Weber; they were both "kindred spirits," but MacMillan was nearer to her own spiritual wavelength.

"I am 26 years old," she told him in this first letter (she was actually twenty-nine—did she feel that a young man of twenty-two might be intimidated by her seven-year seniority?), "and like yourself have been scribbling all my life. Six years ago I began to inflict my scribblings on a public that suffereth long and is kind. I have got on well and make a comfortable living for one small girl by my pen, besides finding a vast deal of pleasure in my work."

Miss Zieber thought her prose was poor. "But I am frankly in literature to make my living out of it. My prose sells and so I write it, although I prefer writing verse. I know that I can never be a really great writer. My aspiration is limited to this —I want to be a *good workman* in my chosen profession. I cannot be one of the masters but I hope to attain to a recognized position among the everyday workers of my time." She had made five hundred dollars this year, one hundred only of which had been for verse.

Though it might be thought a bit egotistical, she felt it

necessary—"especially at the start"—to describe herself for her new correspondent. "Apart from my literary bent I am small, said to be very vivacious, and am very fond of fun and good times generally . . . I am interested in many things and *love living*. I have a camera and enjoy taking photos [she did her own processing] . . . I love *fancy-work*, CATS, horses, pretty dresses and feminine things generally. Revel in books. Don't go in for athletics but love out-of-doors."

In these early letters, Maud gave MacMillan useful information about markets in North America: what editors wanted, length of articles, payment. She sent him copies of her poems. He returned envelopes "fat with clippings and postcards" and some of his *Journal* pieces: Maud liked his "interview" with a sea serpent. He too loved the outdoors. Over the years he sent long and deeply appreciated accounts of holidays spent in various scenic areas of Britain.

They plunged straight into the same animated discussions Maud had been enjoying with Weber: about literature, the possibility of life after death, reincarnation, fairies. *Is discontent helpful to development? Do old people take life less seriously than the young? Why does a trivial event often influence a life more strongly than an important one? Surely all beauty contains a spark of the divine? Is sin in the motive or the act? Will we ever be able to carry out our good resolutions?* ("The next day after never, dear friend," said wise Maud.)

"There is something I want to say right here," she wrote. "If our correspondence is to be really a help and inspiration to each other it is necessary above all else that it should be perfectly frank and sincere. We must feel that we are perfectly free to write as we will, without fear of shocking the other by heresy in any views, spiritual or temporal. You may ask me any question you wish on any subject and I will answer as freely and frankly as there may be light in me to do. Only thus, I think, can a correspondence between people personally unknown be mutually helpful and interesting. In personal intercourse conventional disguises may serve a good and kindly purpose in promoting harmony but I hold them unnecessary in such a friendship as ours."

They exchanged postcards of favourite views (Maud preserved his as bookmarks), copies of favourite poems, clippings of amusing or provocative anecdotes that immediately sparked repartee. Maud sent him a maple leaf, a box of red rose leaves; he sent her a sprig of heather, some flowers which she wore in her hair to a concert, a bit of tansy from the grave of the Black Dwarf. "I could not have been more delighted if you had sent me a whole Scottish 'loch,'" she exclaimed, enchanted. With typical whimsy she went out and bought a copy of Sir Walter Scott's novel "to be able to paste the tansy on the title page!" as she commented to Weber when rejoicing in this gift from "a friend in Scotland," faithfully not naming him.

As the years passed and letters between them became less frequent, but longer, she would write with her diary before her, catching up on events since her last letter, posing some literary or philosophical query, seeking comment on some elusive thought or emotion. Many passages in letters to both men read almost word for word, but to MacMillan she wrote in greater detail and with more intimate revelations of her life's joys and sorrows.

CHAPTER TEN

Behind
the mask

These were not easy years for Maud, though her letters speak of occasional holidays of a month at a time away from home. Nothing in real life ever came up to her early dreams except the world of nature. Maud took possession of earth's beauties and made them her own. Beauty ravished her soul, and wherever else life might fail her, this stood firm to the end.

"When I grew up out of that strange dreamy childhood of mine and went out into the world of reality, I met with experiences that bruised my spirit," she wrote to MacMillan. " . . . The outward circumstances of my life are at present miserably circumscribed and carking—owing in great measure to poor old Grandmama's set ways of age and rapidly increasing childishness. . . ." But she had her retreat. "I am sometimes lonely in the house or when walking with uncongenial company, but I have never known a moment's loneliness in the woods and fields. I have ripe, rich, rare good company there. . . ."

She was fast learning the ability to disguise her real feelings that would stand her in good stead in the years to come—to wear a public face that said nothing of what she felt and thought. "As a rule, I am very careful to be shallow and conventional where depth and originality are wasted. When I get very desperate I retreat into realms of cloudland. . . . I learned that that world and the real world clashed hopelessly and irreconcilably, and I learned to keep them apart so that the former might remain for me unspoiled. I learned to meet other people on their own ground since there seemed to be no meeting place on mine. I learned to hide my thoughts and dreams and fancies that had no place in the strife and clash of the market place. I found that it was useless to look for kindred souls in the multitude. . . ."

At the same time, she was casting an introspective eye on her own personality, and though she might rebel against much of Grandma's Calvinism, some of it stuck. "The trials of an uncongenial environment should be regarded as discipline," she wrote earnestly in March 1906. "I have been led to this conclusion by the marked influence my external surroundings and the life I have had to live for the past eight years has had upon my character. I see now plainly that I *needed* the training very much and that it has done me much good in many ways but chiefly in enabling me to form habits of self-control. I used to be a most impulsive, passionate creature. I do not use the word passionate in the sense of temper," she amended hastily, "for that is not one of my besetting sins. But I used always to *rush to extremes* in any emotion, whether of hatred, affection, ambition, or what not, that came uppermost. It was a very serious defect and injurious to me in many ways, mentally, morally, physically. . . . I cannot certainly say that it has been eradicated. I fear that, given favorable circumstances, it might blaze up as strongly as ever. But it certainly has been much modified and as a consequence I am a much more comfortable person to others and to myself. . . ."

In her self-examination Maud found an entirely understanding friend in MacMillan, who was struggling with the idea that his gift for humour was at war with his religious ideals—its use possibly too flippant for the real and earnest business of living. Maud had cheerful words for him. "I *do* think that we are *always* justified . . . in doing what comes easiest and best for us to do. Do not fear that it is selfish to embark in a life that 'brings the greatest good to yourself alone'. . . . Any life that brings good to yourself must bring good first to other people—and that is enough, even if it be only the good of a laugh, a smile, a moment's relief from the cark and care of existence. . . . You have possibly too narrow a view of what religion really is—perhaps you are too much inclined to regard the *letter* as religion instead of the spirit.

I do not think that you need feel worry because the line of work you take up may not be the highest."

An earlier comment proved to be apt. "I think I would have made a good *preacher*. Only, when I got up in the pulpit, and saw facing me rows upon rows of dull, unresponsive faces, unlit by a single flame . . . of feeling, all my fine sentiments would probably collapse like a punctured balloon and I would come down flat."

To Weber in 1905 she wrote: "There are two distinct sides to my nature. When I go to the woods the dreamy, solitary side comes uppermost and I love the woods best. But when I mingle with other people quite another aspect rules me. I am very fond of society, sparkling conversation, the good *human* times of life. . . . But as to being only 'two of me' as you ask . . . there's a hundred of me . . . some of the 'me's' are good, some *not*. It's better than being just two or three, I think—more exciting, more interesting."

One of the *me's* was the Maud Montgomery few people saw. Witty, vivid and *alive* her letters showed her to be. But she also wrote to Weber of sick headaches, nervous spells; and of unorthodox religious views that must have been simmering behind her controlled public face. She was not—or at any rate was no longer—the bubbly Anne-child of her books. The rapturous, magic childhood had been diminished by reality, though it remained alive in the secret places of her heart and would burst out joyfully in the books by which she would be remembered.

She drew in on herself all the more because she was steadily growing disillusioned by human nature. "People waste any amount of gray matter and nervous energy toeing the chalk-lines prescribed by conventionalities and Mrs Grundy." (Nevertheless, she would toe them herself pretty strictly in days to come, despite her silent inner protest.) "I think the majority of people are prosaic and unideal. . . . The other evening, sitting by myself at the window of my den in the twilight . . . I amused myself by counting up the number of people I knew whom I thought to be really happy. The number was fearfully small—so small that it quite reconciled me to being myself, although a few moments before that I had been full of rebellious discontent, questioning of whys and wherefores."

People who knew her then, those who knew her later in other circumstances and environments, remember her as an outgoing personality, ready with conversation and laughter. She had told MacMillan that she was said to be vivacious, but she also told him that she was not "brilliant and epigrammatic" in conversation. "In *general* company I'm really a dull mortal—having nothing to say and saying it flatly. It is only in a circle where I feel thoroughly at home that I can sparkle at all." When she had become a public figure, she won a reputation for wit and gaiety. She had become more adept by then at sparkling, even when there was no real fire: even when the sparkle covered an aching heart and a weary spirit and tired body.

She took an active part in the Cavendish Literary Society, as secretary, as editor of a "magazine night" (for which she solicited a contribution from MacMillan), as performer, reading papers and reciting poems, but she would never enter a debate. To a cousin—who described her as "a pert girl" at that time—she explained her choice of elocution as a device against being refuted in debate. Repeating someone else's words, she was safe from argument or error. But she told MacMillan, "I could not . . . 'speak' in public if I died for it . . . to get up and *say* anything—horrors, I should die on the spot . . . I just sit like a log while the others are talking eloquently. If I were to get up on my feet I wouldn't have an idea in my head. The worst of it is people won't believe I *can't*. They know I can write slickly and read well and they think that it is just sheer obstinacy that I won't speak in a discussion. But I simply *cannot*. I would stammer and and grope and make grammatical errors that would make the flesh creep on my bones in cold-blooded thought afterwards."

It was a "horror" she overcame in later years. But it may explain why pen-friendships meant so much to her. Here she could discuss calmly, rationally and without stress, and never fear painting herself into a syntactical corner.

At Cavendish she was still the pleasant, community-spirited Maud Montgomery they had always known, who looked after the flowers at Sunday services; church organist, dedicated Sunday School teacher, "a pert girl," a woman who "sat up stiffly," as she wrote of her attendance at a Sunday School convention, "dressed in my best and looked attentive," while "inwardly bored to tears." But at the end of 1908 the girl who had appeared "pert" to her cousin was writing about her "morbid brooding over certain worries and troubles that have been ever present in my life for the past six years. They are caused by people and circumstances over which I have no control, so I am quite helpless in regard to them. . . ." And increasingly she was finding that the narrowness of her moral training and religious upbringing had imprisoned her in a rigid morality against which her inner self rebelled, but from which she could not escape.

What would the good folk of Cavendish have thought, had they known their Sunday School teacher thought her class of half-grown girls "stupid and commonplace"? . . . "Yes, I teach a Sunday School class—but I don't like it much. . . . I have to follow the old traditional paths of thought & expression or I would get into hot water immediately." Would they have been shocked by the woman who was writing when she was thirty-two, "I don't think I have really any belief in any particular kind of a future life. I believe that there is life after death, that's all"? Or would they have been scandalized to know that she was wondering whether religion had been a curse or a blessing, and "*cannot* accept the *divinity* of Christ"?

Friends and neighbours of another writer once boasted: "*They* know you as you write. *We* know you as you are." Maud Montgomery might well have made the reply that came swiftly back: "You who live with me know me as I *seem*. They who *read* me know me as I am." Yet even her books do not reveal the full truth about this complex, deeply introspective woman. Her books bubble. "Nowadays my reviewers say that my forte is humour," she wrote in 1917. She had a sense of the ludicrous, a feeling for the juxtaposition of words that could make a phrase irresistibly comic, and often redeemed an unlucky leaning toward sentimental romance and purple prose.

"Mrs. Emily Frost . . . who . . . had yearned for the Apostle spoons, tried to look grateful for a bed which was too big for any of her tiny rooms . . . Joscelyn Dark got the claw-footed mahogany table Mrs Palmer Dark had hoped for, and Roger Dark got the Georgian candlesticks and Mrs Denzil's eternal hatred.''

"Even Pat [the cat] had a ribbon of blue, which he clawed off and lost half an hour after it was tied on him. Pat did not care for vain adornments of the body.''

But despite her sense of humour and her ready laughter, Maud was no sunny, effervescent Anne. Perhaps in her poems, one of the few vehicles that can carry the expression of deep feeling without embarrassment or pretentiousness—perhaps only in writing never meant for public reading—did she allow herself to lift the veil of conventional reticence. Many of those who thought they were intimate with her might have been surprised to discover the distance at which they stood in her private catalogue of intimates.

"I wish I'd never written about 'kindred spirits' in my book," she wrote savagely to Weber after *Anne of Green Gables* appeared. "Every freak who has written to me about it, claims to be a 'kindred spirit'. I'm going to dedicate my new book to 'kindred spirits'. *You*, therefore, will have a share in it. But many folks will *think* they have who *haven't*.''

Years later, her younger son would recognize the loneliness in which she lived behind a facade of sociability. "She was extremely sensitive, although an excellent dissembler, and though she experienced great peaks, she also fell to great depths emotionally, which does not make for tranquillity. This rigidity and sensitivity prevented any easy camaraderie in the family, but she was capable of inspiring deep affection in all of us.''

CHAPTER ELEVEN

Child's-eye
view

All through these years, a little boy—her cousin Ken Mac-neill—was spending his summers at the farm, recreating (did she realize it?) her own joyous childhood and building up the same wonderful memories. He was also forming a child's-eye view of his cousin Maud, and in his seventies he took a nostalgic look at those years.

"I am afraid I did not ever attain what is now called a *rapport* with Maudie. She was not an outgoing woman, even though well educated and somewhat travelled. She had a small and narrow facial appearance and a somewhat small tight-lipped mouth ["I am a petite person with very delicate features," she once wrote of herself]. Instinctively at first I did not particularly like her, nor, I think, she me. She frequently sort of nipped at me, but I would guess that I was a little brat myself and very likely deserved her feelings about me. The relationship was not improved by two incidents in which I caused her some pain and embarrassment. For some unknown reason I cut off her pet cat's whiskers: and was caught looking at her from a cliff top perch, getting ready to go bathing in the Gulf which bordered our farm. It did not at the time endear Maud Montgomery to me, as she gave me a sort of rough time for a while about it. Eventually it was forgotten, and as I grew up, I think we had a mutual liking and admiration. At least I did not find her so hateful when I attended her Sunday School class later on, and she even sided with my grandmother against my mother on the problem of whether or not I was to be served tea—a privilege that in those days generally was extended at a later age. My mother went down to defeat and I had tea thereafter.

"The front portion of the home we lived in faced the outdoor privy, favourably situated among the apple blossoms. That front entrance was little-used, except for excursions to the privy, as the family itself, everybody who came for the mail, all salespeople, and the peddlers who brought thread, pins, corkscrews, paper, pens, pencils and hard candy for me, used the back door, which faced on the road.

"When I got to be four or five and had some notion of the wonderful summers ahead of me, I could hardly wait until school got out and we started off—my father, a Presbyterian minister, my mother, pretty and fifteen years younger than he, and me. It was an all-day journey from Saint John, New Brunswick, to Shediac by rail, thence by steamer to Summerside, then a train again to Hunter River, the nearest railhead to Cavandish eleven long miles away. We were met there by my Uncle John with a two-seat buggy and room on the back for the trunk we lugged along with us, a most tiresome trip of nearly two hours. And then, finally, there was Grandma Macneill and Maudie, and a fine farm dinner with everything included. I had had nothing but a couple of sandwiches since breakfast, bought on the train.

"There were two homes on the Macneill farm—my Grandmother's, and—about a hundred yards away—my Uncle John's, the only one of Grandma's children who did not seek his fortune in other parts of the country. He stayed and ran the farm.

"The house was between two orchards, with lovely apple, cherry, and other fruits. Maud had her bedroom on the upper floor facing south, with an immense cherry tree for a view. Here she typed daily during my years, and at that time mostly poems, which she dutifully mailed off to magazines in both Canada and the United States. Such half-forgotten names as *Argosy*, *Smart Set* and *Everybody's* come to mind. From these publications she got back small checks, which seemed to my child's mind huge amounts running at times over $100, but mostly less than that."

The variety of publications whose defences Maud stormed —and often breached—show how assiduously she studied the markets of the day, scorning none, however small; nor giving up hope for any poem or story until all possible outlets had been tried. In mid-1907, a poem that had fruitlessly gone the rounds of every American magazine and finally been sent to *The Canadian Magazine* "to get rid of it" brought her an unexpected two dollars. She was not above producing to order what she called "sensational trash." She wrote about a commissioned serial, "I shall be ashamed of it but shall expect a liberal check," and was pleased with the eighty dollars it earned. She also, reluctantly, undertook hackwork, writing stories to fit pictures supplied by a Toronto magazine, *East and West.*

Weber got a triumphant listing in each letter of the "new mags," she had broken into, and the amount she had been paid. The information was, of course, of keen interest to him, looking as he still was for new publications that might accept his own work. He had returned from his unprofitable venture into full-time free-lance writing in Philadelphia, and was homesteading on the prairies again. In 1904, Maud had earned a total of $591.85: at the end of 1906 the year's total was more than seven hundred dollars. The acceptances were becoming more frequent, the amounts larger. December 1906 saw the sale of a five-thousand-word story to *Everybody's* for *"one hundred dollars. . . .* It had also been rejected twice," said Maud smugly, "once by a magazine that pays $30 per story and once by a magazine that pays *ten.*"

Though writing was her major obsession, the daily round occupied more of her time. "She did her share of the housework, including cooking, dishwashing, cleaning and picking fruit for canning, the usual chores on any farm," says her cousin Ken. "I recall that candle making—tallow candles—was one of them. We did have kerosene lamps but we used candles to amplify these. There were no stores within some miles, so we had to depend for food and other supplies on itinerant peddlers. Of course my uncle grew all forms of vegetables, which we used or stored in our potato cellar. One thing I will never forget—the unalterable rule that I should be home by at least eight o'clock at night, and either Maud—or more likely Grandma—would mix up what seems in retrospect a horrible mixture, but which in fact I came to like, a mix of molasses and water. The Coca Cola of its day!"

There is no doubt that she was trapped in the position of the unmarried daughter on whom responsibility devolves for the care of an aged parent. Some days were especially trying. "I have been sizzling over a hot stove all the afternoon making lemon pies—for we have a houseful of company at present— and just getting madder all the time. Then I went out to water my garden and found that some mysterious grub is eating off all my verbenas. That turned my comparative into superlative and I was just *maddest*."

But there was an avenue of at least temporary escape. "I have fled up here to my den where the cares of garden and the deceitfulness of lemon pies cannot enter in. I have got my window wide open and a big jar of garden heliotrope on my table before me. It is mellowing my temper very quickly. I am drinking in its exquisite odor like a cup of aerial wine— and—and—dog-days will pass—and the lemon pies turned out very well—and I'm not over fond of verbenas anyhow and it's a pretty good old world after all!"

Until her grandmother's death released her, the years for Maud were a daily round of pleasure and boredom mixed, to which her writing had always to be subordinated. The summer visitors made extra work—"Uncle Leander and Aunt Mary and their son Kennedy have been here for two months," she wrote in 1909, and as the years went by and Uncle Leander became increasingly a nervous invalid, "his entertainment is a somewhat difficult matter"—but they also brought benefits. Maud loved to bathe, but needed a companion, as the shore was "rather lonely and infested by lobster fishermen." With her aunt she could go almost every evening. "Some of our dips were done in a heavy surf. It was the cream of bathing to stand there and let a wave break up around one's neck in a glorious smother of white foam." In 1904 she had written, "I'm trying to learn to swim and am getting on decently. I can waggle my arms all right and wiggle my legs just so but the trouble seems to be to wiggle and waggle them both together and between times I go ker-souse." She never did succeed. "It seems to me a perplexing business," she was writing two years later.

"Maudie used to go swimming with my mother," recalls

Ken—"I guess you'd call it bathing, they didn't swim, to my knowledge, and they confined this activity to where the rock cliffs ended and the sand beach began. The fabulous beach was called Cawnpore. I never got bored with it, even using it alone. I loved to swim there, and walk the sands, especially when there was a real old-fashioned nor'easter blowing up waves of six to eight feet high. Reading her work, I note that Maud was a little sea-struck, too. She seems to have had a feeling for the gulf and its ceaseless moods, as did I. I simply can't remember seeing her down there too often but maybe our visits just didn't coincide.

"I could watch the gulf shore for hours. The beach ends abruptly as if cut off by a huge knife, and instead of rolling sandhills and dunes, it turned into cliffs some twenty to thirty feet high, all red stone and a peculiar type of clay one could cut out and carve with a knife into various shapes. There was a road cut from the beach up to the field level, and this we used to haul up loads of seaweed to be stored and used for fertilizer. For this we had a little ground sled pulled by a horse. The rocky shore-front also produced treasures like mussels, which I used to pick off and cook over a little wood fire.

"Later I was recruited into the farm work and did my share of hoeing turnips, harvesting grain and hay, running the mower and rake (thrilling for a kid), and always fishing the brook—where as well as swimming I made little dams and water-wheels—the lake and the Gulf of St Lawrence for mackerel and cod."

Maud's greatest pleasure was her garden. Her letters to both Weber and MacMillan are strung with whimsical expressions of her joy in flowers. *Oh, I hope heaven will be all flowers. One could be good if one lived in a lily. . . . I've known roses I expect to meet in heaven. . . . I hope next time I'm born I'll be a Madonna lily. . . . My sweet-peas are lovely —I think they must be the souls of good butterflies. . . . I have a lovely 'mum out—seven or eight great fluffy pale pink flowers out on it. The 'mum is a society lady, all frills and chiffons and languid grace. . . .* Still—"wouldn't you rather be a rose for a fortnight than a 'mum forever?"

Gardening was also one of MacMillan's passions, and both

ways across the Atlantic went bulbs, cuttings, seeds, pressed flowers, received on each side with rapturous expressions of gratitude. MacMillan's gifts over the years, especially books, were carefully chosen to cater to Maud's special interests. "I think you come the nearest of anybody I know to 'inspiration' in choosing your Xmas gifts with regard to the recipient's taste," Maud commented. He sent her Flora Klickmann's *Flower Patch* books, Emily Handasyde Buchanan's *The Four Gardens*, Frances Hodgson Burnett's *The Secret Garden*, *Down the Garden Path* by Beverley Nichols; and for other pleasures, other books: Kenneth Grahame's *The Golden Age* and *Dream Days* and *The Wind in the Willows*; David Grayson's *The Friendly Road*. He sent her calendars each year, and bundles of magazines—the *Westminster Gazette*, *John o' London's*, and when her boys were young, the *Children's Newspaper*, as well as stamps and crests for their collections.

Her own gifts to him were selected with equal care, often North American books he might not otherwise have encountered: poems by Marjorie Pickthall, Sir Charles G. D. Roberts, Bliss Carman, Robert Service; works by Frederick Philip Grove, Oliver Wendell Holmes, Jack London, Ernest Thompson Seton; later, the prize-winning novels of Martha Ostenso and Mazo de la Roche.

From MacMillan, too, came boxes of the souvenirs they both cherished—shells, bits of rock, a piece of the stone from Blarney Castle, the little fossils from Holy Island known as St. Cuthbert's beads. "A certain good man here [the Customs Officer] thinks me a lunatic and probably has the same opinion of you," cried Maud. . . . "He eyed me askance as I opened it and I know I forfeited his good opinion forever by my rapture over its contents. What sane woman . . . could attach any value to such trash and what idiot had sent them all the way from Scotland!"

Did she like music?—MacMillan had asked. Yes, very much. But—"*Color* is to me what music is to some. Everybody *likes* color: with me it is a passion. I revel in it. . . . Everything you say of music I can say of color. . . . On my table is a color effect of yellow California poppies that makes me dizzy with delight every time I look at it." At a recent vaudeville performance she had seen a Rainbow Dance—"a combination of colored lights thrown on a white-clad girl dancing. I never saw or imagined anything so utterly beautiful and *satisfying*. My emotions were exactly what you describe yours as being when listening to music." It was Maud's love of colour that sometimes loaded her work with an excess of ecstatic adjectives.

Letters went on crossing the Atlantic, crossing Canada: ten, twelve, twenty pages of gossip, of philosophical and literary exchanges, discussions of "soul mates," the power of dreams, extrasensory perception, Keats, Kipling and kittens, the disservice done to religion by austere puritanical interpretations. In an April 1907 letter to MacMillan, Maud touched on a subject that would take a firm hold of her mind in later years. "Do you believe such things—'premonitions', I mean? I *don't* and *yet*—well, strange things do certainly happen. I never had any presentiments myself that worked out to anything, although I've had scores that didn't. But I've known odd things in this line." In later years, tormented by the horrors of the war in Europe, she would interpret her nightmares in the light of current events, proving their validity to her own satisfaction. But true premonition (if there be such a thing) eluded her. Meeting a young Island friend shortly before she was drowned, Maud remembered afterwards that she had had "no shattering 'second sight'" to forewarn her of the tragedy.

But, like a child returning again and again to touch, fascinated, a bright forbidden jewel, Maud would hover all her life at the edge of the occult, convincing herself finally that some of her dreams at least were predictive. *I don't believe . . . . but I want to believe and I half believe*: this was the way her thoughts led her, although she was quick to mock herself for credulity. She listed to MacMillan the coincidences that impressed her when some random comment in a letter was followed by the same word or thought in an article or conversation. Telepathy, transmigration and—most of all— reincarnation caught her imagination and offered a reason for hope that the beloved dead might not be gone forever, that known familiar beauties might not be lost in death, that somewhere there was *more*. "How could you and I know each other so well," she marvelled to MacMillan in 1936, "when we have met in person only once and very briefly, if we had not *recognized* some old friend of a former existence—perhaps in this planet, perhaps in one circling round Sirius?"

CHAPTER TWELVE

Anne of
Green Gables

"We are just in the middle of housecleaning!" Maud wrote to Weber on May 2, 1907. ". . . For the past four days I've been scrubbing and whitewashing and digging out old corners and I feel as if all the dust I've stirred up and swept out and washed off has got into my soul and settled there and will remain there forever, making it hopelessly black and grimy and unwholesome. Of course I *know* it won't but knowing is such a different thing from *believing*. . . .

"I wonder if it's absolutely necessary to houseclean? I wonder if nine-tenths of the things we think so necessary really are so! But I shall go on housecleaning and wondering! I may have given up belief in fore-ordination and election and the Virgin Birth; *but* I have not and never shall be guilty of the heresy of asserting that it is not vital to existence that the house should be torn up once a year and scrubbed!"

This letter, however, had other and truly momentous news. "Well, last fall and winter I went to work and wrote a *book*. I didn't squeak a word to anyone about it because I feared desperately I wouldn't find a publisher for it. When I got it finished and typewritten I sent it to the L. C. Page Co. of Boston and a fortnight ago, after two months of suspense I got a letter from them accepting my book and offering to publish it on the 10-per cent royalty basis!"

From Boston had come an austere but encouraging letter to Dear Madam, written on April 8:

"We take pleasure in advising you that our readers report favorably with regard to your girls' story 'Anne of Green

Gables', and if mutually satisfactory arrangements can be made, we shall be glad to add the book to our next season's list.

"Will you kindly advise whether you desire to sell the manuscript outright, or whether you wish it published on a moderate royalty basis, in the former case advising us of the amount you wish to receive.

"We shall be glad also to hear of your plans with regard to future writing, and take the liberty of suggesting that if you are not otherwise at work, it might be a good idea to write a second story dealing with the same character."

The item from her notebook of ideas that had been the hook on which Maud hung her story was a simple two-line entry: *Elderly couple apply to orphan asylum for a boy. By mistake a girl is sent them.* A slight enough theme, but Maud enriched the central idea with an abundance of anecdotal detail and a host of characters shrewdly observed and presented with verve and an amused tolerance for human frailties. The link was the radiant, volatile child who ran like quicksilver through the fictional community of Avonlea.

Maud had not, in fact, actually written the book in the fall and winter of 1906-07. What she had done was revise and expand and recopy an earlier story begun in the spring of 1904, completed by October 1905, and five times sent hopefully out to publishers. From four of them it had returned with nothing more than a printed rejection slip: the fifth commented that readers had found some merit in the story, "but not enough to warrant its acceptance." The disheartened author tossed the manuscript away "in an old hatbox in the clothes room". When time allowed, she planned to cut the story back to its original seven chapters, and assure herself of thirty or possibly forty dollars from its sale as a serial.

But rummaging a year later and discovering the half-forgotten manuscript, Maud "began turning over the leaves, reading a bit here and there. It didn't seem so very bad."

Her old second-hand typewriter bought in 1901 "never made the capitals plain and wouldn't print 'm's' at all." In June 1906 she had invested in a better one—second-hand still, but newer than her former one, and with the standard keyboard the other one had lacked. Typing the revised manuscript was a slow job while she learned the position of the keys. Her writing pattern, she confided to Weber, was three hours snatched from other duties—two hours for writing and one for typing; after her success in selling *Anne*, she kept an hour in the morning for magazine work, an hour in the afternoon for typing, and an hour in the evening for books. "Can you compose on the machine?" she had asked MacMillan. "I cannot do so at all. I have to write everything out by pen first and then copy it."

A year dragged by before Anne made her public appearance. Maud was pleased by her success in finding a publisher, but she had had no illusions about her book. "Don't stick up your ears now," she told Weber, "imagining that the great Canadian novel has been written at last. It is merely a juvenilish story, ostensibly for girls. . . . I did not dream it would be the success it was. I thought girls in their teens might like it but that was the only audience I hoped to reach." By early March 1908 she had sent back the last of the proofs and expected the book to be out within days. Meanwhile she went on shooting her arrows—short stories, serials and poems: some of them hit the target, some did not.

She was well into the sequel the publishers had suggested, though she found it heavy going in an unusually hot summer, not flowing as spontaneously as the first book had done. She was wrangling with the Page Company, she told MacMillan, over her byline. "I want it published under the name 'L. M. Montgomery' as all my work has been. The Page Co. insist on 'Lucy Maud Montgomery' which I loathe. Don't know who will come out on top, probably the publishers."

But they didn't. At last, in June 1908, *Anne* was launched, and an astounded L. M. Montgomery began to understand that she had produced a best seller. "Anne seems to have hit the public taste." By mid-September the book had gone through four editions, by the end of November through six—"and that must mean a decent check when payday comes." By May 1909 *Anne* was in her fifth English edition, and MacMillan was sending her the reviews.

A clipping service provided her with the reviews that came

pouring in from all over North America: at summer's end, Maud had received sixty. "Two were harsh, one contemptuous, two mixed praise with blame and the remaining fifty-five were kind and flattering beyond my highest expectations." Though she would complain in later years that "the only papers who ever give me bad slams are Canadian ones," Maud could hardly find fault with the Montreal *Herald*'s "A book which will appeal to the whole English speaking world—one of the most attractive figures Canadian fiction has produced." Or of the Montreal *Star*'s "The most fascinating book of the season." Or even of her own province's verdict, the Charlottetown *Daily Patriot*'s full column of praise for "the first novel of Miss Lucy Maud Montgomery, who is well known to our readers as a writer of charming verse . . . 'Anne of Green Gables' will appeal to only three classes of readers, those who have imagination, those who have some sense of that rarest of qualities, humor, and those who have not allowed themselves to grow old or to forget that once upon a time they were children. . . . The characters are drawn well and with restraint. . . . The book . . . has running through it a delicate vein of humor; the description of nature throughout is that of a keenly-observant and equally keenly-appreciative lover of the woods and fields and skies. . . ."

Though the New York *Times* said "Anne is a bore," and considered her "a mawkish, tiresome, impossible heroine," the American press outvoted its reviewer. The Pittsburgh *Chronicle* thought Anne "one of the cleverest creations in recent fiction." The Milwaukee *Free Press* remarked "the elusive charm of personality. She is full of flavour." The New York *American* found it "an idyllic story, one of the most delightful books we have read for many a day." And—accolade of accolades—the venerable, seventy-three-year-old Mark Twain sent a personal letter to Maud. "He wrote me that in *Anne* I had created 'the dearest, and most lovable child in fiction since the immortal Alice'. Do you think I wasn't *proud* of Mark's encomium? Oh, perhaps not!"

She could not complain of the publicity the Page Company gave to her work. Only a month after the publication of *Anne* an incident had occurred that Page turned to good account. "A big party of Orangemen were going on a picnic. At the Boston North St. station, they saw a copy of *Anne of Green Gables* bound in green on a newsstand. They took, or pretended to take—they were likely half drunk—the title as a personal insult, marched across to the Page building, the band playing horrible dirges, and nearly mobbed the place. One of the editors came out and told them that although the title might be offensive, 'the heroine, Anne, had hair of a distinct orange hue.' Thereupon they 'adopted' Anne as their mascot, gave her three cheers and went on their way rejoicing." Enterprising Page spread the story in the press from coast to coast, as well as producing posters and booklets to advertise *Anne*.

In the first five years of publication by Page, *Anne* ran through thirty-two editions. The thirty-eighth edition, in May 1914, was a "Popular Impression" limited to 150,000 copies.

In the first three years of publication in England (by Sir Isaac Pitman) *Anne* sold nine thousand copies: but by 1919, the first four titles that followed in the *Anne* series were out of print. From 1921 to 1933, eight of Maud's later books were published by Hodder and Stoughton, and more than a hundred thousand of these were sold.

In 1925, when the *Anne* books had been out of print for some six years, George G. Harrap & Co. Ltd. in England and Angus and Robertson, Ltd. in Australia contracted with the Page Company of Boston to publish them again in a uniform edition, and all the old interest was at once revived. Harrap also published Maud's four last books in 1935, 1936, 1937 and 1939.

In 1956, three million copies of Montgomery novels were circulating in British countries (excluding Canada), and *Anne of Green Gables* accounted for six hundred thousand of these. Since that date, about a quarter of a million copies of the *Anne* and *Avonlea* books have been sold in Britain. *Anne* has been published in more than fifteen languages, including French, Spanish, Italian, Dutch, Finnish, Swedish, Norwegian, Danish, Polish, Japanese, Icelandic and (in English) Braille.

Were she living today, Maud might well marvel, as she was often to do, that this creature of her imagination could live on so vividly through all the years since 1908. She would see Anne in two movies—silent and talking—and in two plays. In 1929 she would hear from a Dutch fan—a missionary teacher in Java—about the performance of *Anne of Green Gables* in a private school for the daughters of wealthy Mohammedan families; and she would be charmed by the accompanying photograph showing the little Javanese faces of the children portraying her sturdy Prince Edward Island characters, Matthew in top hat and swallow-tailed coat.

In 1965, *Anne* moved on to greater triumphs. In that year "a completely Canadian summer festival" was launched to run through July and August in Charlottetown, and has since become what someone has called "the nation's leading showcase for original musical theatre." In the 946-seat theatre of the city's Confederation Centre, opened the year before as a memorial to the Fathers of Confederation, *Anne of Green Gables* was the star attraction—a musical based on Maud's book, written and composed by Donald Harron and Norman Campbell. It was a tremendous success from its first performance and followed its Charlottetown triumph with a sell-out cross-Canada tour in 1967. The Charlottetown company took it to Osaka for two weeks of sold-out performances during Expo 70 and for a two-week Christmas session in New York in 1971. With a company that included three of the Charlottetown cast, with Barbara Hamilton as Marilla, it ran from March 1969 to January 1970 for a highly popular London run. An African production opened in Nairobi at the end of 1969.

And the interest continues. Anne has long been a Japanese favourite; a part of *Anne of Green Gables* is included in one of the junior secondary school Japanese language textbooks. Of the one hundred and fifty Japanese girls interviewed for positions as guides at the Canadian Pavilion for Expo 70, one hundred and forty-nine had either read the book or knew the story. Since 1954, when the Shinco Company began publishing Montgomery books in paperback in Japan (there are sixteen titles in print today), about seven million copies have been sold.

In January 1972 *Anne* was adapted for television by Julia Jones, and shown by BBC-1 in Britain in five episodes, repeated eighteen months later. A sequel based on *Anne of Avonlea* and *Anne of the Island* followed early in 1975.

But in 1908, that was for the future. One has to fall back on the cliché. In 1908, how little could Maud know, as she tried to cope with the immediate overwhelming response to the book, that this response would show few signs of diminishing nearly seventy years later. "I have never, until recently, ever read Anne of Green Gables," confessed her amused cousin Ken, "though Anne was literally written over my head in the room above while I was lulled to sleep to the tune of a tapping typewriter. I was a small boy and nothing could be more beneath me than to read a girl's book, no matter how good. But you know, I really like it. And reading Maudie's own story of her childhood years later, I have come to the conclusion that in certain respects little girls are much like little boys in their imaginations and their fears and embarrassments."

Maud herself had noted certain similarities. When Mac-Millan asked whether she thought men or women recovered more quickly from an unhappy love affair, she replied: "Well, I don't think it is a matter of *sex* at all, but instead of temperament and individual . . . the difference is mostly [one] of circumstance not of sex. I really think that men and women are much more alike than commonly supposed."

Delights and
disappointments

The first royalty cheque, for seventeen hundred and thirty dollars, arrived in February 1909. This represented nine cents of the ninety-cent wholesale price of the book: the retail price was $1.50.

Naturally enough, the reviews had pleased Maud, but something was missing. "One thing surprises me in the reviews and one thing disappoints me," she complained to MacMillan. "I am surprised that they seem to take the book so seriously—as if it were meant for grown-up readers and not merely for girls. The disappointment comes in this:—I had hoped to learn something from the reviews. I knew that the book must have faults which its author could not perceive, and I expected the reviews to point them out. But there is no agreement. What one critic praises as the most attractive feature in the book another condemns as its greatest fault— and there am I, no wiser than before."

By the end of her career she had learned to expect no help from critics. "I gave up trying to fathom the mentality of reviewers years ago. My literary scrapbooks of thirty years make very amusing reading now. They are a series of contradictions."

Despite the heady wine of success, Maud found herself restless and ill at ease. Tourists were demanding to meet her and "I don't want to be met." She resented newspaper publicity about her private life. "I don't care what they do about my book—*it* is public property—but I wish they would leave my *ego* alone," she wrote to MacMillan. To Weber, when he half-humorously suggested that he might write her life if

she predeceased him, she wrote: "No, you won't! Nobody shall. I'd haunt you if you did. Biography is a *screaming farce*. No man or woman was ever truly depicted. Biographies, even the best, are one—or at the most two-sided—and every human being has half a dozen different sides. . . . And I know I wouldn't want some of *my* soul moods depicted—no, nor any of them—for the evil ones would shame me and the good ones would be desecrated by revelation."

Yet she was an avid reader of biographies, and in later years she modified her attitude, giving consent to an article Weber proposed to submit: adding, however, "If I were dead you'd have a better chance!"

She was not physically well, suffering continual headaches, lack of appetite, and weariness, she said, of body, soul and spirit. "We had a houseful of guests all summer"—Uncle Leander and his wife, and cousin Ken again?—"the weather was fearfully hot and I was very much worried in one way or another almost constantly." As well, she was discovering unsuspected jealousies and unfriendliness. "If you want to find out just how much *envy* and *petty spite* and *meanness* exists in people, even people who call themselves your friends, just write a successful book or do something they can't do, and you'll find out!" she told Weber in September, less than three months after *Anne* had appeared. ". . . A certain class of people will take it as a personal insult to themselves, will belittle you and your accomplishment in every way and will go out of their way to make sure that you are informed of their opinions." In December she was still smarting. "I could not begin to tell you all the petty flings of malice and spite of which I have been the target of late, even among some of my own relations."

Many years later, when neighbours were priding themselves on their early friendship with the now famous author, Maud wrote ironically to MacMillan of basing one of her most hateful characters on a woman who had posed to a journalist "as my early friend and helper." She did not spare the journalist either. "I was never in my life called 'Lucy Maud'. My friends called me 'Maud' and nothing else."

She was still sending out stories and poems, cannily "peddling off my old MSS," some of which she was honest enough to recognize had sold only because of her new-made fame. She was also honest enough to recognize faults in *Anne*. The ending was too conventional (but then, how did she know she was going to have to write a sequel, she asked?). Anne's success at school was too good for literary art. "I suppose she's all right but I'm so horribly tired of her that I can't see a single merit in her or the book and can't really convince myself that people are sincere when they praise her."

Nevertheless, she completed her sequel, *Anne of Avonlea*, taking Anne through two years as a teacher, and sent it off to Page early in November 1908, though it was not published until the following September to avoid providing a "rival" while the first book was still selling well. Maud felt that the new book lacked freshness, and she feared that "if the thing takes, they'll want me to write her through college. The idea makes me sick. I feel like the magician in the Eastern story who became the slave of the 'jinn' he had conjured out of a bottle. If I'm to be dragged at Anne's chariot wheels the rest of my life," she concluded in a fine flurry of mixed metaphor, "I'll bitterly repent having 'created' her."

Her fears were only too well justified. Her *Anne* books would bring her fame and fortune (though not as much of the latter as she should have earned, owing to holes—unapparent at the time—in her contract), and she dutifully produced a new one each time her publisher requested it. The writing was to prove a labour and Anne a torment as random gaps in her life were successively filled. "That detestable Anne," she was writing, only a month after the second *Anne* book was finished. In 1915 she plodded restlessly through *Anne of the Island* (Anne in college), published in July, unable to do what she thought of as "real" work because of the war. *Anne's House of Dreams* (her first years of marriage) came out in August 1917. At the end of 1919 Maud completed *Rainbow Valley* (Anne's children growing up) and began work on her tenth work of fiction, *Rilla of Ingleside*. "Then I hope to say farewell to Anne forever." The book, completed in 1920, was to be "positively the last of the Anne series. I have gone completely 'stale' on Anne and *must* get a new heroine. Six books are enough to write about any girl."

The story of Rilla, Anne's youngest daughter, was set in wartime years, and Maud meant it as "a tribute to the girlhood of Canada," she wrote, though she dedicated it in a moment of great personal loss to a dearly loved and recently dead cousin, Frederica Campbell MacFarlane. It was, she said, her only novel written with a purpose. "In it I definitely and for all time conclude the Anne series, I swear it by the nine gods of Clusium." It was delightful to be rid of Anne, "who weighed on me like an incubus when she ceased to be an inspiration."

Yet in July 1936, obediently but "unwillingly," she began work on *Anne of Windy Poplars*, taking Anne back to the days before her marriage when she was writing love letters to Gilbert Blythe. And in 1938 she crammed a "pot-boiler" into four months of writing, published the following year as *Anne of Ingleside*, when Anne's children were in their baby days. That the series was not written in the chronological order of Anne's life probably added to Maud's weary revulsion from each successive task.

She was kept busy explaining that no, *this* particular character was not a portrait of *that* real person. "You can't describe people *exactly* as they are. The *details* would be true, the *tout ensemble* utterly false. I have been told my characters are marvellously 'true to life'—nay, Cavendish readers have got them all fitted to real Cavendish people. Yet there isn't a portrait in the book. They are all 'composites.'"

To her cousin Murray Macneill, professor of mathematics at Dalhousie College, Halifax, and much older brother of Ken, she wrote in July 1909: "I was much pleased to receive your kind letter about my book and am glad to know you liked it. It has been a great surprise to me that Anne should have taken so well with 'grown-ups'. When I wrote it I thought it would be an amusing and harmless little tale for Sunday School libraries and 'kiddies', but I did not suppose it would appeal to older readers.

"However, it seems to have done so and I have received a great many kind letters about it, both from old acquaintances and strangers.

"My second Anne book will be out in September. . . . It will not be as successful as the first. I wrote it, not because I wanted to but because my publisher insisted and I do not think such 'made to order' books ever have much life in them."

She had felt no better at the end of December 1908 than when she wrote to Weber in September, despite a six-week rest from her writing. "Indeed, I think I would have been better at work. I had only more time for morbid brooding. . . ."

Had she resented the call of duty that had brought her back to Cavendish? "The past six years" for which unnamed worries and troubles had bothered her went back to 1902 and her departure from Halifax. She did no more than hint at the existence of or reason for her worries: but she continued to be out of sorts for the rest of the winter, and the "great depths" into which her son would see her fall from time to time in the years to come were a tremendous drain on her spirits at this time, a period when she should have been floating on airy clouds of joy. "I have not been especially well this winter," she wrote to Weber in March 1909. " . . . I've been very nervous and at times somewhat morbid. The doctor says my nervous system is run down. . . ."

Later in the same letter, in a discussion of Christian Science, she confessed that without any expectation of success, she had in the previous November "decided to try to cure myself of sick headaches from which I had suffered every few weeks for eight years." To her surprise, after repeating "Remove the cause of my headaches" several times, an imperious order to some unknown authority, the trouble suddenly cleared up. "I really hadn't the least faith in it. But it is a simple fact that I have never had a headache since I began! I discontinued the 'treatment' after a month but there has been no return of the headaches. I am not *altogether* convinced—it is possibly only a coincidence and they might have stopped anyhow. But I am 'almost persuaded' that it was the mental suggestion which did it. Anyhow 'faith' had nothing to do with it, for I had none."

Cured the headaches may have been, but the "treatment" did not work on what she called her "nervous trouble." Whatever ailed her this year had been caused by more than physical illness.

Perhaps the greatest blow to Maud's morale at this time was the unexpected death in January 1909 of her favourite great-aunt, Aunt Mary Lawson, whose prodigious memory and racy anecdotal talent were the source of so many incidents in Maud's books. She had been "a sort of second mother to me, a sweet, fine, plucky little woman who had lived a more truly heroic life than many of the heroes and heroines of history . . . I felt her death bitterly."

She was a bit more cheerful in September. The summer had been as busy as ever, with "a houseful of company." In the fall, she had had two pleasures. The second *Anne* book came out—though she "took this one very coolly and it caused merely a momentary ripple on the day's surface"—and she had started work on a new book with a new heroine, Sara Stanley. "It's to be called *The Story Girl* and I have the first sentence and the last paragraph written!" Published in May 1911, it would always be Maud's favourite: she thought of it as being more "literary" than *Anne*, a step on the way toward the "mature" books she still hoped to write.

Before *The Story Girl* appeared, her publishers had cashed in on her reputation by producing *Kilmeny of the Orchard*, based on an already published serial, *Una of the Garden*. Reviewers were right when they detected a warmed-over flavour in this fairy tale, with its contrived plot and Garden-of-Eden environment. Maud curled her lips over the comment that the book showed "the insidious influence of popularity and success": she "found it interesting" when Page reprinted it in the mid-1920s, but "it seemed as if somebody else had written it." Yet, though not literally true, the reviewers' criticism had been valid. No character in the book has any of the spicy realism with which Maud could so liberally pepper her pages and in which she gave the truest demonstration of her talent. "You speak of my having *three* styles," she replied to a perceptive MacMillan in May 1909. "I daresay that is true. But the style of Anne is my *real* style. The others are only skilfully assumed garments to suit the particular story being 'built'. I wrote Anne in my *own* style, and I think that is the secret of her success."

She had thankfully turned down an invitation to read a paper at a World's Congress of Women held in Toronto (an activity she would learn to enjoy in later years), though she would have liked to attend the conference for its "broadening influence." She felt similarly deprived by missing the performance of an *Island Hymn* she had written. The composer had been able to respond to curtain calls, but "the author couldn't go. She had to stay home and wish she could."

CHAPTER FOURTEEN

The wider
world

But relief was on the way, together with some of the fruits of success. In September 1910 a telegram came from the Governor General, Earl Grey, who was to visit Charlottetown "and wishes to meet the author of 'Anne.' " There followed much scurrying around to get suitable dresses. Maud always enjoyed new dresses. All her early photographs show a girl and woman who liked pretty things, who cared about being neat and attractive, and her earnings had become more than adequate to allow indulgence in this pleasure. "I'm having a dream of a dress built for the occasion," she wrote to MacMillan once when she was to be a bridesmaid—"all white organdy and silk lace; made up with frills and puffs and shirrings galore; and I'm to carry white carnations and asparagus fern and have lovely little high heeled white satin slippers."

She was delighted with her viceregal experience. She presented Earl Grey, at his request, with autographed copies of her books to date, and got along famously with the "tall, genial, elderly man with a frank, pleasant face and a most unaffected 'homely' manner" and his agreeable family at two dinners, one of them a formal state affair on board the yacht *Earl Grey*—"curtseying backward out of the 'presence' and all that. I narrowly escaped coming to grief over my train."

The *Examiner* included Maud's name in the list of persons accompanying the viceregal party, but the *Daily Patriot* gave her four and a quarter column inches as one whose books the Governor General "has read with much enjoyment. He informed the talented writer that her works were being received with much acceptance in the Old Country." The report mentioned Maud's latest work, *The Story Girl*, not to appear as a book until the following summer, but already receiving bids for magazine serialization.

In *The Story Girl*, Maud had been able to introduce many family and local legends. Though the child-characters were, she said, purely imaginary, no author can fail to draw his material from the whole gamut of previous experience: and many a child from Maud's schooldays, from the classrooms where she taught, from the neighbouring homes, must have contributed a habit, a mannerism, an idiosyncrasy, a physical feature, to the seven youngsters who clustered around Sara Stanley to hear of mysteries and ghosts and star-crossed loves. The original of the old blue chest sat in Uncle John Campbell's Park Corner home. The ghostly bell in an empty house was the newly repaired clock that had raised goose-pimples on Maud and Well and Dave. Peg Bowen was queer Mag Laird, the harmless witch-like creature wandering Island lanes and scaring the three eight-year-olds half to death. The story of Nancy and Betty Sherman featured Maud's own great-grandfather, Donald Montgomery, father of the Senator: and Margaret, whose heart had died with the captain of the *Fanny*, was living and beautiful still, when *The Story Girl* appeared.

The children's chatter is often funny and perceptive, and their characters are neatly differentiated, but the thread on which the story is strung is a frail one, and there is little to move the action forward or to invite continued interest except a gentle pleasure in the mood and setting. Anne and Emily both carry the reader on to new discoveries about developing personalities and life stories, and arouse a desire to learn what happens next. One becomes involved with Anne and Emily as one does not with Sara Stanley and her circle. These children have no passionate problems, no hearts bursting with love and hate and frustration.

In November 1910, Maud was invited to visit Boston, where she was a guest for two weeks at the home of Mr and Mrs L. C. Page, a bit awestruck by her welcome and by life in a big city, entertained at luncheons and dinners by literary and patriotic clubs and delighting all believers in womanliness and modesty. "I lived more, learned more, and enjoyed more in those fourteen days than I had done in the previous fourteen years." She spent a day in the Museum of Fine Arts "and wanted to spend a month." She visited the homes of Emerson, Hawthorne, Thoreau and the Alcotts, and was amused by a placard on a tumble-down house on the Concord road: "This is the original house Paul Revere *would* have stopped at if he had ever ridden this way."

A reception was held in her honour by the Boston Authors Club and in the library of the Page home she was interviewed by a reporter from the Boston *Republic*.

"Miss Montgomery is short and slight, indeed of a form almost childishly small, with delicate aquiline features, bluish-grey eyes and an abundance of dark brown hair. Her pretty pink evening gown somewhat accentuated her frail and youthful aspect.

"It would be easy to exaggerate the retiring manner and untouched simplicity of this already famous woman; nor was it easy to induce her to talk about herself and her books. Her attitude was clearly of extreme surprise at the success of the latter and the interest of the Bostonians in their author."

Yes, Boston was the first big city she had visited. Yes, she would like to travel, but it was clear that her heart was in her Island. Yes, "the background [of *Anne*] is real, the 'haunted wood' is real, the little girl and her chums are leaves out of other lives, and yes, I used to name the places that I especially loved, just as Anne did . . . but except for that there is nothing of autobiography in the book." No, she did not want to do a book about Anne's love story. "I want to leave 'Anne' just as she is forever; in her girlhood."

In the ensuing discussion of women's work and ideals, Miss Montgomery was revealed as "distinctly conservative. . . . For all her gentleness and marked feminity of aspect and sympathies, she impressed [this] writer as of determined character, with positive convictions on the advantage of the secluded country life with its opportunities for long reflection and earnest study. . . . She has no favour for woman suffrage; she believes in the home-loving woman; we could not imagine her as 'a woman of affairs', or aught"—wrote the reporter in a gush of sentimentality—"but the quiet little gentlewoman of the warm heart and the vigorous, creative brain that she is."

The quiet little gentlewoman was, however, much less demure, much more emphatic a personality than she seemed. "Maud could put up, and keep up, a front," says cousin Ken, his pre-adolescent wisdom not far off her son's later judgment of his mother's power of dissimulation. Could her Boston interviewer have seen a letter she had written to Weber a year earlier, he might have had second thoughts. Maud may have had "very little interest" in the specific matter of woman suffrage, but she had views about independence of choice for women and a right to speak for herself. "As for the woman suffrage question, I feel very little interest in it," she had stated, continuing rather contradictorily, "but I do believe that a woman with property of her own should have a voice in making the laws. Am I not as intelligent and capable of voting for my country's good as the Frenchman who chops my wood for me, and who may be able to tell his right hand from his left, but cannot read or write?

"So you wish 'married women everywhere were real companions to their husbands,'" she went on in her feminist mood. "So do I—as heartily as I wish that married men everywhere were real companions for their wives. You can't, as Emerson says, cut this matter off with only one side. It has to have two. As for 'spheres' [today Maud might have used the word 'roles'], I believe anyone's sphere—whether man or woman—is where they can be happiest and do the best work. The majority of women are happiest and best placed at home, just as the majority of men are in the world." (What hackles Maud would raise today by the implication that male occupations are in "the world" and women's are not!) She went on: "But there are exceptions to *both*. Some women are born for a public career, just as some men are *born* to *cook in a restaurant*. Yes, they are! Sex seems to me to enter very little into the question. There is no sex in mind, I do believe, and—'let each one find his own,' and her own, in business as well as matrimony."

Her former professor, Archibald MacMechan, has recalled that Maud was "gratefully remembered for a clever article on the education of women contributed to a 'Dalhousie number' of a local paper" in Halifax. "It is not a very long time, as time goes in the world's history," said Maud in the *Halifax Herald* of April 29, 1896, "since the idea of educating a girl beyond her 'three r's' would have been greeted with up lifted hands and shocked countenances. . . . Could she dream of opposing her weak feminine mind to the mighty masculine intellect which had been dominating the world of knowledge from a date long preceding the time when Hypatia was torn to pieces by the mob of Alexandria?

" 'Never,' was the approved answer. Girls . . . were taught reading and writing and a small smattering of foreign languages; they 'took' music and were trained to warble pretty little songs and instructed in the mysteries of embroidery and drawing. . . . The larger proportion of them, of course, married. . . . But there was always a certain number of unfortunates—let us call them so since they would persist in using the term—left to braid St Catherine's tresses for the term of their natural lives; and a hard lot truly was theirs in the past. If they did not live in meek dependence with some compassionate relative, eating the bitter bread of unappreciated drudgery, it was because they could earn a meagre and precarious subsistance in the few and underpaid occupations then open to women. . . . Their education had not fitted them to cope with any and every destiny. . . .

"But nowadays . . . a girl is no longer shut out from the Temple of Knowledge simply because she is a girl; she can compete, and has competed successfully with her brother in all his classes. . . ."

Maud went on to list the achievements of some women graduates in England, and proudly complimented Dalhousie College on never having barred women students. Since the first two women enrolled in 1881, "a goodly number" had graduated and been a credit to their Alma Mater. This year there were about fifty-eight female students, the largest number so far, and Maud was sure "that, in the years to come, the number will be very much larger." But she thought it unlikely that "girl students at Dalhousie, or at any other co-educational university, will be equal to the number of men."

In a limited way, Maud was one of the early feminists, setting out to earn her own living as a reporter in the early 1900s, and she was certainly one of Canada's earliest successful freelance writers, long before she produced her unexpected best seller. She made brave sounds, this independent, semi-feminist Maud. But she still considered the Victorian wife-and-mother ideal as the first and most important role for a woman, and saw education as a personal enrichment within the happier state of marriage, or at least something to fall back on if she remained single.

"The larger proportion of them, of course, married," she wrote of the earlier women, those who had not been educationally emancipated, "and we are quite ready to admit that they made none the poorer wives and mothers because they could not conjugate a Greek verb or demonstrate a proposition in Euclid. . . ." But Maud Montgomery could never have been totally happy merely as the "home-loving" woman her Boston interviewer saw, even had her own marriage been happy and satisfying, if she had not had her escape door in her writing and the fame it brought her.

In July 1909, Maud had told her cousin Murray Macneill that "Grandma had a real sick spell in May." Her grandmother was then nearing the age of eighty-five. She would live until March 10, 1911.

" . . . The most sorrowful period of my life," Maud wrote to MacMillan . . . "On March 5th my dear old grandmother, who has been the only mother I knew, became ill with pneumonia and five days later passed peacefully away. . . . I knew I could not hope to have her with me very much longer. But that does not make the parting any easier when it came."

Maud moved to Park Corner to stay with her Campbell relatives. "It hurts me so to think of the old house left desolate and forsaken, with no life in its rooms, no fire glowing on its hearth. Yet I am thankful that dear grandma did not suffer and that she died in her own home surrounded by beloved and familiar faces."

CHAPTER FIFTEEN

Affairs of the heart

A few weeks later, members of the Presbyterian Church in the small village of Leaskdale, seven miles or so from the Ontario town of Uxbridge, were diffidently asked by the Reverend Ewan Macdonald, their quiet Island-born minister, for a three-month leave of absence. He would be marrying Miss Lucy Maud Montgomery and he wanted a honeymoon abroad. With what has been described as true Scottish reticence, he did not enlarge on the antecedents and accomplishments of the bride-to-be; but when confronted with a copy of *Anne*, he admitted that yes, he understood she was a writer.

In July 1906, Maud had made casual mention to Mac-Millan of a friend who was about to leave for Scotland. "By the way our minister here is leaving us—Mr McDonald [*sic*]— and is going to Scotland for the winter. He will be attending college in Edinburgh I understand. I suppose it isn't in the least likely you'll ever run across him but of course it is possible. . . . We are all very sorry that he is going away as he was well-liked and a successful pastor."

They were actually engaged at the time she wrote. Ewan Macdonald, born at Bellevue in the eastern part of the Island in July 1870, came from a farm background in Valley-field, and like Maud had Scottish ancestry. Though his engagement to Maud did not take place until three years after his arrival in Cavendish in September 1903, he confessed later that he had "had his eye on her" for some time. "I understood, when I heard of the engagement," recalls an amused neighbour, "why the Reverend used to be seen sitting for long periods, and apparently aimlessly, on the bench outside the post office."

In 1906, marriage was out of the question until Grandma died, and Maud and Ewan were to be separated for much of the following five years, so that one may wonder how much opportunity the couple had for more than a fairly superficial understanding of each other's personality. Ewan spent the year 1906-07 at the United Free Church College in Glasgow, and when he returned to Canada it was not to Cavendish, but to Bloomfield and Bedeque, distant some fifty and twenty-five miles respectively. He was then called to Leaskdale, Ontario, where he was inducted on 15 March 1910.

"I remember distinctly the arrival of Maud's eventual husband, during my years in Cavendish," says Ken Macneill, seven or eight at the time. "I remember that I liked him and talked with him on numerous occasions. Naturally, at that age I would not have had any knowledge of affairs of the heart, and did not associate him with Maudie whatever. He was just a nice minister and a man who was a quarter century younger than my father, and for that very reason a little closer to me."

To MacMillan, Maud wrote her big news on page 12 of a seventeen-page letter: "I have something to tell you which may surprise you a little. Early in July I expect to be married to the Rev. Mr Macdonald whom you met in Scotland. . . . We have been engaged for five years but as I could not leave grandmother as long as she wished to remain in her old home, our engagement was kept secret."

At the end of 1906, in a November letter telling MacMillan that the "very nice and friendly" minister whose name she was still spelling McDonald had gone to Glasgow instead of Edinburgh, Maud had dispassionately offered some rather down-to-earth and unromantic ideas about love. "*Love* is a subject we haven't referred to much in our letters, but I see no reason why we should not discuss it frankly, like any other psychological problem. . . . You ask me if I believe that there is an affinity somewhere for everyone. Well, that depends on what is meant by an affinity. If you mean one who is in perfect sympathy with one's whole nature I don't think I do. I did once in the salad days of my teens but I do so no longer. I think we must take our affinities as we do our happiness—not in one long, uninterrupted stretch as I once fondly believed, but in bits here and bits there, thankful if there be no positive friction or disagreement in the natures of those we meet and mingle with. In an ideal world we might expect to meet with our ideal affinity. But in this real world, whose ragged corners rub the bloom off so many beautiful theories we can hardly expect to."

It would seem to have been impossible—at the least, unlikely—that so intensely emotional a person as Maud could escape the painful, delicious experience of falling in love. With her first sweetheart, she says, she used to sit on the school fence beneath the fir trees when she was twelve, and discuss books, particularly poems by the young man's uncle, the Reverend A. J. Lockhart, who wrote under the name of Pastor Felix (and with what rage, years later, she recorded that the firs had been cut down!). Even before that, when she was only ten, she had fallen instantly in love at a school concert with a slender, golden-haired blind young singer with the face of an angel. Though she never met or spoke to him, she treasured his memory for years.

Ewan was thirty-six at the time of the engagement, Maud thirty-two. Her son has suggested that her single status at this comparatively late age was "due partly to the fact that she had been tied down to care for her grandmother and partly to the fact that in this rural community, in those days, eligible men were few, except for somewhat earthy types." Yet she had had other reasons for remaining unmarried. In April 1907 she moved from her academic discussion with MacMillan about love and marriage into a more personal confidence. MacMillan had asked: "Do you think that love depends upon an admiration for qualities possessed by the loved one? Or is it something more subtle than this?" Maud replied: "In answer to the first question I say most emphatically 'NO'. In explaining why I think so it will be necessary for me to inflict on you a bit of my own experience. . . .

"I loved a man—let us call him A——— — once. It was emphatically the love of my life. Yet, mark this—*I did not respect him*—I did not *admire him in the least*. Before that experience I would have laughed at the idea that one *could* love a man they didn't respect. (The grammar of that sentence is shocking but never mind.) Yet I certainly did. I would not have *married* him for anything. He was my inferior in every respect. This is not vanity on my part at all. He simply was. He had no brains, no particular good looks, in short, nothing that I admire in a man. Yet I loved him as I never can love any other man. There was about him 'the subtle something' you speak of in the second part of your question. This man died and I have always been thankful that it ended so: because if he had lived I daresay I couldn't have helped marrying him and it would have been a most disastrous union in most respects."

In the light of the problems arising from her eventual choice of husband, one is tempted to wonder whether the marriage she refused ("A" was Herman Leard, a young Bedeque farmer) would have been more disastrous than the one she made. But even in the throes of what she felt had been genuine love, and clearly had been a strong physical attraction, Maud was able to subordinate her emotions to her reason. And her reason, when she was courted by Ewan Macdonald, seemed to tell her that her choice was sound. Ewan was a good-looking man with an established position in the community, and even if he had not shown outstanding mental qualities, with his Bachelor of Arts degree from Dalhousie College he was at least educated to a standard beyond that of the local farmers who were now Maud's only possible suitors.

And experience had taught her—or at least she thought it had—that a calm and rational approach to marriage, steering clear of the fatally fascinating romantic idealism and staying safely in the area of pleasant but unexciting companionship, would offer the best chance of successful marriage. She had had her high moments of ecstasy. She had also known the misery of being committed to an unsuitable engagement.

"Before I met A——," she told MacMillan, "I had met a man whom I will call B——. [This was probably her second-cousin Edwin Simpson at Belmont.] He was everything that I admire in a man—he was handsome, brilliant, cultured, successful. A—— was not worthy to tie his shoe laces. Well, I liked B—— very much. I was very young and knowing nothing of love mistook my liking and admiration for love. I became engaged to him—and then I simply hated him. Yes, laugh. I daresay you will. But it was no laughing matter to me —It was a tragedy. That man's kiss turned me cold with horror. . . . I *knew* I could *never* marry him. I tried for a year to be true to him and *hell* couldn't be worse than that year for me. In the end I told him the truth and broke the engagement. Immediately I was free I *liked* him just as well as I had before that dreadful time, but I have been haunted ever since by the wretched conviction that I have spoiled his life. He has never married and says he can't forget. . . .

"I loved one man in whom nobody could see anything to admire. I *couldn't* care for the other who was in all respects admirable. If I had married B. I should have been unhappy all my life. If I had married A. I should I believe have been *happy* but I would have deteriorated in every way. . . ."

Both Anne and Emily would live through a similar experience, Emily's engagement and near-marriage to the charming Dean Priest parallelling Maud's ill-fated affair. Maud was ready now, she thought, to settle for less—for a respected, reliable husband and a life to be lived comfortably on the plains, without the ardours and ecstasies of the high peaks.

What she looked for now, Maud wrote in September 1907, was something more practical. "After all, this is a practical world and marriage must share in its practicalities. If two people have a mutual affection for each other, don't bore each other, and are reasonably well mated in point of age and social position, I think their prospects of happiness together would be excellent, even if some of the highest up-flashings of the 'flame divine' are missing."

Her decision, in the light of the psychological problems that she was not aware of in Ewan at the time, seems to prove —if it proves anything—that reasoned thinking has no greater chance of success in marriage than romantic infatuation. "If I ever marry," continued Maud, aware as she wrote that she had already become engaged to do so, "that is the basis on which I shall found my marriage. *But*—I shall never cease to thank my fate that I *knew the other kind of love too.*"

CHAPTER SIXTEEN

Honeymoon

On Tuesday, 4 July 1911, it was announced in the Charlotte-town *Examiner* that the marriage of "the talented Island au-thoress" would take place on the following day at the home of the bride's uncle. On the same page were American reviews of *The Story Girl*, just published in book form. "It will keep a kindly smile upon your lips and in your heart as well," the Chicago *Inter-Ocean* had said. The welcoming reviews about a book Maud had truly enjoyed writing made a pleasant wed-ding gift.

The ceremony was performed by the Cavendish Presby-terian minister, the Reverend John Stirling, in the front room of Uncle John Campbell's Park Corner home, with about twenty guests present. It was followed by a great feast, prepared by Maud's cousins Stella and Frederica. For her wedding, the bride wore a dress of ivory silk crepe de chine and lace, with a tunic of chiffon and "pearl and crystal garni-ture." She carried a bouquet of white roses, lilies of the val-ley and maidenhair fern. Her veil was of tulle with a coronet of orange blossom, and she wore Ewan's gift, a pearl and amethyst necklace. As she entered the parlour at noon, unat-tended, *The Voice that breathed o'er Eden* was sung.

In the afternoon, the newlyweds left for Montreal and departure for England by the White Star liner *Megantic*. Maud's travelling dress was a suit of steel-grey serge with chiffon blouse, and a matching hat of steel-grey braid trimmed with satin rosebuds.

This trip was an especial joy, enabling Maud—as she had told the Boston reporter eight months earlier—"to verify the

impressions formed by reading": and now, at last, to meet her faithful correspondent in Alloa. A flutter of short notes between June 5 and July 25, including one from the ship and a telegram, kept MacMillan informed of the travellers' plans. Maud's journal for this period was the record of a dream come true, preserving her ecstatic delight in most of the places visited, though a few failed to come up to her imaginings, and none were "more beautiful than can be seen any evening at home." With her usual preference for solitude, she revelled in the wildness of Scottish scenery on the excursion to Oban, Staffa and Iona; with her pleasure in eccentricity, she enjoyed a party of chattering French tourists until seasickness drained all interest in anything at all. But she recovered in time to make a long-dreamed-of visit to Fingal's Cave, whose grandeur silenced even the French tourists.

The Macdonalds visited the Burns country, thinking of *Tam o' Shanter* and *Highland Mary*; the Scott country, thinking of *The Lady of the Lake*—the Trossachs ("far from being the wild, riven, precipitous dell of my fancy"), Loch Lomond and Loch Katrine ("as beautiful as I had dreamed it, but . . . not my Loch Katrine"). They saw Abbotsford, Dryburgh, Melrose Abbey—not by moonlight, although "in that mellow, golden-gray evening light it was beautiful enough, with the little bluebells growing in its ruined courts and over its old graves." They stopped off in Barrie country, drove to Culloden with "a nice old driver who knew all the history and legend of everything." In mid-August they went from Edinburgh to Alloa in Clackmannanshire to visit George Mac-Millan.

MacMillan was now about thirty years old, and a respected *Journal* reporter. "George was really a brilliant man," one of his younger colleagues, John Gardner, has commented, "and if he'd ever summoned up the courage and initiative to leave Alloa and move to a bigger arena, he would have made a name for himself. As it was, he frequently sold small items to *Punch* and the *Strand Magazine*, and his columns and humorous poems, often in collaboration with his chief and my uncle Malcolm Gardner, the proprietor of the *Journal*, were widely enjoyed. But he suffered from a slight hypertension which may have had some bearing on his decision to remain in his home town."

MacMillan was one of four children (three sons, one daughter) of a grocer whose store was on Mill Street at the Alloa Cross. Like Maud's other correspondent, Ephraim Weber, he seems to have been largely self-educated, reared in a home not notably interested in culture, and impelled by an insatiable appetite for literature to go far beyond his ordinary borough school education. Like Maud, he had a lively curiosity about the world and its inhabitants: "conscientious in his work, unfailing in resource, and gifted with an originality which made his sketches and articles on local matters things to treasure for their easy wit and unconstrained humour. . . . He had a faculty for playful rhyming." He also wrote the words for at least one published song, and collaborated with Malcolm Gardner in several weekly features, including *Round the Bandstand, Jottings by the Way*, and *The Man in the Street*. His topical verses and parodies were apt and funny. (In later years, small Stuart, Maud's younger son, would recite some of them at concerts in Ontario's Leaskdale.) He retired in 1946, and died aged seventy-two in 1953.

MacMillan had proved, and would continue to prove to be a uniquely congenial friend for Maud. They shared so many delights, including a strong interest in astronomy: both pondered the deep mysteries of the universe with awe and fascination. "I think astronomy much the most fascinating study in the world," she wrote. She would always be enthralled by "star-hunting." A book entitled *Astronomy with the Naked Eye*, with "a chart of the constellations for every month of the year with the names of all the stars" had sent her out with a pair of good field glasses along the Cavendish roads on starry nights, and "half the time I don't know whether I'm on 'the good red earth' or roaming the Milky Way. . . . I feel as if I had literally been millions of miles away and that all my ordinary surroundings were strange and forgotten." When she read Sir James Jeans's *The Universe Around Us* in 1930, she could not agree with his theory that intelligent, conscious life must be the exception and not the rule. "It would be absurd to think God would waste so many good suns."

MacMillan was not able to offer the visitors the hospitality of his home. Instead, they were generously given accommodation by the parents of a friend and fellow-worker in various church organizations, Jean Allan. He gave the travellers a delightful tour of the beautiful neighbourhood, including Dollar Glen, "one of the wildest, grandest spots we have seen in all Scotland," Maud wrote in her journal, " . . . like a deep gash cleft down through the heart of the mountain." The *Alloa Journal* of August 12 reported her call at the office, and her verdict that "this part of the country was the finest she had yet seen."

They also visited the Glasgow Exhibition. Then, with MacMillan and Jean Allan, the honeymooners set out for a week-long tour to Spittal and the Borders, fanning out from Berwick-upon-Tweed to see the Marmion country and to explore old castles, deserted mills, Flodden Field. In a ravine at Homecliffe Glen they discovered a clump of spruce trees. The two Canadians picked the gum and ate it with familiar relish: MacMillan and Miss Allan thought it was "bitter." They all enjoyed the boat trip to Holy Island, but coming home was not so pleasant. The ladies only just avoided seasickness, and both gentlemen had to retire.

Everything about the Lake District charmed Maud. York Cathedral was "magnificent, a dream of beauty made lasting in stone." Kenilworth Castle was full of ghosts, "gay figures of olden days, living, loving, hating, plotting as of yore." Temple Church and "Poor Noll's grave" in London were outshone by a large and dignified cat, who greeted, welcomed and fare-welled them "in most irreproachable fashion."

Ewan's family tree was rooted in Skye: his father Alexander had come to Canada in 1841 at the age of seven. His mother, Christine Cameron, was Island-born, but her father had been Ewan Cameron of Skye. In Scotland, Ewan and Maud Macdonald had explored the land of their fathers, Ewan's in the Inner Hebrides, her own in Argyll: as always, listening for the ghosts of the past. Now, down the length of England and arrived in Suffolk, Maud sought eagerly for even nearer links, visiting the farm home in Dunwich where her grandmother had been a little girl. "We walked about a mile from the shore . . . until we came to the lane of the Woolner farm, now called Mount Pleasant farm. . . . Tall trees grow all through the yard and almost hide the house from sight. . . . Were these trees there in your time?" she asked her Aunt Margaret, her grandmother's sister. "It seemed as if you and grandma must be somewhere about . . . little girls of twelve and fourteen, and I thought 'if only grandma . . . were alive so that I could write about this'. . . . There is a large garden in front of the house with a hawthorn hedge around it. I picked some flowers from it and pressed them. . . . In what room of the old home were you and grandma born and where did you sleep? . . . Could you see the sea from the house then or was the view of it obscured by trees?"

Shakespeare land, Hampton Court, Stonehenge, Windsor, and London landmarks were covered in a surfeit of sightseeing. A railway strike cancelled a visit to Ireland, but the travellers carried home with them a host of memories and some solidly tangible and treasured souvenirs of their trip. How many Leaskdale old-timers still remember "John Sphinx," the little monster that sat on top of one of the bookcases in the Manse library, bringing back memories to Maud of their visit to Berwick? And there was the pair of china dogs Maud discovered in a happy moment in the shadow of York Minister, with their haunting memories of the green-spotted dogs at Grandfather Montgomery's so long ago. These were bigger, gold-spotted, and more than a hundred years old. She took them back with her when they sailed for home on the *Adriatic* at the end of September, to preside—rather incongruously in a Christian home (though Maud's impish humour would relish the incongruity)—as Gog and Magog, those leaders of the nations warring against God under Satan's direction. Her small son Chester would introduce them gravely to visitors in later years. "This one is God, and that one is *my God*."

CHAPTER SEVENTEEN

Mistress of the Manse

Back in Leaskdale the Manse was being cleaned and painted and decorated for its new tenants. The floors were to be green: an odd instruction to people used to sober greys and browns and yellows, but this was what his lady wanted, Mr Macdonald had said. While the Reverend and his wife boarded briefly across from the church, crates were arriving: books and furniture and china were being unpacked; wedding presents, including the silver tea service presented to Maud by the Cavendish Presbyterian Church, put away.

One box, slatted on top and arriving by express, contained Daffy the Cavendish cat, now about to turn into the Leaskdale cat, so interested in him did the whole congregation become. Three days of confinement had subdued his initial vociferous protests. "He never uttered a squeak all the way from the station. . . . [Then] he climbed leisurely out and stretched himself. He was not at all hungry . . . but he was extremely thirsty and drank three saucers of milk and one of water without stopping. Then he climbed into my lap and kissed me as gravely and humanly as possible."

Most of the Leaskdale congregation hardly knew what to do with Maud, this modest, charming, friendly, unassuming, *famous* swan that had settled in their rural duckpond. They came to greet her with awe and remained to worship. Expecting to find an aloof celebrity, they found instead an unpretentious woman who chatted with them, laughed with them, cared about their joys and sorrows: seemed, in fact, like one of themselves. The congregation welcomed the Macdonalds with warmth and admiration at an official church reception on a night of pouring rain. Maud piled her hair high and wore her wedding dress and charmed everyone with her graciousness.

"Leaskdale is a very pretty country place," she told MacMillan"—would be almost as pretty as Cavendish if it had the sea. . . . It is a farming settlement . . . only fifty miles from Toronto. I find the people here nice and kind. Yes, I like Leaskdale very much. But as yet I do not love it. . . . We have a nice brick manse, prettily situated, though too close to the other houses and backyards in the village to suit my love of solitude and retirement. . . . I love our library—where I hope to see you as a most welcome guest some day. The little plaque you sent . . . adorns its walls, the gilt frame harmonizing admirably with the golden brown of the wall paper."

For fifteen years at Leaskdale and nine at Norval, just west of Toronto, she performed her role in the Manse with scrupulous attention to what she felt was expected of a minister's wife, and never deviated from her script. "There are certain things that cannot be expressed in terms of dollars and cents," she wrote in *An Open Letter from a Minister's Wife* in *Chatelaine* in 1931. "The leadership which the minister's wife can give, especially in rural communities where it may otherwise be lacking, is one of them. From my viewpoint, the minister's wife has a special opportunity for service which is a privilege and not a duty." She might have been Queen Victoria (though she thought Victoria dull, and had got into trouble as a child for being candid about a portrait of that sacrosanct lady) saying "I will be good!"

In June 1912, Maud told MacMillan that she would be "entertaining the stork" next month. MacMillan's news was less happy. For a long time he seems to have cherished a hope that his friendship with Jean Allan might deepen into something more. Now he had finally faced the realization that this was not to be. Maud wrote consoling words. "I am sorry for the suffering the experience has caused you, but I believe it will all be far better for you in the end." She was still comforting him two years later for this disappointment.

Early in 1918 she heard that Miss Allan had married. But not until March 1939 did she discover, to her amazement, that Miss Allan had a brother in Toronto—the Reverend William Allan, minister at Dovercourt Road Presbyterian Church. Maud might well have been amazed. Mr Allan had been a Toronto personality for years; he had initiated the Radio Ministry in 1932 for shut-ins, and was well known for his writings and lectures. "Ever since your letter came," Maud told MacMillan excitedly, "I have been intending to get in touch with him. . . . Some of these days I will get around to seeing him." Mr Allan, unfortunately, did not have many days left. Six months later, returning to Canada from a visit to his eighty-six-year-old mother in Alloa, he was one of the victims of the *Athenia* tragedy.

Maud was nearly thirty-eight when her first son, Chester Cameron, was born in July 1912, nearly forty when Hugh Alexander was stillborn in August 1914, nearly forty-one when she had her third and last child, Ewan Stuart, in October 1915.

As to every mother, but especially to Maud with her passionate emotional intensity, this first child was a breath-taking miracle, "a dear chubby rosy little fellow. . . . I can't imagine life without him now"—her *Punch, Punch-boy, Chester-boy, Peter Pan, little Man Friday.* She noted his every development, reporting to MacMillan the moment of first real awareness in the baby eyes, the baby chatter, the first tottering steps on "small fat legs." But caring for the child, and her other duties, meant less time for writing. *The Golden Road,* published in September 1913, "was written in odds and ends of time and so left a disagreeable impression of 'unfinishedness' in my mind."

Of necessity, a life with so many compartments—mother, housekeeper, minister's wife and author—had to be organized. Without good household help, one or other would have had to be neglected. Maud was fortunate in having capable workers in the home, whose affection she earned by making them all feel welcome and valued, impressing one of them, at least, with her kindness in insisting she should eat with the family. "No, Lily. If you're good enough to be in our home, you must be at our table!"

Without being totally inflexible, housework was orderly—this day for washing, that for ironing, these for cleaning, one for baking and odd jobs, Saturdays for getting ready for Sunday. Maud enjoyed cooking, sewed well, was an expert and innovative needlewoman, designing many of her own handmade needlepoint lace patterns. Years later she was charmed to find a first prize at the Canadian National Exhibition awarded to a lace design she had originated during one long winter evening at the Cavendish farm.

She became an adept at doing two things at once: sewing while she recited or read to her children; working out plots and dialogue as she drove in the cutter or the buggy drawn by Queen, the smart little black mare; or when she travelled by train; or even as she was dressing (parishioners remember hearing "muttering" sounds from behind her closed door from time to time), crocheting or knitting during meetings and pastoral visits. She took her proper part in every aspect of church life: the pastoral visiting, the quilting parties and pie socials, the Women's Missionary Society meetings, the Young People's Guild. She was good with teen-agers, and her pleasure in reciting and reading found a welcome outlet at their gatherings and in helping them produce and act in plays. Sometimes she wrote papers on subjects that were turning over in her own mind. As early as the mid-1920s she was trying to stir up young Leaskdale minds to understand the concept of atomic energy and other deeply puzzling aspects of the universe. Maud never did anything by halves.

Through all the years in this busy round, she managed to keep a couple of hours daily for writing. "She did her writing early in the morning," says her son Stuart, "and reading late at night. As long as I can remember, she slept five hours at night—occasionally six. She was an omnivorous reader and a sight reader. She read and reread all the classic English literature, and with a fabulous memory, could quote most of Shakespeare, Wordsworth, Byron and all the famous English poets, but also read all current books, magazines and news-papers, and ate up one or two detective novels daily."

In 1912 she had published *Chronicles of Avonlea,* a book of short stories, and in 1913 *The Golden Road,* another collection of stories, dedicated to Aunt Mary Lawson. Her children's growing years, her church duties, and World War One slowed her production over the next seven years, but three of the Anne books and *The Watchman & Other Poems* (a volume of what her son has called "mediocre verse" published in Toronto in 1916 by McClelland & Stewart) appeared between 1913 and 1921.

"People around here have a nice feeling about the Macdonalds," says a Leaskdale resident. They earned the judgment. Ewan fulfilled his duties unexceptionably, preached short down-to-earth sermons, posed no intellectual threat to his congregation, was jovial and hearty. The people liked him for his dedication, his rather bluff manner. "He laughed a lot," says someone. "Pleasant, maybe a bit superficial," says another. Perhaps he used laughter to fill in awkward conversational gaps when lack of small talk was a handicap.

But Maud alone knew the depth of his personal problems. If she found him less than the stimulating companion she may have expected, it never showed in her attitude. "The Macdonalds would argue with some spirit, but never became angry with each other," recalls a woman who worked in their home.

Nor did the congregation ever realize, as Maud soon did, how deeply Ewan could sink into a state of nervous melancholia. She wrote casually to friends about his ill health—his "nervous prostration," his insomnia, his low spirits. But only at the very end of her life did she disclose the despair for her husband's state of mind that had filled her heart for most of their life together: and by then, other burdens had combined to bow her down.

CHAPTER EIGHTEEN

Terrors
and triumphs

The war was a dreadful drain on Maud's mental and physical health, aggravated at the very beginning by the stillborn birth of her second child. Her letters to MacMillan during these years make painful reading, full of terrors and turmoil and agony of spirit. "Oh, is it not hideous—unbelievable—unthinkable! . . . Oh, surely, surely, Germany cannot win! . . . It is no joke but a simple fact that I have not had one decent dinner since the war began. Our *dinner* hour is one. The mail comes in at 12.30. If the news is good it excites me, if it is bad it upsets me and I can eat little. While if I decide to exert all my will-power and refuse to look at the papers until after dinner the suspense is worst of all and I can eat absolutely nothing. When I tell this to our comfortable, stolid country people who, from a combination of ignorance and lack of imagination, do not seem to realize the war at all, they laugh as if they thought I was trying to be funny. Those who perceive that I am in earnest think I am crazy."

She was passionately sure it was a righteous war for which she favoured conscription and to which she would send her own sons were they old enough. She argued vehemently with Weber's view that it was a commercial war. "When Germany outraged Belgium and swooped down on France," she shot back, "would you have had England sit still without lifting a finger?" She could not believe that the world would ever outlaw war. "There may be universes—worlds—where this is not the case; but ours is not one." Why argue about it, she told Weber, the idealist; neither would convince the other.

By January 1916, the demands of three-month-old Stuart—"our wee blue-eyed laddie"—were added to work with the Red Cross. Maud filled "every available chink and cranny of time" with sewing and knitting for the Red Cross (she was president of the local branch) and helping pack huge bales of supplies. By this time, reality had brought home to Leaskdale what Maud's sensitivity had made her suffer from the beginning. To Weber, she wrote: "In Uxbridge, our little market town seven miles away a regiment is billeted for the winter, and about seventeen of our finest boys have enlisted right here in our little rural community. Our church on Sunday is full of khaki uniforms, and oh, the faces of the poor mothers! The church is full of stifled sobs as my husband prays for the boys at the front and in training." Many of her own cousins and friends were in the trenches "somewhere in France," including her half-brother, twenty-two-year-old Carl. The following year, Carl would lose a leg, blown off at Vimy Ridge, where he lay on the snow-covered battlefield eighteen hours before being rescued. Yet, back in Toronto, he was "brown and hearty, cheerful and jolly, and gets around quite smartly on his one leg. A cripple in his young manhood!"

In October 1915, Stuart's birth had been followed by Ewan's six-week bout of bronchitis and a series of illnesses for Maud that ended in anaemia and loss of energy. The war news was all bad. "I shall never forget the agony of those two weeks when it seemed likely that the Germans were going to smash their way through! It was just when everything here was at its worst—E's illness and my own break-down. I couldn't eat or sleep. I *grew old* in that fortnight."

For someone whose very nearest and dearest were not involved in the war, and who was far from any scene of danger, her agonizing might be thought self-indulgent, not easy to understand except in the light of her volatile emotional response to every kind of experience. Her intensity transformed and magnified everything that happened to her. It was not hard for Maud's sensitive heart to suffer the pangs of the truly bereaved and the horrors of the battlefield.

She began to examine her dreams for omens and premonitions, drawing what favourable interpretations she could from their various elements: the frightful storm, for instance, from which a khaki-clad soldier had rushed into the Manse for refuge, and the sudden clearing of the skies, when she found herself crowned with flowers. "You may smile," she told MacMillan. "But in the terrible weeks of the Verdun offensive that dream was really my only comfort. . . . But one night during the height of the second desperate effort of the Germans, even my dream failed to sustain me. I seemed to go all to pieces. I walked the floor in nervous agony, picturing the worst . . . but towards morning I fell into a sound sleep. . . . When I awoke I was perfectly calm . . . I felt serene and confident. . . . Whether my subconscious mind really has in some way . . . foreseen the predestimed end of the struggle, time only can show."

Another "storm" dream seemed to forecast the attack on Rumania. "I dreamed that I was in the old sitting room down home with some friends. Suddenly we noticed a gloom and, running to the window I saw that exactly half the sky from the horizon to the zenith was covered with a dense black pall which seemed to have risen up in a moment. As I looked one livid, jagged bolt of lightning rent it asunder. We all ran to do various things as a preparation for the storm— shutting doors, closing shutters, driving in chickens etc. Then when everything was done we discovered that there was no longer *any* storm to prepare for—the sky was clear, the sun shining. I woke at once with the conviction that another German offensive was coming but from what quarter I could not imagine. When the attack on Roumania began I never doubted that Bucharest would fall—I believed that was what the bolt of lightning foretokened. Assuredly the first half of my dream came true," wrote Maud, convinced her interpretation was valid. "The war! Oh, the war!" During the long-drawn-out Verdun offensive, she had felt "as if I were slowly bleeding to death."

Her ninth strange dream since the outbreak of war ("and *every one* has come true") occurred in March 1918, when she held a newspaper whose headline proclaimed "There are 30 evil days in store for us." Next night she dreamed again; she was standing on a great plain "and I held in my arms a man whose face I could not see but whom I knew to be dying. As I held him he died and fell from my arms to the ground. Then I saw his face—and it was the face of the Kaiser's *father*. . . ." For Maud, this foretold the defeat of the House of Hohenzollern.

At every crisis she had spent sleepless nights. Until she heard that Jutland had been a victory and not a defeat, "I walked the floor like a lunatic." The shelling of Paris gave her a night that seemed "an endless agony." On the death of Kitchener, who with Lloyd George was one of her heroes, she felt that "one of the props of the Empire had been wrenched away." At meetings during the conscription election, she spoke twice on Women's Responsibility. In June 1918 she dreamt she met Marshal Foch "and he said simply, 'October 3rd.' " When the war was over, she convinced herself that the dream had been predictive. "You may remember," she told MacMillan, "that on October *4* Prince Maximilian announced before the German Reichstag that it had been decided to ask for an armistice. That announcement was made on the *fourth*. Does it not seem reasonable to suppose that the *decision* to ask for an armistice was made on the *third*?"

Despite the tremendous tensions, the daily routine of home and church and authorship had to go on. In January 1917, Stuart, who "is said to look like me," was walking and talking. Five-year-old Chester, a "chip off the old block," was "about as comfortable to have around as a young elephant": annoyed at his mother for some unappreciated restraint, he had just marched out of the room (Maud wrote to MacMillan) announcing, "If you act like that *at* me, mother, I'll turn you into a pig."

Over the years, MacMillan had been pondering the idea of writing a book, perhaps of essays, or in the form of letters. Maud encouraged him with ideas for topics and titles. The book was never written, but MacMillan's humorous verse earned him a local reputation. Maud liked his "Sweet" song in the *Alloa Journal* in October 1917, a rueful comment on the imminent sugar rationing.

Out-of-town trips for business, for duty and for pleasure, made inroads on her time. Maud was now in constant demand for speaking engagements or to give readings from her own work. She dashed off to Montreal; to Warsaw, Indiana, to visit Ewan's brother; to Boston where an unfortunate lawsuit had been shaping up over a disagreement with her original publisher, the L. C. Page Company. Page had included the right of refusal of all books she might write for five years after the signing of her contract with them in 1907, and she now found other reasons for wishing to be free from their restrictions. They had "kept me in misery for a year," Maud wrote in November 1917.

In 1917, too, she felt she had been too long away from the Island: perhaps a two-year absence had dried up her inspiration. She was writing articles for Canadian publications—this was the year that the story of her career, *The Alpine Path*, appeared in the Toronto magazine *Everywoman's World*. She sent a copy to MacMillan, and little poems by Canadian writers who might never have made the overseas scene dotted the pages of the *Alloa Journal*. But as for serious work, she had no time to produce more than pot-boilers, she said; only when leisure returned did she feel she could try to write something nearer "literature." In 1919 she was writing exultantly of six weeks in Prince Edward Island during the summer of the previous year. And this time she ventured to enter her old home: on an earlier visit, she had dared do no more than gaze at it from outside.

"It was a sad sight. The old maple grove was gone and most of the old birches. How sorrowful, how forlorn the old house looked.

"I slipped around to the back and saw that the door was secured only by a wire easily unfastened. I did what I never expected to do again—I opened the door and once more crossed the old threshold. I stood in the old kitchen. It was quite clearly visible in the dusk. A damp odor of decaying plaster hung heavy on the air. I went through the sitting room and the parlor. In each I shut my eyes and *thought myself* back into the past. Everything was around me as of old—each picture, each chair, each book or flower in its old place. I went up the dark stairs. I stood on the threshold of my old room—my old small illimitable kingdom where I had written my books long ago. But I did not go in. The window was boarded up and the room was as dark as midnight. Somehow I could not enter it. It was too full of ghosts—lonely, hungry ghosts. They would have pulled me in among them and kept me. I would have disappeared forever from the land of living men and nobody would ever have known what had become of me!

"Then I went down and out and away. These pilgrimages to shadow land are eerie things with an uncanny sweetness. I think I will make no more of them."

The Island had never been so lovely, so scented, so alluring, still the hiding-place of fairies secreted in wild columbine bells. As long as she lived, Maud Montgomery would need the Island to refresh her spirit. But such happiness made her apprehensive. "The gods do not give such gifts out of mere wantonness of giving. They are meant as consolation prizes for dark days to follow." Her old haunts still knew her for their own; but she left the Island with the chilling conviction that never again would it be so delightful.

Illness followed on the heels of exultation: a winter of influenza and neurasthenia, another visit to Boston for the lawsuit she had brought against Page. A fatal hole in her original 1907 contract lost Maud thousands of dollars when the movie rights for *Anne of Green Gables* were sold. Who in 1907 would have thought of protecting possible movie and dramatic rights? —and, at that, for a book intended for the shelves of Sunday School libraries? It seems vastly unfair that the creator of the character without whom there would have been no movie should have been denied any part of the profits. But the law came down against Maud this time. She never received one cent from either of the two movies made from the book, nor from the plays that were written from it.

Her grievances against the Page Company were not over. "Next year they're likely to publish a 'new' book by me," she warned Weber, "but be not deceived. It is a collection of old short stories which they held for years under the old contract but would never publish so long as they could get anything better."

Some of the stories had been published before. *The Son of His Mother* had appeared in *The Canadian Magazine* in March 1904; *The Hurrying of Ludovic*, its community of Deland River now transformed into Avonlea and its young plotter Juliet into Anne, had appeared in the same publication in May 1905, and Maud had brought the story of Ludovic and his lady-love Theodora Dix into Avonlea when *Anne of the Island* was published in 1915. *Everybody's Magazine* had used *The Quarantine at Alexander Abraham's* in April 1907. The book was duly published in 1920 as *Further Chronicles of Avonlea*. "Don't read it," Maud advised Weber.

CHAPTER NINETEEN

Lawsuit

This publication initiated nine years of lawsuits in which neither stubborn Maud nor stubborn Page would retreat. In ten pages of a February 1929 letter to MacMillan, when it was finally all over, she recounted the sorry tale.

"And now I am going to expound a dark secret which I promised should be revealed to you in the fulness of time. You remember your surprise when you found on Harrap's list of my books a certain one 'Further Chronicles of Avonlea' which you never knew existed. Well, 'thereby hangs a tale'— a tale that would fill a volume but must be condensed into a few pages. For the past *nine years* my existence has been to a certain extent a nightmare because of 'Further Chronicles.'

"As you know L. C. Page Co. of Boston were my first publishers. . . . When they accepted *Anne of Green Gables* (because a P.E.I. girl on their staff gave them no peace till they did) they asked me if I would prefer a royalty or a certain sum outright. I know now they thought I would jump at 'the certain sum' in which case I would have got $500 for *Green Gables*. But green as I was I was not so green as that so I said 'a royalty.' The contract was a hard one even for a beginner and one clause in it was that I must give them all my books on *the same lines* for a period of five years. I did not think this mattered because I never dreamed Green Gables was going to be a big success so I willingly signed up.

"In 1912 I had no new book ready so the Pages asked me to send them all my short stories for a volume to fill in. I sent them all I had of any value at all. They selected the best and 'Chronicles of Avonlea' were published. They sent back the rest but *unknown to me kept copies of them.* I destroyed the MSS they returned as I did not think they would ever be needed again. I may say that I had rewritten all the stories largely and added a good deal of new material mostly description. These new descriptive bits I kept and used them from time to time in various books that followed—The Golden Road, Anne of the Island etc. etc. This is an important point —keep it in memory.

"By 1916 I found it impossible to carry on with the Page Co. any longer. All their authors had left them and I was compelled to do so too. The time limit had now expired so I went to Stokes. Page was furious and threatened lawsuits to no end but in the end he did nothing because he hadn't the shadow of a claim anywhere.

"The next year he kept back $1000 out of my royalties on the ground that I had been overpaid previously. I needn't go into these details. Page's record is full of these things when dealing with his women writers. He . . . knew most women would submit to anything rather than go to law. But I came of a different breed of cats. I got the Authors League of America to find me a good Boston lawyer, and I entered suit in 1919 and *won it.* The judge gave me the $1000 dollars.

"Page had now found out there was no chance of bull-dozing me and his lawyer . . . (a very fine man by the way) approached me with an offer to buy my rights in the books entirely out. I was as anxious to get rid of them as they were to be rid of me, so I named a sum which would bring me in as much income every year if permanently invested as the royalties on the books were. After long dickering they came up to my price but on one condition. They asked me to allow them to publish another volume of short stories—those stories they had returned in 1912. This is where I made my mistake. I should never have done it. But I was terribly worried at the time, having just got word of the fatal illness of my dear friend Frede Campbell [her cousin Mrs. MacFarlane] in Montreal and I wanted to get away at once and be free, as I fondly fancied of the Page Co. for ever more. Besides they insinuated a vague threat that they could get those stories from the original magazines and publish them any time they liked—the very year I was bringing out a new book perhaps. So, as the stories were poor stuff, I agreed. I was to send copies of the stories. Of course being bound to Stokes I had to get their consent which they freely gave on *condition that there would be no mention of Anne* in the book. So the contract was drawn up and the Pages given the right to publish the book in 1920. I went home, sent them copies of the stories and thought no more about them.

"Then in the fall of 1919 Page wrote me that they had 'discovered in their vaults copies of the stories I had sent in 1912 and were going to publish *them* as the contract gave them the right to do.' I was aghast. Not only were there pages of description in those old MS that by this time had been used in succeeding books but there were several appearances of *Anne* in them—inserted when I was preparing them for possible inclusion in the first 'Chronicles'. This meant a breach of my contract with Stokes and would lay me open to breach of contract suit from them if they wanted to be nasty. Also I would be made absurd by a book coming out under my name containing no end of paragraphs and descriptions which were to be found in my other books.

"I got my lawyer to notify Page that they had no right to publish the 1912 versions and I would bring suit against them if they did. But they did it and brought out 'Further Chronicles' in March 1920. I at once brought suit for an injunction against the book and damages to my literary reputations. The case came up in May 1920. I went down to Boston for it. Page's lawyer thought the case would be over in *two days*. My lawyer was not so optimistic and thought it would take three. *It took nearly nine years!*

"Page's regular lawyer would not take the case so they got [another one]. . . . By the time two days were over it became evident that it was going to be longer than they thought so it went before a 'Master'. This Master hears the evidence at leisure, gives his opinion thereon and hands it to the judge who decides accordingly.

"*I had to stay in Boston until the middle of July*. I was on the witness stand for *three weeks* on end, being cross-examined by the ablest lawyer at the Boston bar. Can you fancy a more nerve-wracking ordeal. But I was telling the truth and not afraid to tell it and he could not break me down. You have heard no doubt of 'the maddening delays of the law'. Well, I know all about them. The hardest thing was their lawyer's 'trick' questions. But, 'though I say it as hadn't orter' he never trapped me once. And when it came to *my* lawyer's turn to grill the Page brothers *we* got some fun out of it—for they . . . would get all tangled up and contradict themselves and each other.

"Of course the whole thing hinged on the interpretation of the contract and their lawyer dragged in something every day to befog the issue. One day my lawyer got George Page to admit a certain thing and after the session he said to me 'We've won our case. I was afraid we couldn't get him to admit that.'

"But we were a long way from winning it. The lawyers would spend *hours* wrangling over the admissibility of certain questions or evidence and for days we would make no progress at all that I could see. Just think of my worry. And one of my boys ill at home! And yet that battle of wits between trained intellects was amazingly fascinating and if I had not been the toad under the harrow I would have enjoyed it.

"*One whole day* those three grave lawyers and myself wrangled over the exact color of *Anne's* hair and the definition of 'Titian' red. Ye gods, it *was* funny. The big table was snowed under with literature and prints to disprove or prove. They had two 'art experts' on the stand who flatly contradicted each other. Years before when I sat down in that old house in Cavendish one rainy spring evening and dowered Anne with red tresses I did not dream that a day would come when it would be fought over in a Boston courtroom. Their lawyer was determined to prove that Titian hair was dark red and that I knew it was dark red. I didn't. I always supposed it was a sort of flame-red and I stuck to it through all his badgerings. One expert said it was 'bright golden-auburn' and the other said it was the color of burnished copper. And so on!

"The raison d'etre of all this was the picture of the redheaded girl on the cover which was a part of our case.

"By the end of June the Pages evidently thought that the

case was not going to be over as soon as they had hoped and decided to hurry it up a bit by scaring me into dropping it. They handed me a writ, suing me for $30,000 damages for libel because of the statements in my 'bill of complaint.' This was absurd of course. A bill of complaint is privileged and they had no case. But the trouble is in the States you have to pay your own fees and costs whether you win or lose and the wealthy Page Co. could afford that better than I could. But my fighting blood was up and I determined to ignore their threat and fight to the end. Still, you can imagine the worry and vexation this inflicted on me.

"Then a Page witness swore to a flat lie—a most damaging lie to our case and my lawyer lost his grit. He said it was such damaging testimony that he thought we'd better offer to settle. I would *not* knuckle down to the Pages after the way they had behaved and said so. So on we went.

"I came home in mid-July a perfect wreck. But the case went on.

"In September Page's lawyer filed his damage suit for the libel. Then the Master took *nearly a year* to make up his report. In September 1921 it came—and it was decidedly adverse to us. I had never expected anything else, of course, after the lies. . . . The report was sent to the judge but it is a *very* rare thing that a judge does not follow the Master's findings. As for the libel suit in August 21 it was thrown [out] of the Massachusetts court on the ground that it was illegal. Then Page appealed it to the Supreme Court of the State. In six months it was thrown out there. Then he carried it to the Supreme Court of the United States!

"As for the Master's report, handed in in Sept. 1921 would you believe it was *April 1923* before the judge gave his decision. Such a thing was never heard of I believe. But—perhaps it was as well for me because what happened was that the judge discarded the Master's report and examined all the evidence himself. There was about a trunkful of typewritten evidence and he told my lawyer he had never met such an interesting case in his life. *And he gave decision in my favour!* I got my injunction against the book and *all* the profits.

"Oddly enough the very same day word came that the Page

appeal had been thrown out by the Supreme Court of the U.S.

"Do you think my worry was over then? Not by a jugful! Of course the Pages at once appealed from the judge's decision.

"And in December 1923 they filed the same old libel suit in the courts of *New York State* and attached my royalties due from Stokes to compel me to fight the case over again there. A New York lawyer had to be engaged also!

"In June 1924 the New York suit was dismissed. Then Page appealed to the Supreme Court of New York.

"On March 4, 1925, the appeal in my case was decided in my favour.

"Then they had to begin the 'accounting' to find out what the 'profits' really were. In October 1925 the New York libel case was finally thrown out and my long withheld royalties paid to me. My N.Y. lawyer wrote me that, since I was not a resident of N.Y. State I had a clear case against the Page Co. for the repayment of all the N.Y. suit had cost me. It had cost me $2000. So I thought I would show Page I had plenty of fight left in me yet and I at once entered suit in New York against *him*!

"In June 1927 the judge gave decision on the profits in my favor. The Pages appealed the amount. In March 1928 I won my New York suit and got back my money.

"And *finally* in October 1928 the Page appeal was refused. *At last* there was nothing more they could do by hook or crook. They paid me $18,000 of profits and the thing was ended after nearly 9 years of worry and expense. The suit cost me $15,000. So I had for recompense $3000, my injunction against the book—*and* the satisfaction of having whipped the Pages to a finish!

"The suit cost the Pages about $75,000 in all. And for the past four years they and their lawyer have not been on speaking terms, though he continued to act for them.

"Those are just the *outlines*! The details would fill a library! . . .

"I began this letter Feb. 10. It is now March 10—and spring —and housecleaning. But, thank God, *no lawsuits*!"

CHAPTER TWENTY

Minister's wife

Perhaps she should never have married a minister. There was more than a grain of seriousness in her rueful comment to MacMillan in 1927 that "Those whom the gods wish to destroy they make ministers' wives!" Certainly she should never have married Ewan Macdonald, whose intense and tragic personal problem—a belief that he was predestined to hell—made itself apparent only slowly to Maud in his increasingly distressing melancholia. Even beneath the shelter of an untroubled marriage, Maud would probably have found difficulty in maintaining the checks and limits on her patience. But once committed, she was not the person to withdraw from the loyalty demanded of a wife—and of a minister's wife at that.

It was not an easy life for a positive person with emphatic views often at variance with what had to be her outward behaviour in a small and conventional community; and now the heavy demands of church work on her time were added to those of her role as a popular author. Her own moral standards, her own willingly shared emotional riches within the bounds of propriety, these brought her well-deserved respect. But for Maud Macdonald too many questions did not find answers, or found answers that could have earned her the scandalized rejection of her congregation had she openly expressed them, though many of them were little more than a sturdy refusal to accept narrowmindedness and meanness of spirit.

It was the legacy—and perhaps the curse—of her upbringing, in which the strength of her own powers of reason and a natural and spontaneous warmth of heart were subordinated to the forbidding Calvinism of Presbyterian dogma. Maud had been an amenable, eager-to-please child, trying to accept the edicts of her elders as right and proper. The adult Maud had learned to question and rebel. But the loyalty to her husband that made her a genuine helpmeet; loyalty to the role she had accepted in society; loyalty to her status as a writer read by the young: all these demanded that no public expression of her inner self, where it deviated from accepted beliefs, should ever be allowed. A tug-of-war conscience did not make for easy balance between training and inclination; she found she was "compelled to play the part by the circumstances of my existence." That no hint of this unceasing internal battle reached those among whom she moved is a tribute to the strength of her personality.

Her congregation would have been astonished by the questing spirit and emphatically unorthodox opinions simmering behind that quiet, friendly face, and they never realized the iron control that kept her at her post, nor understood the pull of weariness and her need for solitude and escape.

She catalogued to Weber and MacMillan the tiresome details of a typical week. Tonight, rehearsal for a play being got up by the Guild. Last night, out to tea. Sunday night to song service. Saturday night a function at Zephyr (the other church in the Leaskdale charge), where she gave an address and presented a gift to a departing member of the Women's Missionary Society. Friday night conducting a Guild social. Thursday night, "practice" again for the play. Wednesday, a trip to Toronto to hear Lloyd George speak. Tuesday night, pastoral visiting. Monday night, practice again.

In 1920, as "a sort of duty" she sat up late at a young farmer's wedding reception. "I had to sit there till two in the morning and talk to scores of the women who were sitting in rows around the room, until I felt like a machine that just talked ever on without any volition. My head ached, my back ached, my mind and soul ached," listening to chatter about hens, eggs, new babies, the high cost of living, "and all the other entrancing subjects of 'conversation' which prevail hereabouts—at least when 'the minister's wife' is present." She suspected that when she was absent the people would talk "racy and malicious and *interesting* gossip, and enjoy themselves much better, but alas, ministers' wives dare not meddle with gossip, else would their tenure in the land be short and troubled."

When she had been a young teacher at Bideford on the Island, she had sent to a Toronto magazine a sample of her handwriting for character analysis. "You are of a rather domineering disposition," she was told, "but knowing how to master yourself as well as others, are very controlled. You are very fond of elegance and luxury, of aristocratic manners, etc. *You know how to suppress and hide your internal thoughts and feelings to such an extent as to appear utterly different from what you really are.* You can be extremely amiable, affable and obliging. You have a will of your own. You like comfort and ease. You are very economical, very politic and diplomatic, suspicious and distrustful. I could tell you a great many more things from your very interesting handwriting."

The italics were Maud's own. While she wondered what "the other things" were that might have been revealed, she commented to MacMillan, "I consider that the underlined sentence marked me out and predestined me for a minister's wife!!!" And though character analysis from handwriting is far from an exact science, this summary was not far from the truth about Maud.

She kept herself beyond criticism, knowing full well the avalanche of censure that would destroy her if she should wander from the accepted paths of behaviour. Those among whom she moved with such cheerful warmth could never have known the tightness of the rein by which she held herself in check, nor the violence with which she repudiated her reputation for social grace, as if she felt it was a mask she was forced to wear. She was not a mixer, though she knew she was considered to be a good one. "I hate the word." She was only "an excellent imitator of one." She *detested* mixers, and despised herself for having to ape them. "I never knew a 'good mixer' yet that was worth a brass farden." The only really worthwhile people were "cats who walked by themselves, rejoicing in their own peculiar brand of cathood and never pretending to be Maltese if they were tortoise shell. . . . You know as well as I do," she told Weber, "that the mixer has no real influence at all"—like a *catalyzer* ("or is it catalyst?") in chemistry, helping but not influencing.

To the young salesman who offered the range of volume as a selling point for irreverent Sunday listening to the Victrola, Maud was sternly the minister's wife. What, she demanded, would her congregation think if they heard her playing *dance* music, even softly, while Ewan was away preaching? Some of them would have understood; many more would have been disillusioned, and she could not risk that—not only for Ewan's sake, but for her own belief in what was a proper example. So she held herself in check. She who had loved dancing denied herself the indulgence as unbecoming to her new role. And "what agonies I have endured betimes when I was dying to laugh" (or criticize, or speak sharply, or contradict, or withdraw?) "but dared not because I was the minister's wife."

What would many of her people have thought, too, of some of her shockingly unorthodox thoughts? Reading W. E. H. Lecky's controversial *History of European Morals from Augustus to Charlemagne*, she agreed with his views on suicide. "Life is forced upon us; we did not ask for it; therefore if it becomes too hard we have a right to lay it down," though such an act would be cowardly if it laid a burden on others. She took issue with Lecky's belief that conscience was divinely implanted. "Conscience is merely the result of our education in right and wrong, and is not in itself an infallible guide. Bitter experience usually teaches us results of words and deeds . . . and so far guides us, but Christians have burned each other quite persuaded that the Apostles would have done the same."

For many years she had been drawn to a belief in reincarnation, the afterglow, probably, of her passion for Zanoni. As early as 1906 she had written: "It is fascinating to suppose that we go from one existence to another, with the restful sleep of so-called death between! To me, the idea is a thousand fold [more] attractive than that of the Christian's heaven with its unending *spiritual* joys." And more than thirty years later she still hopefully clung to the same possibility. In 1937 she confided to Ephraim Weber that she believed the soul to be immortal, but not personalities. When the body was worn out, "the undying spark within us joins the flood of life pervading the universe, seeks and finds another 'robe of flesh' and proceeds to build up another personality. *No* other belief, it seems to me, can explain or justify the problems and pains of life. If this present life is but a *day* in a year of days—they shrink to unimportance . . . in the course of eternity we will live *all* kinds of lives and undergo *all* kinds of experiences, thereby attaining to perfect wisdom and understanding."

But she gave little credence to spiritualism, shattering its claims with shafts of humour. The sudden death in mid-1919 of her cousin Frederica Campbell MacFarlane had given Maud "the most terrible blow I ever had to bear in all my life." They had made a pact years before that the first to die would communicate with the other if possible, but *none returneth again that is gone thither*, and there was no message. "I only know that I am left desolate, bereft . . . whither has she gone? Across the gulf of separation there comes no response. . . . She took away with her the laughter of life for me."

When Maud read *The Twentieth Plane* by Dr Albert Durrant Watson, edited by Dr Albert Holden Abbott, instructor in philosophy and assistant in the psychological laboratory in the University of Toronto, then president of the Canadian Society for Psychic Research, she found it pathetically funny because "so oddly serious." The spiritualists "are choice in the spook company they keep," she commented. "There isn't a single non-famous spirit on their calling list, except Dr. Watson's mother. Shakespeare and Plato, Wordsworth and Lincoln etc. etc. jostle each other for a chance to expound through the ouija board—and all use precisely the same literary style, and a very awful one at that. There don't seem to be any grocers or butchers or carpenters on the Twentieth Plane. . ." And she would prefer more substantial fare than synthetic beef tea and the juice of a rice product, "if one must eat in the world of spirits," and a pleasanter environment in which to consume the food than in a pink twilight under an orange sun.

She came from the tragedy of her loss to the ouija-board craze endorsed by author and editor of the book, and found it unconvincing—"and I was so ready to be convinced." Ouija was remarkably flippant with Maud. When the company stopped asking it questions, it piped up of its own accord.

"Now Laura will dance! Tee hee!"

"But, Ouija, I have no music, I can't dance without music!"

"Oh, Maud will whistle."

For some reason Ouija always spelled phonetically when Maud was at the board ("Why? I detest the idea."). And when asked to name her worst fault, Ouija gave Maud the cryptic reply, *"Ewan knows."* That the board might be right, she admitted. "But evidently some demons have a sense of humor."

In 1924 she was hailing science as the source of the new revelation she felt sure must be coming. "The older revelations have exhausted their mandate. I believe the next one will come through science. What form it will take I cannot guess. . . . Two thousand years ago Jesus Christ burst the bonds that were stifling human thought. Now these bonds are tightening around us again—outworn dogmas, dead superstitions. It will take something as tremendous in its own way as his message for spiritual freedom to destroy those bonds again. But—it will come."

Five years later she was still thinking along the same lines. "Humanity has to pay some price for growing up and becoming wise and rich and comfortable . . . we are, I believe, entering on an age of wonderful scientific development. We will do things that are hardly dreamed of as yet but we will not write great literature or paint great pictures. We can't have everything at the same time. We will fly round the world—and solve the secret of the atom, but there will be no Shakespeares or Homers. They went out with the gods."

As early as 1927 she had been apprehensive about the atomic future. "It will be wonderful and revelatory—but will it be beautiful? The discovery of a way to release the energy of the atom will be the next epochal thing after the dynamic of Jesus. I hope it will not come in my time, nor in my children's. Because it will mean the overturning and passing away of all existing conditions, whether of good or evil. Everything will go—our financial institutions, our standards of value, our ways of living. An utterly new world will arise —which may be a very good thing for those who will be accustomed to it, and who will look back to our age as one lost in darkness and ignorance." But there would be some things still hidden. "God will always keep a few secrets to himself," she added nearly two years later when she was feeling "both infinitesimal and infinite. And a little dizzy," after reading Charles Henshaw Ward's *Exploring the Universe.*

She retained her old abhorrence of "the traditional paths of thought and expression" in teaching Christian ideals. "To this day," she wrote in 1922, her picture of a Christian was not that of someone trying to carry out the ideals and ideas of Jesus, but of an individual like the unctuous evangelist at Cavendish. In time, "I was able to separate this attitude and came into my heritage of reverence for that unique and wonderful personality with its lofty aspirations, its pure conception of truth, its radical scorn for outworn conventions and dogmas." But she found it painful to see her own children in their turn subjected to "false and ugly conceptions of these matters," and to be unable to interfere because her husband's position demanded discretion.

But once, at least, she resolved "to dare the Leaskdale Grundyites." Seven-year-old Stuart, learning his catechism, came to the question *Why did God make all things?* Answer: *For His own glory.* "It seemed to me an abominable libel on God," she wrote in outrage. With scorn for his teachers, "a couple of crude, ignorant old women who never had an original thought in their lives," who regarded as the deepest dyed infidel anyone who did not believe in "the talking snake of Eden," she told Stuart: "That is not how that question should be answered. God made all things for the love and pleasure of creating them—of doing good work—of bringing beauty into existence."

Though she might rage inwardly and despise adherence to the letter where it damaged the spirit, those who knew and loved her in Leaskdale and Norval were not mistaken in their judgment of her. For all her unorthodoxy, Maud Montgomery Macdonald remained an intensely spiritual woman, with a loving heart and an inviolable sense of duty. Everything she wrote rings with a deep inner truth, a hope that decency, morality, beauty will prevail, a revulsion from the limited vision of pettiness, though she knew her own frailties, and sometimes could not cleanse her own soul of pettiness. She had the wisdom to recognize, at least, the unimportance of what she rejected, the importance of what she still believed. Her congregations might have been shocked by some of her views, but the life she lived among them must surely have spoken in a louder voice.

CHAPTER TWENTY-ONE

Demands
of duty

Maud could easily have allowed herself to be remembered differently in Leaskdale. Famous authors can be aloof, superior, condescending—and so, of course, can ministers' wives. But Maud Macdonald—minister's wife and world-famous author—is remembered with love by the people of her congregation: with more than love—a glow of admiration, and a little astonishment that she had seemed like one of themselves.

It was hardly possible for Maud to be unaware of her effect on her congregation, nor to fail to enjoy it, a perfectly human reaction. As a child, she had revelled in being at centre-stage, even if the position had been gained painfully, as when she had so severely burned her hand. She would have had to be aware that she stood on some kind of pedestal—nor, in fact, was it possible for the congregation to look at her with any kind of objectivity. They observed with fascinated attention everything she did, this woman who talked to them and laughed with them and sorrowed with them and moved among them as an equal; with them, but hardly of them.

There was no cold calculation in her own image of herself, nor was it a false image. Duty demanded that she be publicly true to her role, and, as always, duty was her guide. It was a duty that she regarded as a privilege; but it was also a weary-ing role for one who secretly abhorred "mixers," the more wearying because she accepted also the tiresome responsibili-ties of successful authorship. It is vastly to her credit that she juggled a tight domestic routine, a voluminous correspondence, the demands of public appearances and a warm community fellowship with its thousand calls on her time and sympathy, along with her private disappointments and secret rebellions—all without a single crack in the facade of her reputation.

How many times did she subordinate her own desires and preferences to the demands of common courtesy, of duty? A perceptive Leaskdale friend remembers travelling with her by train to a nearby town and being gently requested to forgive her apparent remoteness: she liked to use the time for thinking out some tricky scene in her current work. "Yet, when acquaintances chanced to board the train at an intermediate stop and join us with incessant, inconsequential chatter, no one would ever have guessed, from Mrs. Macdonald's demeanor, how unwelcome their intrusion must have been."

The people of Leaskdale have treasured with deep affection the happy trivia of life in the Manse. The bone-handled pen with which Maud wrote at a table strewn with ink bottle, notebooks, papers and Daffy the cat; her uninhibited enjoyment in what she wrote, rippling over her face in smiles and sometimes breaking into laughter; the little velvet bows she liked to wear on her blouses; her beautiful rose satin dress with lace-overlaid bodice; the sturdy fur-lined coat of blue broadcloth in which she braved winter driving, wrapped around with additional coats and scarves; the graceful movements of her slender fingers, always busy with some form of needlework; the orderly management of the household (Maud was never disorganized)—its punctual mealtimes, its menus carefully planned for two weeks ahead, its snowy linen piled in the closet. They remember the careful provisioning—the two turkeys, four geese and six ducks frozen for winter use, the four pork hams and one "beef ham" (Island terminology) cured and dried for summer meat, the keg of mackerel, box of codfish and six bags of potatoes ordered from the Island each fall.

They were amused by the little boys, restless in church, firmly marched out by their mother after adequate warning;

by Chester's habit of sliding off his chair during family prayers and producing his *Amens* from beneath the table; the little black stick Maud used to rap the boys' knuckles when they needed disciplining. They recall her love of gardening, and the flowers with which she filled the house; her pleasure in picking wild strawberries; the tamarack gum she got from Eaton's, and chewed for the sake of her teeth. They were proud of her interest in the Hypatia Club, the Uxbridge cultural society of which she was honorary president for several years.

They saw a family unity that included good-natured teasing, vigorous and friendly argument, a lot of laughter (especially when the Campbell cousins came up to visit from the Island). They noticed, too, that though she wearied for her beloved Island, Maud found much to satisfy her in the rolling, open countryside of Leaskdale, with its clumps and spreads of evergreens, and its wide skies. "After a snowfall . . . she delighted in watching for the tracks of the various creatures of the woods—here finding a mouse's or a bird's print, and there a rabbit's. She searched for every new beauty nature might reveal. . . . Her conversation was frequently pointed up with 'That reminds me' and off she would go with some 'yarn' for there was always a funny side of things. Because she was witty and gay, young and old enjoyed her company. Rarely one missed hearing some tale about her beloved Island or its people."

Cats were her passion. "How dreadful it would be *not* to love a cat!" she exclaimed to MacMillan. "I wonder if all the spirits of all the pussy folk I have loved will meet me with purrs of gladness at the pearly gates?" But beneath her passion lay an inescapable sense of guilt from a syllogism embedded in her childhood conscience. Grandma and Grandpa had hated cats: Grandma and Grandpa were wise grown-ups: therefore it was not right to love cats. There was always a sense of shame, though adult reason denied it, in her "pleasure in pussies . . . and as for people who say they like cats 'in their place', I know all about them from that one phrase."

At the end of 1907, Maud had written of Daffy, "He's

everything a cat should be, except that he hasn't one spark of affection in his soul. But then somebody has said, 'The highest joy a human being can experience is *to love disinterestedly*. *Daffy*, therefore, gives this joy to me, since I cannot hope for any return of the affection I bestow on him." Yet, as Daffy grew older, the ability to love probably grew in him. When he died in 1920 at the age of fourteen (first thought to have been poisoned, but discovered later to have been shot), he had learned to greet Maud at the gate of the Manse and precede her up the walk. "The house is haunted by him," Maud mourned, stung by her sense of personal loss when his favourite nooks, now empty, caught her eye. This beautiful creature with his coat of silver-grey fur marked with black was not a cat, but a *person*, she said: the last living link with her old life on the Island.

She was still missing Daffy a year later, but confessed that she had "catted" again, though Paddy lacked Daffy's personality. Paddy developed a superlatively fine pair of whiskers after losing his first set to scissors wielded by six-year-old Stuart—just as an earlier cat (could it have been *Daffy*?) had lost his to young Ken Macneill in Cavendish. "When they grew out again they were about twice as long and aggressive as an ordinary cat's."

Ewan Macdonald is remembered as a bit of a tease in a heavy-handed way. One member of his congregation has recalled his attempt to make Scottish oatcakes when he was alone in the Manse on one occasion; no recipe tried by Maud had succeeded in satisfying him. His subsequent chuckling refusal to illuminate the incident led to fruitless searches for remaining cakes, tracking a trail of oatmeal from kitchen to front hall and stairs. He remained silent except to say blandly that the cakes had turned out well. Months later, two of the cakes were discovered when Maud was cleaning out his bureau drawer.

A member of his flock, asking where he got those nice slippers, was told tersely, "Where I left the money." At another time, pointing through a window, he remarked to a member of his Zephyr congregation who (he must have

The house at Clifton (now New London) where Maud was born is now an L.M. Montgomery museum.

Clifton (New London), where L.M. Montgomery was born on 30 November 1874.

Hugh John
Montgomery, Maud's
father, with his second
wife, Mary Ann McRae

Senator Donald
Montgomery, Maud's
paternal grandfather

Grandfather Alexander Macneill

Grandmother Lucy Woolner Macneill

At eleven, Maud was already an inveterate scribbler, an imaginative child with "a passport to fairyland."

Rear view of the old Macneill homestead (no longer standing) which lay between two orchards full of apple and cherry trees. The post office entrance was at the front.

At sixteen, Maud spent a year with her father in Prince Albert.

At nineteen, Maud was studying for her Second Class teachers' certificate at Prince of Wales College.

Maud, aged twenty-eight. Two years later, in 1904, she earned $591.85 from her writing.

Maud was thirty-three when Anne of Green Gables *was published in June 1908.*

Old Prince of Wales College, Charlottetown

Anne of Green Gables.

Chapter 1. Mrs. Rachel Lynde is Surprised.

Mrs. Rachel Lynde lived just where the Avonlea main road dipped down into a little hollow, traversed by a brook that had its source away back in the woods of the old Cuthbert place; it was reputed to be an intricate headlong brook in its earlier course through those woods, with dark secrets of pool and cascade. But by the time it reached Lynde's Hollow it was a quiet, well-conducted little stream, for not even a brook could run past Mrs. Rachel Lynde's door without due regard for decency and decorum; it probably was conscious that Mrs. Rachel was sitting at her window, keeping a sharp eye on everything that pa

N.B. and that if she noticed aught odd or out of place she would never rest

Chapter 1, page 1: Maud begins Anne of Green Gables.

*Ephraim Weber, the first of Maud's two lifelong
pen-friends*

George MacMillan in later years

The Reverend Ewan Macdonald had been Presbyterian pastor at Cavendish. He was forty, Maud thirty-six when they married in 1911.

The Reverend Ewan and Mrs. Macdonald at the Glasgow Exhibition during their honeymoon in 1911. Maud said he looked "fierce."

Ewan Macdonald and George Boyd MacMillan

The Manse at Leaskdale, Ontario, Maud's first married home. Here her sons were born

St. Paul's Church, Leaskdale, Ontario

The Manse at Norval, Ewan Macdonald's second Ontario charge

The Presbyterian Church, Norval, Ontario

*Maud, front and centre,
with one of her amateur
theatrical companies*

L.M. Montgomery

*Stuart (three) and
Chester (six) with their
father in the garden at
Leaskdale*

*Maud's younger son,
Stuart, aged about four*

*Chester MacDonald,
Maud's elder son,
aged three.*

*Stuart Macdonald
became national junior
gymnastic champion
in 1933.*

On our way to "old Kaintuck"

Maud's cousin, Beatrice McIntyre, went with the family on an unforgettable trip in 1924 to the Mammoth Cave in Kentucky

"I love best the flowers I coax into bloom myself." A happy Maud Macdonald in the 1930s

On the gravestone:

MACDONALD

REV. EWEN MACDONALD
1870 — 1943

REV. LUCY MAUD MONTGOMERY
MACDONALD
WIFE OF
EWEN MACDONALD
1874 — 1942

GRAVE OF
L.M.MONTGOMERY

*Maud Montgomery's body has returned to her beloved
Island, where it rests in Cavendish cemetery just across
the road from the site of the Macneill homestead. In the
background is the Green Gables house in P.E.I. National
Park. Green Gables, however, is no longer visible from
the cemetery; in the years since this picture was taken the
trees in between have grown up to obscure the view.*

thought) was being unduly inquisitive: "You see that pump out there? Well, you might pump that, but you can't pump *me*." Though he served diligently, the vivid personality of his wife was to be Ewan Macdonald's chief claim to distinction as a minister.

"They would argue by the *hour*," says a relative, reminiscing. "And *how* they would argue! Aunt Maud could put him down every time. She used to get impatient because he spoke very slowly, and she would be away ahead of him before he got around to his point."

A member of his Norval congregation (he moved there in 1926) recalls Ewan as a plodder. "If it hadn't been for *her*, he'd have been unmemorable. He wasn't a very good conversationalist—a bit slow, a bit absent-minded, a bit offhand. Didn't have much of a viewpoint about anything, at least you couldn't pin him down. His sermons weren't bad, though, good down-to-earth talks, and short. But *her*! Now, *she* was the one who held things together. She was the social part of it. She'd go into the church kitchen and work with the other women—and those strawberry pies of hers! And she kept the young people enthusiastic with the talks she gave and the plays she used to direct, mostly light comedies she'd adapt for the purpose. No one would ever forget Maud Macdonald."

And no one would realize the bone-weariness she suffered as she did what duty demanded. One part of her enjoyed it; one part resented its intrusions. She would write: "Sometimes I get so sick of them [mission bands, missionary auxiliaries, ladies' aids, Women's Institutes, Sunday School teachers' meetings, etc. etc. etc.] that I could hang myself on the handiest gooseberry bush rather than go to another. And yet —it's odd—it's always in prospect only that I hate them. When I get to them I find myself really quite enjoying them. I like 'making things go', having, so I have been told, a 'gift' that way. It is really only because of the inroads they make on my time that I rise up and howl occasionally." Yet she could write, "I have lost the art of living entirely. . . . It isn't right. We weren't meant to live like that." Separately, she could have enjoyed any of her current activities. All together, crammed into one life, they were too much.

Her sons were an abiding joy, at any rate during their boyhood and early teens. On a visit to Leaskdale in June 1936, when Ewan was preaching an anniversary sermon, she found pleasure and pain oddly mixed in her weekend as a guest in the Manse where she had been mistress for fifteen years. The Manse was "full of the ghosts of little boys. . . . The little lads my sons were then seemed to be still somewhere about." In a year when her boys were young men, Chester in law school, Stuart a medical student, she could hear childish laughter in the shadows, light footsteps on the stairs; baby Stuart's "ingratiating chuckle," toddler Chester's "amusing chatter"; the joyous yelling overhead—"probably a pillow-fight," as she wrote to Weber in mid-1919—when they were supposed to be going to sleep; Hallowe'en nights when the boys accompanied their cronies with masks and pumpkins, "dancing in wild abandon round a jacky-lantern on the gatepost and shrieking like tortured savages, as half-civilized man might have, eons ago, round the sacrificial fire"; the time Chester bolted after the cat in the middle of family prayers.

Perhaps, that Sunday, sitting as a visitor in her familiar pew in the small Leaskdale church, so much smaller than the church in Ewan's charge at Norval, a smile would have hovered on her lips, as she remembered the small finger pointing to a word in the hymn-book, and Stuart's voice reading carefully aloud, "Muffer, is that *God*?" at the precise moment his father's head appeared above the pulpit. And the endless questions would come ringing back:

"Mother, who were the father and mother of the first crow?

"Mother, what were pancakes when they were alive?

"Mother, is this the only world there is, *in a sense*?"

The years had become cluttered with responsibilities, to which the war had added its burden. Days that used to be filled with things one *wanted* to do were now full of "things that *have to be done*." Maud longed for the day when the boys would be older, when she could write more often to friends: write, as she hoped to do, more *serious* literature—an optimism that was never justified in her own mind. Meanwhile, she "pegged away" at her pot-boilers.

most hateful of the year, a time of "rush and hurry and worry" with Sunday School concerts and end-of-the-year business meetings. "Can you think of Jesus on Xmas day?" Weber had asked. No, Maud could not. It had become a *horrible* day. She deplored the sending of cards on a false basis of convention—*they* sent us one last year, *we* must return one this year. But "I am as guilty as anybody else. . . . There's something terribly wrong somewhere with most things today, I fear. But I dare say I'm just getting old and tired and that's why things seem to be going to the demnition bow-wows."

She returned to the theme years later. "Isn't it *tragic* that the observance of the birthday of the Founder of the greatest religion on earth should be mainly associated with turkey and geese and plum pudding!!"

CHAPTER TWENTY-TWO

The Wheel of Things

All through the 1920s Maud was hard at work producing new books. Seven titles were published between 1921 and 1931 and none of them truly satisfied their author, except perhaps *Emily of New Moon*. Having completed *Rilla of Ingleside* and finished, as she hoped, with Anne—"I am sick of her and wonder that the public isn't too"—she was writing in October 1921 that she had "a new kind of heroine," and liked her.

"People were never right in saying I was Anne, but, *in some respects*, they will be right if they write me down as Emily." Maud certainly injected into these books incidents and dialogue and characters of her own creating, but Emily's life story—particularly in the first book (there would be three *Emily* books)—and her dedicated intention to be a writer, follow Maud's career closely. Whole chunks of her own life are embedded in the story. The letters written by the ten-year-old Emily to her dead father, as Maud wrote to her own dead mother—written, too, on the backs of letter-bills; Emily's treasured memory of her beautiful mother as she remembered seeing her lying in her coffin; the private language Emily invented, like the language with which Maud and a friend teased their excluded school chums; Emily's unfulfilled longing to wear her hair with bangs like every other girl at the time; the Murray pride in ancestry that mirrored Maud's in the Macneills and the Montgomerys. The saintly, suffering child Anzonetta Peters is there under her own name. Emily's first typewriter copied Maud's—the one that made faint capitals and would not print the letter *m* at all. Emily climbed the same steps in education as Maud did; even Maud's real-life school-teaching is the pattern for Emily's.

Maud saw her new heroine as so different and so fresh that she was affronted by Weber's reaction. "You say 'Of course *Emily* is another *Anne*'. Well, she may be, but if so I have entirely failed in my attempt to 'get her across' to my readers." Emily's background of family and tradition, she felt, was very different from "the hail fellow well met little orphan from nowhere." She could not see any resemblance "except one or two superficial ones in the stage they walk on."

She was amused, however, to read that the only character Weber thought overdrawn was the only one taken from real life—the teacher, Mr. Carpenter. Reaction by readers was almost always the same, she had found. People tended to fit the wholly invented characters to real people and were sure those drawn from real life were imaginary. Was this because life itself is crude and imperfect, she wondered?—inconsistent with our ideas of it? "Does even truth have to have a veil of illusion to make it true?"

Anne and Emily do, in fact, share many similarities. Both are orphans, both are pert, attractive, highly articulate children with a strong awareness of individuality, both strongly imaginative, both passionate in their responses. Both are in the hands of authoritarian guardians and under compulsions that often run counter to their inclination and to their well-developed sense of what is "fair." The adult inhabitants of Emily's world are more often relatives; neighbours fill the gap in Anne's world. But these adults are endowed with similar idiosyncracies of personality—loving or severe, crusty or peculiar, forthright or withdrawn. Some reviewers thought *Emily of New Moon*, which she had dedicated to George MacMillan, was Maud's best book since *Anne of Green Gables*. It is a view shared by many readers today.

After a busy summer in 1922, she was looking forward to a "comparatively leisurely fall," but she was right to add that it would probably turn out to be unsettled and strenuous. "Fate seems to delight in mirages." Her letter to Weber, begun on September 25, was not concluded until October 22, despite her attempt to make "what someone has called a

'Herculaneum effort' to finish it." During the year she had met Nellie McClung, fellow-novelist and ardent advocate of woman suffrage, at a dinner, and liked her, with the qualification that she was "very obvious and lacked subtlety" in a speech that was good until the absence of any real ideas became apparent. She also met the redoubtable Mrs Pankhurst at a Business Women's Club luncheon, and saw only a sweet, tired, gentle face, "like some Presbyterian elder's wife with nothing more strenuous to do than run a village Women's Missionary Society"; it was hard to picture her smashing windows and being forcibly fed in Holloway Prison. Two weeks in Muskoka in the summer were a prelude to a worrying autumn during which the Macdonalds were mixed up in a lawsuit after a car collision the previous year. They lost the suit. And had she said she expected a quiet restful fall? "Humph!" said Maud.

Hardly anyone at Leaskdale or at Norval fails to mention, with a laugh, that "Mr. Macdonald must have been the world's worst driver"—even when he drove a horse and buggy. "Oh dear! He'd dither along, veering all over the road, nearly into the ditch sometimes, hitting every pothole, stopping and starting with a jerk—yes, Mr. Macdonald was no driver!"

In 1918, when they bought their first car, a five-passenger Chevrolet, Maud became a back-seat driver, not without some justification. "I content myself with poking Mr Mac in the back with my parasol if I think he's going more than 20 miles, and saying 'Beware' in a sepulchral voice when I see him preparing to turn a corner." Maud would be involved in her share of car accidents, some of them not Mr Mac's fault; but there were many minor mishaps. "We ran over and killed [a dog] on Yonge St. this summer," Maud mourned.

In October 1923 a letter from the secretary of the Royal Society of Arts of England informed Maud that the Council had invited her to become a Fellow—the first Canadian woman to be so honoured. Maud had now become the kind of "distinguished guest" for whom audiences waited "with some trepidation," and who were astonished and relieved to find her" a comely, comfortable looking lady" with whom the years had dealt kindly. "She quickly made herself at home," said one reporter with relief, "and ere many minutes we were comfortably seated about a cheery fire talking like old friends."

She was an adept at putting people at ease, partly from her own natural good manners, partly because courtesy and kindness were right and proper qualities in a minister's wife. But her pleasant demeanour could be misleading, and the tight self-control she exercised sometimes exhausted her. When Canadian poet Bliss Carman, whose work she had admired, disappointed her by his reputed snobbishness, she commented: "If *I* snubbed as they deserve nine out of ten of the people who plague and drain me with their inanities and ineptitudes, I would have a reputation for snobbishness too As I have learned to suffer fools gladly I escape this imputation: but I sometimes think the cost is too high." Her greatest scorn was always reserved for the people who "know it all." She had no use for snobs.

She needed the rejuvenating, revitalizing power of the Island to restore her spirit. She went back in the summer of 1923 to a shock of amazement that she could have forgotten how lovely it was. "Such fields of daisies and clover! Such sunsets and twilights and fir woods, such blue majestic oceans, such provocative alluring landscapes. Oh, I felt that I *belonged* there—that I had done some violence to my soul when I left it." Perhaps she had. She writes often like a woman thrust out of Eden. In an apologetic note to Mac-Millan in February she had written, "I am as usual very busy —too busy. I haven't time to savor life at all—caught in the 'wheel of things' as *Kim* says. If I were not a coward I think I could better matters. But I am."

Was she never tempted to quit the rat race, escape from the Wheel of Things, persuade Ewan into early retirement, find, perhaps, her dream retreat and live comfortably on the more than sufficient earnings from her pen? Once in 1922, blessedly and miraculously alone on a Muskoka holiday, she peopled an imagined island with her nearest and dearest and dreamed a life of utter contentment. Fourteen years later she would write that "wisest Fate" had always said "no" to her longing to own an island. "I wonder if Fate is so very wise. Sometimes I am tempted to think she is blind and foolish!"

She spoke sometimes wistfully of another visit to England whose literature, in which her early education was rooted, had laid its spell upon her; but she never went back, and Europe seems never to have called to her. Did her driving sense of duty compel her to the frantic pace she clearly resented? For some months in the winter and spring of 1923-24 Ewan was ill with what Maud described as "neuritis and neurasthenia," and for a while she had feared that he would have to resign. She was now into Emily III (*Emily's Quest*); she had found Emily II (*Emily Climbs*) "a bit of a bore," as she always did with sequels. As in earlier days, when she had deplored the necessity to hitch her story to a moral if she hoped to sell it, she regretted the convention that required a "flapper" to be depicted not as she really was, but as a "sweet insipid young thing . . . to whom the basic realities of life and reactions thereto are entirely unknown. *Love* must scarcely be hinted at." Nevertheless, she wrote, "I can't afford to damn the public. I must cater to it for a while yet."

She was back in Prince Edward Island for two weeks in June, this time for a sad occasion: the death of Aunt Annie Campbell, taken from the home "that was the wonder castle of my childhood" and the house in which she had been married. Aunt Annie had "left the world a very much colder place." But at the end of July, Maud made a journey that reached to her heart and stayed in her memory—a family motor trip to Kentucky's awesome Mammoth Cave. The experience impressed her so deeply that many pages of her letters to both pen-friends were given to describing it.

Although throughout their years of friendship, quite long gaps developed in what Maud and MacMillan called "real" letters, they were always in touch with quick notes, gifts, packages of clippings. At the end of August 1924, Maud had been horrified to find that two years had passed since her last "real" letter. "But a friendship as old and well-tried as ours should be able to stand alone without being propped up with apologies." She then started on a massive catching-up chronicle that went off in five parts, ending in October and totalling seventy-four pages. Much of this was taken up by her account of the trip to Mammoth Cave, probably taken straight from her journal, as she wrote to Weber in almost identical words.

Everything about the trip was memorable, even its disasters. They got lost in Detroit. Maud thought there could be no worse hell than to be a traffic cop in Detroit (just think, she told Weber, "when we began exchanging letters there wasn't a single 'traffic cop' in the United States!"). They met bed-bugs in Hicksville, Ohio; they found Indiana monotonous—mile after mile of little villages with hanging baskets, though Maud would never forget the fireflies and the "cold elusive night smells." The red roads of Kentucky, "bright island red," filled her with nostalgia. There was a terrible, endless detour, forty-five miles of dust and potholes. But the cave itself cast a spell on her. She "would be its prisoner forever." Though children and chatter destroyed some of the magic, it was the sort of place to which her imagination could instantly respond. She longed to go through it alone, or "with a kindred spirit."

In the cave costume of jacket and bloomers, each person in the group of fifteen carrying a lantern, they fumbled their way in semi-darkness, strung out along the bank of a black sullen stream in Stygian gloom—"the original Styx couldn't be Styxier"—winding up flights of rock stairs, or "flickering through stately palaces of eternal night" that echoed to the sounds of bells rung by the guides. Maud had expected to find the cave damp and mouldy, and was surprised by the steady fifty-four-degree temperature at three-hundred-odd feet underground, and by the "great wind" that met them at the entrance gates. Along the first route of five and a half miles they passed through a series of caves connected by passages, "great shadowy mysterious avenues, winding stairs of solid rock, narrow, tiny slits": the guides flung up blazing balls of cotton waste to demonstrate the vastness. The boys loved the queer animal shapes of the limestone columns, but for Maud it was not altogether a holy place. "The old gods of the underworld rule it."

The second route of three miles was even grander. In the Star Chamber, with all flares extinguished, came a strong feeling of night sky overhead. Then, after "absolute darkness," the lanterns lit by the guides turned the crystals above them into stars, and dawn noises were introduced: a man chopping wood, cattle lowing, the sound of dogs and cats. Maud sensed the touch of some unfathomable power; felt that she had left a little of herself behind, that it might not be safe to return. "Suppose it kept too much of you?"

Returning home, they were granted a spectacle put on by the gods at Niagara, where for half an hour the worst storm in thirty-seven years flashed over the unlighted Horseshoe Falls, a "ghostly shimmering, blue-white gleam of almost constant lightning, while athwart the mist tore zig-zags of living flame, as if some god were amusing himself by hurling thunder bolts into the abyss." It made the floodlit American falls look tawdry.

CHAPTER TWENTY-THREE

An inadequate spoonful of wine

Norval, Ontario, "is a pretty little village in the valley of the River Credit, which flows just behind the Manse," wrote Maud to Ephraim Weber in July 1926. "We are on a highway midway between Toronto and Guelph—about 28 miles or so from either place."

In February that year, Ewan had been "called" by the congregations of the Norval and Union charge, and had decided to accept, partly because of the disruption in Leaskdale caused by the recent union of some of the Presbyterian congregations with the Methodists and Congregationalists to form the United Church of Canada. After so many years in Leaskdale, Maud found "roots that have been rooted as long as that are not pulled up without pain." And she preferred to forget "the *dreadful* month of packing, moving and unpacking." Next time, she thought, she would just set fire to everything—"it would be simpler." But once settled, she entered into community life with all her old vigour and interest. The Manse was bigger than Leaskdale's, with large airy rooms, high ceilings, and in a charming location. Behind the house the ground runs down to the little river that winds back into country more wooded and steeper than Leaskdale's open hills. The property covers nearly one and a half acres; the church, opened in 1879, has curved pews, and seats about two hundred and fifty, its floor sloping toward the pulpit, the choir and the pipe organ.

Maud was now the author of fourteen published books, including the unauthorized *Further Chronicles of Avonlea* and a book of verse, *The Watchman & Other Poems* (1916). She had also seen the first of two filmed versions of *Anne of Green Gables* (in 1919), and found it disappointing. Though "the photography was beautiful," the atmosphere was not right, New England was not Prince Edward Island, skunks and the American flag were not part of the Island scene, and Mary Miles Minter, who played the lead, was not "my gingery Anne." None of her books so far had truly satisfied its author, who still awaited a day when she could tackle something "serious." What she had in mind was a clan story set in the Maritimes. Knowing clan life "from A to Z" because of the Macneills, Montgomerys and Simpsons in her own background, she felt competent to tackle the theme. The difficulty would be to make it come *alive*, she thought—to get the comedy and tragedy equally balanced. But life at present was too rushed to attempt such a work. She had, however, ventured on a book directed to adults. *The Blue Castle*, out in August 1926, was set, for once, not in Prince Edward Island but in the Muskoka district of Ontario. Though she meant it for adults, it was not what she thought of as a serious attempt at a novel, "merely an amusing (I hope) little comedy." She dedicated this book to Ephraim Weber.

It was hardly a comedy, though enlivened by Maud's talent for depicting robust and pithy characters. It remains a charming and vigorous story: maybe an allegory of Maud's own frustrations, her yearning to live a secluded life in an enchanted natural setting, away from the strains and stresses of a people-encumbered existence, in total harmony with a kindred spirit. Through plot twists and coincidences, its heroine found all her problems solved in the end. Maud would always choose to write happy endings, though she allowed her sense of reality to strew the path of her characters, as in life, with problems physical, circumstantial and emotional, before she allowed them their heart's desire.

As an author of books about girls and therefore expected to be knowledgeable and understanding about youth—perhaps also because of her reputation as a successful worker in the Young People's Guilds—Maud was often asked for an opinion on the youth of the day, particularly girls. "I, alas, have nothing but sons. So what do I know about the problems of daughters?" she asked *Chatelaine* when that magazine requested an article. "[But] I was a girl once myself and have, I believe, managed to retain, even till now a very vivid recollection of what I was, and what I wished to be and how far and why I failed." Reporters who continually demanded to know "What is your opinion of girls of this so-called fast age?" were told "Just as good as those of any other generation. There is a certain proportion of 'high-fliers' in every generation—the ages do not differ radically. Girls are freer to express themselves now. The pressure is off; that is about all the difference there is between our girls now and those of a by-gone day."

Maud had already portrayed the madcap, irreverent, convention-flouting girl in several of her books, notably in Ilse Burnley, Emily's closest friend: a wild girl who nonetheless had the right instincts. She wrote the article for *Chatelaine*, published in the March 1931 issue. It was, in fact, a sound piece of common sense, advising mothers to remember their own young days.

Yes, the young *were* selfish: "Just as the middle-aged of today are selfish; just as the old are selfish—and always have been." Yes, the young *were* thoughtless. "Naturally. You have to learn to think. Nobody is born thoughtful." Youth takes itself seriously. *"Never laugh at her.* Don't blow her little candles out. . . . I have forgiven the people of my youth who advised me and scolded me and lectured me. But I have never forgiven the ones who laughed at me." And "You should respect her personality and never try to force her confidence." Again, "Don't make too many things charming because of a taboo. Especially boys, who are quite charming enough without that to Sweet Sixteen. Don't let your girl pass into womanhood with nothing but starved or stolen youth behind. . . . If she hasn't a beau or two in her 'teens how on earth is she ever going to learn to manage the men?"

Excellent advice, echoing with the frustrations of her own youth. But in private Maud was less tolerant of youth. Over the years she had had long and spirited discussions on the subject with Ephraim Weber, who since 1917 had been a reluctant teacher in Saskatchewan schools. To cheer his pessimistic appraisal of the doltish minds of his pupils, she expounded an argument equally pessimistic—that today was no different from ages past: there had *never* been more than a few minds capable of being educated. So why should he worry?

In 1909, Weber had made a vital decision—to improve his education further and try teaching again, encouraged to do so by Annie Campbell Melrose, the Didsbury schoolteacher whom he married on Christmas Day of that year. Accordingly, he enrolled in the Normal School at Calgary, but found the brief period of teaching that followed as uncongenial as he had back in Waterloo County, Ontario. He therefore set his sights higher, returned to Ontario with his wife, and registered at Queen's University in Kingston for a course leading to the degree of Master of Arts in modern languages. Summer school teaching helped his finances, and he graduated three years later. After a year at Queen's as tutor in German, he spent two years at the University of Chicago, working toward a degree of Doctor of Philosophy. But various difficulties intervened, among them the war and its anti-German bias that shrank classes in German studies and made German texts often inaccessible. He also suffered a great disappointment in finding that months of research for his thesis was rendered pointless by the work of an earlier scholar. Though he acquired a reputation as a scholar, the higher degree escaped him. He could do little other than return to teaching in Saskatchewan. For sixteen years, until he retired in mid-Depression at the age of sixty-three, he taught school—despondently for the most part, although he was rewarded by the success of many of his students.

"My friend, you are growing old," Maud told him toward the end of 1922, replying to a dejected comment about the boy and girl of today. Every generation had said the same thing. "Adam and Eve said that when Cain and Abel were about sixteen. I say it, whereby I avow myself your contemporary. Eheu! Times—manners—morals—customs are not what they were! The present age is degenerate. The boys and girls are not as we were—sage, sensible youngsters that we always were!

"Oh, dear sir, youth is the same in every century. In some it is more rigorously repressed than in others but—underneath the repression it is *the same*—foolish until years teach it bitter wisdom, rebellious until life teaches the futility of rebellion, cocksure until innumerable mistakes have humbled it, selfish and indulgent and hungry—until when—alas, I fear till the grave closes over it. We do not change much; we only grow weaker and wearier."

It was partly herself she was mocking. "Thus saith the Preacher," she ended ironically.

Maud was an odd mixture of realism and idealism, of profound scepticism and undaunted optimism. Weber found it hard to free himself from disillusionment: Maud armoured herself by coming to terms with it. "I suppose our discussion on present day youth gets us nowhere," she was writing a year later, "and might as well be closed. . . . You see youth *en masse*, in the raw, with all its disagreeable qualities intensified by the companionship and backing of its mates. I see it only in my rural environment, toned down by the older people among it and bridled by the conventions that are always to a certain extent in force wherever many older people are. When you meet your pupils out in the society of older people, are they quite as crude and crass and raw and bumptious as they are taken in bulk in your classroom? I agree with you that the present day parent is largely responsible for the shortcomings of our youth. I don't know whether the parent should be blamed too much. The pace of to-day leaves a father and mother too little time for training their children properly. There have been fool parents in all ages who believed their offspring faultless and refused to back up the teacher. I was 'up against' several of these when I taught school thirty years ago. I have worked for twelve years in our Young People's Guild here and I can honestly say that I see no difference between the boys and girls of Leaskdale and the boys and girls I mingled with in my teens. Some of them are stupid and silly and crass. So were some thirty years ago."

She was willing to concede that conditions in the Canadian West might be more lawless, less restrained. But "the evil will right itself in time. And I doubt if teaching school was ever anything but a nerve racking job in any period of the world's history, or if any more than a few pupils in any school repaid the labor expended on them or were keenly interested in study for its own sake."

They were back to the subject three years later. "Teaching has some abominable things about it," Maud agreed, but she did not agree with putting the blame on modern conditions: to some extent contradicting her statement that today's pace had created problems for parents. "I think teaching all down through the ages has been pretty much the same. Only, of course, there are *more* students now when everybody 'goes to High School'. And equally of course I *don't* believe this universal 'education' of everybody is the blessing in practice that it is in theory. To me much of the 'education' of today is like an inadequate spoonful of wine in a glassful of water. The miracle of Cana is not repeated, and the good common thirst-quenching water is spoiled.

"Why ask 'how can we get our pupils to *see* their faults?' You can't. Nobody can. One of the troubles of present day education is that [it] isn't education . . . *a-tall*. It's simply a pouring-in. And why worry because one jug holds a quart and another only a pint. And that most receptacles are sieves, holding nothing at all. Be wise. Just keep on pouring, since pour you have to—and be thankful you have something to pour. Think of the teachers (hundreds of them) who haven't.

"I think 'examinations' are outworn relics of mediaevalism. . . . Why not let everyone go on through every grade? When they get out into the world *it* will examine them very thoroughly and grade them accurately and with no chance of appeal. It may grade (and rightly) some who would have failed to 'pass' the examinations. It may cast out (equally rightly) some who would have made high marks."

Her views were deeply entrenched. She was impatient with those who wasted opportunities, who were incapable of benefiting from the advantages so generously made available to them. Her own passion for learning, her delight in the subtleties of words, her unquenchable curiosity, all made her intolerant of those whose laziness or inattention lost them the reward they could have had. She saw no virtue in pushing it at them. But she saw no advantage in letting such stupidity sour her soul, as Weber seemed to have done, and she found his complaints tiresome. "I have always enjoyed his letters," she told MacMillan, "but of late years the attitude of carping criticism to everything—the aims, politics, schools, etc. etc. etc.—of the age—into which he has allowed himself to drop has rather spoiled them for me. I am heartily glad the years have not brought such a doubtful gift to *you*."

Weber's despair over his students' uncaring attitudes came from an urgent desire to share with them his own deep delight in culture. Their failure to respond he assumed as his own failure to inspire—as if a key existed to open closed minds but he lacked the ability to find it. One senses that his letters to Maud recorded a personal dismay directed more at what must be *his* fault than at *their* limited capacity. When he found an exceptional student, no teacher could give more of himself in guidance, encouragement and friendship. One beneficiary of his kindness was Wilfrid Eggleston, later to become one of Canada's leading journalists and professor of journalism at Carleton University in Ottawa, who has recorded his respect and gratitude to Weber in his autobiography. Maud's impatience with her friend's despondent letters was her own way of handling the same kind of disappointment.

As late as the end of 1927 she was still sparring with Weber, insisting that education should be the privilege of those only who yearn for it, pursued neither for reasons of parental pride, nor for employment opportunities that required paper qualifications. Learning for its own sake was the important thing; no point in worrying about those who didn't care. And anyway, a thought: who would there be, if *all* students were bright and receptive, to do the dull, drab, prosaic, necessary work of the world?

She concluded in disgust: "And an Ontario law *compels* all children to go to school until they are sixteen! It is to laugh!"

Realm of the spirit

In Maud's emphatic elitest theories and Weber's deep pessimism lay a clue to their personalities. Maud was the realist, Weber the idealist. Bruised by frustrations and disappointments, Maud found her escape in the realm of imagination, of humour, of nostalgia: in matters of daily living she accepted disillusionment. She was armoured against things-as-they-are by her ability to live an inner life of mind and spirit in a land of things-as-they-should-be. "Whatever *real* life I have lived has been in the realm of the spirit," she wrote in April 1929.

Her young heroines find their fulfilment in soul-satisfying relationships: not necessarily in success through money or fame, but through perfect communion of the spirit with the right people, in the right environment and the right niche in life, though they often have to suffer before gaining their Promised Land. Jane Stuart (*Jane of Lantern Hill*) had to endure an unendurable old grandmother before finding a father after her own heart and reunited parents. Maud herself made the best of what she had, but in her private letters she sometimes writes like a woman short-changed by life, despite her public success.

Nevertheless, her rich endowments of spirit and imagination were, she must have realized, compensation enough—or almost. Who, with that intense love of beauty, could not be grateful for such a refuge from the slings and arrows? In her mid-fifties, when she was "so tired I didn't want to go on living," she went outside just before preparing for bed, and experienced "one of the rare splendid moments" of her life, hearing the wind sing "in that garden of the wild gods up on the hill called 'Russell's pines' by prosaic people. *Some* Spirit moved there—my soul caught its call and stood mute and rapt as in some vast temple of the night."

And who, with Maud's sense of humour, could not find relief in comedy from darker moods? No wonder Leaskdale folk caught her laughing to herself as she wrote: describing, perhaps, the frigid politeness with which an aspiring Emily and the successful editor she is interviewing suffer the madly destructive living-room romp of an uninhibited dog each believed to be owned by the other; or picturing Aunt Frances, refusing an aspirin to relieve a headache and "still enduring God's will in her bedroom"; or embedding a whole world of shocked folk-morality in one amber sentence: "How would you like to die in your sleep and go before your Maker in *pyjamas*, Patricia?"

She had another refuge—her lifelong personification of inanimate objects, a trait shared by her youthful heroines: the child in her flower-girl finery who runs upstairs to comfort a weekday dress for temporary neglect; the little girl who ached for the lonely, tumble-down house that needed to be loved and lived in; Emily saying goodbye to her trees—"to the Rooster Pine and Adam-and-Eve . . . to the spider crack in the kitchen window—to the old wing chair—to the bed of striped grass—to the silver birch-ladies."

And of course, for Maud, there was also the intoxication of words and phrases. "Why have some lines of poetry a potent and indescribable influence not conditioned by their merit?" she asked, quoting a verse by Felicia Hemans that always made her shiver with profound delight:

> "The sounds of the sea and the sounds of the night
>   Were around Clotilde as she knelt to pray
> In a chapel where the mighty lay
>   On the old Provençal shore."

Did her strange response go deep "to some former life and some intense moment in that life?" She was stabbed "suddenly and piercingly" with memories of her own gulf shore, by Milton's lines "odours from the spicy shore of Araby the blest." And, she asked Weber, "Were you ever haunted by a couplet of verse for no seeming reason?" For instance;

"The little dog-angel's eager bark
  Will comfort his soul in the shivering dark. . . ."

There could be worse things, she thought, than jolly little ghost-dogs. And—having just heard an owl hooting in the pines—could you call an owl anything but *owl*, she wondered? or a frog anything but *frog*? such a "funny, dear, charming word."

And of course, there was always *wonder*. Maud never outgrew wonder. Not too many years off sixty, she was marvelling at a delicate greenfly that had alighted on her hand. "What Power made it so lovely for only me to see?" And why, she asked ruefully, did that same Power also make so many hideous humans and so many bitter and ugly human lives? "Why???"

There were other puzzles, on the lighter side, and eternally fascinating to her agile mind. She compiled a list of questions she would ask the famous dead, and tossed them for comment to both Weber and MacMillan.

St Paul: *What* was your thorn in the flesh?

Pilate's wife: What did you dream of the Nazarene?

Queen Elizabeth: Were you, or were you not, secretly married to Robert Dudley?

Mary Queen of Scots: Did you know about Darnley's murder?

The Man in the Iron Mask: Who were you?

Charles Dickens: Was Edwin Drood really murdered or not?

Homer: Was there only one or half a dozen of you?

Beatrice: Did you know Dante loved you, or did you care?

Mona Lisa: What are you smiling at like that?

Abraham: Just why did you leave Ur?

Vashti: Were you ever sorry you didn't obey Ahasuerus?

Judas Iscariot: Why did you really betray him?

Weber returned a list of his own:

Beethoven: How did you create those symphonies with a stone-deaf ear?

Brutus: Were you ever sorry you stabbed Caesar?

Hamlet: Which of all the theories about you is right?

Bishops Ridley and Latimer: Is it true that in getting burned to death, the nerves are soon seared to insensibility, then easy dying?

Lucy Gray: "What became of you when you got to the middle of the bridge?

Maud too wanted to know about the fate of Lucy Gray. "The awful intriguing mystery of that phrase, 'And further there were none,' haunted me all through childhood." Oddly enough, the shadow-Lucy who had lived behind the glass doors in the Cavendish parlour had never been associated in Maud's mind with Wordsworth's mysterious lost child.

At Norval, Maud's forceful personality was making the same impact as at Leaskdale, especially—as before—on the young people; and whatever may have been her opinion about the mental level of those she worked with, and their possible capacity for receiving higher education, no one was ever hurt or slighted by Maud Macdonald. The ability to feel superior about *something* is a necessary and important part of self-esteem, and Maud had much about which to feel superior. Yet she never hurt anyone, or made anyone feel less than important.

"Last winter I had some pleasure and a great deal of worry training a group of young people to give a play," she wrote in December 1927. Norval people remember the plays she directed with as much pleasure as Leaskdale people do. "Those plays she put on were a tremendous hit everywhere. The group used to give a performance at several different places—in church basements, school halls—and the proceeds would be split between the Norval group and the host community." From the first year's performance they made $500.

Careful as she was in choosing her plays (mostly light comedy), Maud sometimes was faced by the kind of criticism that always revolted her. In one play, the part of a woman who had to climb through a window was given to a boy to forestall adverse comment about an inevitable and unseemly display of leg and underwear. The forethought did not protect her from the scandalized disapproval of a minister in the audience that a *minister's wife* should be responsible for such an outrageous impropriety. "Ah, but you must remember," Maud flashed back, "that it *isn't* the minister's wife who directs this play, it's L. M. Montgomery." And it was L. M. Montgomery who would pillory this kind of thinking in the biting little sketches—sometimes no more than one-sentence portraits—that are scattered through her pages. The mean-spirited and the narrow-minded got short shrift from Maud.

It was Maud Macdonald who sat decorously in the pew each Sunday, who attended church meetings, church socials, church bazaars, taught in Sunday School. But it was L. M. Montgomery who was writing: "I don't number public prayers as necessary. I don't care for any kind of public prayers, not even in a church. These are nearly always farces and generally unpleasing farces." It was L. M. Montgomery who felt that perhaps "a *little* evil is necessary to give spice to existence. . . . Wouldn't it be a frightfully tasteless world if there were absolutely no evil?" It was L. M. Montgomery who agreed that historic Christianity was "ghastly," and religion condemned if "by their fruits ye shall know them": who, writing of the United Church a year after it was established in Canada, said, "Personally, I really believe the day of the church is done. . . . But—a tree that took 2000 years to grow will be a long time a-dying, and I think both United and Continuing and all other churches will function for centuries yet before they finally 'peter out.'"

Until Ewan's car crash in 1920, when he had collided with the Sunday School superintendent of the Methodist Church in Zephyr, he had been all in favour of church union. Losing the subsequent lawsuit soured him on Methodists, and consequently on having any part of the United Church when it was set up. Maud had no high opinion of the new church, though "I know little of it, being of the continuing Presbyterians, thank God." It was not the birth of a new church, but the wedding of a couple of old churches too old to have offspring. "Many United Church friends are already bitterly disappointed. They say it is going to be a bureaucracy, ruled by a few at the top. . . . A too big church is *not* a good thing. It becomes clumsy and unwieldy. . . . It is no use to say that people want a church for a 'social community centre'. They don't—not to the extent of sacrificing for it and paying for it, anyhow. If . . . Jesus of Nazareth is shelved, then the church will crumble, for he was her 'one foundation' in whatever sense you take it. If the new church 'tries experiments' I fear they are foredoomed to failure. People can get moving pictures and dramatics without keeping up a church to get them. They want something else and if a church cannot give it, it may as well close its doors."

By seeking a false and fictitious strength in uniting, Maud continued, the two groups were only propping each other up "and hoping to find in numbers what they have lost in quality. Well, we—or our descendants—will see."

Twenty years before, Maud had written: "I call myself a Christian, in that I believe in Christ's teachings and do my poor best to live up to them. I am a member of the church believing that with all its mistakes and weakness it is the greatest power for good in the world and I shall always do what I can to help its cause." And "the idea that Christ must have been a wilful impostor if he were not divine does not disturb me . . . it does not disturb me to believe that he, in common with most great teachers and reformers, had an element of fanaticism—for want of a better word—in his character."

Perhaps it is significant that Maud wrote more often of *gods* than of God: she never quite escaped the spell of *Zanoni*, all beauty and terror and magic, hinting at indescribable, supernatural grandeur of soul and spirit in a universe of total knowledge and wisdom. It was as if she had sometimes caught "a glimpse of the enchanting realm beyond—only a glimpse—and heard a note of unearthly music." She had been too thoroughly repelled by the stark severity of the Presbyterianism with which she had been indoctrinated to feel other than revulsion from a strict belief in its tenets: even *her* imagination, trying to conjure up Marie Corelli's view of angels as "creatures shaped of rainbow light" was defeated by her Sunday-School-paper version of angels "wearing a sort of nightgown with big goosy-looking wings branching out from their shoulders and a mop of untidy hair streaming over their backs." She would hold fast to the church as the most powerful agency through which weak and wavering humans could be directed to ethical and moral behaviour, but she found her spiritual ecstasy and the answer to many of her questions elsewhere. Maud returned again and again, moth-like, to reincarnation: half-believing, but unable to find a firm and totally satisfying answer.

"That idea of the immortality of *character* never appealed to me. Too few of our characters would *bear* immortality. I would *like* to believe in a personal immortality but find it difficult. I *do* believe that the spark of life within us we call the spirit is immortal and indestructible and that when it is released by the decay of the body it joins again the great tide of life that flows through the universe until its next 'incarnation'—which happens, I believe, whenever some fit organism seizes it and holds it. And so on in unending cycles. But I can't believe much as I would like to that it retains aught of our memories and personalities. However, all our curiosity will be satisfied some day—or there will be no curiosity."

Many books, re-read, made her wonder how she could ever have enjoyed them. But re-read in 1924, *Zanoni* kept the old enchantment "as subtly delightful as of yore—as full of romance, inspiration, suggestion, gramarye." Had MacMillan read it?—if not, she would send him her copy. She quoted sonorous, turgid sentences to MacMillan in pure remembered delight. . . . "Child of heaven and heir of immortality, how from some star hereafter wilt thou look back on this ant-hill and its commotions. . . .Ho, young Chaldean, young in thy countless ages, young as when, cold to pleasure and to beauty thou stoodest in silence on the old fire tower and heard the starry silence whisper to thee the last secret that baffles death, fearest thou death at length?"

Zanoni gave up his immortality for mortal love and vanished at death into the eternal life-stream. Only Mejnour, the emotionless Master Mystic, retains his personality. How did *Zanoni* ever find its way into a strict Presbyterian home in the remote little village of Cavendish?

CHAPTER TWENTY-FIVE

A squirrel running...

At the end of 1927, Maud was more than ever caught on the Wheel of Things. She had no time, she would never catch up: "there's something terribly wrong somewhere with most things today, I fear." She really needed a secretary, but was sure she could not find one who would consent to live in such a quiet little spot as Norval. Some of her home duties had decreased, however, as the boys grew older. Only Stuart, now twelve, was at home: Chester, at fifteen, had already been a boarder at St. Andrew's School in Toronto for two years. A year previously he had been as tall as his father and wearing size sixteen clothes.

Maud had not been well this fall: in her next incarnation she hoped she would be "one of the daughters of Mary. The daughters of Martha have decidedly the worst of it!" She had been writing a series of short stories for the *Delineator* about a little girl called Marigold who found life "int'resting," but four of them would not now be published because a new editor wanted more sophisticated fiction. Maud felt let down. She had hoped that publication in the *Delineator* would have helped to advertise *Magic for Marigold*, the book made from the series in 1929. One chapter appeared in *Chatelaine* in April that year. Maud was entertained by the illustration in the Italian version, in which the hired man wore a splendid uniform, and a picture of the Virgin Mary adorned the wall over Marigold's Presbyterian bed.

But there still remained the Island, and July had been "a blissful month. . . . I have never been away. And oh, how

lovely—and lovelier—and loveliest—it was. How satisfying."
Though cars were now raising red dust on Island roads, Maud
rejoiced to find herself once again on *buggy* rides, just poking
along in no hurry to get anywhere, "past little hollows full
of scented fern, past little 'pole' gates under spruce trees, past
stone dykes hung with wild strawberries, and over looping
blue rivers and through valleys where amber brooks called—
and always the fragrance of dead fir coming unexpectedly
every little while—that fragrance which is as the wine of old
romance to me and always opens some floodgate in my soul."

During this visit to the Island, a letter to Maud from
Number Ten Downing Street gave startling proof that her
readers were not necessarily girls, or young. The Prime Minister of Great Britain, Stanley Baldwin, was travelling to
Canada to attend the diamond jubilee of Confederation.
Could he meet her? He had specifically asked the Government of Canada to include Prince Edward Island in his
itinerary. "I cannot," he wrote to Maud, "come home without
having seen the Anne country . . . I know I should be perfectly at home at *Green Gables.*"

She missed him on the Island, for she had to return home
before his visit, but she "purred real loud" at the honour.
Back in Ontario, however, she received an invitation to the
Garden Party at Government House in Ottawa to meet the
Prince of Wales who, with his younger brother George (later
Duke of Kent), was also in the Dominion for the anniversary
celebrations. She found the Prince "a bored young man" and
his brother "a duck of a fellow"; and she had her chat after
all with her Ministerial fan in the grounds of Rideau Hall.

Another British prime minister would bring another purr
from Maud in the 1930s when Ramsay MacDonald told one
of her friends how much he regretted missing Prince Edward
Island on a recent visit to Cape Breton: he had always wanted
to see the Island since reading Montgomery's books.

"Oh, you read her books?"

"Yes . . . I've read every Montgomery book I could get my
hands on two and three times over."

In July 1928, Maud and Weber met face to face for the

first time, when Weber and his wife were motoring through eastern Canada. They would meet again twice, in October 1930 in the West, and in the East again in the summer of 1935. After the 1930 meeting, Weber made brief comments about her to his friend Wilfrid Eggleston, who later edited, in *The Green Gables Letters*, those written by Maud to Weber between 1905 and 1909. On her 1930 trip to the West, she gave a reading at the Battleford Collegiate (but though she described the trip to MacMillan, she did not mention meeting Weber). Weber thought "she reads well and has an impressive presence on the stage, though she is short. . . . [She] seems to be hardened both to praise and blame, though she can still appreciate appreciation. . . . She is so modest that one has to ask to learn much."

Maybe Maud was reticent in general conversation but in her letters she revealed much of herself.

She wrote to Weber in April 1929: "No, I am not dead, dumb, nor demented—though sometimes I wonder if I am not on the verge of the latter!" She had felt, she said, like a squirrel running endlessly around a wheel. A week in Muskoka in August 1928 had been almost the only happy event she could record, when she and Ewan had slept one night in a little cabin on a sandy shore. She had sat on a log in the dreamy twilight to bask in restfulness, the tree-shadows in the rose and silver water "lovelier than the trees themselves," and had got up early to watch dawn mists over the lake. But fall and winter had been a catalogue of illnesses and mishaps. Three weeks of influenza in September had been followed by a fall down some stairs in the church and a sprained arm for seven weeks, three of them in a sling. December brought a bad cold, January intestinal flu and a mysterious rash on her face, February tonsilitis. She was, she said, feeling like a demoralized dish-rag.

Stuart joined Chester at St. Andrew's in September 1928, and Maud found the house lonely, "as if someone had died . . . that dark silent room where he had slept! . . . The halls that echoed to his whistle!" She had seen much of herself in Stuart, touched when one night, with her own gift for assigning emotions to inanimate objects, he had sleepily asked to be reassured that he had set his boots together under the bed "so that they will be company for one another." And who could resist the child who hoped "if I am ever born again *you* will be born again as my mother"?

She had completed *Magic for Marigold*, and in response to a demand for another adult novel, she was collecting material for a story about an old heirloom jug. She had also got through a varied programme of reading, some of which inspired her, some disgusted her. Reading poems by Wilson MacDonald—though she found them "very beautiful"—made her sad for the lost days of great poetry.

Nor would there be any more great hymns, which "come out of a deep and fervent belief in the supernatural. Our age has lost that belief—and I do not believe it will ever return. Which is a great pity. Because mankind are lonely creatures without gods, and without gods no great hymns can be." She said she had never written a hymn and never would. Perhaps she did not remember her *Island Hymn*, or did not count it worthy of recall.

She thought free verse was simply laziness. There could be no such thing: the very essence of verse lay in its bondage to certain rules, otherwise it could be nothing but readable prose. To MacMillan she wrote disgustedly:

"I feel
Very much
Like taking
Its unholy perpetrators
By the hair
Of their heads,
(If they have any hair)
And dragging them around
The yard
A few times
And then cutting them
Into small, irregular pieces
And burying them
In the depths of the blue sea.
They are without form

And void,
Or at least
The stuff they produce
Is.
They are too lazy
To hunt up rhymes
And that
Is all
That is the matter with them."

This was the year she was reading *Exploring the Universe*, which had made her feel breathless by its scope. She felt, she said, "a little as if I would like to give up such astounding explorations and squat down in a grassy corner and play 'knifey' without thinking about the staggering processes that attend 'first fingery' and all the rest of the motions." (Strange, she mused, how such games survive, outliving dynasties and kingdoms. Children were still playing 'knifey,' a game for boys, but Maud had played it too: going through the ritual motions of her childhood, *first, second and third fingery, front-handy, back-handy, fisty, breasty, eary, nosey, mouthy, foreheady, right and left shouldery, over heady and 'shoot the pigeon'* . . .) And yet, she said, nothing in the book explained the fundamental mystery—"how, when I decided to do 'first fingery,' the decision gets from my mind to my muscles. I don't think the scientists will ever discover that. God will always keep a few secrets to himself."

Though Maud accepted the realities of ugliness in the world, she could not bring herself to portray them in her writing. Literature, to her, meant the exposition of beauty, an escape from what was all too evident and inescapable in life. Ugliness, she recognized full well, but was it necessary to fasten one's eyes on it to the exclusion of all else? Hence she was repelled by "that much be-trumpeted novel"[*Strange Fugitive*] from the pen of a new Toronto writer, Morley Callaghan, whose idea of literature "seems to be to photograph a latrine or pig-sty meticulously and leave nothing else in the picture." It was "the deadliest dull thing" she had ever tried to read. She too was aware of pigsties and latrines, but what she saw at the same time was the garden before them, the blue sky over them, the velvety pines behind them, the "misty hills of glamor beyond"—just as real, she insisted, as the latrine and the pigsty, and just as visible. She was probably visualizing the Cavendish privy in its orchard setting as she wrote.

Maud was sensitive enough to criticism of her "lack of realism" to defend her approach in public speeches. "Sunsets are just as real as pigsties," she told the Toronto Women's Press Club defiantly in 1936. Or was it less sensitivity than a blow struck against what she genuinely saw as a growing "uglification" of literature? She had been brought up on the majestic, ringing prose and poetry of the masters, from the Bible down through the ages, whose themes had been grandeur, whose canvases had shown sweeping visions. "I'm learning [Byron's] Prisoner of Chillon by heart," she had written in 1905, "because I want to remember it in the next world." Every year now she had difficulty in finding a book she thought MacMillan would like.

She did not think, as Callaghan seemed to, that you were a "sentimentalist" if you dwelt on beauty. When Weber replied that he thought the book "wishy-washy," Maud howled. "Why, you benighted Philistine! [Callaghan] thinks he is the only person writing real 'he-man' fiction in Canada!!!!"

The year 1929 was, like most of Maud's years, one of mixed pleasure and pain—"many pinpricks and some delights. Which is the common lot of humanity. Selah." Abcessed teeth had been removed in November 1928, and she had had to wear a temporary set until the following August. In December a neighbour rushed in with appalling news. There had been an accident as the radial car was proceeding to nearby Georgetown: it had collided with a snowplough and Mr Macdonald was "broken." Where? His back, his limbs, his head? A distracted Maud was getting into coat and wraps when a cutter delivered her husband, whose knees had been sprained, keeping him in bed for three weeks and at home for six. Had the accident occurred two minutes later, however, the car would have been on a bridge over the Credit River and dumped its passengers into the sixty-foot gorge below.

CHAPTER TWENTY-SIX

Fans and critics

Of Maud's most famous book, *Anne of Green Gables*, her former professor, Archibald MacMechan, wrote in 1924: "The . . . book just misses the kind of success which convinces the critic while it captivates the unreflecting general reader. The story is pervaded with a sense of reality; the pitfalls of the sentimental are deftly avoided; Anne and her friends are healthy human beings; their pranks are engaging; but the 'little more' in truth of representation, or deftness of touch, is lacking; and that makes the difference between a clever book and a masterpiece. . . . Miss Montgomery has created her public and she supplies it with what it wants. The conclusion to be drawn from Miss Montgomery's achievement is that the great reading public on this continent and in the British Isles has a great tenderness for children, for decent, and amusing stories, and a great indifference towards the rulings of the critics." All through the years that followed *Anne of Green Gables*, Maud continued to receive a massive fan mail, as English and Australian and European readers were added to her North American audience. At Leaskdale, her mail continued to arrive in bundles and basketsful, demanding some kind of acknowledgement in almost every case. "[She] maintained a voluminous correspondence," says her son, "writing by hand every fan letter reply and a detailed daily diary over 55 years."

One fan letter had been addressed to Miss Anne Shirley, care of Miss Marilla Cuthbert, Avonlea, Prince Edward Island, Canada, Ontario. One correspondent addressed Maud as "My dear long-lost uncle"—Uncle Lionel—believed by the writer to be an L. M. Montgomery who had disappeared years before. Maud was offered plot ideas by people willing to sell their own life stories for "half the proceeds." An illiterate letter in 1909 had considerately warned her against false hopes: the writer's motive was friendship only—he was a married man.

A young girl asked whether Anne kept a diary and, if so, would she publish it? An eighty-five-year-old man kept worrying that he would not live to read the next book. Years later, at a Toronto convention, a woman told Maud how she had been helped through labour pains by gales of laughter when her husband read *Anne* aloud.

In 1922, Maud was disgusted by a fan ("a male prig") who, convinced by her books that "a real Christian can still write books"—this brought a spatter of exclamation marks from Maud—"then went on to warn me my nefarious habit of marrying off my characters 'tends to lower the conception of the holy state of matrimony'. . . . I wonder if he thinks it would be better if I let them mate up without marrying . . . or sent them into convents!"

Mid-winter had seen the arrival, in one day, of eighty-five letters from Australia where, without her consent, a girl had published Maud's address. She answered them all (more than a thousand altogether dribbling in until May), but rather curtly. Probably run-down (she was also about a third of the way through her "jug" story), she had a bad attack of influenza in June 1930. The arrival of the boys for the summer vacation cheered her up: Stuart had led his class in his first two years at St Andrew's, and was already thinking of a medical career; Chester, about to enter university, had decided on mining engineering. In April 1931 his parents drove him to the "Dantean landscape and barren rocky hills" of Sudbury to work for the summer with International Nickel.

That fall, Maud had her first personal experience of broadcasting, reading a couple of poems over the air, and found she missed a live audience. The novelty of radio had hit her first in 1923, but with apprehension rather than with pleasure. "These discoveries treading on each other's heels give me a sense of weariness and *homesickness* for the slower years of old. . . . Those of us living now have to speed on with them willy-nilly. . . . And none of these things really 'save time'. They only fill it more breathlessly full."

Her winter had been the usual rush of social functions, crowded with too many events she considered useless and pointless. But she had kept up with her reading, going through Pope's *Iliad* for the first time ("a gigantic fairy tale") and not able to resist chortling to Weber that even a thousand years ago Homer was lamenting the degeneracy of modern days:

"A mighty stone such as in modern days
  No two of earth's degenerate sons could raise."
Yet her own disillusionment about modern days went quite as deep, in many ways, as Weber's.

The new book (the "jug" book) had gone off to the publisher in February 1931 with a great flurry of indecision about a title. It finally appeared as *A Tangled Web* in Canada and as *Aunt Becky Began It* in England, after going through *Aunt Becky* (absurd, said Maud, because Aunt Becky dies in the first section); *The Moon Man* ("ridiculous"); *Crying for the Moon* (didn't sound like a Montgomery book, said the publishers); *Roses of Love* or *Ribbons of Moonlight* (nice, sentimental, blue-and-pink sweet-sixteen titles, scoffed Maud, for a humorous story about middle-aged people); *The Quest of the Jug* and *The Fun Begins*. The different English title was to avoid confusion with *The* Tangled Web just published by another house.

The plot of *A Tangled Web* sounds an unpromising one to sustain a whole book, dealing with the behaviour over a full year of people who all hope to inherit a rather hideous but valuable heirloom jug. In fact, Maud managed to inject so much humour into her characters and situations, putting her finger unerringly on small foibles and small mishaps, that the interest is maintained even though the sub-plots are contrived to work out everything for everyone's best. One could find less interesting character studies than Aunt Becky's self-written obituary, which her terrified relatives feared she might actually arrange to have published:

". . . Her temper was about the average, neither worse nor

better, and did not sweeten as she grew older. She always behaved herself decently though many a time it would have been a relief to be indecent. She told the truth almost always, thereby doing a great deal of good and some harm, but she could tell a lie without straining her conscience when people asked questions they had no business to ask. She occasionally used a naughty word under great stress and she could listen to a risky story without turning white around the gills, but obscenity never took the place of wit with her. She paid her debts, went to church regularly, thought gossip was very interesting, liked to be the first to hear a piece of news, and was always especially interested in things that were none of her business. . . . She longed for freedom, as all women do, but had sense enough to understand that real freedom is impossible in this kind of a world, the lucky people being those who can choose their masters, so she never made the mistake of kicking uselessly over the traces. . . ."

And there is something richly comic in Tom Dark's acquisition of a dislocated shoulder. "The night before, as he was sitting on his bed . . . he had absently put both feet into one pajama leg. Then when he stood up he fell on the floor in what his terrified wife at first thought was a fit. Very few of the clan sympathized with him . . . they thought it served him right for wearing new-fangled duds. If he had had a proper nightshirt on it couldn't have happened."

This was the only book, apart from *The Blue Castle*, that Maud wrote for adult readers. As far back as September 1908 she had recognized her limitations, though she was not ready to give up her aspirations. "Some day I shall try to write a book that satisfies me wholly," she wrote then, but she added: "I do not think I'll ever be able to write stories for mature people." Her subsequent fan mail from adult readers gratified her but did not satisfy her sense of literary achievement. She might have been taken aback, however, to know that *The Blue Castle* would be published in 1972 for young readers in one of a series, *Canadian Children's Favourites*.

Critics continue still to differ in their assessment of her work. Desmond Pacey, writing in 1952 on *Creative Writing in Canada*, dubbed the 1910s and 1920s as "the age of brass" in Canadian literature, including Maud's name as a bestselling author of the period, although he exempted her first book from the cutting dismissal given to her later work. A. L. Phelps, a year earlier, had been more generous in *Canadian Writers*. "Coming at it freshly and with an attempt at open mindedness, to my surprise, I enjoyed some of it as a relief from the tension and self-conscious craftsmanship and experimental techniques of many contemporary works presumably much more important and widely read . . . L. M. Montgomery's work . . . is unpretentious to the point of being naive. Its innocence seems always on the edge of suggesting close cousinship with ignorance . . . of life. Yet, as one reads, the sophisticated reader is uneasily aware that the argument might turn and go in another direction. The unpretentiousness and innocence may be the kind of honest simplicity that does have life and even art in it. . . . It may be that L. M. Montgomery, one of our popular so-called mediocre story tellers, should not be dismissed too casually just because she has been popular."

Elizabeth Waterston, writing in 1966 (*The Clear Spirit*), has been more penetrating and even kinder. "[L. M. Montgomery] may . . . lay increasing claim to our attention as adult critics. . . . Writing 'for children', she could re-enact the rituals of childhood. Recreating her own remembered yearnings and anxieties, she could create a myth of the hesitant desires and worries of the virginal years. . . . Re-reading the . . . books with even a reserved acceptance of Freudian symbolism would surprise most of us. . . . Such a Freudian re-reading, besides increasing our interest in the 'Anne' and 'Emily' books, may lead to a revaluation of *The Blue Castle*, where many of the suppressed themes are directly stated."

An intelligent, educated woman of today has privately confessed that *The Blue Castle* remains one of her favourite books. So it does of this writer. The plot contrivances are incidental to the charm of the setting and the neat and witty character portraits. And there is no doubt about Maud's ability in the mind of Dr Moncrieff Williamson, director of the Confederation Art Gallery and Museum in Charlottetown, where the original manuscript of *Anne* is held. He says unhesitatingly: "*Anne of Green Gables* is an extremely sophisticated book."

CHAPTER TWENTY-SEVEN

Old books
and new views

The winter of 1931-32 was remarkable for mildness. Maud picked lettuce, cosmos, marigolds, lupins and roses in December; even in mid-January, tulips were up two inches and crocuses were blooming. At the 1931 Canadian Authors Association in Toronto she had been both bored and interested, "though whether it helped the cause of Canadian literature the gods alone know." She enjoyed several luncheons, and was saved by interesting table companions from the "boring and long-winded programs" at government-donated and city-sponsored dinners. *Interesting*, in her terms, did not always mean free from flaw. She was secretly amused (though doubtless careful not to show it) by Wilson Mac-Donald's "naiveté" as he gravely informed the group that, like Rabindranath Tagore and Walt Whitman, he never ate meat—" 'it was not fit food for genius.' " Maud, free from any pretensions to genius, "ate all the good things I could get."

There was an eighteen-month gap between her letter of December 27, 1931 (not completed until January 17, 1932) and her next dated July 16, 1933. She liked the freedom to write at will, without apology; her diary and notebooks enabled her to recall and comment on past events of importance. Personal news was limited. She was working on another book "like Anne," called *Pat of Silver Bush*. Stuart would be entering university in the fall to begin his medical education; he had been for two years junior gymnastic champion of Ontario, and the previous year placed second in the national contest at the Canadian National Exhibition (he would win the national title in September 1933). She had dropped away from Canadian Authors Association affairs and hardly saw any of the members. She was having the greatest fun with a movie camera, her gift for acting as a judge in a Kodak-sponsored international photography competition in September 1931. She was utterly entranced by the films she took on her visit to the Island in the following month—she had never wanted to be a millionaire before possessing this plaything. It was "spooky"—as if you had got out of your body—to see yourself walking and talking, feeding the cats, looking at Lover's Lane trees. Island friends flashing across the screen *must* hear you if you called to them.

But if personal news was uneventful, Maud could always find other things to write about, though not very happily. These were the years of the Depression: she had been helping to make up bales and boxes for distressed churches and institutions in western Canada (a little resentful of what she called the "crickets"—things were hard in the East too, but "we 'ants'" had managed to carry on without help). She was even sicker of the word "Dee-pression" than of the reality, she told MacMillan. Russia was looming darkly over Europe. Her own generation had seen wrenched from its pedestal and hurled to ruins everything that had been believed immovable, "our whole world turned upside down," stirred up in a welter of doubt and confusion and uncertainty: she envied her mother and grandmother their "unchanged and practically unchanging world," when religion, politics, society, all were nicely mapped out, arranged, organized.

She had been growing gradually more despondent about the prospects for a better world, retreating into the comfortable world of the classics, re-reading old favourites, for refuge from "modern hysterics." She saw no hope for a warless world; the pacifists had not invented any conclusive answer yet. "But then there are no longer any gods," she wrote with bitter sarcasm. "And our fathers were only mistaken old fools who didn't know beans. Why die for their ashes? Far better make fertilizer out of them."

She was turning back to older books, since "good fiction seems to have died the death"; like the man who had said " 'whenever a new book comes out I read an old one.' " In this mood she had enjoyed reading Samuel Butler's *The Way of All Flesh*—not a modern sex novel, she assured Weber, but "a mordant, ironic arraignment of everything. It's a book full of *half-truths*." Living in a world she saw as upside-down, with its traditions ripped away and its beliefs shattered, she found solace, too, in Trollope's world of fixed and unquestioned social patterns.

Recoiling from the licence of the modern novel, Maud was reading more history and biography. A new life of Charlotte Bronte by E. F. Benson enthralled her, though she thought it probably did not present the author any more truly than Mrs Gaskell's "saintly" portrait did. Charlotte, she commented, had an unenviable talent for disliking almost everyone she met—"no gift for suffering fools gladly."

She had written once to Weber, "Perhaps a *little* evil is necessary to give spice to existence—like the dash of cayenne that brings out the flavours of a salad and saves it from vapidity? Wouldn't it be a frightfully tasteless world if there were absolutely *no* evil?" It is refreshing to find the dash of cayenne in the bland flavour of the character Maud herself offered to her world. It could not be said of her that, like Charlotte Bronte, she disliked almost everyone she met; but she did not care for as many people as her manner indicated and, like her Aunt Becky, she enjoyed spicy gossip. Her private judgments were candid and not always kind, both about personal acquaintances and her literary contemporaries. Though she liked some of Wilson MacDonald's poetry, she did not like the man himself; Bliss Carman was a disappointment, Nellie McClung had no substance, Edna Jaques was "personally uninteresting." Though she had found Amy Lowell's prose "delicate and beautiful," she had been shocked to discover that "[she] is a perfect *giantess*, very masculine, *smokes, swears*." When she discovered who had designated her work as "the nadir of Canadian literature," she passed on to Weber some unpleasant gossip about the *Globe and Mail* critic William Arthur Deacon. And she was touchy about Mazo de la Roche's success, rearing up at a suggestion that *her* dominating grandmother in *Magic for Marigold* had been modelled on the Whiteoaks matriarch. Marigold and her dominating grandmother had been in the *Delineator* long before and, anyway, Maud said, she hadn't read the *Jalna* books. Did no other Canadian dare depict a dominating grandmother for the next hundred years? Had Miss de la Roche taken out a copyright on the idea?

"Dear, dear!" she had written in 1927, "the gods shouldn't come to earth at all. One can't help suspecting that they are only half-gods after all."

Her letters, like a confessional perhaps, were a safe outlet for private disillusionments: her increasing weariness, her reputation as a good mixer maintained at such a cost of energy and distaste, her treasured traditions considered unimportant in this brash new world. Perhaps, too, she had finally accepted with resignation the limits of her talent. She would not, after all, write the great book, give to the world the deathless poems that surged in her mind beyond her powers of expression. It was in another life that she had written in her journal, in her twenties: "Oh, I wonder if I shall ever be able to do anything worth while in the way of writing. It is my dearest ambition"; and from some cold boarding-house during her school-teaching years, "Oh, I love my work!" She had been wildly successful, but she had not met her own literary standards.

She was becoming a "latitudinarian," she said, as she grew older. Yet she had always been secretly a liberal thinker. Perhaps she meant her ardent idealism and optimism for the human spirit had now hardened into a vain expectation— "Why kick against the pricks?" Human nature would not change: as it had been in the days of Rameses, so it would be in 10000 A.D. A sense of being trapped—somehow betrayed by life—permeates her letters. But not until the very end of her life did she give a clue to her greatest despair.

She need not have spent herself on church duties, public appearances. Her famous-author status would have excused her from all but a token performance as minister's wife. But Maud was Maud Macdonald before she was L. M. Montgomery: latitudinarianism did not go far enough to undermine her loyalty, her view of what was right and proper behaviour.

The winter of 1933-34 was a terrible one, perhaps to pay for the mild one the year before: unbroken cold from early November until early March. Maud was beset by colds and the ceaseless effort to keep warm. Only two notes went to MacMillan in 1934, "quite the most terrible year I have ever lived." In January 1935 a massive fifty-four-page letter went off in two parts, giving more details, mostly about Ewan's health, which (Maud explained) from March until the end of the year had gone through influenza and insomnia to a complete breakdown, with nearly four months in a sanatorium, two more months at home in misery, and a month of recuperation on the Island. No wonder that Maud "staged a little breakdown of my own and for six weeks couldn't sleep or eat or work."

At the end of 1935, Ewan resigned from the ministry, and in July 1936 Maud was writing from "Journey's End" at 210A Riverside Drive, Toronto, "on a winding road on the banks of the Humber River." The house backed onto a deep ravine where pines, oaks, bracken and wildflowers delighted her. She was charmed to discover that the wind howled around the house in storms. And she was happy that both boys could now live at home again.

A new movie (this time a talkie) of *Anne* had just been released, approved in general by Maud. She liked the little actress who played Anne, whose real name was Dawn Paris. She had been using the stage name of Dawn O'Day, but thenceforth adopted the name of Anne Shirley. It made Maud feel "a bit like Frankenstein" to see the name on theatre marquees. She saw the film four times. But an enthusiastic MacMillan topped her record. "You actually went to see the Anne film seven times!" she marvelled.

Matthew and Marilla Cuthbert were "good in their own way," though Maud thought this Marilla was actually more like her own concept of Rachel Lynde. She did not like Gilbert, and "Diana was a washout." And if anyone had told her all those years ago that one day a man would *fly* across the continent to take the part of Matthew in "a moving and talking picture . . . I would have wondered why the poor prophet was being let wander about loose." The actor, O. P. Heggie, died shortly after making the picture. In 1936, when *Anne* was being shown at a local theatre, Maud's twenty-year-old maid was mystified. "But how can they put it on now?—when that man is dead?"

Probably the highlight of Maud's 1935 was her investiture by the Governor General, Lord Bessborough, with the insignia of the Order of the British Empire. Each of those to be honoured was given "a sort of hooked pin" to wear, on which his Excellency hung the medal, a handsome one in the shape of a gold Maltese Cross about two inches square attached to a richly coloured bow. The medal bore the order's legend on the front: on the back was engraved the King's monogram. It could be worn only when "a representative of the King" was present, but a miniature could be made and worn to any full-dress evening affair. Maud found herself amused by the accompanying warrant signed by the King. "I wonder if the poor man ever heard of his 'trusty and well-beloved Lucy Maud Montgomery Macdonald' before he signed it."

It was typical of Maud to notice and be tickled by the two inches of white underslip showing beneath the elegant dark blue dress of a gorgeous lady who proceeded up the long "throne" room at Rideau Hall to curtsey to the Governor General in blissful ignorance of the mishap to her clothing. Maud's own progress and curtsey, she was told by friends later, came off "nicely." She was more interested in the ceremony of dubbing the knights, a ritual much more elaborate and lengthy than that for Officers of the Order of the British Empire.

CHAPTER TWENTY-EIGHT

The gleam
and the glory

Like her Emily, Maud had felt near to the secret heart of
the mystery, only a fragile veil's-width away from all the
answers she would never find in church. Her gods were
beauty and truth; and reality, for her, lay in her writing
where, through the thoughts and actions of her characters,
she could safely express unorthodoxy, hit out at remembered
injustices, and re-live the joyous world of her youth. Yet in
that world, her sharp eye saw the human flaws, her keen ear
heard the note of protest. Few writers have better portrayed
the plight of sensitive children under the authority of uncom-
promising adults. All her heroines are hag-ridden to greater
or lesser extent by these guardians, well-meaning but obtuse:
they are adolescent girls alone in a world more or less hostile,
unprotected by the parents with whom they had once lived
or (they passionately believed) would have lived in close and
sympathetic companionship. Only Jane Stuart, of all Maud's
heroines, once she had discovered her charming father—and
perhaps Pat, with her happy home life at Silver Bush and full
complement of parents—really escaped the tyranny of nagging
adults. Anne and Emily and Marigold constantly ran head-on
into the prejudices of the period in those small, infinitely
important crises erupting in the daily round of life in school
and home. All too well Maud understood and was able to
depict the soul-destroying power of the trivial, and the incur-
able scars small stabs can leave. "I think the little things in
life often make more trouble than the big things," said Anne
with Maud's own insight.

Her books, by their very nature, are more powerful than her short stories (which she continued to write and sell throughout her life): especially those with romantic plots frequently based on the emotional reconciliation of people who had let some stupid tiff keep them apart into middle age, a theme that appealed to her romantic nature. Stories featuring children are much more successful. Maud's child characters are natural little creatures with human flaws, neither all bad nor all good, and she uses them skilfully for sly digs at absurd adult behaviour or the prim conventions of the day. The children scold each other with the virtuous morality they have imbibed from their elders.

"You ought to be ashamed, speaking of such things," says Felicity primly in *The Golden Road*, echoing sex taboos, shocked by the mere mention of the unborn children the future might bring. (Emily, too, came under fire from an outraged aunt for bringing the word *bull* into drawing-room conversation.)

"If he's converted, he oughtn't to get mad," remarks another small prig—answered philosophically by a realist, "Well, lots o' people do."

In every book the children endlessly attempt to fit the concept of a kind God to the petty tyrant their elders seemed to believe in, and to the cross old man of religious illustrations. They know that Presbyterians are the elect of God, but they wonder why the Bible had no mention of either Presbyterians or Methodists, though it did mention at least one Baptist. Ministers are sacrosanct, even when unlikable.

"A common man would be queer, but when it's a minister, it's eccentric."

"Uncle Roger says that if he had been a Roman Catholic he would have become a monk, but, as he was a Presbyterian, all he could do was to turn into a crank."

"They're going to make a minister of him. . . . He's bound to have all the fun he can before he begins to be a minister, 'cause he doesn't expect to have much afterwards."

"I don't think it's right to tell a funny story about a minister. It's not respectful."

"You shouldn't speak of the—the—*devil*". . . . "Well, that's just what Mr Scott said." "Oh, it's all right for a *minister* to speak of him. But it isn't nice for little girls."

"It's no wonder we can't understand the grown-ups," says the Story Girl, when the children's sermon contest has brought a scolding for jesting about "sacred things," "because we've never been grown-up ourselves. But *they* have been children, and I don't see why they can't understand us."

In her almost plotless books—a series of anecdotes and incidents strung on the thread of a child's journey to adulthood—Maud's strength in capsule characterization is particularly marked. She has made telling and effective use of the kind of detail every reader will recognize. Every story she was ever told, every person she met, every human situation she encountered, every phrase she read or heard, all were noted down, stored away, to be used unchanged or brought to sparkling new life by the touch of her darting imagination. Everything was the stuff of stories for Maud. Even those terrible premonitory dreams during the war were used, grafted onto the schoolteacher Gertrude Oliver in *Rilla of Ingleside*.

The inescapable power of natural beauty to haunt and compel her, the tormenting need to purge her soul of its ecstasy in verbal expression, led her often into the excesses she was able to mock through the characters she created, but could not correct in her own writing. Her purple patches, and the clichés of her romantic and frankly commercial short stories have led many critics to overlook the real flashes of insight and often wit in her characterizations, especially those of adolescent girls and crusty eccentrics.

"You're too fond of purple, Emily," the young Emily is told by a candid teacher. "Cut out all those flowery passages," was Anne's teacher's advice. "And I'd let the sun rise and set in the usual quiet way without much fuss over the fact."

But when it came to sunsets and sunrises, Maud was lost. Morning and evening were new miracles that had to be captured and recaptured on her pages. In one book alone (*Anne of the Island*), sunset after sunset trailed glory through successive pages. "The sun began to burst out goldenly now and again between the rents in the clouds, burnishing the grey seas with copper-hued radiance. . . . The perfect half hour that follows the rose and saffron of a winter sunset. . . . What a beautiful sunset . . . it's just like a land in itself, isn't it? That long, low bank of purple cloud is the shore, and the clear sky further on is like a golden sea. . . . The sky faded out, but the strip of yellow along the western horizon grew brighter and fiercer, as if all the stray gleams of light were concentrating in one spot; the distant hill, rimmed with priest-like fire, stood out in dark distinctness against it. . . . The fine, empurpling dye of sunset still stained the western skies, but the moon was rising and the water lay like a great, silver dream in her light. . . . Beyond, the harvest hills were basking in an amber sunset radiance, under a pale, aerial sky of rose and blue. The distant spruce groves were burnished bronze, and their long shadows barred the upland meadows. . . . They all sat down in the little pavilion to watch an autumn sunset of deep red fire and pallid gold. . . . They lingered in the park until sunset, living in the amazing miracle and glory and wonder of the springtide. . . . The girls wandered down a long pineland aisle that seemed to lead right out into the heart of a deep-red, overflowing winter sunset . . . pausing in an open space where a rosy light was staining the green tips of the pines.''

It was impossible for Maud to leave natural beauty well alone. With Anne she would cry, "Spring [or sunset, or sunrise, or autumn, or wind or moon or sea] is singing in my blood . . . I'm seeing visions and dreaming dreams." But then, this is part of her continuing appeal. She speaks for so many inarticulate people in the grip of emotions they cannot release, particularly the young for whom she writes who are making their own first discoveries about the joy of living.

She was aware of her failure to reach the heights. "I wanted to put something of the beauty I felt into the words of my poem," she says through Emily, "and now . . . the words seem flat and foolish and the picture I tried to draw in them not so wonderful after all. . . . It seems to me there is something beyond words—any words—all words—something that always escapes you when you try to grasp it—and yet leaves something in your hand which you wouldn't have had if you hadn't reached for it.''

Nevertheless, some happy inspirations succeed in creating instant and unforgettable pictures. *A December fir wood . . . where I've heard harps swept by the fingers of rain and wind. . . . A little room . . . where old dreams hang thick . . . silky thin paper [from Japan] with dim cherry blossoms on it like ghosts. . . . Long hills scarfed with the shadows of autumnal clouds. Windy meadows harvest-deep.*

And Maud's work is leavened by laughter. She knew how to set down with risible effect small incidents from her own experience or her imagination—though she was indignant ("Gods, how I ground my teeth!") at a critic's suggestion that the incidents and droll sayings in *A Tangled Web* must have originated from many hours of talking with the old folk of the Island. Nevertheless, it is not to her discredit that she made clever use of much of her own experience in all her books. Milty Boulter's belief that heaven was in his Uncle Sam's garret came straight from her own childish location of heaven in the Clifton church attic. The child Davy's assumption that there would be jam in heaven surely came from an encounter with a real-life child's misreading (perhaps her own) of the catechism: *"Why should we love God? Because He makes preserves and redeems us.* Gog and Magog, endowed with the green spots of Grandfather Montgomery's china dogs, turn up in *Anne of the Island* at Patty's Place, on either side of the fireplace. And the mournful Methodist minister's wife of Maud's own childish writing buried her brood of children again from Newfoundland to Vancouver in Anne's story *My Graves*.

Some of the funny schoolroom episodes must have come straight from Maud's own teaching days, student howlers carefully jotted down in her bulging notebooks: Thomas à Becket canonized as *a snake*: the definition of honeymoon as "an extra nice kind of bicycle": of a glacier as "a man who puts in window frames." And she had a refreshing ability to bring soulful sentiment crashing back to earth with practical realism. "I like to lie in bed and hear [the rain] pattering on the roof and drifting through the pines," says poetic Anne. "I like it when it stays on the roof," replies her friend forthrightly. "It doesn't always."

Though she was furious at the unauthorized publication

of *Further Chronicles of Avonlea*, Maud should have been pleased by the introductory flattery about her one-sentence characterizations, followed by examples. There was Aunt Cynthia, who "always gave you the impression of a full-rigged ship coming gallantly on before a favourable wind"; the lady who was "good at having presentiments—after things happen"; the lady who "looked like a woman whose opinions were always very decided and warranted to wear."

The people in Maud's pages seldom stand alone; over the shoulder of each of them peer the faces of a dozen inquisitive neighbours, fascinated by the foibles of their fellows. James Baxter, who had stopped talking to his wife, "and *nobody knows why*." Systematic Luke Elliot, who marked on a chart every New Year's day "all the days he means to get drunk on —*and sticks to it*." Mrs Stirling, who "would sulk for days if offended, with the airs of an insulted duchess." Aunt Wellington, "who always enunciated commonplaces as if uttering profound and important truths." Mrs. Frederick, who ate her breakfast in sulky silence, "offended with Providence for sending a rainy day when she wanted to go to a picnic." And the generally accepted view in the society of which she wrote that "It was permissible, even laudable, to read to improve your mind and your religion, but a book that was enjoyable was dangerous."

No wonder young and old the world over delightedly recognized the silly and irritating taboos of their youth and the quirks of their associates in the figures of Maud's fictional world.

Green Gables
enshrined

The sequel to *Pat of Silver Bush* had been published in 1935 as *Mistress Pat* (Maud had wanted *The Chatelaine of Silver Bush*). She had undertaken it with her usual reluctance— "inspiration always goes after the first book." Reluctantly again, she started another Anne book, to appear as *Anne of Windy Poplars*. Again she lost her choice of title: she had wanted it to be *Anne of Windy Willows*, but though this title was used for the English edition (later, much to her delight, chosen as "the romantic book of the month" by the *Daily Mirror*), Canadian publishers evidently feared a confusion with Kenneth Grahame's *The Wind in the Willows*.

The book brought some unexpected dividends. For one sentence—"I was just moonlighted into thinking I loved him" —she was paid three dollars by *Reader's Digest* in 1937. "*That* was the *highest price* I was ever paid for a single line in my life!" In 1939, Twentieth Century Fox paid her $150 for the use of a title from a story she had incorporated into the same book, *The Man Who Wouldn't Talk*. Titles cannot be copyrighted, so the payment was a precautionary measure to avoid possible lawsuits; but "I have never made $150 so easily before," chortled Maud, "dying of curiosity" to see how the title would fit the eventual film.

She would sign a film contract of her own in 1939 with RKO for the rights to *Anne of Windy Poplars*, "after living in a hail of air-mail letters for two months. . . . Or rather, I signed *five* contracts, each in 19 different places—ninety-five times in all!!" The tightness of the contract had the kind of piquancy Maud would enjoy: once bitten, by the loss of the rights for *Anne of Green Gables*, she had learned to be twice shy in the matter of future dramatic rights.

In July 1936 she was doing the spadework on a book with a new heroine, Jane Stuart. The book, *Jane of Lantern Hill*, appeared a year later. Set partly in Toronto, but chiefly in Prince Edward Island, it was an idyllic Cinderella-story with a vindictive grandmother playing stepmother-and-ugly-sisters, and a delightful new-found father as stand-in for Prince Charming. It was the stuff of dreams-come-true, the repressed child blossoming in the care of an understanding companion in a delicious little house full of joys and delights. "Magic! Why, the place was simply jammed with magic. You were falling over magic." The title was dangerously near one of Nellie McClung's, *Leaves from Lantern Hill*, but Maud defiantly refused to change it. She had picked it, she said, before Mrs McClung's book appeared. Later she was intrigued to hear that a girl in Montreal had asked for "that Montgomery book *A Chain of Lantern Hills*."

For four years, Maud had not managed to get back to her Island. On a visit in October 1936 she found the old scenes unchanged, but many old friends were gone. Truly, she was "haunted by many ghosts." She was at first dubious about a plan to develop a national park embracing Cavendish and centred on *Green Gables*, now grown into a legend, though the house the tourists flock to see as Anne's Green Gables is not, specifically, the house Maud had in mind. *Her* Green Gables, she has explained, was in fact a composite of several dearly loved houses from her childhood. Nevertheless, for a fictional character, it does not seem out of place to have a fictional house, and enough of it is genuinely associated with the book to give it authority. The bedroom over the front door was Anne's room in Maud's mind. It is now equipped with furniture of Anne's period, chosen to fit as nearly as possible the description of her room in Maud's book. Lovers' Lane runs through the woods nearby, part of the farm then owned by Ernest Webb, whose wife was a Macneill and whose home, where Maud stayed for a few days on every visit, is now the house known as Green Gables. A daughter of the house, Anita Webb, lived with Maud in her Toronto home for several months in 1939-40, helping her with the management of the house.

But in 1936, Maud felt it was *"sacrilege"* to throw open to desecration by the public "all of those lanes and woods-encircled fields where I roved for years. . . . They will never —can never be the same to me again." Sensibly, however, she recognized that the government action had saved the area from being broken up and sold to individual and possibly uncaring owners, who might cut down the trees and destroy the lanes. "Now they are to be preserved exactly as they are."

"She was really very pleased and proud," says Miss Webb. "She was all set to listen to the broadcast when the park was opened officially—and nothing came through. When she telephoned the CBC, they had to tell her apologetically that there had been a blind spot in the transmission."

When she returned three years later, she felt even better about the project. All her old beloved haunts had been maintained, and new beauties added. Down a flight of stone steps she was charmed to find a cup hung on a birch tree for all who would drink from the water of the Dryad's Bubble, now surrounded by a stone wall.

In 1937 Maud was devastated by the death of her latest cat Good Luck. She had sat up with Lucky for three cold April nights six years before when the cat had double pneumonia: wrapped in a blanket by an open window for the fresh air the vet had said was imperative for recovery. Always, the latest cat seemed to have been the dearest, most lovable, most human of them all, but perhaps Lucky meant more to Maud than any of them. He had been (she told Weber) "for the greater part of five thousand nights and days my inseparable companion. . . . I loved other cats *as cats*. I loved Lucky as a *human being*. He was the most beautiful and uniquely marked cat I have ever seen, with *human* eyes. . . . Whatever Luck was he was *not* a cat. A cat's body, true! But it was not a cat soul that inhabited it . . . I buried him under a little pine tree in my rock garden and no cat was every more deeply missed or sincerely mourned." Maud's letters to MacMillan (also a cat-lover) are touchingly full of loving references to her pet, and her account of Luck's death ran to six heart-broken pages.

In mid-1937, her publishers, with *Jane* due to appear in a couple of months, had begun demanding another Anne book. Maud thought she might begin one, but her heart was not in it. Each month of the year had brought her new and depressing problems—"worry over many things, some of them the kind that can't be told to the world but must be hidden and not spoken of," wrote Maud to MacMillan. Ewan's health had continued to deteriorate. "It was more than nerves this time—for about two months in the summer he was a mental case, and among other symptoms, lost his memory completely. I could not bear to have him go to any institution for I knew no one could understand him as I did, for I have nursed him through so many of these attacks."

As a result of worrying, and following a debilitating attack of influenza in the winter of 1937-38, Maud herself had a nervous breakdown—that convenient term the doctors employ, she said sardonically, when they can't find out what is wrong. The will to work, her appetite, her ability to sleep all fled. She was obsessed by a dreadful restlessness—"for 4 months I lived in a sort of hell on earth"—walking the floor to try to gain control of her nerves. She endured the condition for four months before the autumn brought the beginning of improvement and, at last, in the spring of 1939, she found herself (stopping to rap on wood) better than she had felt for years. But "I shall never forget the terrible nights."

Maud had seen *Anne* turned into two three-act plays in 1937 (one by Alice Chadwicke, one by Wilbur Braun) without any reward to herself because of the loss of dramatic rights in her original contract. She felt the Chadwicke version was done "fairly well," but she had criticisms. She could not see puritan Marilla exclaiming "No siree!" She did not like "the silly and unnecessary love story" injected into the play. Anne would never have used big words improperly, especially when she was a grown-up college girl. But at a performance she had attended in a nearby centre, where "Josie Pye stole the show," Maud found Anne "capital," Matthew "excellent," Mrs Lynde "good though too thin," and Gilbert "a dreadful stick." The audience had seemed to enjoy it, however.

Fan mail was still coming to her from around the world. From the beginning she had heard from "men and women who are grandparents, boys at school and college, old pioneers in the Australian bush, missionaries in China, monks in remote monasteries, and red-haired girls all over the world . . . telling me how they loved Anne and her family." A letter from a woman in Jerusalem in 1939 about Jane had given Maud a thrill that reached far beyond its kindly comments, and set her imagination soaring. "To think of a book of mine being read in that ancient city where David and Solomon reigned and the Great Teacher worked. . . ." An odd little note came from a sixteen-year-old American girl to say that "the joy of life would be killed for her" if a rumour that the author of the books was married turned out to be true. Had she developed a passion for an L. M. Montgomery she believed to be a *man*?

World
upside down

Maud had started on what would be the last *Anne* book in September 1938, completing it in December by doing nothing else for the whole four months. Concerned with the baby days of Anne's children, it was published as *Anne of Ingleside* in 1939. Maud, who had been ill in August that year, spent a month in the Island and came back, as always, renewed. But she was on a downhill path. The outbreak of World War Two had further depressed her already low spirits. "I am not going to talk about the war," she wrote to Weber. "I can't! It is not *fair* that we who went through all this before should have to go through it again. That is childish, of course, but it is exactly how I feel."

With what horror, at the war's very beginning, did she open her paper on the morning of Monday, September 4, to read the savage story of the torpedoed *Athenia* and learn that among the unreported passengers was the Reverend William Allan, Jean's brother? With his son Andrew (to become known Canada-wide in later years as a top CBC broadcaster) and Andrew's fiancée Judith Evelyn, Mr Allan would have been on another, earlier ship, had not reluctance to leave his mother postponed his return. One of the survivors who crammed into an overloaded lifeboat, he was tossed into the sea when the propellor of a Norwegian rescue ship cut into the small craft, killing eighty who had escaped the original disaster. Did Maud, for Jean's sake, bring herself to attend the memorial service in Dovercourt Road Church in October, when hundreds stood in the aisles to join the fifteen hundred seated mourners and the hundreds more standing outside?

Neither of her sons was immediately threatened. Chester, who had given up mining engineering in favour of law, was rejected on account of shortsightedness, and Stuart, refused permission to join a medical unit by a Medical Council decree that held back all students not yet through their course, did not join the navy until after his mother's death. But the enormous waste and tragedy of war, added to her husband's deteriorating mental health, bowed her down. Ewan went to Florida in January 1940 hoping for improvement, and Maud, writing to Weber in February, was expecting him to stay until the end of March.

This was the last letter Maud wrote to Weber in her usual style of high courage. She did her best to hold onto the two good friends of half a lifetime, with whom she had explored ideas, discussed books, exchanged gossip, confided fears, shared a treasured communion of the spirit.

Through the year she tried to continue her writing, working on a sequel to *Jane of Lantern Hill* that would never be completed. In mid-1940 she had again become victim of a "dreadful nervous breakdown" that followed a bad fall and the depressing war news. She had injured her right arm, but she managed to send a letter to MacMillan in both July and August: not quite "notes," but not "real" letters either. In the August letter she was showing signs of her old resilience after her "intolerable distress. . . . I really think I have turned the corner. . . . Several things including my fall came all at once with the breaking of France and caused [my breakdown]. But now I really have some hope of recovering, things do not look so black. But even yet I very often wonder what God can be thinking about!!!"

At the end of December 1940 she wrote to Weber: "Dear Friend . . . I do not think I will ever recover. . . . Let us thank God for a long and true friendship." Three more letters would reach him, one of them merely a note from her nurse to thank him for the plant he had sent her, the others a few scrawled lines penned in hopeless dejection.

In 1941, MacMillan received five scribbled postcards, each more pathetic than the last. "I am no better. . . . I have had a very bad year. . . . We have lived to see beauty vanish from the world. . . . Am no better dear friend and never will be.

You do not know the blows that have fallen on my life for years. I tried to hide them from my friends. I feel my mind is going. . . . I am very ill and still not able to write."

For six months Maud struggled with what she had once called "all tears and fears that haunt the halls of night." By December 1941 only a hypodermic enabled her to write at all, and she penned her last letters to her two friends. And at last allowing her guard to drop, and stripped of all hope, she uncovered the torments with which she had so bravely coped throughout most of her marriage. To Weber she wrote on the 26th: "My husband is very miserable. I have tried to keep the secret of his melancholic attacks for twenty years, as people do not want a minister who is known to be such, but the burden broke me at last, as well as other things. And now the war. I do not think I will ever be well again."

And to MacMillan: "Thanks for your gift. I am no better and never will be. But I thank God for our long and beautiful friendship. Perhaps in some other incarnation in some other happier world we will renew it. This past year has been one of constant blows to me. My eldest son has made a mess of his life and his wife has left him. My husband's nerves are worse than mine even. I have kept the nature of his attacks from you for over 20 years but they have broken me at last. . . . I expect conscription will come in and they will take my second son and then I will give up all effort to recover because I shall have nothing to live for. May God bless you and keep you for many years. There are few things in my life I have prized as much as your friendship and letters. Remember me as I used to be and not as I am now. Yours in all sincerity and perhaps for the last time. . . ."

Long, long ago, she had written to Weber: "I . . . hope that death will come to me *suddenly*. I don't want to *know* it is coming. I envy those who die in their sleep." And later: "I have a horrible fear that I'll die by inches." Her fear was only too justified. For the last months of her life she watched death coming, in real agony of mind and spirit.

She died on April 24, 1942. Perhaps at this moment she was glad to lay down the terrible burden of living. Obituaries in Canadian newspapers were shorter than they would have

been had not war now screamed from the front pages and
column space limited their length; but most of them ran to
several inches, usually with a portrait of the "beloved Canadian author." (*The Canadian Author and Bookman*, journal
of the Canadian Authors Association for which she had done
so much, so willingly, did not bother with an obituary until
September 1944, reprinting a Canadian Press report from two
and a half years before.)

Her sons and her husband accompanied her body to the
Island where her spirit had always been, for burial in the
little Cavendish cemetery on Wednesday, April 29; she would
be joined nearly two years later by Ewan, who died in December 1943. "A great concourse of people" thronged the Presbyterian church or stood outside for Maud's memorial
service. It was a day of windy sunshine, with snow still holding in patches and gulf ice visible in the distance. Some birds
had returned already—wild geese, a few songbirds. The minister who had married her, the Reverend John Stirling,
presided at her funeral: her poem about the Resurrection,
The Watchman, was read, as well as extracts from *Chronicles
of Avonlea*, "in support of the view that she was possessed of
a mind of unusual range and soundness, and understood the
evangelical as well as the cultural and ethical side of the
appeal of the Gospel."

The Reverend Dr Frank Baird, representing the Modera-
tor of the General Assembly of the Presbyterian Church in
Canada, added his tribute. Among the many important and
distinguished names adorning Island history, he said, "I do
not think any will outshine the star that shone, and will continue to shine down through the ages in Lucy Maud Montgomery Macdonald. If service to Prince Edward Island be
accepted as a criterion of judgment, if I mistake not, and I
think posterity will concur—she places first . . . the palm for
all the Maritimes should go to the distinguished authoress
robed 'in the white majesty of death' [her own phrase] here
before us today."

"What a strange thing this death is," she had written to
Weber more than thirty years earlier. ". . . Theologians have
done much to surround death with horror and dread. If we

listened to Nature's teachings we should be happier, truly believing (I hold) that death is simply a falling asleep, probably with awakening to some happy and useful existence, at the worst an endless and dreamless repose. Isn't the Christian (?) doctrine of eternal torment as *hellish* as the idea it teaches? . . . I admit that a consciousness of sin and remorse is a hell in itself. . . . Nobody wilfully chooses evil. . . . Sometimes, in the case of bad habits, we cannot turn from it. But I believe that only lasts while the physical body on which the habit is impressed lasts. When it is destroyed the habit will also be destroyed and the liberated soul will get 'another chance', with the warning of its bitter experiences."

In March 1931 she had written to MacMillan, "Yes, I suppose we must both face the fact that we are 'growing old'. ["I have got fat!" she had complained. "I weigh 150 lbs.— quite as much as my height can carry. . . . If it goes on I shall have to diet or exercise. For the first I have no liking . . . for the second no time."] For my own part I have never *felt* old till this past year. And I admit that several times during its passage I *have* felt rather wearily 'old'—as if courage had run low and there was little to look forward to in existence. This may have been merely the result of my poor health and if I were to recover fully I might not feel that way at all. And, in any event, I say to myself 'I believe in a series of re-incarnations. If that is true I am really nearing the time *when I will be young again.* Just as often after noonday we really get nearer to another morning with every passing minute.' Though, when I feel very tired I catch myself hoping there will be a good long restful *sleep* between the evening and the morning. As no doubt there will. What other truth is our night and sleep meant to teach us?"

Maud Macdonald had a talent for companionship that stood her in good stead when her whole being cried out to be alone, not to have to *mix* with people she did not much care for. But the rigid control demanded of her patience and temper, even though friendliness came naturally to her, doubtless contributed to those periods of nervous tension that finally overcame her.

Not many of us would be able to maintain the outward face of modesty Maud presented to the world after the accolades she received. She can be forgiven, or at least granted understanding, for an inward arrogance. And with the knowledge of her terrible private problems, we can forgive, perhaps even admire, the control that hid them from most of her neighbours and enabled her to receive the genuine admiration and love of the people of her congregations. This is no mean achievement for a tempestuous, contradictory personality that was at once critical and warm-hearted, forgiving and yet not a little spiteful, courageous and fearful, and perhaps above all else, loyal to her own personal code; but using the very human defence of self-mockery as a forearming against the darts of criticism from others that could all too easily hit their target.

Without doubt she felt tethered by the need to behave circumspectly (though it was no effort for her to behave with dignity). The respect she received as famous author, supplemented by her personal intelligence and charm, probably would have saved her from the kind of ungenerous and small-minded censure she had seen vented on other luckless ministerial wives. The *Open Letter from a Minister's Wife* she wrote in 1931 was based as much on her youthful observations of ready-to-pounce congregational attitudes in the ingrown little fundamentalist communities of the Island as on her own experience. "[The minister's wife] expects that the congregation will concede to her a right to her own opinions, tastes, methods of housekeeping and child training. To be the target of endless criticism along these lines would take the joy out of any life." She gave as example a minister who had been rejected by a congregation for no more reason than that his wife had been frivolous enough to turn up with a red rose in her hat. "Even if her dress were dowdy and her hat swore at her nose, she wouldn't be a bit the better wife to the minister or help to the congregation."

Yet of course there had been compensations for her. "I look back and see many lovely things. . . . Houses that always seemed pleased to have you come to them. Frank, ungrudging tributes, appreciative, priceless words that cast a sudden rainbow over existence. Dear gentle souls who never once made me feel that I had said the wrong thing. . . . Little friendly, neighborly offerings now and then—the jar of cream or jelly, the box of eggs, the root of an admired perennial. . . . And the dear, dear women I have known!"

But despite her huge and unexpected success, despite the "many lovely things" she could look back on, one is left with the feeling that Maud Macdonald did not find in life what she had so ecstatically expected in those golden days of her childhood. Possession of so rapturous a response to beauty is not always the enviable gift it seems to be when life allows no real control of one's destiny, and the "great peaks" so often mean "great depths" as well. In 1908, "circumstances over which I have no control" brought her morbid brooding. In 1923, she was "compelled . . . by the circumstances of my existence" to play the detested part of a "mixer." Was she too deeply indoctrinated to escape without guilt from an interpretation of religion she could not accept? Her heart told her that God was not the God her grandmother had directed her to, not the God of the tight-lipped holders-to-the-letter-of-the-Law, but she could not break free. She was bound inescapably to her early training, though she stirred restlessly within its straitjacket.

"She was very religious," writes her son, "although in a rather rigid way, and although in her writings she gave the impression of broad tolerance of human weaknesses, she did not condone any such elasticity in herself or in her family. I think she derived comfort and strength from her religion, but it was a rather bleak and forbidding one."

Man is a worshipping animal, she knew, and Maud Montgomery Macdonald's strength had to be derived from this knowledge. She had a worshipping soul that found only beauty fit to worship, and there was not enough of that. Like Anne, "If I really wanted to pray . . . I'd go out into a great big field all alone or into the deep, deep woods, and I'd look up into the sky . . . into that lovely blue sky that looks as if there was no end to its blueness. And then I'd just *feel* a prayer."

In many ways she found it a dark world, but she had the courage to whistle in the dark.

No wonder her Island rejuvenated her. All of Cavendish was a prayer. She could offer up a soul-ful of worship, from the days of wonder she had known there from her very first breath. Her cousin Ken, had she but realized it when he was a pesky small boy around their grandmother's home, was living out the same dream, to be stored away and brought out to be dreamed again when the years had moved ahead and the spirit needed refreshing. In 1974, one hundred years after she was born, nearly eighty years after his own birth, Ken Macneill would write with his cousin Maud's nostalgia of the Island's unbreakable spell.

I sometimes want to return to Cavendish again and sometimes I don't. I know I'll never find the kerosene lamps again, nor the tallow candles, nor the root cellars, not the giant built-in ice-boxes that farmers used to cut ice for and fill up each spring with sawdust, nor the all-dirt red roads . . . and the daily milk run to Stanley Bridge to the cheese factory, nor the voyages out a mile or two with my uncle in his dory, and a line and hook to get an odd mackerel or even a stray haddock, to say nothing about hauling up his half dozen or more lobster traps: or the sand-pipers on the beach which I flung pebbles at and never hit, or going to bed with a cup of molasses and water, nor the twelve-mile buggy trip from Hunter River station, twice a year, and Maudie's rat-tat-tat upstairs long after I went to bed, and climbing trees for cherries and apples, usually not quite ripe but so what, and my early morning arising to go to the brook and haul up a few four or five inch trout for breakfast. . . . All gone, and all enjoyed when it happened, and now we go there in an hour or so and in the air. . . .

Cavendish still has its magic. Maud was right—she never should have left it. But then perhaps she never really did.

Bibliography

Books by L. M. Montgomery (in order of first publication date):

Anne of Green Gables, L. C. Page & Co., Boston, 1908

Anne of Avonlea, L. C. Page & Co., Boston, 1909

Kilmeny of the Orchard, L. C. Page & Co., Boston, 1910

The Story Girl, L. C. Page & Co., Boston, 1911

Chronicles of Avonlea, L. C. Page & Co., Boston, 1912

The Golden Road, L. C. Page & Co., Boston, 1913

Anne of the Island, L. C. Page & Co., Boston, 1915

The Watchman & Other Poems, McClelland & Stewart, Toronto, 1916

Anne's House of Dreams, Frederick Stokes & Co., New York, 1917

Rainbow Valley, Frederick Stokes & Co., New York, 1919

Further Chronicles of Avonlea, L. C. Page & Co., Boston, 1920

Rilla of Ingleside, Frederick Stokes & Co., New York, 1921

Emily of New Moon, Frederick Stokes & Co., New York, 1923

Emily Climbs, Frederick Stokes & Co., New York, 1925

The Blue Castle, Frederick Stokes & Co., New York, 1926

Emily's Quest, Frederick Stokes & Co., New York, 1927

Magic for Marigold, Frederick Stokes & Co., New York, 1929

A Tangled Web, Frederick Stokes & Co., New York, 1931 (English title: *Aunt Becky Began It*)

Pat of Silver Bush, Frederick Stokes & Co., New York, 1933

Courageous Women (in collaboration with Marian Keith and Mabel Burns McKinley), McClelland & Stewart, Toronto, 1934

Mistress Pat, Frederick Stokes & Co., New York, 1935

Anne of Windy Poplars, Frederick Stokes & Co., New York, 1936 (English title: *Anne of Windy Willows*)

Anne of Ingleside, Frederick Stokes & Co., New York, 1939

Jane of Lantern Hill, Frederick Stokes & Co., New York, 1937

The Road to Yesterday, McGraw-Hill Ryerson, Toronto, 1974 (Posthumous publication)

Arranged in chronological sequence of Anne's life the complete series is as follows:

Anne of Green Gables (1908): Anne's childhood.

Anne of Avonlea (1909): Anne as teacher.

Anne of the Island (1915): Anne goes to college.

Anne of Windy Poplars (1936): Love letters to Gilbert Blythe during her term as school principal.

Anne's House of Dreams (1918): Marriage and first child.

Anne of Ingleside (1939): Birth of five more children.

Rainbow Valley (1919): The children grow up.

Rilla of Ingleside (1921): Anne's daughter and the war years.

Short pieces by L. M. Montgomery:

"On Cape Le Force" (poem), Charlottetown *Daily Patriot*, November 26, 1890

"A Western Eden," Prince Albert *Times*, June 17, 1891

"A Girl's Place at Dalhousie College," Halifax *Herald*, April 29, 1896

"The 'Teen-Age Girl," *Chatelaine*, March 1931

"An Open Letter from a Minister's Wife," *Chatelaine*, October 1931

Various poems and short stories (some of which were reprinted in *Chronicles* and *Further Chronicles of Avonlea*) in such publications as *Everybody's*, *McClure's*, *Canadian Magazine*, *Chatelaine*, *Maclean's*, *Delineator*, *The Criterion*, *Youth's Companion*, *Forward*, *The Congregationalist*, *Christian Advocate*)

"The Alpine Path." *Everywoman's World*, Toronto, 1917

Articles about L. M. Montgomery:

Campbell, Hon. Thane. "Address at Cavendish on the unveiling of a memorial in memory of L. M. Montgomery," September 12, 1948

Chapman, Ethel. "The Author of Anne," *Maclean's* Magazine, 1919.

Fitzpatrick, Helen. "Anne's First Sixty Years," *Canadian Author and Bookman*, Spring, 1969.

Hill, Maude Petitt. "The Best Known Woman in Prince Edward Island," *Chatelaine*, May and June 1928.

Pacey, Desmond. *Creative Writing in Canada*, Toronto, 1952

Phelps, A. L. *Canadian Writers*, Toronto, 1951

Presbyterian Record. Obituary, June 1942

Sclanders, Ian. "Lucy of Green Gables," *Maclean's* Magazine, December 15, 1951

Weber, Ephraim. "L. M. Montgomery as a Letter Writer," *Dalhousie Review*, October 1942

Weber, Ephraim. "L. M. Montgomery's 'Anne,' " *Dalhousie Review*, April 1944

Newspapers (relevant years):

Alloa Journal
Charlottetown *Daily Patriot*
Charlottetown *Examiner*
Charlottetown *Guardian*
Halifax *Herald*
Halifax *Chronicle*
Manitoba Evening Free Press
Montreal *Star*
Ottawa *Citizen*
Prince Albert *Daily News*
Prince Albert *Times*
Saskatchewan, The
Saskatchewan *Herald*
Toronto *Globe*
Toronto *Globe and Mail*
Toronto Star

Other sources:

Bolger, Francis W. P. (ed.). *Canada's Smallest Province.*

P.E.I.: The Prince Edward Island 1973 Centennial Commission.

——. *The Years before "Anne."* P.E.I.: The Prince Edward Island Heritage Foundation, 1975.

Bulwer-Lytton, E. *Zanoni.* London: Chapman & Hall, 1853.

Eggleston, Wilfrid. *The Green Gables Letters.* Toronto: Ryerson Press, 1960.

——. *While I Still Remember,* Toronto: Ryerson Press, 1968.

Historical Sketch: 100th Anniversary, Leaskdale, Ontario: St. Paul's Presbyterian Church, 1962.

Historical Sketch of Norval Presbyterian Church, Centennial 1938

Holland, Norah M. *Spun-Yarn and Spindrift.* London and Toronto: J. M. Dent, 1918.

Lockhart, A. J. *The Papers of Pastor Felix.* Toronto: William Briggs, 1903.

L. M. Montgomery as Mrs. Ewan Macdonald of The Leaskdale Manse, 1911-1926. Leaskdale, Ontario: St Paul's Presbyterian Women's Association, 1965.

Lucy Maud Montgomery, The Island's Lady of Stories. Springfield, Prince Edward Island: The Women's Institute, 1963.

Meacham's Atlas of Prince Edward Island (1880). Reprinted Mika Publishing Co., Belleville, Ontario: 1973.

MacMillan, George Boyd. Letters from L. M. Montgomery (unpublished).

Opie, Iona and Peter. *Children's Games in Street and Playground,* Oxford at the Clarendon Press, 1969.

Public Archives of Canada. RG—15, B1, Box 1089, file 137340.

Ridley, Hilda M. *L. M. Montgomery.* Toronto: Ryerson Press, 1956.

Simpson, Harold. *Cavendish: Its History, Its People.* Truro, 1973.

Wallace, F. W. *Wooden Ships and Iron Men.* London: Hodder & Stoughton, 1925.

Watson, Albert Durrant (ed.). *The Twentieth Plane.* Philadelphia: G. W. Jacobs & Co., 1919.

Weber, Ephraim. Letters from L. M. Montgomery (unpublished), PAC: MG 30 D 36.

Index

Other Canadian Lives you'll enjoy reading

Canadian Lives is a paperback reprint series which presents the best in Canadian biography chosen from the lists of Canada's many publishing houses. Here is a selection of titles in the series. Watch for more Canadian Lives every season, from Goodread Biographies. Ask for them at your local bookstore.

Something Hidden: A Biography of Wilder Penfield
Jefferson Lewis

The life story of a world-famous Canadian surgeon and scientist — written by his journalist grandson who has portrayed both the public and the private sides of Penfield's extraordinary life of achievement.

"One of the most valuable and fascinating biographies I have read in many years." — Hugh MacLennan

Canadian Lives 1   0-88780-101-3

Within the Barbed Wire Fence
Takeo Nakano

The moving story of a young Japanese man, torn from his family in 1942 and sent with hundreds of others to a labour camp in the B.C. interior.

"A poet's story of a man trapped by history and events far beyond his control." — *Canadian Press*

Canadian Lives 2   0-88780-102-1

The Patricks: Hockey's Royal Family
Eric Whitehead

A first-rate chronicle of the four-generation family of lively Irish-Canadians who have played a key role in the history of hockey for more than 70 years.

"A damn good story." — Jack Dulmage, *The Windsor Star*

Canadian Lives 3   0-88780-103-X

Hugh MacLennan: A Writer's Life
Elspeth Cameron

The prize-winning bestseller that chronicles the life of one of Canada's most successful novelists.

"This impressive biography does justice to the man and his work." — Margaret Laurence

Canadian Lives 4   0-88780-104-8

Canadian Nurse in China
Jean Ewen

The story of a remarkable young adventurer who went to war-torn China in the 1930s, met all the heroes of the Chinese Revolution, and survived the terrors and dangers she encountered with her ironic sense of humour intact.

"A remarkably candid book by a no-nonsense nurse."
— Pierre Berton

Canadian Lives 5   0-88780-105-6

An Arctic Man
Ernie Lyall

Sixty-five years in Canada's North — the story of a man who chose the Inuit way of life.

"The main reason I decided to do a book about my life in the north is that I finally got fed up with all the baloney in so many books written about the north." — Ernie Lyall, in the preface.

Canadian Lives 6   0-88780-106-4

Boys, Bombs and Brussels Sprouts
J. Douglas Harvey

One man's irreverent, racy, sometimes heart-breaking, account of flying for Canada with Bomber Command in the Second World War.

"Tells more about what it was like 'over there' than all of the military histories ever written." — *Canadian Press*

Canadian Lives 7   0-88780-107-2

Nathan Cohen: The Making of a Critic
Wayne Edmonstone

A giant of a man, a legend, Cohen had a vision of what Canadians could achieve in the arts and entertainment — and he convinced both audiences and artists that Canadian work should and could equal the world's best.

"A man of vision, prophecy and insight." — *Ottawa Revue*

Canadian Lives 8   0-88780-108-0

The Wheel of Things:
A Biography of L.M. Montgomery
Mollie Gillen

The remarkable double life of the woman who created Canada's best-loved heroine, Anne of Green Gables.

"A perceptive and sympathetic portrait of a complex personality." — Ottawa *Journal*

Canadian Lives 9   0-88780-109-9

Walter Gordon: A Political Memoir
Walter Gordon

The gentle, passionate patriot who became an Ottawa insider and fought for his principles in a cabinet of politicians all too ready to abandon theirs.

"Valuable insight into our political history and a revealing portrait of the man himself."
                    — CBC newsman Norman Depoe

Canadian Lives 10   0-88780-110-2

Troublemaker!
James Gray

The memoirs of a witty, warm-hearted, irreverent newspaperman who witnessed the golden age of Western Canada, 1935-1955.

"A book of great immediacy and appeal — wise and extraordinarily revealing about ourselves." — Jamie Portman, Southam News Services

Canadian Lives 11   0-88780-111-0

When I Was Young

Raymond Massey

One of Canada's most distinguished actors tells the story of his aristocratic youth as the offspring of the most Establishment family of Toronto. The first of his two-volume memoirs.

"An urbane, humour-inflected and sensitive recollection."
— *Victoria Times-Colonist*

Canadian Lives 12   0-88780-112-9

Having trouble finding a copy of a book in this series?

If you're having difficulty finding a copy of a book in Goodread Biographies' Canadian Lives series, send us a stamped, self-addressed envelope and we'll put you in touch with a bookstore that stocks all titles in the series.

Write to:

> Goodread Biographies
> 333 - 1657 Barrington Street
> Halifax, Nova Scotia
> B3J 2A1

Be sure to enclose a stamped, self-addressed envelope with your letter.

"You brought me here, Jake. You got me into this. Now help me figure it out."

He opened his mouth to protest, studied her for a moment, then he sat down and huffed out a huge sigh.

"I'm only the Haven's handyman, Gem," he said weakly.

"You're the fixer—that's why all those people called you. Now help me figure out how to fix things for this child that my husband loved so dearly, when I can't even remember my own name. Wait a minute. That picture."

"Gem, are you okay? You look…weird."

"The picture that was in my wallet. That must be Alexa." Suddenly the sun felt too hot, the problems too large, the decisions too overwhelming. Somewhere in the recesses of her brain she thought she could hear a man's voice calling. *Take care of her. Take care of Alexa.*

The world wobbled. Had she really heard that, or was she dreaming? She felt so strange.

"Jake?" she whispered.

"Yes, Gem?"

"Have I ever fainted before?" Gemma didn't hear his reply as she slid off her chair onto the patio.

Lois Richer loves traveling, swimming and quilting, but mostly she loves writing stories that show God's boundless love for His precious children. As she says, "His love never changes or gives up. It's always waiting for me. My stories feature imperfect characters learning that love doesn't mean attaining perfection. Love is about keeping on keeping on." You can contact Lois via email, loisricher@gmail.com, or on Facebook (loisricherauthor).

Books by Lois Richer

Love Inspired

Rocky Mountain Haven

Meant-to-Be Baby
Mistletoe Twins
Rocky Mountain Daddy
Rocky Mountain Memories

Wranglers Ranch

The Rancher's Family Wish
Her Christmas Family Wish
The Cowboy's Easter Family Wish
The Twins' Family Wish

Family Ties

A Dad for Her Twins
Rancher Daddy
Gift-Wrapped Family
Accidental Dad

Visit the Author Profile page at Harlequin.com for more titles.

Rocky Mountain Memories

Lois Richer

HARLEQUIN® LOVE INSPIRED®

Recycling programs
for this product may
not exist in your area.

LOVE INSPIRED BOOKS

ISBN-13: 978-1-335-47933-4

Rocky Mountain Memories

Copyright © 2019 by Lois M. Richer

www.Harlequin.com

Printed in U.S.A.

And we know that all things work together for good to them that love God, to them who are the called according to his purpose.

For whom he did foreknow,
he also did predestinate to be conformed
to the image of his Son, that he might be
the firstborn among many brethren.
—*Romans* 8:28–29

This book is dedicated to those who strive tirelessly to make a difference in their world. Shut out the naysayers, the negativity and the nonsense. Keep on keeping on. It's worth it.

Chapter One

He would have recognized her anywhere.

Oblivious to the May long weekend crowds throng-
ing the Canadian airport in Edmonton, Jake Elliot
strode directly toward Gemma Andrews, her gorgeous,
waist-length tumble of auburn hair drawing him like
a homing beacon.

"Hello, Gem," he said when he reached her. "Welcome home."

Her forest green eyes widened as she surveyed him,
studying him as though he was a complete stranger.

"Uh, thank you." The lack of energy in her response
bothered Jake.

"Are you all right?" He glanced at the strip of gauze
covering her left temple. "Your head...?"

"Wh-who are you?" The pure panic in her words
floored Jake.

"Excuse me." Only then did Jake notice Gemma's
companion. "I'm Celia Shane from the Canadian embassy in Lima. You are?"

Unease skittered across his nerves. An embassy official had escorted Gem? Because she couldn't manage the trip on her own or…?

"Jake Elliot. I'm here to take Gemma home."

"I was told someone, um, older would meet us." Celia's phone pinged. She checked it and returned a text. "Apparently there's been a change. May I see some credentials?"

Jake fumbled for his wallet to show her his driver's license.

"Thanks. Hello, Jake." Celia's calm demeanor offered some serenity to Jake's whirling thoughts and apparently to Gemma, too, because her scared look eased. "Now, let me explain. As we notified the family, Gemma was at Machu Picchu with a tour group when the earthquake occurred. Subsequent to that notification, we learned she'd been struck by tumbling rocks, had fallen and, as a result of that, she's lost her memory. Because her head injury was minor and she's otherwise in good health, the hospital released her. They feel she'll recover best at home. Besides, they need the beds."

"Lost her memory?" Jake was stuck on that.

"Temporarily." Celia smiled. "Her doctors are convinced her memory will return in time."

"Will she—?"

"You two do know I'm standing here, right?" Gemma interrupted indignantly. "I *can* speak for myself."

Ah, that was more like the feisty woman Jake had known.

"Sorry, Gemma." Celia smiled at her. "Hazard of the job. I tend to take over."

"I am fine." Gemma's eyes met Jake's with the same directness she'd always employed. "I have a cut on my forehead and my brain is a little dinged up, but as Celia said, supposedly things will return to normal soon. In the meantime, I'm sorry but I don't know you."

"Sure you do. I'm Jake, your foster aunts' handyman." To his dismay, even that brought no flicker of recognition to her lovely green eyes.

"My *foster* aunts?" She studied him curiously. "Not my parents or my family?"

"They *are* your family, Gem." He hesitated, but maybe more information would reassure her. "Some years ago Tillie and Margaret Spenser brought you and three other foster girls to their home, The Haven, in the foothills of the Canadian Rockies."

"Um, okay." Gemma's blank look remained so Jake pressed on.

"Your sister Victoria lives at The Haven permanently, with her husband and family, and the aunts, of course. Your sister Adele and her husband and kids live next door, while your other sister Olivia and her husband and family live on a nearby acreage." Still no comprehension. Jake added a little desperately, "They can all hardly wait to see you again."

"You've known me for a while?" she murmured, her expression pensive.

"I came to The Haven six years ago when you were seventeen. I've been there ever since." Jake caught Celia checking her watch. "You need to leave?"

"That text said I'm to fly to Ottawa in an hour to accompany someone back to Peru." She glanced at Gemma. "If you're all right?"

"She will be as soon as I get her home." Jake glanced around. He saw only a battered backpack and a small duffel. "Luggage?"

"Duffel's mine. The other is hers." Celia indicated

the battered canvas with its multiplicity of stickers. "Authorities found it at the site. The hotel where Gemma and—where she was staying was flattened."

Gemma and Kurt. That's what Celia had been going to say. Why had she pulled back?

"The embassy will be certain to forward anything else they recover." She touched Gemma's arm. "Is it okay for me to leave you with Jake?"

"You have to go. You need to do your job, help someone else. I understand." Clearly summoning her pluck, Gemma thrust back her narrow shoulders.

Jake noted the thin cotton shirt she wore was far too large for her lithe frame and not at all her usual style. Well, it hadn't been, but things changed. Then her smile faltered and he forgot about what she wore as compassion for her suffering welled.

"You're going to be fine, Gemma." Celia must have sensed her uncertainty, too.

"Yes, I'm sure I will be." She cast him a sideways glance. "With Jake."

He didn't think Gemma looked or sounded fine. She appeared nervous and uncertain, but in these circumstances, who wouldn't? Though Jake had wished many times for God to blank out the horror of his own past, he couldn't begin to imagine how it must feel to have forgotten everyone and everything. It would take time for Gem to feel secure again.

"You'll feel better once you're home." He hoped she could relax. "It's a long drive to The Haven. If you need to make a stop here, get some coffee or lunch, we'd best do that before we leave."

"All I want is to freshen up. The flight was long and

tiring." She automatically headed for the ladies' room, as if she'd done it a hundred times before.

"How did she know where to go?" He stared at her retreating figure.

"Some things she does from rote. I guess that part of her memory is intact. Recent events are a blank though." Celia shrugged. "She can recite tons of information about lots of different locales she's taken tours to, but she can't tell you anything about the earthquake, what happened before or after it, or her personal past. Which reminds me, I need to talk to you before she returns."

"Okay."

"Gemma doesn't remember that she was married," Celia warned in a low voice. "She doesn't remember Kurt at all."

"How could she forget her own husband?"

"It's part of her injury, I guess." Celia shrugged. "Anyway, you need to be aware that she also has no idea that he died in the earthquake. My office contacted her family as soon as they found out, but apparently you'd already left to come here. I didn't feel it was my place to tell her," the woman explained.

"Why not?" he asked, brow furrowed.

"I couldn't gauge what her response might be. I was worried that if she reacted badly, there wouldn't be any-one to support her." Celia chewed her bottom lip. "Of course, hearing of Kurt's death might trigger her memo-ries, too. Either way, I believe she needs someone who knew them both to help her through her loss and grief. The important thing, according to her doctors, is that with her type of brain injury, the fastest way to recov-ery is no stress."

"You want me to tell her." Jake's heart sank as he

read between the lines. "You don't think her aunts should do it?"

"It's your decision, of course, but I do think it should be you, for several reasons." Celia frowned. "Gemma will find it difficult enough to deal with the family she doesn't remember. Four sisters, aunts, nieces and nephews. It's a lot. I believe it would be simpler for her if she'd already faced the complication of her husband's death when she meets her family."

Inwardly Jake groaned. How was he supposed to tell Gem that Kurt, the man she'd loved and married less than a year ago, was gone?

"Mostly I believe you should do it because you're her friend, her very good friend. Aren't you?" Celia seemed pleased by his nod. "Excellent. To regain her memories, Gemma's going to need someone she can lean on, depend on and talk to without worrying about offending them. I think that's you, Jake. Perhaps during the journey home, you can work it in that she's now a widow. I—" She stopped. "Here she comes."

Work it in? Like, "By the way, Gem, nobody told you but you're now a widow?" Jake's brain scoffed.

He stood by Celia, watching Gemma stride toward them. She moved easily across the space, making her appear confident and assured. Though appreciative heads turned to admire her beauty, Gemma appeared unaware of the attention. Her intense gaze rested on them.

"I'm ready to go," she announced, though there was the faintest wobble in the words and her eyes were red. "Thank you for everything, Celia. I appreciate your assistance so much."

"It was my absolute pleasure, Gemma." Celia hugged

her, a trace of her own tears showing. "I put my card in your pack so that we can keep in touch. I want to know how you're doing. If you need anything," she added as she drew away, "anything at all, you let me know and I'll try to help. Maybe one day you'll return to Peru and we'll have lunch together. *Adiós o hasta pronto, mi querido amigo.*"

"Hasta que nos encontremos de nuevo," Gemma responded in a very quiet tone.

Jake blinked at her automatic Spanish rejoinder before remembering Gemma was fluent in several languages. Another reason why becoming a tour guide had seemed so perfect for her.

Celia waved, picked up her duffel and hurried away. Gemma watched her leave as though she was losing her best friend.

"Things will get better, Gem," he reassured her, trying to sound cheerful.

"Promise?" She gave him a half-hearted smile and then slung her pack over one shoulder. "I have a hunch they're going to get much worse first. I'm ready. I guess."

Jake had never heard Gemma sound so uncertain. She'd always been full of confidence and assurance.

Had been.

"I could take that—" He immediately choked back his offer to carry her backpack when her chin lifted and she glared at him. "Right. Let's go." He pulled his keys out of his pocket as they walked toward the exit. Outside in the clear sunlight he hesitated, concerns rising at her fragile appearance. "It's quite a hike to the car."

"Do you know me well, Jake?" Gemma's green eyes challenged him.

"Pretty well," he said. *Not that well*, his brain rebuked. *You never thought she'd elope.* "You've been away for a while, but I used to," he clarified.

"If you know me at all, then you know that I can quite easily manage a little walk across a parking lot. Right?" One auburn eyebrow arched imperiously.

"But you've been—right." He stifled his objection and pointed. "I'm parked over that way."

Gemma walked beside him, her head swiveling from right to left, taking in the sights of fully leafed trees scattered here and there, and the sound of chirping birds. "It's summertime." She sounded surprised.

"Late May. Springtime in North America and not quite summer in the Rockies," he explained. "The days are much longer but remember our nights are still chilly."

"That's the thing—I don't remember." She sighed. "So many things I've forgotten."

"So many things to rediscover now that you're home." As they reached her foster aunts' big, roomy SUV, Jake hit the unlock button and opened her door.

His phone dinged with a text which he ignored. Someone needing his help, no doubt. The community had gotten in the habit of calling on him for aid with lots of things, but he was busy helping Gemma right now and she came first. He waited until she was comfortably seated with her backpack on the floor, before he closed her door and took his own seat.

"It's not going to be a fast trip out of the city," he warned.

"Rush hour in Edmonton is never fast." Gemma blinked. "I have no idea how I know that," she muttered. "Actually, I'm not sure about a whole lot of things.

I know what they told me, but I can't recall any personal details, like my birthday or when I started leading tour groups or—anything."

"I can tell you a little," Jake offered. "After you graduated from high school, you studied languages. You were always good at French in school."

"Le printemps à Paris est le meilleur moment pour visiter," Gemma murmured. Her eyes flared with surprise. "Uh—"

"See? Your memory is there, Gem. It just needs to wake up." He grinned at her as they sat at a red light.

"But why do I remember that when I can't remember my own name or where I live?" She sounded irritated. "Or these aunts you mentioned. Or the sisters. Or this haven place."

"You'll love The Haven. It's a big old stone manor house perched on the top of a hill with the most wonderful view of the valley and in the distance, the Rockies. It's surrounded by untouched forest." He felt the intensity of her focus on him. "That's what makes it such a perfect place for your aunts' ministries."

"Ministries?" She blinked. "Like they lead a church there or something?"

"No." Jake chuckled. "The ladies have faith—very strong faith—in God. They spent years as missionaries in Africa. Now they're using their home and land as a place for troubled foster kids to come for respite. Your sisters run the programs for them."

"How old are these aunts?" Gemma asked.

"Seventy-six, but you'd never know it. They are very active and extremely involved in their community. I doubt Tillie and Margaret Spenser will ever truly retire because they love helping people." Jake paused before adding, "I should know. They saved my life."

"I'd like to hear that story." Gemma pressed back against the seat, as if she was finally comfortable with him.

"Maybe some other time," he said, trying to gird himself for adding to her pain. "First there's something I need to discuss with you."

The serious note in Jake's voice warned Gemma that whatever he wanted to talk about would not be pleasant. Internal warning signs flared. She was so weary of bracing herself for the unknown. Yet what alternative did she have?

Just then Jake's phone rang. She waited while he answered it.

"Hey, Marv," he said after pressing a button on the dashboard.

"Hate to bother you, Jake, but I'm at Gerda Brown's place, trying to fix her water heater. Except it can't be done. The thing's finished and she can't afford a new one. I already used the spare one you found at O'Shea's place for someone else last month. Any ideas?"

"I'm tied up at the moment, Marv. Why don't you go pick up one at the hardware store? Put it on my tab. I'll figure it out later." After a few moments he ended the call. "Sorry about that."

"You're buying a water heater for somebody who can't afford one?" When he nodded, she asked, "Why?"

"Because they need it." He shrugged his wide shoulders as if it didn't matter. "Anyway, as I was saying. I need to tell you—" His phone rang again and then a third time. His lips pursed but he didn't answer either call. When Gemma tilted an eyebrow at him, his face reddened and he muttered, "They can wait till I get back."

She giggled when the phone rang again. "Maybe not."

"It's from three different callers. Probably three different issues." Jake sounded impatient. She guessed he wanted to say whatever was on his mind.

"I'm listening." She shifted when he didn't immediately speak. "Tell me what you need to, Jake."

"It's sad news, actually." He licked his lips and then pressed them together. "You were married, Gem. To Kurt Andrews. You eloped about eight months ago."

The way he said it, in short staccato bursts, revealed his distress in telling her. But she didn't feel distressed. She felt...empty? The yawning unknown threatened to overwhelm her until she looked at Jake, and some part of her brain calmed. He was a nice guy who bought water heaters for needy women. He'd probably been pressed into duty on her behalf, though he obviously wasn't comfortable with explaining this. She touched his arm.

"Just tell me," she murmured. "Then I can deal with it."

"Kurt was killed in the earthquake." Jake huffed out a breath. "I'm sorry, Gem. I don't have any details. Celia only told me that the embassy is certain he did not survive."

"Oh." Gemma frowned. It didn't feel as if they were talking about anyone she knew, let alone a husband. What did it mean? "Does his family know? Will I have to tell them?"

"You are his family, Gem. His parents died in a car

accident just after you were married." Free of the crush of traffic and now on the divided highway, Jake accelerated.

"No siblings?" Gemma mused, struggling to sort through her building questions.

"You are Kurt's only remaining family." Jake frowned when she didn't immediately respond. "Are you all right?"

"Actually, no." Gemma couldn't control her burst of irritation. "I was married less than a year to a man I loved?" She glanced at Jake, relieved to see his firm nod. "I was his wife, yet I feel blank. I'm sad that he died, of course, but it doesn't feel *personal*. Isn't that shameful?"

"No. It's part of your injury. Truthfully, I'm sort of relieved you don't remember him yet," Jake said, a hint of sternness coloring his voice. He looked embarrassed by his admission.

"You are? Why?" Gemma's curiosity about this unusual man grew.

"Because you're going to need your strength to deal with your living family," he told her, his voice very gentle. "Mourning will come later."

"Did you know Kurt?" Gemma sensed something in Jake's responses that didn't jibe with her impression of him as open and honest. It felt like he was hiding something.

"I knew Kurt the same length of time as I've known you. He was a local, born and raised in Chokecherry Hollow, that's the town near your foster aunts' home." He shrugged. "I liked him a lot and I know he loved you very much."

"Oh." There were a hundred questions roiling inside

her head, but suddenly Gemma didn't want to ask them. She needed time to absorb the fact that she had been a wife—and was now a widow.

To escape the miasma of her whirling brain, she retrieved her backpack. She knew her passport was tucked into the exterior zippered pocket because she'd put it there. She saw Celia's card there, too. But she'd been too tired and too muddled to open the pack that had been handed to her right before she'd left the hospital.

Now curious about what might lie inside, she unzipped the main cavity and began withdrawing the contents. A wallet of soft white leather came first. A driver's license tucked under clear plastic revealed her own face staring back at her. She looked so happy. Behind it was a small snapshot of her and a blond-haired, blue-eyed man.

"Is this Kurt?" She held the photo so Jake could see.

"Yes." A muscle flickered in his jaw. "He's—he was very attractive. You two looked good together."

Gemma didn't respond. She was too busy staring at another photo that was partially stuck to the back of Kurt's, as if the wallet and pictures had been damp. A little girl, also blonde, also blue-eyed, gazed back at her. She wore a fancy dress like children wear at Christmas or on their birthdays. Perhaps four or five, she appeared happy as she clutched a small brown teddy bear and grinned at the camera as if it was her best friend.

"Do you know who this is?" She held up the photo.

"No. I've never seen her before." Jake glanced at her before suggesting, "A foster child you adopted maybe? You used to support several."

It was a good guess, but it didn't feel right to Gemma. Since she had no idea why, she set the photo on the console between them while she checked out the rest of the contents in her backpack, including a metal tag with her name embossed on it. *Gemma Andrews, Tour Director, WorldWide Tours.* It bore deep scratches.

"I think I was wearing this when they found me," she murmured, her fingers tracing the marks. "I have a bruise this shape near my shoulder..."

A memory flickered on the fringes of her subconscious. People gathered around her, laughing as she told them a story, but she couldn't quite recall the entire memory.

"That tag is probably how they identified you. Anything else that's interesting in there?" Jake asked.

"A sweater." She drew out the lime-green cardigan and fingered the soft wool. "Alpaca. I'm guessing I got this at Arequipa. That's where you find the best alpaca garments." The words spilled out spontaneously, shocking her.

"Did you often take your tour groups there?" Jake's question shook off her surprise.

"Usually. They always gave our guests these wonderful gift packs of Peruvian coffee" Gemma stared at him. "Hey, I remembered that and I didn't even try."

"Perhaps that's the way it's going to be," Jake murmured. "The less you strive to think about it, the more relaxed your brain will be, and you'll recover quickly."

"Maybe." It sounded good, but Gemma couldn't shake an ominous sense that things were going to get a lot tougher. She replaced everything in the pack, except the sweater which she pulled on, and the picture. The little girl's joyful face gazed back at her. "She looks so happy, as if she loves whomever she's looking at." A wave of wistfulness swamped her.

What was it like to feel so loved? To love someone and know they loved you? Frustrated by her inability to recall anything personal, Gemma tucked the photo into her pocket while she searched for a topic of conversation. Jake beat her to it.

"You must be wondering why I came to get you instead of your family. Your aunts intended to come, as if anything could have stopped them."

"They're not here and you are, so something must have," she pointed out.

"True, though I would have driven them anyway because Margaret—well, let's say city driving's not her thing." He chuckled.

"So they changed their minds." Gemma shrugged. "It doesn't matter."

"No, they didn't change their minds. Tillie woke up with a sore throat and a fever." Jake paused to ask if she wanted to stop for anything. When Gemma declined, he continued. "Margaret intended to come until a guest showed up unexpectedly, a military man she'd been corresponding with for some months. He was desperate to speak to her and she was worried about his mental state. She sends her apologies."

"Oh." Gemma didn't understand what he was talking about. Jake must have realized that because he explained.

"For years your aunts have conducted a letter-writing campaign to our overseas military troops to offer them encouragement, prayers and someone to talk to. The ladies have a huge list of correspondents." He shrugged. "When they get leave, those folks frequently come to The Haven for a visit, to talk to the ladies personally."

"I see." So her aunts had several ministries. Which

didn't explain why one of her foster sisters hadn't come in their place. Gemma had no sooner had the thought than Jake addressed it.

"Your sisters wanted to be here, too," he told her.

"But?" Was it wrong to feel disappointed that her family had sent their handyman to get her, even though Jake seemed a very nice man?

"Victoria's going through a difficult pregnancy. She struggles to deal with anything before eleven o'clock in the morning." Jake grimaced. "Best for her to be sick at home. Adele offered to take Margaret's place until she got an emergency request to foster two orphaned infants who'd just lost their parents. Olivia's in hospital because yesterday she gave birth to a brand-new baby daughter. So you're stuck with me."

"Not stuck," Gemma protested. "It's very kind of you to sacrifice your time—say, what exactly is it that you do at The Haven, Jake?" It felt strange to say those words, as if she should know. But Gemma couldn't form a mental picture of her family's home or his work.

"I do whatever your aunts need me to do." A muscle twitched in Jake's jaw. "I owe them big-time for saving my life, so fulfilling their needs is my job and my pleasure."

Saving his life.

Gemma was about to ask about that when she realized they were taking an exit off the highway. And his phone was ringing again.

"Sounds like somebody else needs you," she said.

"Apparently." He checked the number before letting it go to voice mail. "I don't think it's serious, but I'll get some coffee and call them back. I was up very early," he said, obviously aware of her curiosity. "How about you?"

"I don't mind stopping." She knew it was an excuse so he wouldn't have to say more about his past, but that didn't mean she intended to let the subject go.

Gemma was stymied by her reactions to him. Why did she feel so comfortable with him? What was with this keen interest in Jake? And why did she feel compelled to discover why this strong, competent man would need two elderly women to save his life?

It was natural that she had a lot of questions about herself, important knowledge like who she was, where she'd grown up, her childhood, her foster aunts and sisters, especially her husband. She couldn't remember any of that. What kind of a woman forgot her own wedding?

But now Gemma also had growing questions about Jake Elliot. A good-looking man, he was tall, solidly built and radiated an empathetic aura of strength and confidence. Rather like a young John Wayne in a very old movie, though this handyman was definitely not old. He was probably close to her age, which was twenty-three according to her passport. He seemed perfectly comfortable in his well-fitting jeans, cotton shirt, cowboy boots and battered leather jacket, while his mussed brown hair and piercing blue eyes made him seem vibrantly alive, unlike the dull blankness that hung over her mind.

Besides all that, Jake was apparently the go-to guy for the community's needy folks.

A strange combination to be sure, though why he should intrigue her so was a puzzle Gemma couldn't fathom. The only thing she did know was that Jake wasn't like her. He knew exactly who he was, where he was going and, unlike her, exactly where he belonged.

It might take time, but she was determined to discover exactly who this poised, handsome handyman was behind the friendly, self-effacing smile.

And somehow she intended to learn why he had needed saving.

Chapter Two

Spurning an offer of coffee, Gemma elected to stretch her legs while Jake returned his calls. Tactfully, he deferred the concerns of each person, assuring them he'd handle their needs when he returned. By the time Gemma reappeared at the car, he'd come up with solutions to each problem presented. The outreaches he did were mostly busy work for his brain, but they helped suppress the barely buried memories of his past. That was exactly why he'd taken on the role of community problem-solver.

"Everything okay?" Gemma asked as she fastened her seat belt.

"Yep. Next stop, The Haven."

While he drove, Gemma slept. Every so often she would call out or startle and waken herself. Then her long, lush lashes would droop, and she'd doze again.

Jake had a thousand questions. Had she been happy with Kurt? Had marriage lived up to her expectations? Did she regret not having a big, fancy wedding? In the past she'd have told him all of that without his asking. He yearned to rebuild the old camaraderie they'd shared.

He was thinking about her too much. He needed to adjust his thoughts.

In six years of living at The Haven, this was one of a handful of times that Jake had left the place. Was that why he felt so antsy? At The Haven he could bury himself in other people's issues because there was little about the place to remind him of Lily or of the reason for her death. The folks at The Haven and in Choke-cherry Hollow had become a bandage over the pain of his loss.

As Gemma now was?

I promise, Lily. I will never love another as I did you. I will never risk another woman's life through my selfishness. Never again. I promise.

He was Gemma's friend and he'd do whatever he could for her, but friendship was all they could ever share.

Jake switched on the radio for distraction, glad when he turned off the highway that Gemma would arrive home in daylight. It wasn't the Andes in autumn, but springtime in the Canadian Rockies *was* pretty spectacular.

"Time to wake up," he said when there were only a few minutes left in their trip. "You need to see this, Gem."

"I haven't done a thing and yet all I do is sleep." She sat up and rubbed her eyes, wincing when her fingers brushed the injury on her forehead. She yawned and stretched her neck, twisting and turning to get a good look at her surroundings. "Spectacular," she breathed.

"It is," Jake said with smug satisfaction, as if the land was his own. "We'll soon be home. Then you can climb into bed and really rest, if you want."

He wanted to ease her transition, but how could you help someone who couldn't remember anything about their past? Maybe he should have let her sleep.

"I've always loved the snowcaps on these mountains." She paused. "I mean, I think I have."

"You don't have to monitor every word. Just take it as it comes, Gem. And I know exactly how you feel." The serenity of the vast forest surrounding The Haven filled Jake's soul. He loved it here. This was *his* haven and he never wanted to leave, though technically it wasn't *his* home. He'd lost that the day—

Jake shoved away the guilt and drove uphill toward the big stone house where the aunts lived.

"Jake?" Gemma's voice came soft, breathless.

"Yeah." He glanced at her. Worried by her pallor, he pulled to the side of the road. "Feel sick?"

"Yes. What if I don't ever remember them?" She grabbed his arm and clung to it. "What if this never feels like home? I'm so scared."

"Don't be." He wrapped her icy fingers in his and held on to them, trying to ease her discomfort the way a movie hero would simply because Gemma—the old Gemma—had always admired white-knight heroes. "Everything is going to be fine. There's no rush about remembering. You'll do it when you're ready. No one will pressure you. Everyone will understand. All they care about is that you're home and unhurt—well, mostly unhurt," he corrected with a smile, wishing she'd lose that terrified expression.

"But—but—"

"Gem." He gave in to his longing to comfort her and slid his palm against her cheek for just a second. "You used to have a special verse you'd recite whenever you needed to encourage yourself. Do you remember it? It starts, 'God is our refuge and our strength.'" He removed his hand and waited for her to finish it.

"'A tested help in times of trouble.'" Eyes wide, she nodded. "I do remember that."

"Now think about the words," he suggested while his brain called him a hypocrite. *God hasn't been your refuge or strength, Jake. Not for years.*

She remained silent for a few moments before huffing a sigh.

"Okay. Guess I'm as ready as I'll ever be."

"Atta girl." He shifted into gear. "The Haven's gorgeous, isn't it? All that stonework with those towers and—" One glance at Gem's face and Jake cut off his commentary, sensing that she needed silence to gather her pluck for the reunion ahead.

He sent up a prayer for her, for strength and a calm spirit, and then wondered at himself. He didn't talk to God anymore. Hadn't since... Anyway, Gemma Andrews wasn't his responsibility.

Yet from the first day he'd arrived at The Haven, Jake had felt protective of her, as if he had to be there in case she needed him.

"There are so many of them!" Gemma gasped, drawing his attention to the house and the folks assembled on the driveway.

"Those aren't all your relatives," he sputtered, amused by her shocked expression. "I'm guessing your family arranged for whatever kids' group is visiting The Haven to form a welcoming committee. Relax," he chided as her fingers tightened around her seat belt. He parked, turned off the car and waited a moment before asking, "Ready?"

"As I'll ever be," she whispered. She lifted her hand to open her door, pausing when Jake shook his head.

"Wait." He climbed out, strode to her side and offered a hand to help her exit the car. Her hair had loosened from the topknot she'd tied it in earlier and now tumbled past her waist. Her face was strained and the jeans she wore had seen better days.

But Jake thought she had never looked lovelier.

"Welcome home, Gemma," he said softly, and then he drew her forward to meet her family.

Gemma licked her lips as she mentally reminded herself, *They're my family. My family.*

She didn't feel like she belonged with them.

"Our dear, dear girl." One of the elderly women, an auntie perhaps, wrapped her in a gentle, fragrant embrace. She brushed a kiss against Gemma's brow before holding her back to examine her. "We are so thankful you're home, dear."

"I—er, I'm glad to be here," she whispered. It wasn't home—not yet—but how could a mere hug feel so wonderful? She glanced from one lady to the other. "You're twins!" Her face burned at the peals of laughter around her.

"Guess I forgot to tell you that, Gem. This is your Aunt Tillie," Jake explained.

"Hello. Jake said you were ill." As Gemma squeezed her hand she noticed the woman's red nose. "I hope you're feeling better."

"A simple case of the summer sniffles. Some people worry too much," Tillie said with a glare at her doppelganger.

"You are Aunt Margaret. It's very nice to—" Gemma

had been going to say *meet you.* But that was hardly appropriate. "To be here," she finished.

"My dear, you should be resting in bed." Margaret wrapped tender arms around her in a second hug. "You've had a dreadful ordeal."

"I'm fine." Gemma had never felt more on show.

"Margaret tends to fuss," Tillie murmured.

"It's nice to be fussed over, but I'm truly all right." She wanted to get this over with. "Thank you for the welcome," she said, scanning the assembled group. One glance at Jake and he immediately understood. He nodded at someone and after the group of children had sung a welcome song they hurried away, apparently to other activities.

"These are your sisters, Gemma." He introduced each woman, her husband and her children.

Her foster sisters at least resembled the descriptions he'd given her during their long ride here. Their children's names would require memorizing.

"I should have brought gifts," Gemma whispered to Jake when the silence stretched too long.

"No, you shouldn't have, Gem," Victoria said. "All we care about—all we've been praying for—is that you'd come home safely."

"I care about presents, Auntie Vic!" A little girl glared at her aunt until her mother—Adele?—hushed her. "Well, I like 'em," she muttered defiantly.

Gemma grinned at her. "I like presents, too," she said.

"We're so sad about Kurt, Gemmie." Olivia, a tiny baby snugged against her chest in some type of sack, embraced her. "I'm sorry you had to go through that alone."

"Thank you." *Go through? Oh, she means losing my husband. But I can't even remember what Kurt looked like, just as I can't remember any of you.* "Jake said your baby is brand-new," she murmured, staring at the delicate face and wondering if she'd ever wanted to be a mother. "Congratulations."

"Thanks. This is your niece, Mirella. She's pleased to meet you."

"Me, too, Mirella." Gemma stirred at the touch on her shoulder. Jake. Her protector. When he smiled, her tension eased.

Thank You, God, for Jake. Funny how natural it seemed to pray. Was she very religious? How could she not *know* something like that?

As if sensing her confusion, Jake asked, "How about some lemonade on the deck, Gem?"

"Great idea! What's wrong with us, keeping our girl standing here?" Tillie smiled at Gemma before turning to Margaret. "Come, sister. Let's savor this blessing of having our four girls home once more. It's been forever, or so it seems."

"Thank you all for your warm welcome," Gemma repeated politely.

Her family—how strange that word felt—sat around her on a huge deck overlooking a picturesque valley. Everyone chattered at once. It should have sounded like bedlam, and yet to Gemma, the loving, teasing voices and laughing children who played boisterously nearby were a balm to her jumbled mind. With the warm sun on her face and several delicious cookies in her stomach, her eyelids soon drooped.

"Gem?" Tension underlaid Jake's husky drawl.

"Yes?" She blinked before forcing herself to sit up

straight. "Did I fall asleep again? I'm so sorry," she apologized to the group who now stared at her with sympathy. "Is my hair a mess?" When she lifted her hand to smooth the strands she noticed an older man in a three-piece suit standing at the edge of the patio. "I'm sorry if I should know you," she began to apologize. She stopped when Jake's fingers squeezed her shoulder.

"Gemma, this is Wilber Hornby. He's a local lawyer." There was a graveness to Jake's tone that she didn't like. "He's here about Kurt."

"Now?" She frowned. "But I only just got here—"

"I'm very sorry," Mr. Hornby said in precise diction. "But Kurt was most insistent that if anything happened to him, I was to speak to you immediately. I promised I would do so, therefore I have come."

Only then did Gemma notice that, one by one, her family had silently left. Only her aunts, Jake and the lawyer remained with her. This must be serious. Funeral plans?

"O-okay." As she drained her glass of lemonade, she realized that Jake was about to depart, too. "Please stay?" she begged. "Please?"

Jake glanced at the aunts. They nodded. He appeared to consider something but finally shrugged and sat down. Gemma mouthed *thanks* before turning to face the sober-faced lawyer.

"What is this about?" she asked.

"It's about a girl," Mr. Hornby said. "Your husband's four-year-old stepdaughter. Her name is Alexa."

Gemma had steeled herself to hear something important, perhaps something about Kurt's final wishes or... Wait a minute.

"My husband was married before me?" She turned

questioningly toward Jake and was astonished by his outraged glared at the lawyer.

"Kurt Andrews never had eyes for anyone but Gemma for as long as I knew him." Jake glowered at the lawyer. "He was always crazy in love with her. What are you saying?"

The way Jake said the words, fiercely, with his blue eyes glittering, jaw clenched and his back ramrod straight—it was as if this man was indignant on her behalf, Gemma thought wonderingly. That made her feel special, valued, precious.

"I have a letter from Mr. Andrews to his wife that will explain," Mr. Hornby began, drawing an envelope from his briefcase.

He held it out, but Gemma couldn't take it. She wasn't sure exactly why, only that she didn't want to have to deal with anything more right now, especially not a letter from a husband she couldn't remember.

"Can't it wait?" she begged, sending Jake a pleading look.

"Kurt's direction to me was to proceed as quickly as I could." The lawyer's set face told Gemma he would do his duty no matter what.

"Perhaps in this instance, Wilber," Aunt Tillie said softly, placing her hand on his arm, "we might dispense with her reading the letter right now. Couldn't you just tell Gemma the gist of it?" She glanced at her sister for support. "After all…"

The two women shared a look that told Gemma they knew, or at least guessed what was in that envelope.

"Those are not the terms—"

"I know, Wilber. And you've been most circumspect in coming here as soon as our dear girl arrived home,"

Margaret soothed. "But Gemma isn't herself. She's been through an earthquake and she has amnesia. The doctor's orders are for her to minimize stress."

Even Gemma could see the lawyer weakening under the genteel ladies' soft words and beseeching expressions. She had a hunch that there weren't many people who could deny these aunties whatever they asked for. They were characters. It would be fun to get to know them.

"If you could just explain to Gemma what you need from her, sir," Jake added quietly. "Once she knows whatever it is, she can think about it and come back to you if she needs clarification."

She threw him a grateful look. He was such a sweet man to always keep smoothing the way for her.

Always? Jake had smoothed her way before?

"Is that your wish, Mrs. Andrews?"

Gemma glanced around, wondering whom he was addressing and found everyone staring at her. Oh. *Mrs. Andrews.* That was *her* name. How strange.

"Gemma?" Mr. Hornby pressed.

"Yes, please. Just tell me the basics," she said, nodding.

"Very well, though it's rather difficult…" Mr. Hornby paused, gathered his thoughts and then began speaking. "Your husband—you remember he went to college after finishing high school?"

"I'm afraid I don't remember anything," Gemma told him. "Just pretend we never met before and tell me what you think I need to know about, um, Kurt."

"All right." Hornby cleared his throat. "He told me he was uncertain about his next step and went to college to try to figure things out. While he was there he met a woman, Anna, a law student in her final year, who became a good friend. Kurt learned she was pregnant and desperate to finish school. She felt she had no way to raise a child and adoption was out because she couldn't pay for a delay in her education. She intended to have an abortion."

"I see." *So the stepchild must be the Alexa he's talking about. But why would my husband...?*

"Kurt was totally against abortion. He said he tried desperately to talk Anna out of it, but she would not be swayed. She saw no other option." Hornby paused for breath, then continued. "To be brief, Kurt persuaded her to marry him, insisting he'd support her until the child was born and continue to work to ensure the child was cared for while Anna finished her schooling. Nothing romantic about it, Kurt said. His whole concern was for the child. Anna finally agreed to marry him on condition he told no one about their arrangement."

"Where was I during all this?" Gemma asked, struggling to absorb the information.

"Overseas, at language school," Jake said immediately. His face reddened at the surprised looks from the aunts. "I remember that's where you went after high school."

"You are correct, Jake. Gemma spent time mastering languages in Europe," Margaret agreed somberly.

Mr. Hornby cleared his throat.

"Please go on." A sudden chill made Gemma shiver. *Now what?*

"When the child, Alexa, was born, Kurt took care of her. He loved her, but he hated the secrecy of not being able to share her with his family. So after Anna graduated, Kurt came home one weekend to tell his parents the truth. When he returned, Anna and her child were gone." Mr. Hornby took off his glasses and polished them on his handkerchief.

"Gone where?" Gemma realized she was perched on the edge of her lawn chair. "And how do I fit in?"

"Anna later called Kurt to explain that she'd arranged for them to divorce. She had a new job and wanted a fresh start for herself and Alexa, and for Kurt. Anna was adamant that Kurt belonged with you. She'd always known he loved you." Mr. Hornby managed a smile.

"Easy for you to say," she muttered, a little embarrassed. It didn't seem like the lawyer was talking about anyone she knew.

"Mrs. Andrews, Kurt told me he loved you dearly and that there'd only ever been friendship between him and Anna." The lawyer's hard face softened. "But little Alexa had stolen a piece of his heart. Kurt had no legal or biological claim to her, of course. Still, he felt that if ever she needed him, as his mother had needed him, there should be funds available for her. That's why he set up her trust fund. His request was that if he was not able, you should manage the fund for Alexa. Kurt had great faith in your ability to protect her." He held up the letter. "This is his explanation to you about the matter."

"But why didn't he just tell me himself? Why did he keep it a secret?" Gemma's head ached as the knowledge whirled round and round inside it. The letter in her hand felt heavy, full of problems, and she already had too many of those. "What am I supposed to do with this fund? Make sure it's invested properly—something like that?" She glanced at Jake for help, but he appeared as puzzled as she felt. "I don't know anything about investing or trust funds."

Something clicked in her brain, like her words weren't quite true. But she didn't understand how that could be. And suddenly this world of everything unknown felt like it was closing in on her.

"May I say something, dear?" Tillie's soft voice broke through Gemma's confusion. "Margaret and I knew about Alexa. Kurt's parents confided in us."

"That was one of the reasons for the disagreement," Margaret chimed in.

"What disagreement?" Gemma read disapproval on the ladies' faces.

"My dear, you came home to announce your elopement and we were very happy for both of you." Margaret's smile eased some of the tension gripping Gemma.

"But when we asked your husband privately if he'd told you about Alexa, he insisted that he wanted you to meet the child first so you could bond, but Anna and Alexa were away that weekend." Sadness edged Tillie's words. "We disagreed with Kurt's decision. We felt he should have explained about the child before you agreed to marry him. I'm afraid it caused a bit of a rift between us and him."

"He certainly should have told me the truth before we got married," Gemma said, feeling indignant for Kurt's wife. Wait, that was *her*! "But since he didn't, it's a moot point."

Everyone was watching her, including Jake. She shifted uncomfortably, waiting for someone to speak. When they didn't, she blurted out her thoughts.

"So what now? Am I supposed to do something about Alexa? Is she okay? And what in the world could I do anyway? I haven't even got a job." Worried and muddled, Gemma fumed. "I can't help myself, let alone a child."

"May I suggest something, Gem?" Jake's smile somehow calmed her. "Maybe you could find out about Alexa, make sure she and her mom are all right. At least then you'd have peace of mind."

"I guess I could do that," she agreed, then frowned. "What do I do after that?"

"If Alexa doesn't need Kurt's money, you could ensure it's wisely invested and then leave it to grow until she does need it," he said with a shrug.

"That sounds advisable," the lawyer agreed.

"Yes," Tillie said, though she was frowning. She looked at her sister.

"It does *sound* good. Only, Alexa and her mom aren't all right," Margaret blurted.

"How do you know that?" Jake studied the sisters with narrowed eyes.

"We've kept tabs on them. Kurt and Gemma were away so much, you see." Margaret cleared her throat. "We felt it our duty to watch over the child."

"And so?" Gemma replied automatically. She felt so confused and muddled and her headache was back.

"I'm sorry to tell you that Anna was accidentally killed three days ago in a drive-by shooting." Tillie's sad voice was hushed.

"The day of the earthquake," Gemma whispered, aghast.

"Yes." Margaret sighed. "Apparently Anna had a will that named Kurt as Alexa's guardian in the event of her own death. Because there are no other relatives and Kurt was unreachable, Anna's daughter, Alexa, was placed in foster care. We've been praying and praying for a way to help the child."

"Yes," Margaret exclaimed. "And now you're home, Gemma. A true answer to prayer."

"Me?" Gemma blinked. She glanced sideways at Jake and found no help in his shrug. So she studied her aunts. "I'm an answer to prayer? What am I supposed to do?"

"We have no idea, dear," Tillie said, her smile sweet.

"Not yet. But we'll think of something," Margaret said confidently. "We always do." She rose. "Or you will. Oh, dear, look at the time. I'm so sorry, Gemmie, but Tillie and I must leave. We have an appointment in Chokecherry Hollow that we simply cannot cancel, but it shouldn't take too long."

"My dear girl," Tillie said, rising and moving close to pat her shoulder. "You're safe now. Jake will show you around The Haven and your room is waiting for you. As always."

Gemma sat stunned as the ladies kissed her cheek and told her again how glad they were to have her home. Then they bustled away. The lawyer rose, too.

"I must also depart. As Kurt's executor, I'm happy to answer any questions you may have, Mrs. Andrews— Gemma. Call on me anytime." He, too, left.

Gemma felt like Dorothy in Oz, right after the tornado had touched down. Wait, how did she remember that?

"Well, I guess I'd better get started answering those calls—" Jake started to say.

"No you don't!" He was her lifeline and she wasn't about to let go of him in this sea of confusion. "You brought me here, Jake. You got me into this. Now help me figure it out."

He opened his mouth to protest, studied her for a moment and then poured himself another glass of lemonade. He sat down, huffed out a huge sigh and swallowed half of the pale yellow liquid.

"I'm only The Haven's handyman, Gem," he said weakly.

"You're the fixer, that's why all those people called you," she said, struggling to make sense of everything she'd learned. "Now help me figure out how to fix things for this child that my husband loved so dearly, when I can't even remember my own name. Wait a minute. That picture." She blinked, remembering the photo of the smiling child.

"Gem, are you okay? You look…weird."

"The picture that was in my wallet. That must be Alexa. Maybe Kurt did tell me about her and I just forgot. Along with everything else." Suddenly the sun felt too hot, the problems too large, the decisions too overwhelming. Somewhere in the recesses of her brain she thought she could hear a man's voice calling, *Take care of her. Take care of Alexa.*

The world wobbled. Had she really heard that or was she dreaming? She felt so strange.

"Jake?" she whispered.

"Yes, Gem?" His voice came from a long way away.

"Have I ever fainted before?" Gemma didn't hear his reply as she slid off her chair and onto the patio.

Chapter Three

For the next two days, Jake stayed away from The Haven, trying to catch up with his work and hoping to give Gemma time to absorb everything in her world. But with each day that passed, his concern about her ramped up. Somebody had to do something.

Though he'd called the local doctor after Gemma had fainted, though she'd been given a thorough checkup and she had pooh-poohed his concern, he worried. She did look and sound fine, yet she seemed somehow diminished. Apparently her interest in Alexa had also lapsed because she remained silent on that issue.

"Want to check out our fishing hole this afternoon?" Jake had asked yesterday when he'd seen her sitting on the deck. He'd pointed out the spot, expecting she'd jump at the chance to resume her favorite activity.

"I just showered. I'll get dirty scrabbling down that hill," she'd mumbled, barely meeting his gaze. "Anyway, Adele's a chef. She doesn't need me to bring home supper."

Excuses made, Gemma had resumed staring across the valley.

It seemed to Jake that she couldn't muster the strength to move on with her life. Since Tillie and Margaret gave the impression they were perfectly content to let their foster daughter float through the days, Jake felt it was up to him to help her snap out of it. Which was why when he found Gemma in the kitchen near noon today, still swathed in her bathrobe, he discarded his white-glove treatment.

"Since you're not busy, can you help me out?" He was relieved that his peremptory tone jarred her from her vacant stare through the massive window to the distant mountains.

"Help you out with what?" Though Gemma looked at him, her gaze was hazy, unfocused.

"With my work here at The Haven." It was the only thing he could think of to motivate her. "I'm behind."

"Because you took time off to come get me." As he'd expected, Gemma immediately jerked upright. Twin dots of color appeared in her cheeks. "I'm sorry, Jake. I've been selfish, haven't I?" She sounded more like herself. "I don't know that much about your work, or anything else for that matter. But I'll help however I can if you'll show me what to do."

"For starters, get dressed. Old clothes. We'll be working in the dirt." Jake lifted one eyebrow when she simply sat there. "Well?"

"Dressed. Got it." Gemma rose and strode across the room. When she reached the doorway, she stopped and turned. "Will you wait here, or should I find you?"

"I'm already late," he told her in a brusque tone that he despised but used because it seemed to be shocking her out of her dazed lethargy. "Find me in the garden."

"The garden." She didn't move. "Uh, the garden is…?"

He pointed.

"Right. I'll be there in five minutes," Gemma promised.

"Wear a sun hat," he called after her retreating form.

"Do you think that was wise, dear?" Tillie murmured.

Jake whirled to find the aunts standing behind him, both wearing disapproving frowns. They'd obviously overheard his less than gentle tone. Jake mentally grimaced, hating that he'd caused that look of strain on their sweet faces.

"Gemma needs to be busy, to be doing something," he explained gently. "Sitting around, waiting for her memory to return isn't helping her."

"What if it doesn't return?" Margaret's hushed tone revealed her concern.

"Ladies," Jake chided with a smile. "Where's your faith?" He was rewarded with their nods. "Until Gemma's memory returns, she needs a purpose. Maybe gardening will give her that." Did he sound more certain than he felt? "It's better than doing nothing," he offered belatedly.

"Yes, it is," Tillie agreed.

"Thank you for trying to help, Jake," Margaret added. "We've been afraid to push Gemma. Shame on us for our lack of faith in God."

"It's time we prayed about this in a different way, sister." Tillie slipped her hand in Margaret's arm and drew her out of the room. A moment later Gemma appeared clad in raggedy jeans, a T-shirt, a hoodie and a sun hat he hadn't seen for years.

"I thought you said you weren't waiting," she accused, her megawatt smile flashing. "The aunts," she guessed. "They waylaid me, too." She waved a piece of delicate pink notepaper.

"A Bible verse?" Jake guessed as he held the door for her to exit The Haven.

"Uh-huh." She handed it over so he could read the spidery script.

Whither shall I go from thy spirit? or whither shall I flee from thy presence? If I ascend up into heaven, thou art there: if I make my bed in hell, behold, thou art there. If I take the wings of the morning, and dwell in the uttermost parts of the sea; Even there shall thy hand lead me, and thy right hand shall hold me.

"Psalm 139." Jake handed back the note which Gemma folded and tucked into her back pocket.

"You know it?" She seemed surprised, yet her stride matched his and she never faltered.

"Sure, I know it." Jake hesitated to say more, but being Gemma, he figured she'd keep pressing for the why. "It's a good verse. I looked it up after someone said it to me once." He glanced her way and almost smiled at her raised eyebrows. She'd always been full of questions.

"Why did they quote that verse to you?"

"It was after a funeral." Two funerals, actually. *Change the subject, Jake.* "Did you think more about Kurt's stepdaughter?"

"Alexa. I haven't been able to think of anything else. I'm almost certain she's the child in that picture I found in my wallet. Maybe Kurt told me about her or maybe I found out." She shrugged. "Guess I'll never know."

"Either one sounds plausible." Relieved she hadn't brushed off the orphaned child, he asked, "Are you going to apply for her guardianship?"

"Me?" She gaped at him. "What do I know about kids? I was thinking more along the lines of bringing Alexa here for a visit. I've been watching the kids who come. They all seem to have a wonderful time."

"Yes." Jake had hoped for more, hoped for Gemma to interact with the child. Maybe if her focus wasn't on what she'd forgotten…

"You want me to weed?" Gemma stood at the fenced entrance to the garden, surveying it.

"Do you want to?" He smothered a laugh at her eager nod.

"Yes! I love weeding." As soon as the words were out, her forehead pleated. Her expression faltered. "Don't I?" she asked hesitantly.

"You did." He handed her a pair of work gloves she'd left behind long ago, and grinned as she slid them onto her slender fingers. "You've loved weeding ever since the first time the aunts sent you out to weed as punishment for some misdeed. You were supposed to work an hour. You were here for three and I didn't have to do it again for a week. You used to beg them to send you out to weed." He chuckled. "I often wondered if you sometimes broke a rule or misbehaved just so you could get your fingers in the dirt."

"Sounds like I was a brat." Gemma knelt and with a touch born of long experience, eased a thistle out of the ground from between tender carrot shoots. "Was that why I eloped, do you think, to break a rule?"

"I don't know the answer to that, Gem. You never said." Jake sank to his knees in the next row and began extricating the unwanted green invaders from around his beans.

Silence stretched between them, a comfortable peace The Haven always seemed to engender in him. At least it had until Gem's return. For some reason Jake now felt like he had to keep up his guard, had to keep reminding himself of his vow to Lily.

"There's something wonderful about weeding," Gemma murmured more to herself than him. "It's exciting, like you're preparing the way for something. You can't see exactly what's happening, but you know the end result will be so good. We'll have carrots." She said it almost triumphantly.

"And peas and beans and…" Jake let it trail away, amused by the satisfaction filling her face.

"I remember once when I was in Italy—" Gemma stopped, blinked and stared at him. "I remember something!"

"Good. What is it?" He kept on weeding, waiting to hear whatever thought was emerging. Listening to Gemma speak about her travels had always fascinated him.

"I was in a garden there." She leaned back on her heels, her gaze on some far distant place. "There were the most massive tomatoes and I was picking the best." She stopped and grinned at him. "To make sauce for lasagna. Or rather, Mamma Francesca was teaching me how to make it. Those tomatoes were so delicious."

"Cool," he murmured, watching the wash of sun light up her face. Gemma was gorgeous. Then shadows filled her eyes.

"I don't know what else happened," she murmured. "I can't—"

"Remember," he finished for her and winked.

"Exactly!" Gemma exclaimed. She burst out laughing and the tense lines dissipated.

They worked together for a while in a genial silence that required no speaking. Jake had a hunch she was remembering more, but he remained quiet, loathe to interrupt.

"I must have been to Italy several times," she eventually murmured. "In my mind I can see the Coliseum, the tower of Pisa and a spot on a mountain where there was an eruption."

"Vesuvius," Jake offered.

"No. Mt. Etna. Three days after Kurt and I left, there was an eruption. It was a big tour group and we were so glad we hadn't delayed…" Gemma blinked several times, then twisted her head to look at him. "Why can't I remember my husband, Jake?"

"You will. But you have a lot of memories tucked in that lovely head. I guess they can't all come at once." He kept working.

"What am I supposed to do until I do remember?" A hint of bitterness colored her voice. "That's part of what bothers me with the whole Alexa thing. What do I have to offer her? I don't remember how to lead a tour anymore, but even if I did, how could I travel *and* care for a child? Or am I supposed to stay here and freeload off the aunts until I remember my life? If I ever do, that is."

"Gemma," Jake scolded. "Last year your sister was injured while rock climbing. Nobody thought she was freeloading when she stayed in bed to let her leg heal. Olivia happily took over her job."

"Victoria always did love scaling the most treacherous places," Gemma muttered, apparently unaware that she'd identified which sister without any prompting. "But this is different. I don't work here."

"Maybe you could for a while," he suggested.

"Doing what?" she asked, eyebrows arched. "Showing people around? Kind of hard since I don't know my own way around the place."

"You'll figure it out. Give it some thought. I'm sure you'll find a niche in The Haven's ministry that only you can fill." He paused before asking, "What will you do about Alexa?"

Gemma rose. She studied the group of kids playing dodgeball nearby in a grassy meadow. Then she considered the circle of stones they'd gathered around last evening to roast marshmallows. Lastly she surveyed the play equipment her sisters used for their own children. She remained silent for some time. When she did speak there was a hesitancy to her words that told Jake she was struggling to sort out her emotions.

"I think I'll ask Victoria to find out if Alexa can come here for a visit."

"That's a great idea." Jake hoped she wouldn't change her mind. A lonely child could be exactly what Gemma needed to take her mind off her own problems.

"We can get to know each other. I don't want to abandon this child whom my husband apparently cared for so deeply," she murmured, forehead pleated. "But what if—?"

"I'll help you," he interrupted, wondering why he was doing this when he'd spent the past six years basically isolating himself at The Haven. Now he was going to help with some orphaned little girl he didn't even know? *Yes.*

"Thank you, Jake." Gemma's smile somehow made it all make sense. "What will we do with her?"

"Help her join in the activities with all the other kids," he said, glancing over her head at a group of kids now flying kites. "There's always something to do here."

"I suppose." The way Gemma dragged out the word proved he'd missed the intent of her question. "I actually meant what will *I* do with her? What kind of things would help me get to know Alexa?"

"You were always good with kids, Gem. You'll think of something. And you do have Kurt in common. But I'm not sure you need to plan it all out ahead of time," he cautioned. "Maybe you wait, watch to see what she enjoys and build on that."

"How did you get to be so smart about kids, Jake?" Gemma moved farther down the row, annihilating weeds as if driven.

"I'm not smart about kids," he denied as the familiar surge of loss bloomed inside. *I didn't get that chance. Don't go there.* "Hey," he challenged, desperate to change the subject. "Are you doing the corn rows or am I?"

"You take forever. I'll do it." She shot him a cheeky grin. "You always baby the seedlings too much. Once they're out of your greenhouse and in the ground, they'll toughen up. You have to be strong to live in the foothills of the Rockies."

"So now *you're* the gardener who's giving *me* advice?" He relaxed, comfortable with their familiar banter. "Any suggestions you want to share about the rhubarb? Your aunts want three more plants."

"What on earth for?" Gemma's nose wrinkled with distaste. "It's so sour."

"Not when Adele mixes it with my strawberries and adds a big dollop of ice cream. What?" he demanded when she hooted with laughter.

"You can't grow strawberries here, Jake." She looked so alive, so vibrant, so... Gemma.

He'd forgotten she hadn't visited last summer because she'd been escorting a group on a cruise through the Northwest Passage. So now, of course, she razed him mercilessly about trying to grow delicate strawberry plants at this elevation. Jake endured it for a little while, but with his pride at stake, he finally rose and beckoned.

"Follow me, oh doubting one," he ordered.

Gemma had always been lousy at hiding her emotions and right now her curiosity was in control. She dusted off her grubby gloves against her dirty knees and hopped across the rows to follow him.

"Where are we going?"

"Wait for it." He led her around an outcropping of stones. "Feast your eyes on my strawberry garden, doubter." He drew one fat red fruit off its stem and ensured it was relatively clean before setting it on her palm. "First berry of the season."

Wide-eyed, Gemma inspected the fruit before popping it into her mouth. A flush of satisfaction filled Jake when she slowed her chewing to allow the flavors to permeate her taste buds. Her zest for life, her eagerness about everything it offered, that's what he wanted her to recover.

"Well?" he demanded, stupidly eager to hear her opinion.

"Amazing." Her big expansive smile did funny things to his stomach. "How did you get them to survive?"

Jake figured his explanation probably went into too much detail and droned on for too long, but Gemma seemed to listen to every word. This was the old Gem. This intense interest in life was what had first drawn him to her.

"So by packing those stones around to soak in the heat, and by raising the beds, you create a warmer, sheltered area." She clapped her hands together. "Bravo, Monsieur Horticulturalist."

He'd missed her enthusiasm.

"Yield?" She bent to study the way he'd laid the new runners.

"Last year was good. It's too early to tell this year." Funny how pleased he was by her interest. "I'm hopeful we'll get enough for Adele to freeze for next…"

Suddenly Gemma wasn't listening. She gazed over the valley, but Jake doubted she was seeing the meadow with its wildflowers waving in the wind. Something else was going on inside that auburn head.

"Why do I keep thinking about roses, Jake?" She turned to frown at him, green eyes dark and swirling. "Is it something to do with my past?"

He shook his head.

"Mine," he said very quietly. Of all things, why did she have to remember that?

Eyes stretched wide, she waited for an explanation.

"I grow roses in the greenhouse." He pushed past a tide of memories. "I experiment with them."

"The Lilian." Her frown deepened. "I keep hearing that name."

"We should finish up weeding. It will soon be time for dinner." He wanted to walk away, to ignore her question, to retreat to the silence that he should never have left.

Jake wanted to leave, but he couldn't ignore Gem's question, not when she was so desperate to learn about her past. Besides, The Lilian was part of her past, too.

"I'm sorry if I said something wrong." Her hand touched his fleetingly. "I didn't mean to."

"It's okay. The Lilian was a prototype of a rose that I used to work on when you lived here before. In memory of—someone," he substituted at the last moment.

"Which has to do with the funeral you mentioned, doesn't it? I'm sorry." Gemma said it so quickly that Jake figured he must have visibly reacted. "We don't need to talk about it."

She walked to the corn rows and began industriously weeding between stalks. Jake watched her for a few minutes, but he couldn't stay. Mention of The Lilian had brought back his old restlessness along with a wealth of excruciatingly painful memories. He had to get out of here before they overwhelmed him and turned him into a weeping wimp.

Take them tomorrow, Jake. Don't go today, please? What does one more day matter?

Lily's voice.

Teeth gritted, he wheeled around and strode out of the garden enclosure, carefully latching the gate to keep out invaders before he race-walked to his small cabin. Inside he made himself a thermos of strong coffee, grabbed a couple of protein bars and changed into his hiking boots. Backpack secure and walking stick in hand, he stepped onto the trail he hiked whenever he needed to break free of his past.

When Jake reached the top of the first incline, he ignored the voice in his head and turned back. Gemma was still in the garden, but now she stood, one hand shading her eyes as she looked directly at him, motionless for several moments. Then she knelt and continued with her weeding, as if she understood that he wanted to be alone.

Wanted to be alone? No.

But that's the way it was. Would always be. *Had* to be.

Gemma set the foil-covered dishes on the counter in Jake's cabin and moved toward the door. She didn't want to look around, didn't want to invade his personal space when he wasn't there. But she couldn't help noticing how clean, how sterile everything seemed.

No pictures of loved ones. No books on side tables. Nothing left lying around. Nothing to hint at the intriguing man who'd abandoned her in the garden earlier and hadn't yet returned.

Her fingers were reaching for the door handle when it opened.

"Hi." Jake stood there, studying her.

"Hi. You missed dinner, so the aunts sent me over with some," she blurted, feeling the heat singe her cheeks. "I didn't mean to intrude."

"You're not. But you shouldn't have gone to the trouble. I'm not very hungry." He stepped inside, set his pack on the tiny table and faced her. "Thank you though."

"It's Adele's lasagna and it's amazing." She blinked, then grinned. "You probably already know that. See you."

Gemma scurried back to the house, feeling like a frightened rabbit. The barrenness of Jake's quarters and his earlier reticence after she'd asked about The Lillian frightened her. Was that because subconsciously she knew that if he answered all her questions, if he was completely honest with her, she'd know for sure that she didn't belong at The Haven?

But if she didn't belong here, then where did she belong? Certainly not in the cheap Toronto apartment the aunts had described. Not anymore. From their description she'd figured it was a tiny place where newlyweds constantly ran into each other and enjoyed it. That romantic place belonged to another newly married Gemma.

This Gemma didn't want to go there, didn't want to feel even more out of place, even more distanced from the woman whom everyone but she remembered. More than that, she didn't want to *not* belong anywhere else. So during dinner she'd asked her aunts how she could have her things moved without physically traveling to Toronto. Of course they had a friend who had a friend and by next week everything she and Kurt owned would supposedly arrive here at The Haven. And then what?

Her mind immediately turned to Jake. He'd help her deal with it. She didn't know why she was so sure of that, she just knew it was true. But was it fair to ask him?

Gemma had so many questions about her rescuer and very few answers. So far Jake was the only one who'd expressly said she belonged here.

If only she could believe him.

Chapter Four

"Relax, Gem. You're going to love Alexa."

Jake hoped he sounded confident because he'd grown as nervous as Gemma while they waited for the arrival of a new group of foster children looking forward to a weekend of fun at The Haven. Alexa was traveling with them.

"You don't know that. But anyway, here they come." Gemma patted her ponytail as if there could be any improvement on that reddish-gold swath of glistening waves. "I hope—"

She didn't finish that sentence, but her longing was visible to Jake. That's how well he knew her. He knew she wanted a fresh start, to make a connection with someone who knew as little about her as she did them, someone who had no preconceptions about her. Someone she didn't have to remember.

When Gem's hand slid into his, Jake startled. She must have felt that because she glanced at him.

"Do you mind?"

Mind? How could he? Holding her hand, helping her however he could, made him feel ten feet tall. It also worried him. He was hoping she'd take a keen interest in Alexa, and not only for the child's sake. But he needed to make sure he didn't get too involved with Gemma.

"Hang on to me whenever you want," he said in a breezy tone.

Gemma frowned at him in that discerning way that said she suspected his genuineness.

"I mean it. Oh, oh. Those three boys look tough, don't they?" Jake spoke mostly to calm Gemma. "Those four girls are just as tough looking. But where's—ah." His breath escaped in a rush as the last passenger, a boy of perhaps twelve, helped a young girl down the steps. "That must be Alexa."

"Really?" Gem pulled the small picture from her pocket and studied it. "I guess. Someone cut her beautiful hair. Badly."

The boy said something to Alexa who nodded and remained in place. He hurried toward Victoria who was directing children toward their counsellors. Alexa clung to a ragged doll as she peered around curiously. The other kids had obviously visited The Haven before and knew the routine. Alexa kept scanning the area. Jake knew the exact moment she recognized Gemma because she began walking toward them.

"You're Gemma," she said, stopping in front of them.

"Yes, I am." Gemma blinked her surprise. "How did you know?"

"Kurt tol' me all 'bout you an' he gave me a picture. Is he here? I want to see him. I didn't see him for a long time 'cause he was workin'." Alexa scanned the area hopefully.

"I, uh." Gemma gulped and glanced at Jake. All he

could do was nod for her to continue. "He isn't here, sweetheart. He had to go away and—"

"Like Mommy had to go 'way?" Tears pooled in Alexa's big blue eyes at Gemma's nod. "The lady tole me Mommy's never coming back. Isn't Kurt c-comin' back neither?"

Her obvious pain touched Jake's soul. Poor little orphan girl.

"I'm so sorry, Alexa, but Kurt died," Gemma said very gently. "He wanted to see you, but there was an accident and—"

"A acc'dent. Jus' like Mommy." Alexa's sad sigh of resignation brought tears to Jake's eyes. Such a tiny child to have experienced so much grief in her short life.

"Everybody's gone away, 'cept me. I don't like bein' alone," she said to Gemma, her voice wobbling as if she was ready to burst into tears.

"I know exactly how you feel, Alexa." Gemma beckoned the little girl to join her in sitting on a rock. "I feel like I'm all alone, too."

"Why? You gots this big house an' this man here an' everythin'." Alexa managed a watery smile for Jake. "I'm Alexa."

"Nice to meet you," he said with a chuckle. "I'm Jake."

"Hi, Jake." She held out her tiny hand to shake his and then returned to the subject. "This is where you an' Kurt live?"

"No, we never lived here together. We lived in a big city, but I can't remember that." Strain etched spider lines at the corners of Gemma's green eyes. "I can't remember Kurt or The Haven or Jake either. A rock hit me," she explained before the child could ask.

"An' that made you not remember nothin'?" Alexa's blue eyes grew huge.

"Mostly nothing." She nodded. "So I'm all alone, too, Alexa. Maybe we could be friends?"

Jake didn't like hearing Gemma say she was all alone, and yet her words had emerged without thought, as if that was how she really felt. He'd have to think about changing her perceptions without letting their relationship develop too deeply. It wouldn't be easy, but he'd done it before. He could do it again. Couldn't he?

"You're too big to be my friend." Alexa giggled. "My friends are s'posed to be little like me."

"Well, Kurt was your friend and he wasn't little." Gemma raised her eyebrows at Alexa as if to ask what she thought of that.

"Yeah. 'Kay." Alexa shrugged before looking around. "Arthur tol' me we're gonna have juice and cookies. I want some."

"Arthur is...?" Gemma waited while Alexa explained about the boy who had stayed with her for the entire ride.

"He's over there by that lady. Arthur din't wanna come here," Alexa murmured after she'd waved at him and yelled that she was okay. "He likes hockey better. C'n he play hockey here?"

"If it was wintertime our creek would be frozen and we'd have a party skating on it. But it's almost summer now so the ice is all melted. It's still lots of fun though." Apparently unaware that she'd revealed knowledge of her past, Gemma rose and held out her hand. "I can see Arthur's going inside. Let's go join him, Alexa. Coming, Jake?"

"I guess I've got time for a quick break, though by

the looks of that bed, I should do some more flower planting." Jake walked with them toward The Haven's kitchen because he wanted to watch their interaction a little longer.

"C'n I help you plant? I love flowers," Alexa asked enthusiastically.

"Sure. But maybe not today," he said. "I've got something else I need to do first."

"What're ya gonna do?" Alexa studied him.

"I think I know." Gemma's snicker told him she understood his dour expression. "My aunts just bought a new cow. Her name is Sweetie, but I think Jake calls her something else, something not nice."

"Why? Is she a bad cow?" Alexa wondered, grabbing both their hands and skipping between them. "Maybe she don't like it here. Maybe she don't got no friends here neither."

"Maybe she won't make any if she keeps swatting me with that tail of hers," he mumbled and then realized they'd both heard him. "Sweetie—terrible name by the way—and I have some discussing to do."

"You c'n talk to a cow?" The child's big blue eyes gaped at him. "C'n you teach *me* cow talk?"

Gemma burst into laughter and Jake had to join her. This child was going to be good for Gemma. Maybe for him, too?

"First, snack time. Then we'll see," he said, noting Gemma's big smile. "Perhaps by then you'll remember how to clean the barn."

"Ew! I don't want to remember that!" With a toss of her auburn ponytail, Gemma grasped the little girl's hand and led her inside. "Come on, Alexa. I'm told

Friday's doughnut day at The Haven. I snuck one and they're scrumptious."

"Did Kurt like 'em?"

Gemma paused. Her gaze flew to Jake, a question in the depths. Then she took a deep breath and hunkered down to Alexa's level.

"How could he not?" she murmured, her face troubled as she traced one hand over the badly shorn strands of shiny blond hair.

"I can tell you Kurt loved doughnuts." Jake spoke past the lump in his throat. "And Gemma. And you, Alexa. He was a very smart man." Satisfied that both females were now smiling, he said, "Let's eat, ladies."

Gemma spent all afternoon with Alexa, shocked by the comfort she found in the child's company, even though the little girl had boundless energy and just as many questions—about everything.

"Is Jake your boyfriend?" she asked as they planted some flower seeds in pots.

"What? No. I hardly know him." Flustered, Gemma tried to interest the little girl in watching birds. "Besides, I was married. To Kurt, remember?"

"Jake likes you," Alexa insisted.

"How can you tell?" Curious to hear the child's response, she sank onto the grass and watched the little girl stab seeds into the soil.

"'Cause he got you a big glass of iced tea an' the best chair an' the doughnut with the mostest icing on it." Alexa nodded wisely. "That means he likes you."

"Jake's nice," Gemma agreed, hoping they could leave it at that, because she didn't want to examine her friendship with Jake too closely. Not yet.

Finished seeding, they wandered around The Haven until Jake showed up with a couple of fishing rods and cajoled them down to the river. At first Gemma protested that she didn't want to fish, but she gave in when Jake insisted. With the sun waning over the western mountains, she found a certain calm in sitting on a rock and casting her line into the bubbling water. That tranquility quickly dissipated when a fish jerked her line.

"Why choose mine?" she mumbled, feeling stupid and inept.

"'Cause it's tryin' to be your friend. Turn the thingamajig," Alexa advised, almost bouncing on her toes as she watched the fish flip in and out of the water, ignoring her own rod, which was in danger of falling into the creek.

"Jake!" Gemma desperately wished she'd chosen to read a book this afternoon.

"Stop yelling. You'll scare away all the fish and I haven't caught any yet," he grumbled from behind her left shoulder, his voice reassuring. "Slowly reel the line in. You've done it a hundred times before, Gem."

"Maybe, but I don't remember that." And then, all at once she knew exactly what to do. She slowly turned the handle on the reel, judging the distance. When the fish jerked, she gave it some line then resumed winding. Finally, without even realizing her intent, she leaned over and drew it from the water just before the fish could take off again. "Okay. Now what?"

"Now we put it in our bucket." Jake calmly disentangled the hook and plopped the fish into the pail of water. "We'll clean them later. That's your job, by the way."

Clean fish? Gemma couldn't dredge up a single memory of doing that.

"Doesn't The Haven practice catch and release?" she asked desperately.

"Not when it's my dinner." Jake grinned. "You can cast again now."

"Uh-huh." With him watching her so closely, Gemma had to do something. She deliberately miscast and landed her hook in the rocks. "Oh, dear."

Jake's smirk and the shake of his head told her he knew she was avoiding catching more.

"Mine's stuck," Alexa muttered. "I can't—oof!" She jerked the rod so hard, it pulled the line out. A flapping fish passed over their heads to land on a rock behind them. "I caught a fish," she said, dumbfounded.

"You sure did, although your technique needs a little refining. Let's take a picture." He pulled out his phone and snapped a shot of Alexa holding her fish. "Good work, kiddo. Now, let's put it in the bucket."

"Hey, mine's the biggest," Alexa pronounced. "Can I try again?"

"Sure." Jake reset her line, offered encouragement when her first few casts had no results and then resumed his own fishing. "She's a great kid, Gem," he murmured. "No wonder Kurt loved her."

"You're really good with her." Gemma hadn't thought of Jake as the fatherly type, but somehow it seemed right.

"You didn't expect me to be good with kids when I work at The Haven where there are kids around all the time?" He chuckled. "No-brainer."

"You should have your own kids, Jake," she said, thinking how lucky that child would be.

"I did once." Barely audible, the words seemed

squeezed out of him. Immediately his lips pursed as if to stop any further revelations.

"Where are they now?" Gemma regretted asking when his whole body froze.

"*He* died." Cold, stark, void of emotion.

"The funeral you spoke of. It was your son's." She reached out and touched his arm. "I'm so sorry, Jake."

"Thanks." He withdrew his arm on the pretext of helping Alexa who was happily reeling in her second fish.

Gemma pretended to concentrate on her own rod while she tried to make sense of what she'd learned. Jake was a dad who'd lost his son. How? Where was his wife? Did her aunts and her sisters know about his past? Had she known? Questions abounded, but his closed expression deterred her from asking.

She shivered, suddenly chilly though the temperature hadn't changed. Jake and Alexa caught more fish while Gemma let her hook dangle in the shallow water as her tired brain tried to put the pieces of Jake's past together.

"We've a good catch of fish." His voice drew her out of her reverie. "Time to clean them now. Then we'll cook them up."

"I think Adele's cooking ribs for dinner," Gemma murmured.

"That's good because I was thinking we could share these with a friend of mine. He lives in town." Jake smiled at Alexa. "Would you like to have a fish dinner with my friend?"

"Is Gem comin'?" Alexa glanced her way anxiously, obviously relieved when she nodded.

"Maybe I am. Who's your friend?" Gemma asked.

"Billy Hooper." Jake grinned at her gasp.

"He's still alive? He must be nearly a hundred now." Gemma blinked. How did she know that when she couldn't even conjure up Billy's face?

"Ninety-seven. And you know how he loves fish dinners." Jake stored their hooks and bundled the rods into their leather bag. From it he extracted a filleting knife and a honing stone, which he used to sharpen the knife. "See that big, flat stone over there?" he said to Alexa. She nodded. "That's where we'll clean the fish. Then we can leave what we don't want for the birds to eat."

"'Cause they get hungry, too, right?" Alexa seemed not at all squeamish as Jake slit open the fish.

For some reason Gemma caught herself paying close attention to how he achieved the first fillet. While he slipped it into a plastic bag, she found herself rising.

"I'll do it." She stared at him and gulped. Where had that come from?

"You're sure?" Jake inspected her, a twinkle glimmering in his eyes.

"Actually, no," she admitted, her mouth dry. "It just seems like… I should fillet," she told him after a moment's pause.

"You should," he agreed with a smile and handed her the knife. "You're much better at it than I am. Another gift you've remembered. Let's see if your hands remember the skill."

Gemma stepped in front of the rock. She considered the fish he'd laid there. Blankness filled her brain.

"I don't know—" And then suddenly she did know. Almost of their own accord, her fingers slid the knife under the slippery scales, automatically freeing perfectly smooth, thin filets. When the fish was deboned she looked at Jake and grinned. "Who knew?"

"You did." He laughed at her smug smile. "You've got a ton of other talents, Gem. You just need to let them out."

When all the fish were in the bag, they washed the knife and pail and their hands in the creek water. Jake dumped the fish remains on a pile of stones downstream. No sooner had they moved a few feet away than gulls, eagles and ravens homed in on the food.

"They like it!" Alexa exclaimed, clapping her hands. "Don't fight," she yelled and waved her arms for emphasis. "Hey." She frowned at Jake. "They're goin'. Did I scare 'em?"

"No. It's spring, so they're taking the food to feed their babies. There won't be a scrap left." His face as he gazed at the little girl made Gemma's stomach clench. How gentle and kind he was. Perfect for working with kids at The Haven. He clearly belonged here.

But where did she belong?

"Can we stop by the house before we go to Billy's?" Jake asked.

"We don't need to," Gemma began before noticing his expression. "But we can. Why?"

"Billy doesn't eat that well. I usually take along extra food for his lunch tomorrow. Adele will have it ready." He waited for them to precede him up the hill. At the top Gemma agreed that Alexa could skip ahead.

"How did you get so involved with Billy?" she asked.

"I work with a church group who help seniors who want to stay in their homes but need a little support to do it." He shrugged. "Fix a roof, empty eavestroughs, find someone to clean or do laundry, organize meals or shopping, visit and share a meal. Simple stuff like that."

"But isn't there a women's group…" Gemma paused

as a memory flickered to life. "Never mind. I doubt Billy would tolerate a female in his home."

"I told you it would all come back to you." Jake grinned at her. "There are several senior men like Billy in our little community who are quite capable of living alone but have other needs. Sometimes all they really need is coffee time with another male and some good, strong man-stuff discussions."

"Man stuff?" she teased, one eyebrow lifted.

"Just sayin'. Billy grew up almost a century ago when it was different for men and women. Besides, there's Ethel." His nose wrinkled.

"Ethel Denman?" She saw Jake nod and frowned. "Why, she must be as old as him. They should have lots in common."

"Not so much. Ethel's mostly interested in husband hunting Billy. He is *not* interested in that, even though she keeps baking her special prune-and-bran custard pie for him."

"Prune and bran pie?" Gemma gaped at him in disbelief. He wore such a comical expression she burst out laughing. "No wonder he's not interested. It sounds awful. So you really are a white knight."

"Me? No, just not well equipped for other services in the church. I tried ushering but I dropped the offering plate. Can you say *fired*?" He grimaced comically, but she knew he was minimizing his abilities. "I want to be involved and this allows me to help yet still have some flexibility. Hopefully I don't mess up too badly."

"So that's the reason for all those phone calls on the drive here. I think it's wonderful. You must be kept very busy." She called to Alexa who was petting her aunts'

rescue dogs, Spot and Dot. "We're going to visit someone so we should wash up first, kiddo."

"'Kay." The biddable child followed Gemma inside.
She asked such a plethora of questions that Gemma
was glad when they returned to find Jake waiting by
his truck.

"She doesn't take *I don't remember* for an answer,"
she whispered after he'd fastened the car seat he'd bor-
rowed for Alexa.

"Neither did you once," he reminded. "You two are
a matched set."

Gemma thought about that as Jake drove to Billy's.
Had she been like Alexa? It was so frustrating trying
to remember when her stupid brain only recalled dumb
stuff like filleting fish.

"You're doing fine, Gem. Don't force it. It will—oh,
boy." Jake parked quickly and jumped out of the truck
to intervene between a red-faced Billy Hooper who was
thumping his cane on the doorstep, apparently trying
to silence Ethel Denman who was pretending to wash
windows while trying to peer inside Billy's home.

"Come on, Alexa," she said, unfastening her seat belt
and doing the same for the child. "It seems we're going
to be peacemakers for a while."

"What's a peacemaker?"

Gemma rolled her eyes at the nine-hundredth question before stepping forward to greet the elderly woman
and divert her attention. She thought she heard Jake
mutter thank you, but since he kept his expression totally blasé it was hard to tell.

"I'm stuck," Ethel said with a glare at Billy. "This
garden is a mess, like everything else around here."

"Then why do you keep coming here?" he demanded in a growly tone.

Gemma helped Jake ease Ethel's skirt off the long rose thorns that had trapped her.

"Isn't this fun, Gem?" Jake muttered.

Oddly enough, with Jake it really *was*.

Chapter Five

"You gots a really dirty house, Mr. Billy," Alexa said bluntly after her first step over the threshold. "We gotta clean it."

Wonder of wonders, after choking back his surprise, Billy agreed. He also agreed that Alexa and Gemma could dust, but only *if* Jake made their entire dinner. So now Jake was at the stove.

"Billy, if you keep forbidding Ethel entry, she'll only grow more eager to get inside," he argued as he fried their catch of fish. Gemma's snicker was low but he still heard it.

"As if anything could stop that determined woman," she muttered.

Jake didn't disagree. But the place was a disaster and he figured Billy had agreed to let the females dust only because he thought it was a woman's place to do so and because Ethel had threatened to call the health department. Thank the Lord Gemma hadn't minded pitching in, though now she was swiping her cloth across the fireplace mantle with a disgusted look that said she figured Ethel's idea was spot-on.

"Nobody fries fish like you do, Jakey." While everyone else labored, Billy happily lounged in his tattered recliner.

"Jakey?" A wicked grin played with the corners of Gemma's mouth. She turned her back, but her shaking shoulders told Jake she was enjoying his embarrassment.

Jakey ignored her to concentrate on his cooking. He had everything ready just as Gemma and Alexa pronounced the main area dusted, though not, he noted, dust-free. Still, it was a first step. When everyone was seated around Billy's heavy oak table, Alexa insisted on holding hands before they said grace. Jake liked the feel of Gemma's soft fingers curling around his as the old man offered a fulsome prayer of thanks for the food. Then they ate.

"Ooh, this is so good. I can remember when last I..." Gemma shook her head once. "It's very good, Jake."

"I never had this kinda dinner afore," Alexa told him. "An' I never caught no fish neither." She studied Billy for a moment before asserting, "You should'a comed fishin' with us. Gem's good at—" she turned to Gemma "—whad'ya call it again?"

"Filleting," Gemma responded. She held out Billy's tiny antique glass pitcher and suggested, "Try a bit of this vinegar on your fish. It's delish."

"That rhymes." Alexa's giggle made everyone smile.

After dinner Gemma insisted Jake and Billy sit outside with their coffee while she and Alexa cleaned up. Seeing the glint in her eyes, Jake knew better than to refuse. If he knew Gemma, she intended to load that seldom-used dishwasher to the brim. While it ran, he figured she'd coax Alexa to help her turn the dingy kitchen into a gleaming space. It was like old times. Gemma fit in wherever she went and managed to help someone along the way. Jake liked that. A lot.

Outside, when Billy plied him with questions about her, Jake told him about the earthquake.

"So when's she going to be normal again?"

"Gem's normal now, Billy. She just can't remember some stuff." Some people might have taken Billy's aggressive questions the wrong way, but Jake had known him long enough to recognize the glint of concern lurking in the back of the old fellow's amber gaze. "Doctors say her memory will return when her brain's ready. Nothing to do but wait."

"What's she going to do till then?" Billy demanded. "Doing nothing while staying with those two old ladies will drive her bonkers. Least it would me."

To Billy other seniors were old. The description did not apply to himself.

"I'm not sure," he said quietly.

"She sure is a good-looking girl, Jakey. You interested?"

The meddling old codger! Half amused, half irritated, Jake shook his head. "No."

"Why not? She's sure as shooting pretty. Bible says a man ought not to be alone," Billy quoted.

"You're alone, Billy," Jake pointed out. He almost groaned as he realized Gemma could probably hear every matchmaking word through the open kitchen window.

"That's different. Ain't nobody can replace my Irma." Billy's chin thrust out.

"No reason you have to replace her, but a little companionship would be good for you." Stubbornness set the old guy's face into rigid lines. "Besides, you've forgotten something," Jake mused, tongue in cheek. "Those ladies who'd like to come calling on you are fantastic bakers. Seems dumb not to take advantage of that."

It wasn't just that Billy didn't eat well. Jake also worried his friend was alone too often. Using the pretense of food, visitors could keep him interested in community life and thereby divert a lapse into loneliness and depression that often overtook solitary seniors. If Billy would let them in.

"Bakers, huh? Never thought of it that way. Now that the place is cleaned up some—" A cunning grin flashed across his weathered face. "Maybe I'll let that know-it-all Ethel come calling if she brings me a pie. An' I don't mean that prune thing."

Jake shook his head. No sense remonstrating with the man. Billy had his own way of doing things. At least he'd agreed to allow a visitor. That was progress.

His serenity was shattered a moment later by Alexa's raised voice.

"C'n I stay at The Haven all the time?"

"You mean permanently?" Gemma sounded shocked. "I—who would look after you?"

"I don't need nobody. That dumb ol' Kurt tol' me I was a big girl an' could look after my mom an' me." Belligerence laced the girl's voice.

"Are you mad at Kurt, sweetheart?" Gemma asked in a very soft voice.

"Yeah." Alexa's sobs came through the window clearly.

"He didn't leave you on purpose, Alexa. He couldn't help that there was an earthquake and he died. He didn't *want* to go away." Gemma's certainty made Jake think of Lily. She hadn't wanted—

"Those old aunties said Kurt's in a better place now." Alexa sniffed. "They musta been talkin' 'bout heaven 'cause that's what people said when my mom died, but I don't think it's better."

Jake figured memory or not, Gemma was hunkered down in front of the little girl, ready to listen and, if possible, help her. That was Gemma. Heart of gold.

"Why isn't it better?" she asked in a soothing voice.

"'Cause I'm not with her!" Alexa wailed. Then a pause. "D'you think Kurt an' my mom *like* not havin' me with them?" she demanded incredulously. Her sad sniff said her little heart was breaking at the thought.

"That's not what the aunties meant. Of course Kurt and your mommy would like to be with you, but they are also glad to be with God. Where they are, there is no pain, no sadness, no wishing things would be better. Where they are is wonderful. I don't think they'd want you there though, at least not right now."

"Why not?" Alexa demanded. Jake visualized her tiny fists planted on her hips.

"Because it's not your time to be there," Gemma said quietly. "The Bible says there's a time for everything. A time like now for leaves to grow and seeds to grow. And then there's a time for the leaves to turn color and fall off."

"An' then it's time for snow," Alexa chirped happily.

"Yes. There's a season for everything," Gemma said. "Right now is our season of missing Kurt and you missing your mom. You want it to be like it was before, but it can't be. I know it's hard to understand, honey, but I believe God wants you to stay right here on earth."

"Why?" The barrage of kid-questions made Jake grin.

"I can't tell you why. You'd have to ask Him to tell you that. I will tell you what I believe." Jake could hear the smile lacing Gemma's voice. "I think here is where you belong, at least right now. You helped me get through the awful time today when I couldn't remember filleting and you cheered me up. I think that for now you belong at The Haven, Alexa."

That sounded exactly like the old Gemma. He could hear her voice from the past. *God knows what He's doing. Get with His program.*

"Where do you belong, Gemma?" the little voice squeaked.

A long silence followed. Jake tensed. Then Gemma murmured, "I don't know. Yet."

As they drove back to The Haven, Alexa nodded off. That was okay because Gemma's head whirled with the day's events. She was going to talk to Jake about it when a call came through his dash screen.

"Hey, Olivia. How's it going?"

"I'm in a pickle, Jake, and hoping you can do me a favor." Gemma frowned at Olivia's harried tone.

"Name it." Jake pulled to the side of the road and set his flashers going so he could fully listen to her request.

"A friend took Eli to soccer practice. I'm supposed to be there in half an hour to pick him up because Gabe's with a trail-riding group from The Haven. But the baby's really fussing and won't settle and—"

"Say no more. We'll go watch Eli practice and then bring him home," Jake quickly offered.

"Who's we?" Olivia wanted to know.

"Gemma, Alexa—who is Kurt's stepdaughter—and

me," he explained. "We just came from sharing our fish dinner with Billy Hooper."

"Hey, Gem. So you're back fishing. Your most favorite activity. How's Alexa?" Olivia asked.

"Sleeping right now. But she's fine. Who's Eli?" Gemma asked and then felt silly for not knowing. "I don't think I met him."

"Eli was away on a school field trip the day you came home. He's Gabe's son from his first marriage. He's a great kid—" Olivia paused midsentence before saying hurriedly, "That's Mirella again. I have to go. Thank you so much, you two. I appreciate it."

"Our pleasure, Livvie. See you later." Jake pushed the off button. Then he glanced at Gemma. "You don't mind, do you?"

"Of course not. I'd like to meet Eli. Besides, you *are* the local fixer," she teased. "This is just another wrinkle for you to smooth."

Jake shot her a droll look before turning around and heading back to town.

"Do you think my sister is happy with her life?" she asked.

"Very." Jake needed no deliberation over that. "I think all four of you found happiness in your marriages."

"Did you?" The question slipped out before Gemma could think about it. Given the grim look on Jake's face, it was obvious the subject was painful. "Sorry, I—"

"I was very happy," Jake muttered. Then he clamped his lips together so tightly Gemma knew not to ask more. They drove through town. He pulled into a parking spot by the soccer field where the players were already going through their drills. "That's Eli," he said, pointing. He waved at the gangly boy.

"Good-looking kid," Gemma said, hoping to break the tenseness between them. "Wake up, Alexa."

Once she'd explained what they were doing and Jake had told Eli they'd take him home when he was finished practice, they found seats in the bleachers and watched the players. Most of the parents seemed to be coaching which meant that after a few greetings they were virtually alone in the stands. When a bored Alexa asked to join three children kicking a ball behind them, Gemma agreed. Jake remained silent.

"I wasn't trying to pry," she apologized when it seemed he'd never talk to her again. "It just kind of slipped out. I'm sorry. I shouldn't ask so many questions."

He stared at her for several moments, his blue eyes stormy. She didn't look away. Finally he sighed.

"Look, if I tell you, can we let it go? It is not something I want to rehash ever again."

Gemma nodded, afraid to speak lest he change his mind.

"I was married and we had a baby son. I was starting a new business, a greenhouse business, and I was in debt up to my neck—past it. I had a contract to deliver a truckload of my best poinsettias three weeks before Christmas." He closed his eyes. His low voice grew forced, as if each word took an enormous amount of courage. "The plants took a ton of time and effort, but they were gorgeous and at their peak. I had to deliver them on time because fulfilling that contract meant we'd have enough cash for my bedding-plant season, and it meant I could concentrate on my specialty."

"Roses." Gemma wondered how she knew that.

"Yes." Jake gave her a sidelong glance. It was several moments before he spoke again. "I was totally focused on getting the poinsettias to market at the promised time. No way could I return the deposit I'd been given. We'd already spent most of it on new stock and house renovations. I felt I had to show up as contracted."

"Okay." What was so terrible about that? But as she waited, Gemma's misgivings grew. "You don't have to tell—"

"I delivered the plants with no problem. But on my return I got caught in a freak ice storm. I slipped off the icy road and had to spend the night in my truck with no cell coverage to call home. It was a deserted road so no rescuers." His voice sounded edgy. "Lily hadn't wanted me to leave. She was ill and the baby had a cold. She begged me to put it off one more day, but I was so sure I could make the run and get home with no problem." His face hardened. "Instead I got stuck in the ditch, helpless until the storm spent itself. In the morning, help finally came, but it was too late."

His voice had dropped and his face had hardened into a white strained mask. Gemma knew that whatever was coming wasn't good.

"When I got home I found Lily and Thomas dead from carbon monoxide poisoning from the fireplace, which I'd loaded up before I left."

"Oh, Jake." She touched his arm, her heart aching for his devastating loss. "I'm so sorry."

"I killed them, Gem." His eyes, now hardened chips of Arctic ice, glared at her. "It was my fault they died. Lily had been complaining for ages about the fireplace not being right. I kept promising her I'd fix it. That day

I'd even told her I'd do it when I got home." His eyes looked dead. "I put my wife and child's safety second and business first. What kind of husband—father— does that, Gem?"

She wanted to tell him it wasn't his fault, but Jake suddenly lurched to his feet and stalked away. When Alexa would have followed him, Gemma called her back, sensing that the handyman needed privacy.

"Jake's thinking about something, honey. Let's leave him alone for a while, okay?" Relieved when the child nodded and returned to her playmates, Gemma visually tracked the handyman until he disappeared from sight. "Oh, Lord, please. His burden is so great. Help me know what to do to help him."

She didn't know where the words came from, had no idea if her prayer was even appropriate. She only knew Jake was suffering and she had to do something. And that she felt better after asking God to help.

Her attention divided between her thoughts, Alexa and Jake, and whether God cared about her lost memories, Gemma shivered when a chilly wind washed over her. She began climbing down the bleachers to retrieve her sweater from Jake's truck.

That's when the flashback hit.

Machu Picchu. Gemma knew it instantly, recognized the path she'd taken to the exact spot where she now saw herself standing. She knew the exact words she'd say to her tour group. Everything was so familiar.

Then suddenly the ground was moving and she couldn't find firm footing on it. Everything wobbled and tilted. Great gaping cracks opened up. Terror grabbed her by the throat as she ordered her guests to take cover against the side of the mountain. But she couldn't hide. She had to find Kurt. She screamed his name and moments later saw him just below her on a crumbling step. His eyes locked with hers and he mouthed something.

I love you, Gemma.

Then he was gone, his voice drowned out by a loud rumbling behind her. Rocks and debris tumbled down from above, piling around her feet. Someone grabbed her arm and yanked her forward in the same moment as she turned. Fierce pain radiated from the back of her head and blinded her.

Then the memory was over and she was huddled on the bleachers, shaking.

"Gemma! Gemma, wake up. You're okay. You're safe."

"Jake?" She blinked and found him peering down at her, his face haggard. Alexa was there, too, white-faced and scared. "I remember Kurt," she whispered. "I remember the earthquake."

Tears came then, oceans of sadness, filling her eyes, dripping down her cheeks and soaking her clothes. There was nothing she could do to stop them.

"Is Gem okay?" Alexa whispered.

"She's going to be fine, sweetheart. She just needs to rest. Let's get her to my truck." Jake scooped her into his arms and carried her across to the parking lot. Tenderly he set her in the vehicle before his fingers closed over hers. "Relax, Gem. You're safe now."

"Kurt knew he was going to die," she whispered, unable to stop the words from streaming out. "He knew and all he could think of was me. He kept repeating that he loved me. He loved me."

She remembered feeling that love, the safety and security of it, the certain knowledge that she wasn't alone, that she didn't have to be afraid because Kurt was there, that he would take care of her because she belonged with him. In the awareness of that knowledge came the understanding that she'd sought for that security her entire life, and that when she had finally found it, she'd been desperately afraid of losing it.

And now she had lost it, because now she belonged to no one, belonged nowhere.

"I'm alone."

She couldn't tell if she said it out loud or in her heart. It didn't matter. It was still true.

Chapter Six

As soon as Eli's soccer practice ended, Jake drove to Olivia's ranch. He was desperate to get Gemma home to The Haven, as if that would somehow ease the agony of her memories. Eli and Alexa talked quietly in the back seat, perhaps sensing that Gemma needed space to process her thoughts. Jake guessed she was trying to make sense of her memories, though how much she'd actually recalled wasn't clear to him.

What was clear was the fury he felt at the words she'd whispered.

I'm alone.

Gemma *wasn't* alone. She had friends, family, tons of people who loved and cared about her. The plethora of cards, letters and bouquets from well-wishers proved that, even though Gemma had left everything stacked in the office because reading the names and trying to remember the senders stressed her.

But she was not alone. She had him.

Jake immediately revised that. They were friends. He'd always had a soft spot for Gemma, yes. He'd also always known that friendship was all there could be. So he'd do whatever he could to help her now—everything but let his heart get over-involved. Because no matter how much he cared about her, he could not step beyond those invisible bonds. He'd promised Lily.

Anyway, Gemma only wanted a friend. So that's what he'd be.

"I'm going inside with you and Eli," she said when they arrived at Olivia's.

"Are you sure?" He'd hoped they'd drop off Eli and then leave. Jake immediately dropped that plan when he saw her chin jut out in determination.

"I want to hold her baby," Gemma insisted.

Alexa asked Eli to show her the birdhouses he'd been talking about, leaving Jake and Gemma to enter the house alone. When Olivia placed Mirella in Gemma's arms, Gemma's complete focus rested on her niece. Jake used the opportunity to take Olivia aside and explain what had happened.

"She seems okay now, just enthralled." Olivia smiled at her sister's rapt expression. "Which I totally understand because Gem always liked kids."

"Maybe your daughter is triggering more memories, Liv." Frustration gnawed at Jake. "There's no schedule or plan to this memory thing of hers. All I can do is assume she knows what she's doing."

"She always did," Olivia agreed, grinning. "Sit. Have a cup of coffee while Gemmie admires my beautiful daughter. Tell me what you've been up to in your community work."

"You name it, I'm trying to do it. Or get it done. I'm up to my ears," Jake confessed. "The list of needy folks never shrinks. It's a good thing the aunties aren't obsessive about my work schedule."

"You know they love having you at The Haven. You've been their lifesaver, especially when we girls couldn't get home to help them." Olivia plucked a list off the fridge. "As I mentioned last Sunday, I noted some folks I believe could use your help. None of them need physical assistance. In my opinion they're mostly lonely."

"Long list," he muttered.

"Since you have such a knack for building community connections between people, I thought you might know someone who could pay them a visit." Olivia's smile warmed his heart. "You provide a wonderful service, Jake."

"A service? All I wanted to do was keep folks in this community caring about each other, though I'm not really qualified for it," he confessed.

"Your qualifications are that you care about our community." Olivia touched his cheek with her fingertip. "That's more than lots of people do and we're all grateful for what you do." She began loading the dishwasher.

Sure he cared, Jake mused. But there was getting to be way more than one man could do in his spare time to help folks.

Jake sat at the kitchen island, nursing his coffee as he thought about it. For a guy who'd tried hard to avoid getting involved, he was becoming pretty heavily vested in the locals' welfare. Not that it was personal. It was just…helping. Yet that weak word didn't fully express what he wanted to achieve. Maybe because he hadn't clearly defined it in his own mind? Maybe because he was trying to help in a personal way without getting personally involved.

Jake figured his crazy yen to fix things for folks

who couldn't do it themselves probably stemmed from years of watching the aunts reach out to anyone who needed them. They'd often drawn him in, too. It hadn't taken him long to recognize that the elderly ladies were swamped and wearing thin. So he'd pitched in. And then he couldn't *not* help because reaching out to folks brought sanity to his life more than it helped anyone else. He felt like it was one way he could atone for causing Lily's and Thomas's deaths.

Cheap atonement. It didn't cost Jake anything but a couple of pieces of lumber to turn Mr. Gertz's stairs into a ramp so he could get in and out more easily. No need to bother the aunties about visiting Billy or lots of other shut-ins around Chokecherry Hollow either. Nor did it take a genius to see single-mom Nancy Filmore needed help fixing her ramshackle home, though Jake wasn't certain that what he was doing was enough. Same thing with Alexa. The kid needed someone to give some stability to her world, but *him*? And how was he supposed to help Gem?

By not getting too involved.

At least his meager efforts to help others hadn't required talking to God. That gave Jake the freedom to tamp down his past and the *why* questions that would not be silenced. The ones God never answered.

Recently, however, he'd begun to feel less and less capable of helping others and more aware that he needed to help himself. Oh, he still saw the issues around him. He just wasn't certain he was making enough of a difference anymore. And now too many folks were looking to him to remedy their issues.

Jake was breaking his own rule. He was getting too involved.

So he'd try to scale back. But the one person Jake had to help was Gemma. She needed her life back.

"She's such a beautiful child," Gemma whispered, drawing his focus to her.

The myriad of expressions floating across her face—curiosity, joy and pleasure—all seemed to jumble together as she touched the tiny fingers, brushed her thumb against the baby's tipped-up nose and breathed in her scent.

"She'll make a great mother," Olivia murmured. Jake thought so, too.

Then Gemma lifted her head and smiled at him.

"What kind of a mind must God have to create such a miracle?" she breathed.

"A mind that is far greater than we can think or understand," Olivia murmured.

"Agreed." Because Mirella began to fuss, Gemma brushed a featherlight kiss against the baby's cheek before she handed her back to Olivia. "Thank you for sharing her," she murmured. "Does it feel strange to be a mother?"

"Sort of." Olivia snuggled her baby with a chuckle. "But remember, Gemmie, I've been waiting for her for a while. Would you like some coffee?"

"No, thank you. This is Alexa's first day at The Haven. I think we need to get her back so she can settle in." Gemma's wide smile spread as she watched the children through the patio doors. "She's had a busy day."

"Come again, anytime," Olivia invited them. "Mirella and I would love to see you."

"You have a beautiful place. I will come back." Gemma seemed bemused as she walked with Jake to the truck and climbed in. She waited while he buckled Alexa into her seat, hands folded in her lap, her eyes gazing at something he couldn't see.

"Are you all right?" he asked when they were half-way to The Haven.

"I think so." Gemma said nothing more until they arrived at the big house. Once there, she politely said thank you before they walked inside. She shared a few words with the aunts while Alexa gave him a hug that made his throat choke up.

"I love you, Jake," she whispered in his ear. Then she followed Gemma up the stairs, wondering aloud if her suitcase was already there.

When they'd disappeared, Jake gently closed the kitchen door and faced the aunts.

"Gemma remembered the earthquake and losing Kurt," he told them.

"She did seem rather quiet. It must be so confusing for her," Tillie said thoughtfully.

"Perhaps we'll go and help settle Alexa," Margaret said. "No doubt it's been a difficult day for our dear Gemma."

The ladies disappeared to help their foster daughter. Because Jake wasn't sure if Gemma would need to speak to him again tonight, he went out to wait on the back patio and got lost studying the twinkling stars.

"The Big Dipper's very clear tonight," she murmured a few moments later from behind him.

Jake rose. "Are you all right, Gem?"

"I'm fine." She sat down in the chair beside his. "I told Alexa a story about when I first went to Europe alone. That seemed to help her relax."

"Your stories never made me sleepy," he teased.

"They made me want to go there." He tried to read her mood and figure out if the memory of the earthquake had rattled her. "Can I do anything for you?"

Please let me do something so I won't feel so useless.

"Thank you for offering, but what is there to do, Jake? Everything's the same as it was, only now I can remember," she mumbled.

"Everything?" he asked as he sat down beside her.

"No." When she shook her head, her gorgeous hair shivered in the moonlight. She pushed the rosy strands behind her ears before facing him. "I remember the earthquake. I remember Kurt's face and that he said he loved me. But that's it. Only bits and pieces of other stuff."

"You were wrong, you know." He needed to say it, even if it did shock her.

"I was?" Her green eyes widened.

"You said you're alone. You're not." He had to erase those thoughts so her brain would be open to embrace the next set of memories. "You're among family, people who love you."

"I think I've always been alone." The pathos in her whisper gutted him. "I think that if I asked the aunts, they'd tell me that I never had a family—no mother, no father, no siblings. I'm just…here," she said after a short pause. "By myself."

"I'm here. Your aunts are upstairs with Alexa. Your sisters are nearby," he argued.

"Yes." She didn't debate him.

"You are loved and surrounded by those who love you. What does your past matter?" he demanded in frustration.

"What was your childhood like, Jake?" Her whispered appeal begged him to answer.

"Happy, I guess. My parents owned a nursery and I grew up among the plants, which I loved." He shrugged. "Mom got breast cancer when I eight. She died when I was twelve and Dad missed her terribly. When I finished school, he sold his business but kept on working for the new owners. He died of heart failure a year after I left home."

"I'm sorry. No brothers and sisters? Cousins?" she murmured.

"My parents were only children. There was no one else. Until—" *No! Don't go there.*

"Until Lily," Gemma murmured, a tender smile turning up her lips. "I think that's how it was with me, Jake. Kurt was my anchor when there was no one else."

"You had your aunts, your foster sisters," he protested.

"*We* had *our* aunts, *our* foster sisters," she corrected. "It's not the same as having someone special of your own."

"Gemma—"

"The thing I don't understand is why Kurt loved me like that." Her forehead wrinkled as she struggled to express herself. "What I saw—he knew he would die, Jake. And yet his focus stayed on me, on making sure I knew he loved me. I can't absorb that. It was life and death. Why wasn't he worried about his own safety? Why didn't he call for help? At that particular point, what did loving me matter?"

"You were the only thing that mattered to Kurt." Jake leaned back in his chair, smiling at the cascade of memories of Gemma's husband. "That was always obvious."

"It was?" She frowned.

"Yes, because that's who Kurt was. A man who loved others. Nothing mattered to him as much as people, especially you, Gem." Jake smiled at her. "Love was the reason he had to make that trust for Alexa. Because she mattered to him. I've never known anyone with a bigger heart than Kurt Andrews."

"He sounds nice. I wish I could fully remember him." Gemma squinted as a star flashed through the sky. "Every time I say his name I see Christmas cards. It's really weird."

Jake shouted with laughter which he quickly muted because of their guests.

"What's so funny?" Gemma asked.

"Christmas cards. Surely you remember that list of Kurt's? Every year he'd send a photo card to everyone on his list. It had maybe a couple hundred names of people, including the folks who'd been on every one of his tours. He was nuts about ensuring people knew he remembered them." Jake glanced at her. "You once told me that's why he had so many return clients, that they loved his personal touches."

Jake had always envied Kurt, partly for his sunny disposition and the way he'd lavished himself on other people, partly because it seemed so easy for him to give love, and partly because he gave of himself wholeheartedly, without reservation. Mostly because he genuinely loved Gem. Kurt hadn't had anything to atone for.

"Did I love my husband, Jake?" Gemma whispered.

"What?" He blinked his surprise at her doubt, but given her pleading gaze, he knew she was serious. "Yes, you loved him."

"Oh." Her head bowed.

"Why did you ask that, Gem?"

"Because I don't feel anything. It's like I'm a shadow, not really here. I'm dead inside. Or frozen." She glanced over one shoulder, as if to check if anyone was near. "My aunts. They're wonderful, giving women who've tried their best to make me feel at home. They're amazing ladies."

"They are," Jake agreed. "But?"

"But I don't *feel* love. I *like* them, but…" Her voice trailed away on a sigh.

"Love seldom comes immediately to anyone, Gemma," Jake said. "You've just met the ladies. You don't know them well yet. Given time, you will love them just as everyone else does. You won't be able to help it. That's the way love works."

"Maybe." She didn't sound convinced.

"It's like faith." Jake stopped. He was hardly the right person to be talking about faith. He'd avoided communication with God since Lily and Thomas had died. "Not that I'm any expert."

"You mean, the more we pray, the better we get to know God?" she asked.

"Maybe that's what I'm trying to say. Badly." It was late. Gemma needed her rest. So did he, if only to stop himself from spouting any more homilies.

Apparently Gemma thought so, too, because after several moments of contemplation, she rose, smoothed her wind-tossed hair off her face and smiled at him.

"Everything is going round and round in my head." Tiredness leached into the words. "I hear you, but nothing computes in my brain. I *should* love those two old ladies, if only because they have loved me and raised me, given me a wonderful home here at The Haven."

"Are you sure you don't?" Jake asked.

"I'm not sure I know what love is. Everything is so mixed-up, so confused and out of place. Nothing seems quite real." She exhaled on a long sigh. "I can't figure out what I feel, Jake. Or maybe I'm afraid to."

"Afraid?" He stared at her. "What are you afraid of, Gem?"

Minutes yawned between them.

"That I'll disappoint them," she whispered, her voice ragged. "That I won't fulfill their expectations, won't be the daughter they want."

Jake didn't move. He didn't make a sound because he knew there was more coming.

"The Gemma they knew disappeared in the earthquake," she said starkly. "I'm terrified I will never remember how to get her back."

Before Jake could reassure her she rushed away, leaving him alone in the night.

One by one the lights in the old stone house extinguished until only the exterior yard lights illuminated the vast grounds. Jake rose and stretched to ease the crick in his neck. He pulled his arms across his body to loosen the tautness in his shoulders. But no amount of stretching could dissolve the tight band in his gut. Gemma was hurting.

He walked the short distance to his cabin, but he didn't retire. There would be no rest for him tonight. His mind whirled with thoughts of Gemma and how he could make her see that she was who they claimed, that even if she had changed, she would still be Gemma, still loved, still cherished, still needed.

Sure, he could repeat stories about her past, tell her how she'd shown her heart of love a million ways. But they were just words. What Gemma wanted, needed, was inner certainty that she wasn't alone. That was not something he could give her.

As Jake sat on a bench outside his door, thinking, two young deer appeared and began grazing under the wavering spruce trees. Maybe it was because his barriers were down that his brain suddenly filled with memories of Lily, of their simple wedding and of her promise that nothing would ever come between them.

Promise me we won't ever let anything matter more than we do to each other, Jake.

How foolish he'd been. He'd let his work, business pressures and the pull of everyday life take precedence over the preciousness of his family. Of love. He knew that now, knew how easily one could forget the things that really mattered.

"But why did Lily and Thomas have to die for me to learn that? Why couldn't You have taken me instead?" he asked.

There was no answer. There never had been. That was why he had no answers for Gemma. Jake had no answers for himself.

In her darkened room, Gemma sat on the window seat in her room and stared across the valley. The full moon provided enough illumination for her to identify hills and knolls she'd probably tromped over in the past, but she couldn't remember now.

Two deer foraged for food near the perimeter of the woods. Mesmerized by the way their gazes darted from side to side between bites, she relived the warm, fluttery feelings of security when Jake had held her in his arms and carried her to the truck.

He'd held her as if she was precious cargo to be protected. He'd set her on the seat so gently, fussing to ensure her comfort, his face very serious, as if she was an important part of his world, someone he had a duty to care for.

Before he disappeared, Kurt had given her the same look, an intense, cherishing stare that said she was vital to him. But now Kurt was gone and Gemma couldn't feel anything but a sense of loss.

Was that because of his letter which the lawyer had given her? She'd read it earlier, confused by the way Kurt had ended it. His words were engraved on her brain.

I know I should have told you about Alexa before we were married, Gemma. Your aunts accused me of hiding her out of fear that you wouldn't accept her without knowing her. Perhaps that's true. In retrospect, I think you'd have understood because you have a truly loving heart. People matter as much to you as they do me. That's what bonds us, Gem.

I love Alexa. From the first time I saw her, I felt compelled to be the father she doesn't have. Please, please, darling, now that I'm gone, take up that duty for me. Make sure she's safe and happy, but most of all loved. Teach her about God, how He loves us. How He's always there, always caring for us no matter whether we can see Him working or not. Then, when she's missing me, when she cries because I'm not there to hug her, she will remember your assurance that no matter what happens, God is on the job. Take care of Alexa for me, sweetheart.

I love you, Kurt.

God is on the job? Then what was He doing when the

earthquake happened? Where was He when the earth swallowed Kurt and left her brain empty of everything that mattered? Gemma couldn't accept Kurt's words because she couldn't make them make sense.

Why? The word resounded in her head over and over.

Gemma was tired and so weary of trying to figure out herself. The answers to who she was wouldn't come and that left her more frustrated. Now she had a child to consider. What was she to do with Alexa? It was fine to give her a holiday here at The Haven, but then what? Send her back to foster care? She hated that thought, but what had Kurt expected her to do with the little girl?

If only she could sleep, let the cares and worries roll away in sweet oblivion without the recurring nightmare of the earthquake invading her rest. Defeated, yet knowing she needed to rest, she began to rise but paused when she spotted a lone figure walking around the garden enclosure.

Jake. She recognized the relaxed way he strode over the uneven ground, never faltering or stumbling. Apparently he couldn't rest either. Gemma thought she knew why. Lily and Thomas. Such a sad story.

Was God working then, too?

Fed up with her thoughts, she turned down her bed. Her glance rested on the framed cross-stitch picture on the wall, illuminated by a shaft of moonlight.

And we know that all things work together for good to them that love God, to them who are the called according to His purpose. Romans 8:28

All things work together for good—Kurt's death? Alexa's mom's death? Lily and Thomas dying? How could any of that be made into good?

Frustrated by the lack of answers, Gemma made a mental note. Come morning, she'd ask the aunties about it. Then maybe she'd be able to offer Jake solace.

Chapter Seven

The next morning Jake paused outside at the corner of the house because he heard the aunties speaking. Sensing the importance of their words in the quiet solemnity of the early morning, he stayed where he was, loathe to interrupt but curious.

"We've always felt that cross-stitch picture wasn't finished, dear," Tillie said.

"Yes, because who wants to hear that verse when they're in pain or grieving? 'All things work together for good,'" Aunt Margaret said with a frown. "It doesn't help you much, does it? You're still hurting terribly. You want to know why."

"Exactly," Gemma agreed.

Jake heard a note of hopelessness in her response.

"The thing is, God doesn't leave us hanging like that. Verse 28 is only half the thought," Tillie explained. "You have to link it with verse 29 to completely understand what's meant."

Jake had never heard this before. Though Romans 8:28 had been recited to him many times after Lily's and Thomas's deaths, he'd always resented the words. As if their horrible deaths were somehow good. Now, intrigued by the ladies' explanations, he leaned a shoulder against the stone wall, prepared to hear their clarification.

"You see, dear, the very reason for verse 28 *is* verse 29," Margaret explained. "God *does* work all things together for good according to His purpose. But what is that purpose? Verse 29 tells us that God is making us more like His Son."

"Let me put it this way." Tillie's chuckle warmed a spot in Jake's heart. "After we become Christians, why doesn't God send us to heaven and thereby save us the heartache and pain we feel? Then we'd avoid all the bad stuff in life."

Jake had often wondered the same thing.

"God doesn't rescue us and spirit us away because He wants us to exercise our faith, to depend on His power and thereby develop maturity and strength. To become like Jesus," she finished.

"If you never face adversity and figure out how to get through it with God, you won't grow as a Christian or develop enough depth to withstand the next storm in life," Margaret agreed. "And there are always storms, my dear."

"You're saying that this memory-failure thing of mine…" Gemma's words came slowly, thoughtfully. "That God is somehow using it to make me like Jesus?"

"Yes!" the ladies exclaimed together.

"So what you're really telling me is that no suffering is wasted." She sounded stunned by her conclusion.

Jake was, too. Except in his case it was worse. It meant Lily and Thomas had died because of him. But then, he already knew that.

"To help us through this suffering, verse 28 assures

us that we *know*. We don't think or hope or feel," Tillie emphasized. "We *know*, even if we can't understand how or why or when, we know that God is going to benefit us."

God was using Lily's and Thomas's deaths to *benefit* him? Jake couldn't see how. Apparently Gemma felt the same.

"How could my not remembering anything help me?" she demanded.

"We don't know. It's God's plan, not ours," Margaret said crisply.

"Maybe it's to help you learn things about yourself you otherwise would not have learned," Tillie suggested. "Or maybe it's to help you help others. You may never know. The thing to hang on to is the Bible's promise that God is working for your good." Confidence laced her words.

"Also, remember Psalms tells us God puts our tears in a bottle. In Isaiah it says we are inscribed on the palms of His hands. He knows every detail of our suffering." Margaret's smile infused her voice. "You're not suffering pointlessly, Gemma. God hasn't abandoned you."

"Even if I can deal with that, what's next?" Gemma sounded hesitant. "Where do I go from here? What am I supposed to *do*?"

"Darling, we'd like to tell you that, but *we* don't have the answers. You need to seek God, wait for His direction," Tillie said.

Jake peeked around the corner of the building. The aunts were seated on either side of their foster daughter, hands clasped, heads bent together.

"For right now, do whatever you can to make a difference in someone's world. Pitch in wherever and whenever you can to help others. God will show you His way, dear, but it may take time." Margaret patted her shoulder. "Perhaps you can use that time to spend with Alexa."

"I'm just supposed to keep living here, doing nothing?" Gemma's indignant voice rose. "I'm sponging off you."

"No. You're spending time with your family," Tillie corrected. "And we love that. Why not just enjoy it while you wait for God's next move?"

"I understand now why Jake said I'd love you." Tears muffled Gemma's words. "You don't judge, you don't chastise, you don't push. You just…" She paused as if searching for exactly the right word. "Love."

"That's what Jesus did. That's what God tells us to do, and we do love you, dear. Very much." Margaret brushed the wind-tossed strands off her face. "Now rest in God's promise as you begin reforming your life. He is at work."

"I believe I hear your little Alexa calling." Tillie chuckled. "Spending time with her is going to keep you very busy."

"Yes, it will. Thank you, Aunties." Gemma rose and walked inside.

"You can come out now, Jake," Margaret called.

He felt his face burn to the roots of his hairline as he stepped around the corner.

"I'm sorry. I wasn't trying to eavesdrop," he hurriedly assured them. "What you were saying intrigues me though."

"Because of your family." Tillie nodded. "You suffer greatly over their loss."

"You're like our Gemmie, fussing about the past and the outcome of your troubles instead of learning the lessons." Margaret's disapproving face chastised him.

"Lessons? Outcome?" He shook his head. "I don't have an outcome. I'm just a handyman."

Tillie sputtered with laughter.

"My dear Jake, you are a child of the most high God." A very serious-faced Margaret studied him. "Do you know the first things children do when they get hurt?"

He shook his head, not wanting to remember Thomas hurting.

"They lift their arms to be picked up and comforted," Tillie said. "They're humble. They don't let pride or anger get in the way. If they need food, changing, comfort, they reach for it. We need to do the same because God's hands are always outstretched toward us."

"Rather like yours are to the people of this community," Margaret murmured, her intense gaze searching his. "Perhaps it's time you allowed someone to hold *your* hand and comfort *you*, Jake."

Excusing themselves, the ladies bustled off to a day filled with ministering to others. Jake intended to find a solitary place and think about what they'd said until Gemma's voice stopped him.

"Good morning, Jake. Can Alexa and I help you with anything?"

"Good morning." He studied her face, saw need. "Have you already run out of ideas to entertain her?"

"According to Alexa, I'm not very knowledgeable when it comes to a four-almost-five-year-old." Auburn waves flowed over her shoulders as she gazed at him with what he interpreted as shame darkening her green eyes.

"Me, neither. I guess we'll learn together. I have

some odd jobs around here that I need to complete this morning, but you can't help with those," he said.

"The bank wants me to go see them. I guess I could take Alexa with me. That would fill in an hour or so," Gemma mumbled. "But I can't think of what to do with her this afternoon. She doesn't seem interested in joining any of the kids' groups."

The look of distress on her face made Jake mentally revise his schedule.

"This afternoon I need to visit a single mom who has three kids and laundry problems."

"Not a good combination." Gemma made a face.

"No. Want to come along?" He wasn't sure what Gemma would do, but at least she and Alexa would get some social interaction.

"That would be great." Relief washed across her sculptured features. "Maybe later this morning I'll take Alexa with the group who's going horse riding at Adele's ranch. Alexa said she's never done that."

"Sounds like a plan." Jake grinned when she waggled her fingers and almost skipped into the house. Looked like the former, bubbly Gemma was on her way back. Had the aunties' advice helped her?

As Jake dealt with Sweetie the cow, mowed the front lawns and tilled the flower beds, he struggled to make sense of what the aunts had said.

How was it possible for the deaths of his beloved family to make him more like Jesus?

Maybe, for the first time, the aunts were wrong.

"So, tell me about this single mom." Having settled Alexa with her phone and earbuds so she could listen to music, Gemma waited expectantly.

"Her name is Nancy Fillmore. Last year she came home after having given birth to her third child to find a note from her husband." Jake's teeth automatically gritted. "He'd abandoned them. The idiot has no idea what he's thrown away."

"But—why?" Gemma gasped.

"Said he couldn't take the responsibility. So Nancy was left alone with three kids to support while recovering from a C-section."

"What a rat!" Gemma gaped at him, shocked by the new dad's actions.

"Nancy had no time to think about that. Her maternity leave was extended because of the surgery so at least she's been able to stay home and help her kids adjust," Jake explained.

"Wait. Let me guess." Gemma pursed her lips, considered what she'd learned about Jake and said, "You got the community involved to help her."

"Nope. That would have embarrassed Nancy. She's very proud. She didn't want anyone to know she was struggling. I wasn't sure what to do until Adele said Nancy needed to feel cared for." He shrugged. "She and Liv organized a baby shower. Victoria said new clothes would help Nancy. Your sisters brainstormed a little more and eventually came up with the idea that folks could give gift cards so Nancy could get whatever she needed."

"Smart ladies, my sisters." Gemma applauded proudly.

"Things kind of snowballed after that." Jake chuckled. "Your aunts got into the act by arranging for Nancy's two eldest children to attend summer camp at The Haven.

That gave her time to adjust to single motherhood. Now she's managing."

"Wow." Gemma gazed at Jake appreciatively. "And you were the one who got the ball rolling. Good job. So why are we going to her house now?"

"Nancy is getting her life on track, but her house isn't." Jake seemed to hesitate.

"Whatever you tell me will remain confidential," Gemma assured him. He'd never divulged many details of what he did for the townsfolk, but maybe that was because he wasn't sure he could trust her. "I'm not a gossip."

"I know that, Gem." Jake's smile sent a current of warmth through her. "Fortunately Nancy doesn't have much of a mortgage because her great-aunt left her the house. But it's very old. Even if Nancy returned to nursing full-time, her salary wouldn't be enough to cover needed improvements."

"What are we talking about?" she asked curiously.

"Basic stuff. A new roof, new windows and replacement of the rest of her nearly dead appliances, including a new furnace. Paint. Minor repairs on just about everything else." His grimace revealed the direness of the situation.

"How are we going to help her today?" Gemma liked that this seemed like an opportunity to do something, to be part of something instead of waiting on the sidelines to remember a tidbit of her past. "What can I do?"

"From time to time folks give me—uh, let's call them anonymous donations to use to help somebody," he said carefully. "Today, thanks to a donation, Nancy is getting a new washer and dryer, and trust me, she desperately needs both. With a baby and two little kids, she can't afford the time, money or energy to keep running to the laundromat."

"You have a wonderful ministry, Jake." Gemma fell silent for several moments before asking, "Can anyone contribute to your work?"

"Sure." His face revealed his puzzlement. "Why?"

"Mr. Hornby asked me to go to the bank because Kurt's insurance has been settled. Apparently there were several policies, including a very generous one from his—our employer. It's in an account in my name." Gemma studied Jake. "From what everyone's told me about Kurt, I think he'd like to know some of his money is being used to help others."

Jake pulled into Nancy's yard, stopped his truck and stared at her.

"That's amazingly generous of you, Gemma," he finally said. "But you should keep that money for yourself, for your future."

"I don't need it. Apparently I was also a very good saver. At least that's what the accounts the aunts helped me transfer here from Toronto show. And I'm living free at The Haven." Her voice softened. "Trust me, there's more than enough money for anything in my future." He still looked dubious so she added, "I want to share in helping Nancy, even if it's only with money." She told him how much money she wanted to contribute.

She wasn't going to tell him the rest of her newly forming plan. No yet. Not till she'd thought it through.

"If you're sure, then thank you, Gemma." Jake's grin was all the thanks she needed. "You just fixed another problem. I have a pensioner who can't afford a refrigerator. She's been living without one for months. This will be an answer her prayers."

"Living without a fridge?" She couldn't imagine it. "That's awful."

"It was easier when the weather was colder, but now you've settled my concern about the summer. She'll get a new fridge to keep her medication cool thanks to you." Jake's face shone and his eyes glowed with excitement. He was so handsome. "If you're willing, you can be an even bigger part of things for the next few hours."

"Okay?" She blinked. "How?"

"Keep Nancy's kids busy while the old appliances are removed and the new ones are installed. Of course, that can only happen after the flooring people replace her wrecked linoleum," he explained with a grin. "Might take the whole afternoon."

"Good. Alexa and I will do whatever we can to help." Slightly abashed, Gemma gulped but hid her inner worry about failing.

"Just give me a minute to phone the appliance store to see if they can deliver Mrs. Burns a fridge today. Then I'll introduce you to Nancy."

While Jake spoke on the phone, Gemma thought about all the money from Kurt's estate. She was his beneficiary on the policies, but she didn't want that money. It would feel somehow wrong to hoard it when she already had so much of her own, though she had no idea where it had all come from. She'd learned she had numerous stocks and bonds and other investments. She'd study the papers in her purse when she was alone tonight, see if she could figure it out. Tour guides must be much higher paid than she'd imagined.

She'd already instructed Mr. Hornby to increase Alexa's trust fund, and now ideas to use even more per-

colated. She could help Jake with his community work
in a way that really mattered.

"They can deliver the fridge today," Jake said, pock-
eting his phone. "Come on, Gem. Let's go meet Nancy."

The new mom welcomed Gemma and Alexa, introduced her kids and then showed them where the new
washer and dryer would go.

"Jake's been such a sweetheart to help us out," she
told Gemma, eyes brimming with pride as she watched
her two eldest children invite Alexa to play in the sand-
box Jake had built. "I can't imagine how I'd have made
it through without him."

Gemma muttered some response she hoped was appropriate, but her focus was on Nancy's eldest, Jeremy,
whose face was distorted by a harelip. She knew there
was surgery available to correct such an issue. Why
hadn't Nancy had it done? She couldn't want her child
to go through life so disfigured.

Alexa tugged on her skirt. She beckoned Gemma
to bend down.

"That boy," she whispered, when Nancy was busy
with the baby. "His face is hurted. Isn't nobody gonna
fix it for him?"

"I don't know, sweetheart. But let's not mention it,
okay?" She smiled to soften the words. "It might hurt
his feelings and we don't want to do that."

"Nope. But when he goes to school, the other kids
are gonna call him names." Alexa nodded wisely as if
she'd experienced the phenomenon herself. "Sometimes
kids aren't nice," she proclaimed. Lips pressed together,
she rejoined the other kids.

Gemma stood mesmerized by a scene in her head.
A circle of boys yelled *carrot top* at her while they

ran round and round, refusing to allow her to escape. The shame, embarrassment and pain hit like a physical blow in the pit of her stomach. Alexa was right. Jeremy would suffer from the other kids' teasing. Kids always picked on the weakest one, the most different one, the *orphaned* one.

When she'd asked yesterday, the aunts had told her she'd been an orphan. Meaning she'd once had a family of some kind, but they were gone. That's why she'd been in foster care. She'd been suddenly afraid to ask more. And yet the lack of knowledge stymied her. These little flashbacks were so annoying, but apparently being teased about her hair was the only memory her brain would release today.

While Jake and Nancy discussed removing the old appliances, Gemma went to find the back door and the children. She was appalled by the state of the house. Old wooden windows didn't close properly. They'd be a nightmare in the winter. The heating bill must be through the roof. How did you keep kids healthy in a drafty old place like this? The back screen door was propped open because it was broken and the glass in the door had long ago cracked. The kitchen appliances looked like relics from the 1950s, though they sparkled clean and bright. The house was immaculate, but no amount of cleaning could disguise tattered floorboards showing through the ancient linoleum.

And then Gemma saw the quilts. Three of them, hanging in a small room in the corner. Drawn by their beautiful designs and gorgeous colors, she moved closer, fingering the fabrics as she studied the delicate stitches that held each together. Hand-quilted.

"I see you found my weakness," Nancy laughed.

"I'm so sorry. I didn't mean to pry. I was looking for Alexa—these are amazing," she interrupted herself to exclaim. "You did all this?"

"My great-aunt raised me," Nancy explained, waving a hand. "She was an extraordinary quilter. She taught me to love it, too. So whenever I have a spare moment, I come here and let my brain daydream."

"Your dreams are stunning." Gemma let go of the fabric. That's when she noticed a detailed wall hanging depicting happy children playing in the snow, two appliqued pillows and three backpacks with puffy faces and bright eyes that stared at her. Each item was unique. Gemma couldn't stop staring. "You're very talented, Nancy."

"It's my passion," the other woman breathed, a misty fondness in her eyes. "I've had to resort to completely hand stitching everything though."

"Why?" Dazed by the beauty she saw, Gemma thought this woman should never stop creating.

"My great-aunt's sewing machine is broken and this time I can't cobble it together. I think it needs a specific part that is probably either obsolete or crazy expensive." She laughed and shrugged it off. "Can I get you coffee?"

Just then someone rapped on the front door.

"No coffee, thank you, Nancy. I'll go find the kids and keep them busy while the workmen do their jobs."

Asked about the baby, Nancy told her Sophie was now fast asleep. Gemma went outside and when the children grew restless, she took them for a walk to the park to enjoy the playground equipment.

But she couldn't forget that sewing room. Or the amazing talent that had been silenced for lack of a part on an old machine.

The afternoon flew past. When the floor had been installed and the appliances, gleaming and bright, were finally in their places, the washer already running, Jake ordered pizza while Nancy made a huge pitcher of fresh lemonade.

The warm day had cooled by the time they returned to The Haven, with Nancy's thanks ringing in their ears. Alexa had fallen fast asleep in the back seat. Gemma knew exactly what she wanted to do next. But first she needed information.

"Why doesn't Nancy get surgery for Jeremy?" she asked. "It should be done before he starts school, so he'll be like the other kids. Does she need money for that?"

"No, time." Jake smiled at her surprise. "The doctors in Edmonton will do it as part of their health care, but she will have to stay with him for between ten days and two weeks. Nancy can't afford that."

"But there are places which offer almost free lodging. Anyway, does she have to be there the entire time?" Gemma wondered.

"Nancy would never leave Jeremy by himself." Jake heaved a sigh. "But she also can't take the other two along—especially Sophie—and she doesn't want to ask anyone to babysit if she can't pay them properly. I've been trying to work out something, but so far…"

He didn't finish. When they arrived at The Haven, he returned Alexa's hug, smiling as she hurried toward the aunties.

"Well, guess I've got chores to do." He grinned at her. "Thank you for all your help, Gem. You are a blessing."

"My pleasure." She frowned, wondered if he'd accept her idea. "When you've got some time, say later tonight around nine thirty, will you meet me on the patio?"

"Sure. Why?" He frowned as he stared at her. "What do you need?"

"Help," she said simply. "See you later."

Her mind brimming with plans, Gemma ate with Alexa, supervised her bath and then tucked her into bed. Alexa wouldn't sleep until she got another story about Gemma's travels.

"Will you take me there someday?" she asked, barely smothering a yawn. "I'd like to see the kids in those costumes you talked about. And hear them sing."

"We'll plan on it," Gemma promised. "Good night, sweetie." She savored the little girl's fierce hug and brushed a kiss over her brow, her heart welling with love. *Thank you for Alexa, Kurt*, she whispered inside her head.

Then Gemma retired to her room to make a list. That had always been the way she thought best.

When she was finished, she leaned back with a satisfied smile.

Jake had no idea what he'd unleashed today.

Chapter Eight

Three weeks later Jake once more sat outside Nancy's home with Gemma, this time in her brand-new car.

"Are you sure about this?" he asked, trying to hide his concerns. There was so much involved...

"We can do this, Jake. You're the detail man and you've organized everything. I'm the sitter. If I need help with the kids, I can call on my sisters or my aunts. I have a vehicle to transport the children to their activities. I have their car seats. I can do this," she said, her megawatt grin blazing. "Can you?" she asked, one golden-red eyebrow raised.

"I sure hope so." Truthfully, he wasn't certain they could carry off this magnificent plan of hers. But he was determined to try.

"Then let's get Nancy and Jeremy on their way to the hospital in Edmonton. Nothing can happen until they're out of here," Gemma reminded.

"True." Jake exited the car with a heart full of admiration for her intentions, but a gut full of worry about all the things that could go wrong with her incredible plan.

"We prayed about this, remember?" Her big green

eyes dared him to voice one doubt. "Are you going to trust God or not?"

As rebukes went, it was a good one. Jake shut down his nagging uncertainties and grinned.

"Well?" she demanded.

"Lead on, Gem. You're in charge."

"And don't you forget it," she shot back and then spoiled the smartness of that remark with a wink.

Half an hour later, after an abundance of directions and many hugs—some tearful—Nancy and Jeremy were on their way. Ten minutes after that, just as Jake finished loading the children's suitcases in Gemma's car, a hoard of tradesmen began arriving.

"You're sure the kids will be okay overnighting at The Haven?" He eyed Sophie and Donnie dubiously. "I doubt they've ever slept anywhere else but here, and I don't remember you doing much babysitting in the past—"

"Shh!" Gemma glared at him. "If this place is livable, we'll come back and stay the night. If not, we'll sleep at The Haven," she whispered. "You do your part and I'll do mine." She raised her voice. "Right now we're off to preschool. After that we're having lunch in the park."

"Sounds fun." He knew baby Sophie wouldn't be a problem. She seemed most adaptable. Donnie worried him. The kid wasn't quite finished with the terrible twos and didn't mind expressing his dissatisfaction with his world—often loudly and sometimes for lengthy periods of time.

"This afternoon we're going to have ice cream in the park," Gemma said, apparently as aware as Jake of the glower on Donnie's face. "I'm having maple walnut. Sophie wants vanilla. Donnie's still deciding what flavor he'd like."

"I'd choose chocolate," Jake said. "With fudge topping and lots of sprinkles."

Donnie's mutinous expression turned thoughtful as Gemma buckled in the kids. Once she was in the driver's seat, she rolled down her window.

"You can do this, Jake," she said cheerily. "With God's help. See you later."

With God's help. He hadn't even asked for that. He stood there, staring at her disappearing car, thinking what a wonderful encourager Gemma was, until a major crash echoed inside Nancy's house.

"I know I haven't been talking to You regularly," he mumbled as he crossed the yard. "And I have no right to ask anything. But this idea of Gem's—it's a massive undertaking and she's so gung ho on it. Could You please help us make it work?"

There was no clap of thunder or even an inner voice to guide him. Jake figured that meant God expected him to just get on with it.

"Why did you offer to do this, Jake?" he muttered when at noon his muscles loudly protested the hard work of removal. "Next time mind your own business."

"You talkin' to me?" the electrician asked.

"No." Jake clamped his lips together and concentrated on tearing out the kitchen cabinets that were probably installed long before Nancy's great-aunt had even been born.

"Two bathrooms and a kitchen reno, rewiring, replumbing, new flooring and painting the whole place, inside and out." Marcus the electrician rolled his eyes.

"And you're expecting it to be done in ten days? You're dreaming, Jake."

"Maybe."

It didn't matter how hard it was. This was Gemma's dream. He would work his butt off to make it come true if only because Gemma was finally dreaming again. As a bonus her dream was going to totally change Nancy's life. Jake shrugged.

"Piece of cake, Marcus."

"Wow!" Two days later Gemma surveyed Nancy's now open-plan first floor, turning in a circle that made baby Sophie burble with laughter. "This is amazing, Jake."

"It's a mess," he corrected, his smug grin tugging up his downturned lips. "At least the tear-out went faster than I expected. We uncovered a few issues while installing those support beams, but there wasn't anything we couldn't handle."

Gemma only partly listened as he described eons-old cast iron plumbing pipes that had to be replaced, service lines he'd dug up so the tree roots could be removed and a host of other mechanical issues necessary to bring the old house into the modern era.

"We had ten men show up to help install the new windows and doors yesterday, so that got finished very quickly," Jake continued. "Do you like them?"

"I love them, especially those French doors to the backyard. Nancy will be able to see the kids when she's working in the kitchen." Gemma licked the tip of her finger and made an invisible number one then struck a pose. "Score one for me. I'm not just a useless former tour guide, you know."

"Never useless," he said. "You're a very generous woman who's making a mom's unspoken dreams come true. You are extraordinary, Gem. Paying for all this— it's really amazing."

"Shh!" She glanced around to be sure no workmen were nearby to overhear, while trying to disguise her pleasure at the praise Jake was heaping on her. "The money thing is between us, remember? As far as everyone else is concerned, an anonymous donation is paying for this."

"But if Nancy knew she would—"

"I don't want her to feel beholden every time she sees me." Gemma shook her head, her auburn mane rippling with the action. Sophie clamped chubby fingers around a hank of it and giggled. "I just want to be part of the team that helps make this come true." Gemma winced as she freed the strands from the baby's fingers. "A silent part."

"A very big part," Jake corrected.

"What's next?" she asked, intrigued by the process of renovating such an old house.

"Plasterers have been in once to begin repairs. They'll work overnight and probably finish tomorrow morning. When that's dry we'll paint. After that we can begin to put things back together."

"It's going to be lovely, isn't it? Just like Nancy and her kids." Gemma pressed a kiss to Sophie's cheek, loving the feel of the child's downy-soft skin. "And apparently Jeremy's surgery went well, too. The aunts told me."

"I heard that from Nancy this morning. Where's Alexa?" Jake laid out an array of paint colors.

"I begged the preschool place to let her attend while

she's visiting." Gemma smirked, eager to share her secret. "She's helping Donnie fit in there."

"Yeah? Why would she do that?" Jake's knowing look made her blush. "What are you bribing her with?"

"Cowboy boots. Well, I have to buy them for her anyway," Gemma argued, blushing at the smirk on his face. "She loves riding."

"Uh-huh." Jake shook his head. "You're a pushover for a strong-willed kid like Alexa, Gem."

"Probably, but I need to make up to that little girl for all she's lost. If cowboy boots can help do that then I'm in." She didn't like the way his brow furrowed or the way he cleared his throat.

"I know you want to heal everyone's hurts, Gem, but please be careful."

"Of what?" she asked. But she knew what he'd say. "Don't love Alexa too much? Don't let her have a piece of my heart? I can't help it. Everything else in my world is upside down. I can't make sense of or remember most of it. But this bond Alexa and I are building—it's mine. It's something I don't have to try to remember. It's here and now. It's real. For you, too," she charged.

He opened his mouth to interrupt but she wouldn't let him.

"Admit it, Jake. You're crazy about that kid. Otherwise why would you have spent last evening, when you were stiff, sore and tired, showing her how to plant her flower garden?"

"I like Alexa very much." His face was so serious. "But we have to keep our feelings in check."

"Why?" she demanded.

"Because what happens when Alexa leaves?" he asked quietly.

"Hopefully we'll have built a connection we'll all cherish and we'll keep that going into our futures. Don't you think that's why Kurt asked me to watch out for her?" Gemma didn't want to hear Jake's warning. She sure didn't want to think about Alexa leaving or about being alone. Again. "It's almost time for Sophie's nap and I need to pick up Alexa and Donnie."

"What treat are you spoiling them with today?" he asked, one dark eyebrow lifted.

"I'm not spoiling them," she snapped. Then backtracked. "Okay, maybe a little bit. We're going to do some finger-painting and make pictures for their bedroom walls."

Jake shook his head as if stunned.

"What's that look for?" Gemma demanded.

"I'm amazed at the ideas that fill that pretty head of yours. I had no idea you would be such a fantastic surrogate mom." Something in his words made her look, really look at him. But she had to quickly avert her eyes because a nervous shiver made her knees weak when he added, "You're quite a lady, Gemma Andrews."

"Oh, phooey. I'm an ordinary female who likes kids and wants to keep them happy," she said, uncomfortable with his fulsome praise. "Don't make me out to be some kind of hero."

"I don't have to," Jake said very softly, his probing blue-eyed gaze holding hers. "It's just who you are."

She quickly turned the conversation to the paint samples, pretending to check that he'd ordered it in the shades she'd chosen.

"Nancy loves that pale turquoise that's so popular now," she explained. "You can see it in her quilts and cushions. And when her sofa's recovered, it's going to fit in perfectly against that pretty wallpaper." Gemma had no idea where this interior decorating knowledge came from. She only knew that every morning she prayed God would help her to choose things Nancy would like. And then she followed her heart.

"You're the boss." Jake tickled Sophie under her chin and chuckled when she reached her arms out to him. "I'm too dirty to hold you, little one," he protested, but Gemma slid the child into his embrace anyway. "I need to get something from her room upstairs," she said, making the excuse on the spur of the moment. "I'll be right back."

As she climbed the stairs, she could hear Jake talking to Sophie. Tears filled her eyes at the depth of tenderness in his voice as he showed off his work.

"This is what I did this morning. I'm not a carpenter, but I can do odd jobs. Mostly though I just tell the other people what we need done and they do it." Sophie babbled something and he laughed. "Yeah, Uncle Jake is lots better with plants than he is with building. I've got a ton of lovely plants coming. You can watch me plant them. Do you think your mommy will like this room? It's special because it's your mama's quilting room."

Upstairs Gemma paused inside the kids' room.

Jake would have been a wonderful father. She could imagine him cuddling his newborn, promising to ease his path, smiling with delight as his son reached a milestone. He would have been a fantastic husband, too. He was the kind of man who cherished a woman, the kind who gave her space to be herself but was there when she needed him.

Gemma gulped. How did she *know* these things about this man she'd met such a short time ago? Yet she was certain she had a handle on Jake's character. Why was that? Had she known him so well before? Again the desperation to remember settled on her heart. All the unexplained issues she struggled with—how much easier life would be if she could just remember her past life.

She recalled her talk with the aunties, how they'd insisted that God was working in her life to make her more like His son.

"I don't know how my forgetting could make that happen," she whispered. "But I guess I need to trust You, don't I?"

With a weary sigh she rose, picked out three sleeper sets and returned downstairs. At the bottom she heard a faint hum. She stepped around the corner silently and froze at the tender scene.

Jake was perched against a sawhorse, rocking Sophie in his arms as he sang to her, telling her of God's love for children. It was a praise song Gemma faintly recalled. As she listened to the words, she marveled at the tenderness of his voice. Sophie's rapt gaze held his for the entire time. When he stopped singing, she reached up to brush his chin with her tiny fist.

Tears welled in Jake's eyes as he gazed at the child. Gemma stood frozen to the spot as moisture wet his cheeks and dripped off his agonized face.

"I miss you, Thomas," he whispered, his voice raw with emotion, eyes squeezed closed. "I'm sorry I failed you and your mom. I'm so sorry, son."

Gemma stepped back out of sight. This was a private moment Jake wouldn't want her to see. He was in a world of his own, a past he'd lost. Her heart ached for the pain he still suffered.

Why? she asked silently. *How could You be using such a loss for Jake's good? Can't You see how awful it is for him? Can't You help him?*

There were no answers. The same blankness that shielded her past also concealed whatever God was trying to tell her. It was so hard to trust when there was never any reassurance that answers would come. It must be doubly hard for Jake because he blamed himself.

Gemma so wished she could help him. Yes, she had plenty of money. She could buy a lot of things. But with deep clarity, she knew there was no *thing* that could help Jake.

Or her.

There was only trust.

God is our refuge and our strength. A tested help in times of trouble.

If ever there was a time of trouble, it was now. The aunties would say that the best, the only hiding place from all the doubts and worries that assailed her, was God.

"I will trust You," she whispered and marveled as a gentle peace quieted her heart.

"Gem? What's taking you so long?" Jake called.

"Trying to find a bag to put this stuff in," she said cheerily as she rounded the corner. "Guess Sophie's diaper bag will have to do."

There were few remaining traces of his emotional storm, but Gemma knew from the lines carved around his eyes that Jake's suffering continued. He'd merely shelved it for now.

God, please help Jake as he walks this lonely path.

Gemma prayed that over and over as she collected Alexa and Donnie and drove to The Haven. When she finally burst out laughing as the kids plastered themselves in paint after creating pictures for the renovated home, she was able to give Jake into God's care. Then, for the first time in ages, her heart felt light, happy.

It was only after she'd tucked the kids in, told them all another story about her overseas travels and was sitting on the back deck with the baby monitor, watching the stars come out, did she wonder why it seemed so imperative that she help Jake.

Of course he was her friend and she wanted happiness for him, but...

Only a friend? her brain wondered.

"I don't know if I can spend very long with you this morning, Alexa." Jake pointed out a weed that had taken root in her seedling flower garden. "Maybe just until Gemma gets back from her appointment."

Always Jake was concerned about getting too close, about letting his affection grow into something more. There was no permanence in life. He couldn't count on this child being here tomorrow and he didn't want Alexa to count on him. He was just a handyman.

Aren't you getting tired of pretending you don't want more? He ignored the query in his head.

"Gem's makin' a m'orial for Kurt," Alexa said. "What's a m'orial?"

"It's a time to remember someone," Jake explained.

"My mom din't gots one of those." Alexa looked sad. "She din't have nobody to do it. Our fam'ly was Mommy an' me, an' sometimes Kurt." She sniffed before digging into the earth with a firm shove of her tiny spade.

"I'm sorry. That must have been hard for you. But

you have lots of good things to remember about your mom." Jake smiled, hoping she'd talk about her memories because so far Alexa had not often spoken about her mother and he had a hunch that she needed to.

"Mommy loved God. Kurt helped her know how. He tol' us lots 'bout Him an' said we gotta never forget God loves us. No matter what." The child peered across the valley at the distant Rockies.

"Hey, you two. How's the gardening?" Gemma's cheerful voice startled Jake out of his musing. "You're not working very hard."

"We're talkin' 'bout m'orials," Alexa explained. "I'm m'orialing my mommy."

"That's nice." Gemma shared a look with Jake, but he couldn't translate the unasked question in her green eyes.

"Where are Sophie and Donnie?" Jake asked.

"With the aunts. Just for a minute. I need to ask Alexa something." Gemma squatted so she was at eye-level with Alexa. "Would you like to have a memorial for your mom at the same time as Kurt's? You could tell us about all the wonderful things you remember about both of them."

"Really?" Excitement chased away Alexa's sadness. "I could say 'bout how she always made water-lemon 'sert on hot days."

"You mean watermelon dessert," Gemma corrected.

"S'what I said." Alexa glared at her, then shrugged. "An' I could say 'bout how Mommy liked red. An' how I miss her."

"You could do all of that and we could share your memories. That's the best way to remember people who can't be with us anymore." Gemma glanced at Jake before adding, "I'd love to hear your memories about Kurt, too."

"'Kay. I'll do it." Alexa picked up an earthworm, studied it, then plopped it back on the ground and buried it. "When's it gonna be?"

"Not till after we finish Nancy's house," Jake said quickly.

"'Kay. I'm goin' to see Donnie now." Alexa skipped toward the house.

"I'm a little stressed," Jake confided. "We only have a couple of days left before Nancy and Jeremy come home."

"You'll get it all done." Gemma's smile warmed a part deep inside him that had stayed safely hidden for a long time, a part that he'd forgotten existed. "If anyone can do it, you can, Jake."

"I hope I live up to your faith in me." He felt totally inadequate, though he desperately wanted to prove her right. That was the Gemma-effect. She made people want to be better. She personified the love of God that the aunts spoke about.

Jake could almost believe in that love, except for his family. The kind of love that had taken them was something he couldn't comprehend. Maybe he never would.

"If I'm going to finish at Nancy's, I need to get to work." He rose with a sigh as he realized that while he'd been with Alexa, the black guilt cloud had lifted. All he'd felt was love. He smiled as the little girl raced Donnie to where they were. He patted her head, enjoying her cute smile. "Bye, sweetie. Bye, Donnie."

"Donnie don't feel like talking t'day," Alexa explained. "An' he jus' eated a worm."

"Ew." Jake rolled his eyes until she giggled. "See you later?" he asked Gemma.

"After preschool. We're coming to hang the kids' pictures, remember?" She cocked an eyebrow at him. "The bedrooms *are* ready, aren't they?"

"Did you doubt my promise that they would be?" he snipped, liking the way her cheeks colored. "The bedrooms are refloored, re-windowed and freshly painted. They're ready."

"Then what's wrong? Not the quilting room?" Worry darkened her gaze. That room was Gemma's personal project and she'd gone to great lengths to ensure it would be exactly what Nancy would need.

"No. The *big deal*," he emphasized with a grin, using their code words, "will be delivered and installed today. It's the bathrooms that have me worried. The tiles are still missing."

"I'll be praying for you and them." Gemma's megawatt smile sent a flicker of warmth to his heart. "We're almost there, *Jakey*," she said and giggled at his grimace. "God's not going to let us fail now."

"From your lips," Jake murmured. He figured her prayers were probably a lot more effective than his.

Gemma's reassurance had kept him going when issues seemed certain to stall progress at Nancy's and derail their surprise. In fact Gemma seemed more like her old self every day, even without the return of her memory.

Jake's affection for her was growing, too. So much so that it was becoming difficult to imagine a day without Gemma's sweet smile and cheery encouragement.

Warning, his brain squealed.

Chapter Nine

"It's amazing." With tears rolling down her cheeks and her kids clinging to her, Nancy gave a huge smile that erased the strain and tension from her face. "How do I say thank you for all this?"

Gemma figured her reaction was worth everything they'd struggled with.

"Your thanks will be your enjoyment of your home." Jake grinned and pointed at Gemma. "But if I got the colors wrong or whatever, blame her. She's the decorator."

"Not decorator. I only suggested a few things," Gemma said, eager to deflect attention from her part in the renovation. "Jake's the one who got it done."

"Thank you both. There isn't one thing I'd change." Nancy hugged The Haven's handyman for what Gemma figured was about the fiftieth time, then said, "I don't know where the funds to do this came from. Or those that paid for our trip for Jeremy's surgery. Or for the gorgeous trees and flowers planted all around the place. Amazing." She began listing all the changes but then shook her head when there were too many. "I wish

I knew who's paying for everything so I could say a proper thank you."

"Enjoy your home," Jake said. "That's all the thanks anyone wants. That and seeing Jeremy get the care he needs."

"His prognosis couldn't be better. He won't have to hold his hand over his mouth anymore." Again tears welled in Nancy's eyes. Baby Sophie pressed her face into her mother's neck as if to console her.

"That's what we need to thank God for." Gemma stuffed down her desperation to know if she'd chosen appropriately for Nancy's quilt room.

"I know how you c'n thank people." Alexa, her hand firmly holding Donnie's, stood in front of Nancy.

"How, sweetie?" the woman asked with a smile.

"Make 'em a quilt. You got lotsa stuff to do that an' that big new machine." She gave Gemma a quick glance.

"Alexa, honey, quilts are expensive and they take a lot of work," Gemma explained, praying the child hadn't figured out she was responsible for ordering the longarm quilting machine, *the big deal* as Jake called it, that now sat in the quilting room.

"Alexa, you are a very smart cookie." Nancy hugged the child until she wiggled to be free. "It's an amazing machine and I can hardly wait to use it. Thank you for thinking of that."

"Welcome." Alexa pursed her lips. "Kurt usta say God gave us stuff so we'd use it ta make other people happy."

"He was right. I can hardly wait to get some time in that quilting room and try out everything." Nancy's longing look was interrupted by Jeremy's plea for a snack.

"The kids have missed you and Jeremy." Gemma laid a hand on Alexa's shoulder. "We'll go now so you can spend some time together."

"Okay. But tomorrow I'm going to have a big party and everyone who had any part in fixing this house is invited. Can you spread the word, Jake?" Nancy asked, smiling when he nodded. "Thank you."

Moments later they left Nancy inspecting the new children's play set that had been installed in her backyard.

"It's a good day t'day," Alexa pronounced with a yawn.

"It certainly is." Gemma shared a smile with Jake after he'd buckled the little girl into her car seat and helped her plug in her earbuds. "You did amazing work," she murmured so Alexa couldn't hear. "Thank you."

"Gemma, it was completely my pleasure to partner with you in improving Nancy's home." Their gazes locked. His smile did funny things to her knees. Thankfully his phone rang and drew his attention. "What? Oh, no. Okay, thanks. I'll be there shortly."

He hung up. All the elation from Nancy's surprise had drained from his face, leaving it a pale mask.

"What's wrong?" she asked.

"We need to get back to The Haven." Once they were moving, Jake explained, the lines of strain around his eyes revealing his concern. "One of the kids wandered away from his group and now they can't find him. I should have been there," he said, eyes narrowed. "I'm taking too much time off from my job, getting too involved in other people's stuff. Your aunts should have called me on it a while ago."

"Jake, that's silly. Even if you were there, you can't monitor every single visitor," Gemma protested. "Besides, you've always put The Haven and my foster aunts before everything, including yourself. Getting involved in other's people's stuff isn't wrong. It's a blessing to the community."

A muscle in his jaw flickered but he did not respond. She was glad Alexa was humming to her music so they could talk.

"What's really going on with you, Jake?"

"A reality check. What happens when I'm not around anymore, Gem?" he growled. "What happens when there's no one to help out these folks who keep calling me?"

"You're leaving?" she gasped. Suddenly the sun dimmed and her world seemed bleak.

"Not today, but sometime. Then what?"

"Do you think you're the only person God has in His arsenal of helpers?" Gemma demanded as a wave of relief rushed over her. *Jake's not leaving.* "He placed the community's needy folks on your heart. If you're not willing to help, don't you think He can find others who will step in and fill in the gap?"

"You think what I've been doing was directed by God?" He gave a half laugh. "I doubt that."

"Because?" she demanded.

"Because I never asked Him for help, never sought out His leading on who to help."

She studied him, working it out in her mind and blinking at her conclusion.

"You don't think God's with you at all, do you, Jake?" she asked, stunned by that. "You believe He totally abandoned you the day Lily and Thomas died."

"Didn't He?" he demanded, his anger visible.

"No, Jake, He didn't." Somehow Gemma had to make him see God in a new way. "First of all you can stop taking all the credit for their deaths. I know you didn't leave your loved ones behind knowing that carbon monoxide would kill them." She continued, ignoring his attempt to interject. "You knew that chimney had been a problem and you were going to fix it, but first you needed to secure your family's future with that delivery. Correct?"

Jake shrugged. He didn't disagree, though his expression clearly showed he didn't accept her rationalization.

"You couldn't have known they'd die, Jake. There was no way to know. That's the thing about carbon monoxide." She thought of something. "Did you have an alarm?"

"Yes. They said it never went off, that it may have been faulty." His eyes grew hard, cold.

"And that was also your fault?" Gemma guessed with a groan. "You were supposed to know that how?"

"I bought the thing, Gem," he said through clenched teeth.

"But…" She couldn't argue with that because she couldn't think of a way to offer him a new perspective. He'd been hanging on to his grief and blame for too long.

So she remained silent until they were almost at The Haven, her brain desperately sorting through each detail she knew, searching for something to hang on to, something to prove to Jake that he could not have done more. Something to prove he was innocent of his family's deaths.

Only there was nothing.

"Gem?" Alexa's tone said there was a question coming.

"Yes?"

"Who do I b'long to?" the little girl demanded. "This song says we all b'long to someone, but I don't. I don't b'long to nobody."

Before Gemma could respond, a deer skittered across the road in front of them. She thrust out a hand just as Jake slammed on the brakes. The force sent her hurtling forward in her seat. Her head collided with the dash. For a moment she saw stars.

And then Gemma was a child, in a room, *her* room. It was nighttime. There was a beautiful, sparkly light shining over her princess bed. A woman hugged her close.

"Sleep well, darling," she whispered. "Tomorrow we'll fly to Hawaii and you can play on the beach for as long as you like."

The lady smelled like the flowers the florist brought every Friday and set in pretty jars all over their house.

"Daddy and Mommy love you so much, pretty girl. Here's a kiss, sweet Gemma." A man's strong arms lifted her up and a scratchy face brushed her cheek. "Sleep well, darling girl. See you tomorrow."

"Don't go, Mommy. Daddy, don't go." But they were gone. Gemma was all alone.

Then, in a tidal wave of memories, it all came cascading back. Her uncle waking her up, saying that her parents had gone away, that he'd take care of her. Only he'd gone away, too. One of the servants said the police had made him go to jail, but Gemma thought he'd gone to wherever Mommy and Daddy were. She didn't know where that was. She only knew they'd left her behind.

She'd cried and cried until a grumpy lady took her away and made her stay with people she didn't know, people who didn't understand that she wanted her teddy and her own clothes and her special shoes that Daddy said made her a beautiful ballerina. She didn't belong with any of them. She belonged with Mommy and Daddy. Why didn't they come back? Didn't they want her anymore?

Gradually Gemma's brain realized a voice was calling her name, but she ignored it to focus on remembering. She'd gone to other foster houses, lots of them. But they weren't home. Some places seemed so awful she couldn't stay, so she'd run away. She remembered her social worker bawling her out for getting in trouble. She remembered coming to The Haven, to her foster aunties and her foster sisters and desperately hoping that perhaps here she could finally belong.

But she hadn't really belonged here either, not until she met Kurt. He'd made everything okay. Dear, wonderful Kurt had soothed and comforted her battered spirit, made her feel safe. When she confided her feelings of not fitting in, of not belonging anywhere, he'd shown her—though it had taken weeks, months, even years—that she was a child of God, that she belonged to God.

That He loved her.

"Gemma?" A hand on her shoulder brought full awareness. Jake stood by her open truck door, his fingers around her wrist, taking her pulse. "Are you all right?"

"Yes." She shook her head, winced at the faint tenderness on her brow and then glanced around. "I'm fine. Where's Alexa?"

"We're at The Haven. Alexa's with Victoria and her children. She's okay. She's just worried about you." His face tightened. "I'm sorry I hit the brakes so hard that you got hurt."

"I'm not hurt." Gemma would think about it all later. For now she picked up her purse off the floor and slid out of his truck, enjoying the feel of his helping hand under her elbow. "Why are you wasting time with me? We need to go look for that little boy."

"They found him. He's fine. He was with Sweetie." Outrage filled Jake's face. "The dumb old cow cornered him in the barn and wouldn't let him out."

A bubble of laughter inched up from inside. Gemma smacked her hand over her mouth. It wasn't nice to laugh when Jake was so serious, but she couldn't help it. She pulled her hand away and let her laughter spill out. It felt so good, as if all the worries and fears she hadn't been able to answer for so long now floated free.

"Uh—Gemma? Are you hysterical?" That made her laugh even harder. Poor Jake looked so confused.

"No, but a c-cow caused all this fuss?" She waved a hand to indicate the number of people who were returning to their cars, obviously searchers who'd come to help.

"Yes." His brow lowered. "Sweetie's not getting any oats tonight, trust me."

"Oh, Jake, your face." His glare made Gemma laugh again. "If you could only see your f-face," she said, trying not to giggle.

Finally he managed a laconic grin, though his eyes still searched hers.

"Tell me," he said after several moments had passed.

"What do you mean?" She brushed back her hair and exhaled, feeling freer than she had for weeks.

"Something's different about you." Jake studied her for an instant more before his mouth split into a huge grin. "You remembered," he crowed.

She nodded, unable to conceal her delight.

"Everything, Gem?"

"I think so. More than I realized I knew. I did have parents, Jake. We lived in a big house. They were going to a party and they kissed me goodbye." She touched her cheek with her fingertips, almost able to feel her parents' caresses once more. "They were killed that night, but I didn't know that. Everyone said they were gone. They talked about me being left behind, so that's what I thought had happened."

"That they'd deliberately left you behind," he murmured. He let his breath out between his teeth. "That explains a lot."

"Alexa's question was like a trigger. I always thought they'd abandoned me. Ever since they died I've been trying to figure out where I belong."

"Until Kurt," he said softly.

"Kurt offered me security," she agreed quietly, wondering if she should reveal her long-hidden secret. "I clung to him because with him I felt safe. And then the earthquake stole that sense of security and I couldn't find it. Still haven't," she mused sadly. "Still can't quite figure out where I belong."

"You belong here, at The Haven."

"Perhaps." She gave Jake a sad little smile. "At least I finally figured out why I've felt alone for so long." Gemma closed her eyes and visualized the past. "They said my parents had gone, Jake. They never said *died*.

They said gone. I was only four, around Alexa's age. I couldn't understand why the ones I loved so much, the ones I thought loved me, would go somewhere without me, why they'd leave me on my own and not come back."

"Oh, Gem." Jake's arms drew her close as tears rolled down her cheeks. "You didn't understand that they hadn't abandoned you."

"Eventually I did," she sniffed. "But by then those feelings of not belonging were deeply rooted. Maybe my brain knew that my parents hadn't abandoned me, but my heart couldn't accept it." It felt so good to relax in his arms and release the fears that had lain inside for so long.

"Loving Kurt helped you through that," he murmured as one hand smoothed her long hair down her back.

"Mm, more like he helped me shelve it, stop worrying about my past and get on with my life," she answered. Dare she tell Jake the truth? Would he understand or would he feel she'd betrayed the man who'd loved her with his whole heart.

"He knew what you needed," Jake said as she regretfully drew away. "He loved you a lot."

"I know." Gemma exhaled then admitted, "The thing is, I'm not sure I loved him the same way."

Shocked and certain he'd misheard, Jake pulled back to get a glimpse of Gemma's face.

"What did you say?"

"You heard me right." She glanced around, saw a huge boulder nearby and pointed to it. "Can we sit down while we talk?" She needed some distance between them.

"Sure." He made sure she was comfortable before lifting one eyebrow. "Start with your memories."

Gemma remained silent for several moments, though her gaze never left him.

"My parents were wealthy. Aunt Tillie and Aunt Margaret told me my family history when I turned eighteen because that's when I got control of my trust fund. It's huge," she said, green eyes stretched wide. "It pays dividends directly into my bank. That's why I have so much money in my accounts. From dividends. Not because I save so well." She rolled her eyes. "Sometimes I am so dumb. I told myself a tour guide must make a lot of money. From what? Tips?" She snorted in disgust. "Call me clueless."

Gem, gorgeous, smart and funny Gemma was a wealthy heiress. Jake needed time to process that. For now he nodded encouragement for her to continue while he appreciated the way she tilted her head to one side and lifted the shiny strands off her slender neck.

"After the aunts explained, I read online that my uncle embezzled a lot of my parents' assets when he was settling their estates. He was my guardian until some accountants figured out what he was doing. Then he went to jail and I became part of the foster system."

"Your uncle didn't get your money?"

"Some of my parents' estate, sure." She shrugged. "My father had most of my inheritance locked up until I reached eighteen though. That's why the aunts chose to tell me on my graduation." Gemma's smile faded. "It rocked me, I can tell you. So much so that I begged them not to tell anyone else. I didn't want my world to change any more than it already was."

"Change?" He couldn't figure out what she meant.

"Yes, I didn't want to not belong again. Remember, I was finishing school and planning on going overseas. Kurt couldn't decide what he wanted to do. We were going to be separated. He wouldn't be there when I needed him. I was terrified that I was making a mistake by leaving." She huffed out a sigh. "So I asked the aunts to oversee the details of my inheritance."

"And you've never touched it?" Jake asked.

"Didn't have to. Dividends, remember?" She needed him to understand. "I think that I deliberately kept these details suppressed because I've been subconsciously angry that they left me behind."

"You were angry at your parents?" he said, brow furrowed in confusion.

"At them, God, the foster system, my uncle, Kurt. All the people who failed me." She bit her bottom lip. "Maybe that's why I never quite believed Kurt when he said he loved me," she whispered. "Inside I was scared he'd leave me, too. The aunts didn't like that I'd eloped or that I'd never told him about my money."

Jake struggled to understand what she was saying.

"And they thought Kurt should have told you about Alexa," he murmured. "So you were both keeping secrets."

"Yes." Gemma sighed. "It wasn't right, but not telling Kurt—that somehow allowed me to enjoy what security I had, to let myself relax and savor being loved for myself. I thought it would never end," she added very quietly. "I was stupid."

"So when you say you're not sure you loved Kurt as he loved you…?" He had to ask, had to know.

"Kurt was very special to me. And I did love him

dearly. He was gentle and kind and he taught me so much."

"But?" Jake couldn't have stopped himself from saying that if he'd tried.

"Kurt gave and gave. He did everything he could to be the husband any woman would want. He always made me feel special, cherished, wanted. Most of the time I was certain that I belonged with Kurt." Gemma studied her hands, head downcast.

"Most of the time?" He caught his breath when she looked at him. Her lovely face was now ravaged with grief.

"He gave me so much. What did I give back? Nothing but friendship." She rubbed her wet cheeks with her palms. "It was all I had to give. I realize that now. And Kurt never once complained, never said he wanted more. He always seemed happy. But then I heard…"

Gemma's words died away. Jake tensed. He knew she was going through some traumatic event that had set off this whole chain of self-doubt. But he wouldn't ask, wouldn't probe. If she wanted to tell him, he'd listen. As a friend.

"I overheard him praying once," Gemma whispered. Her gaze was far off, in the past. "We were escorting a tour through France last year. Our hotel room was the most gorgeous room with Louis XIV décor and the loveliest balcony. I woke up and he was sitting out there, probably so he wouldn't disturb me. He had his Bible open but he wasn't reading." She gulped. "He was weeping, Jake. Weeping for me. Begging God to let me love him as much as he loved me. Asking God to heal me so we could have a real marriage."

She twisted her head, eyes brimming with tears, her

sadness tearing at his gut. Jake wanted so badly to wrap his arms around her and draw her close, to ease the pain of that memory and her guilty feelings.

"I think that's why Kurt never told me about Alexa," she whispered. "He wasn't sure he could trust me enough to love her the way he did. Because I couldn't love him enough."

His brain told him not to do it, but Jake ignored the warning. He couldn't stop himself. He slid his hand over hers and drew her upward, straight into his arms. All he wanted was to comfort her, to soothe this tortured woman, to take some of her suffering so she could once more be the special person he knew she was. At least that's what he told himself.

"I don't believe you didn't love Kurt, Gem," he murmured, his cheek pressed against her lovely hair, his lips near her ear. "Maybe you didn't love him the way you thought you should, but I think you loved him just as much as you could. And I also believe Kurt knew that."

Gemma leaned back to stare directly into his eyes.

"Do you really believe that, Jake?" she said, her lovely green eyes dimmed. "Or are you only saying it to make me feel better."

"*I* believe it," he said firmly. "The question is, do you?"

Chapter Ten

On the day of Kurt's memorial, Gemma rose before dawn. She took her cup of coffee to the deck and huddled under one of her aunts' afghans to watch the sunrise while her mind recalled the first day she'd met him.

I'm Kurt Andrews and I'm going to be your friend.

Snapshot after snapshot clicked through her brain, sometimes making her smile, sometimes making her weep until that last precious moment before he'd disappeared.

"Thank you for giving me such a wonderful friend, God," she whispered as the pale pink fingers of sun crept over the horizon.

"Gem?" Jake stood at the corner of the patio, an insulated cup cradled in one hand. He studied her, those compassionate blue eyes dark with concern. "What's wrong?"

"Nothing." She dashed away her tears and managed a smile. "Just remembering Kurt."

"If it's going to be too much for you, you don't have to give the eulogy. I could do it for you," he offered quietly.

"Thank you, but no. I have to do it. I owe it to Kurt." She motioned to a chair, glad when Jake sat down. "It's the least I can do for him."

"You know Kurt would never say or think that. He wasn't much into accolades." A smile hovered over Jake's lips. "He once told me there were far too many people all taking credit for the same thing."

She nodded. "That was Kurt."

"What will you say, Gem?" Jake asked, his voice very quiet.

"That's why I came out here to think. I'm not sure exactly what I should say." She looked at him as her thoughts gelled. "Kurt liked to laugh. He loved God and he made a point of sharing his faith. That's the man I'm going to talk about. He wouldn't want a maudlin service. He always told me he was allergic to tears."

"You'll do great." Jake said it with such deep intensity that she got caught up in examining his handsome face. He looked tense, she realized, as if he was struggling with some inner demon.

Understanding dawned.

"You don't have to be there today, Jake." She touched his hand, trying to transmit her empathy. "Not if it will bring painful reminders of Lily and Thomas and their funerals. There's no reason for you to relive that."

Jake squeezed her hand but quickly released it. His shoulders went back. His chin lifted and he looked directly at her. "How do you do that?"

"Do what?" Gemma frowned at him in confusion.

"Worry about me when you've got your own emotions to deal with on this of all days?" A hint of anger underlaid his words. "It's I who should be comforting you, Gem."

"There's no *should* about today," she contradicted. "We've all lost a very good man. Whatever we can do to help each other deal with that loss is what we'll do." She paused before asking, "May I tell you something?"

"Of course. We're friends," Jake murmured.

"A year after I first came to The Haven, one of my schoolmates died tragically. I had a horrible time dealing with it. It reminded me of losing my parents, I guess. Anyway, I kept bugging Kurt about how I felt it was so terrible and how she'd had such big dreams and she'd never get to fulfill any of them. He listened to me babble about it for a week. And then one day he sat me down and said, 'Look, kid, accept it. None of us know how long we're here for.'"

"Okay." Jake's dark eyebrows rose in an unspoken question.

"He'd always quote James 4:14. Do you know it?"

"Not offhand. What's it say?" Jake asked.

"'Ye know not what shall be on the morrow.'" Gemma smiled at the memory. "Kurt said that was his life's verse. I didn't understand it until he told me that he needed that reminder daily because nobody knew how long he'd have to make a difference in the world. He said that every day he got out of bed he needed to do whatever he could to make a difference. To me that sums up Kurt."

"I'm not sure exactly why you told me this."

"Because, Jake, if coming to his memorial upsets you or reminds you of how you lost your family, you shouldn't come," Gemma explained. "In fact doing so goes against everything he stood for. Kurt was about life, not death."

Jake stayed a few moments longer before he made

some excuse about jobs he needed to do before the memorial. Watching him stride away saddened Gemma. When would he let go of his past? When would he stop blaming himself?

"Please show me how to help him," she prayed. "And give me strength today so I can encourage others."

Then she went inside to prepare.

Since talking to Gemma this morning, Jake had vacillated between attending Kurt's memorial and staying at The Haven. It wasn't just the memories such a sad occasion roused. It was also worry that his presence would divert Gemma's focus. His heart told him to be there for her, comfort her. His brain said to stand back, let her deal with this with her own strength.

He finally temporized by slipping into the church after everyone else was there. From his position in the corner he could still see Gemma, but he doubted she'd notice him.

A huge picture of Kurt, surrounded by dense jungle vegetation, Panama hat in hand, and grinning his trademark smile, took center stage. Pure white lilies in a tall vase stood in front. Jake gulped. He'd ordered lilies for Lily's funeral. Lilies and roses.

There was no picture of Anna, but her name was printed on a huge board next to Kurt's picture. A massive vase of lilies guarded it, too. Memories of the man he'd known, a man who'd dedicated himself to caring for Anna and Alexa and Gemma swamped Jake until he suddenly realized the organ music had stopped.

Gemma rose and walked to the podium.

"Welcome," she said, her voice rough. She cleared her throat and began again. "Kurt Andrews didn't like accolades, attention or applause. What he loved was showing off the world his Father, God, had created. That's why I chose this picture. Kurt was never happier than when he could share his appreciation of God's handiwork."

Gemma paused, seeming to struggle with her throat. Jake mentally cheered her on.

You can do it, Gem.

"Two months ago today Kurt's earthly life ended with an earthquake in an Incan citadel in the Peruvian Andes. I believe he's now appreciating God's creation in a whole new way."

Soft chuckles echoed around the sanctuary.

"As I told someone this morning," Gemma's eyes found Jake and stayed on him. "Kurt's mission in life was to make a difference every single day of his life. For as long as I knew him, he did that. And the world is better off for him having been part of it."

Come on, Gem, Jake said internally when she faltered.

"Perhaps the best way we who loved Kurt can show our love is to pass on his legacy of making a difference in our world. Our actions affect others."

Only then did Jake notice that Gemma used no notes. She spoke directly from the heart, her voice firm yet tender.

"Kurt was many things to me. Friend, spiritual leader, companion, husband. I've been realizing lately exactly how much he brought to my world. He made it so much better. A very long time ago, when I first arrived at The Haven, Kurt taught me a song. It's called 'Brighten the Corner Where You Are,'" she told them. "And its words are as relevant today as they were when

it was first published in 1913. They were words Kurt
Andrews lived by. Let us honor Kurt's life by bright-
ening our corner of God's world."

Jake wanted to applaud, but Gemma wasn't finished.

"Now I'd like to invite Alexa, Kurt's stepdaughter,
to talk about him and her mom, Anna, who died tragically on the same day as Kurt. Alexa, honey?" Gemma
remained in place, smiling encouragement as the little
girl joined her.

"I'm scared, Gem," she whispered loudly, her fingers reaching for Gemma's.

"You don't have to be scared. We all loved Kurt.
Didn't you?" Alexa's head tipped up and down in a
strong nod. "Tell us about him and your mom. I'll be
right here."

Alexa took her time, but finally heaved a huge sigh
and smoothed out her pretty blue dress, which Jake
knew Kurt had bought for her. Then she began.

"Kurt was my for-real dad," she said, her voice clear,
not requiring any amplification by microphone. "He
wasn't my borned dad, but Mommy said Kurt was better
'cause he choosed me to be his kid. My mom was going
to uni—school," she substituted after stumbling over the
word. Chuckles again filled the room. "Mommy din't
have no money and she coun't 'ford to have me. She
said Kurt got them married 'cause he wanted to help us.
He helped lots. He teached me how to walk, an' how to
read the picture cards he sended me, an' how to print
in my special book."

Jake had never been more proud than he was now
of this sweet child, as if she was somehow his to be
proud of.

"Kurt buyed me lots of stuff, but I din't love him

'cause of that," Alexa said emphatically, as if daring anyone to argue. "I loved Kurt 'cause he loved me. He tole me that's how we're s'posed to love, like God does. Kurt tole me 'bout God an' how He loved us, even if sometimes we get bad. He learned me how to pray. Mommy said Kurt knew lots 'bout God. She readed me stories from the Bible he gived her. She tole me God was our bestest friend. Me an' Kurt an' Mommy always had lotsa fun." She gulped. "Kurt liked to laugh. It was loud, an' when I was little, sometimes it scared me. But then he'd hug me an' it would be okay."

Alexa stopped suddenly. Her head bowed. Everyone could hear her soft sobbing. Jake ached to race to the front, lift her into his arms and comfort her. But sweet Gemma already had a hand on the girl's shoulder and was whispering something. When Alexa lifted her head, Jake saw her face was wet, but her blue eyes shone with love.

"When Kurt laughed—" The little girl giggled through her tears. "Mommy did, too. So did I. Everybody did. He was the bestest dad." She turned to Gemma. "C'n I tell them all 'bout Mommy, too?"

"Go ahead, sweetie." Gemma's encouraging smile made Alexa grin.

"My mommy was so pretty. She had long brown hair, not long as Gemma's but pretty long," she said. "An' she liked water-lemon. She liked it lots."

Jake smiled at the smothered laughter. How could you not love this sweet child?

"Mommy liked ta sing. She had a pretty voice, kinda like a bird. Sometimes Kurt'd sing with her." Alexa shook her head, eyes twinkling. "That wasn't so nice 'cause Kurt didn't sing good. Mommy said it was like hearin' a crow. She tole me I should sing louder to cover up his singin'."

This precious child had the entire room enthralled.

"My mommy tole me 'bout Gemma. She said Kurt loved Gem very much. That's why Mommy got 'vorced. She said Kurt'd always be my daddy, but he'd helped us 'nuff and now he had ta marry Gem. Mommy tole me that I had ta share Kurt's heart with Gemma. I din't wanna at first," Alexa admitted honestly. "But Kurt tole me he had 'nuff love to go around, for me an' for Mommy an' for Gem. He said I'd love Gem an' he was zackly right."

Alexa stopped. She seemed to suddenly realize that everyone was looking at her. Her face crumpled and she began crying.

"I miss Mommy an' Kurt," she bawled.

Immediately Gemma scooped her up into her arms and held her close.

"We all do, darling," she said, her voice wobbling over the words. She squeezed her eyes closed and then reopened them to focus on the audience. "My aunts, Tillie and Margaret Spenser, will now read God's promises to us."

Carrying Alexa, Gemma returned to her seat, her red-gold head bent. She cuddled the little girl close as the aunts softly read the thirteenth chapter of I Corinthians, the love chapter. It seemed to Jake no scripture was better suited to the man he'd known as Kurt.

Ten minutes later, after several people in the audience had also shared their memories of Kurt, the pastor reminded everyone of the luncheon in the church hall, pronounced a blessing and thanked everyone for attending the memorials.

Jake rose to his feet, suddenly aware that since he'd seen the lilies, he hadn't thought of Lily and Thomas once. His whole focus had been on Gemma and Alexa, and their loss.

All he wanted to do now was make sure they were okay, but since it seemed everyone wanted to talk to them, he stayed in the background, serving coffee where needed and chatting with folks he knew while his gaze constantly returned to the slim, auburn-haired woman and the blonde child at her side.

In that moment Jake knew he'd do anything for them.

"It was a great tribute, Gem." That evening Jake sat across from her on the patio, no longer wearing his serious blue suit, but clad now in his familiar jeans, T-shirt and cowboy boots. "You and Alexa both did very well."

"Thank you." Gemma sipped her well-creamed coffee and let the strain roll away. "I'm not sure I said everything that should have been said. I probably needed notes. But I guess it's too late to fuss about that now."

"Alexa says you're having two headstones set in the local cemetery, one for her mother and one for Kurt." Jake's voice warmed her, though the evening wasn't chilly. "That was kind of you."

"Celia said there's no chance of recovering Kurt's body," she murmured. "I don't know about Anna, but I wanted a place where Alexa would be able to come to and think about both of them. And I wanted something to mark Kurt's life. I only wish we had pictures for Alexa. She worries she'll forget her mom."

"Why not contact her social worker?" Jake suggested. "Social services must have done something with Alexa and Anna's belongings, especially the personal stuff."

"How did you get to be so smart about this?" she teased. "And why didn't I think of it?"

"Well, you do have a lot on your plate, although…" He paused meaningfully.

"If you're going to say you're smarter than me, don't," she warned. "Am I not the one who solved Mr. Marten's housing situation and Mrs. Janzen's income shortage at the same time?"

"Yes, you are," Jake agreed with a grin. "I can't fathom where you got the idea that the woman should run a boarding house for senior men, but it certainly has worked out for everyone involved."

"Just a part of my brilliance," she snickered. "Wait! There's more to come."

"That's what I'm afraid of." Jake's droll expression made her chuckle. "Gem, you do understand that my expertise is plants and not renovating houses?"

"Oh, fiddle. You are a handyman, aren't you? And Mrs. Janzen's place only needed a few handy things done." How she enjoyed this repartee with him. "Ever think your problem is maybe you're too old to be doing such hard work, Jake?"

"Too old?" He glared at her, pretended to rise and then flopped back into his chair. "Oh, my back," he groaned in pseudo pain. "You could be right. Lugging those ancient iron bed frames down two flights of stairs nearly killed me."

"Poor baby. You need a good woman to look after you." Aghast at what she'd said, Gemma gulped. "Ah—"

"Are you offering?" Jake asked, with one dark brow arched.

Relief whooshed out of her. Surely it was a good sign that he could joke?

"Actually, I'm going to suggest you move into Mrs. Janzen's place." She couldn't help giggling at his outraged expression. "Why not? She'll feed you three square meals a day, do your laundry and get the other men to chat with you. She still has a vacant room on the bottom floor you could rent. No stairs. Sounds perfect."

"She takes seniors," he reminded, eyes rolling with disgust. "Which I am not."

"Then I guess you won't be whining when I tell you about my idea to fix the preschool's bathroom problems?" Gemma hadn't felt this carefree in eons. Was that because Kurt's memorial was over?

Jake studied her as silence yawned between them. Gemma was about to speak but he beat her to it, his voice quietly droll.

"I don't believe I fully understood the meaning of the word *minx* before today."

"Now you like it?" she asked, tongue-in-cheek. There were too many shadows to allow her to read his expression.

"I *like* you."

Had he really said that, or had she imagined it? And if he had, what exactly did he mean and what was she supposed to do about it?

"I like you, too," she responded. *Liked him too much?*

"Are you really okay, Gem?" Jake's gentle question reminded her of the tender way he'd held her that day at the soccer field, after she'd remembered the earthquake, when she'd bawled all over his shoulder.

Gemma cherished that sweet memory, though his comment still lurked in the back of her brain.

You loved Kurt as much as you could. I think he knew that.

Gemma hoped, no, prayed, that was true. But she wasn't certain and that nagged at her. Kurt had loved her so much. Had she shortchanged him?

"What I'm really asking is if you're struggling with Kurt's death, with letting him go?" Jake's rich blue gaze seemed to penetrate through to her thoughts.

"No. That day at Machu Picchu is pretty hard to deny. I saw him die." She managed to smile, suddenly weary of explaining. "He's gone to a better place. That's settled in my mind."

"Then?" Jake looked at her expectantly.

"Just a lot of *I wish* going on at the moment." She dragged her fingers through her hair, trying to shake off the jumbling emotions. "I wish I'd appreciated him more. I wish I'd told him how much his friendship meant to me when I first came here and after."

"You did. I heard you say it often," Jake assured her.

"Maybe. But—"

"Don't go there, Gem," he said gruffly. "Believe me, I know going over and over it in your head doesn't do anyone any good. Rest in the knowledge that he loved you and knew you loved him. Remember the happy times you shared."

"Is that what you do, Jake?" The question slipped out. She bit her tongue, worried she'd hurt him by probing his pain.

"There were happy times." He exhaled heavily. "Thinking about them reminds me of what I've lost. So I try to forget."

"But that's wrong!" She was aghast. "Lily and Thomas are part of you, who you were, who you've become. You can't just stuff them away in some forgotten corner of your brain. That doesn't honor their memories."

"I don't want—"

"To remember? I know," she said gently. "But I'm pretty sure that in remembering lies healing." He didn't want to talk about them, but she pressed him anyway. "Tell me about Lily. What was her favorite color?"

"Pink." The response came automatically. "She always wore something pink. It suited her dark hair and dark brown eyes. She wasn't very tall, only up to my shoulder, but she was beautiful inside and out."

Jake was actually talking about Lily! Gemma could hardly believe it. Because she wanted him to continue, she asked another question.

"And Thomas? Did he take after you or his mother?"

"Both of us." A tender smile curved his lips as he stared into some distant place. "He never cried much, only when he was hungry. Or if he was cold. That kid hated being cold. He had dark hair, curly like Lily's, but my blue eyes. At least we thought they'd stay blue." Jake's voice broke off. He gulped and clenched his hands together, maybe to force down the pain. "I'll never know," he whispered.

"You can't forget him, Jake. Ever," she whispered.

"As if." He cleared his throat, only speaking when he'd finally regained his equanimity. "But remembering is too painful. It's better to suppress it all."

"Is it?" Gemma shook her head. "I think it only hurts more. Talking about Kurt, about what he liked, who he was, it soothes the ache of his loss."

"It's not the same," Jake snapped.

"You think not?" Gemma wouldn't push it because

she wanted Jake to ponder what she'd said, not work even harder to keep his grief inside.

"Can we talk about something else?" Jake asked, a certain desperation underlying his voice.

"Sure. Let's talk about Billy and Ethel." She lifted her hand to hide her smile. She'd shocked him. Good.

"What about them?" Jake uttered the words hesitantly, as if he was afraid of what he'd hear.

"I stopped by Billy's the other day to drop off a pie Adele had made for him. Ethel was there, and they were not arguing. They were laughing."

"Good." Jake's eyebrows rose as his eyes stretched wide. "So?"

"I think we should play matchmaker." Gemma was sure she couldn't have surprised him more.

"Uh, our projects have always been about meeting needs." Jake blinked.

"No difference with this one," she assured him.

"What needs would our matchmaking meet?" *Dubious* didn't begin to convey the skepticism in those blue eyes.

"Companionship, affection, friendship, camaraderie."

"And love." He frowned at her. "That's your ultimate goal, isn't it?"

"Not exactly a goal." Gemma deliberately chuckled as if he'd said the funniest thing in the world, instead of hitting the nail on the head. "If they fall in love, that's their business. I just want to make it easier for them to be together."

"Why?" Suspicion lurked in that one word.

"I recently learned that Esther has hated living alone since her husband passed. She stays in that big old house of his family's, even though it's depleting her resources, because she believes she's doing her duty to the family."

"How *do* you find out these things, Gem?" Jake shook his head. "Guess I should be glad you're not suggesting we renovate it."

"Are you kidding? It must be over four thousand square feet on those three levels." Gemma shook her head. "Billy's place would be perfect for them both."

"Billy's place was also Irma's place," he reminded.

"That's where you and I come in." Jake's aggrieved expression sent Gemma into peals of laughter. "It's nothing bad. I just think we should help Billy sort through Irma's hundred million knickknacks. Not to get rid of, but perhaps to *bequeath* to his daughter or daughter-in-law."

"I have no words to describe the conniving brain tucked under your mass of beautiful hair," Jake murmured after several moments had passed.

"I'm not conniving." Gemma didn't like that he might think that of her. "I want to help. We both know Billy's very lonely. And Aunt Margaret isn't interested in him."

"Huh?" Jake sat in rapt attention as she related Aunt Tillie's confidence about Billy's crush on her sister.

"See? We'd be helping him get over that. Besides, lately Billy and Ethel seem to have plenty to talk about. And she loves cooking for him."

"Not that prune-pie thing?" he asked in disgust.

"Try prime rib with Yorkshire pudding. Peking duck. Southern-fried double-dipped chicken." She watched Jake's lips curve into an O-shape of surprise. "Those are only three of eighteen recipes Ethel got from Adele."

The Haven's handyman appeared completely taken aback. When he finally spoke, his voice brimmed with awe.

"What do you want to do?" he asked meekly.

"Put the health authorities on him." Gemma held up a hand to stop his protest. "I mean, *pretend* to do that."

"How?"

"By spreading a rumor that they're coming to investigate. You saw how Billy reacted when he suspected Ethel would summon them. He was afraid and he let us dust." She frowned. "I don't think he enjoys the mess his house is in now, but I believe even thinking about changing it overwhelms him. Perhaps the threat of the health department is the one thing that would force Billy to act, especially if we generously offer to help him get the place sorted *before* authorities can show up."

"You are a very devious woman." Respect echoed in those words.

"No, I just want to help Billy and Ethel. This happens to be the only plan I can come up with to achieve that. Well?" she demanded when Jake kept gaping at her. "Say something."

"Do you know what I appreciate about you, Gem?"

"Huh?" She frowned, not following.

"Actually there's a lot. First, you don't mind going into an old man's dusty, dirty place, where no woman has lived for eons, and helping clean it up so he'll have a second chance at love. Your temerity-slash-compassion is awesome." He pretended to clap.

"Oh, stop it." She blushed.

"Of course there's the little issue of lying. I should tell your aunts on you," he warned.

"It wouldn't be a lie. It'd be—a rumor," she substituted.

"Also, what if all that mess and dirt is what attracts Ethel? You never know. Maybe Billy's magnetism for her is that she'll get to make that place sparkle."

"I can't imagine—oh, you're joking." She heaved a sigh of relief. "So what are you saying? Will you help me?"

"How could I refuse?" He rose. "As it happens I'm going over there now. The church ladies asked me to take him a box of leftovers from the luncheon after Kurt's memorial. Want to come? We could drop your, er, hint about the health department."

"Isn't it too late to visit?" she asked, glancing at her watch.

"Not for Billy. He stays up for the really late, late news." Jake glanced around. "I haven't seen Alexa this evening."

"She went to bed early. She was worn out." Gemma stood. "Can you wait while I ask Victoria to listen for her?"

"Yep."

She felt his eyes track her until she was inside The Haven.

"Going somewhere?" Victoria asked from her perch by the kitchen table.

Gemma quickly explained their errand, though she said nothing else. Victoria's eyes glowed with a knowing look, but she merely nodded.

"Don't be too late," she said in a motherly way. "Kurt's memorial took a toll on you, Gem, even though you might not feel it yet."

As she sat in Jake's truck on the way to Billy's, Gemma assessed herself. She didn't feel worn or tired. She felt revitalized. Was that because she was with Jake or because they were on their way to trying to help someone else?

Whatever the reason, she felt like she was beginning a brand-new chapter of her life and that Kurt would have wanted that for her. Wouldn't he?

Chapter Eleven

With summer now in full swing and what Jake called their "Matchmaker" project underway, life at The Haven became busier than ever. As hordes of kids arrived to enjoy days, weekends, or a whole week of riding, hiking, singing, camping and learning about God, Gemma kept volunteering for extra jobs.

As if running herself ragged could ease her brain's unease about her growing attraction to Jake.

Most afternoons they worked with Ethel and Billy, sorting a lifetime of possessions into what was needed and what wasn't. To Gemma's surprise, the threat of the health department became unnecessary after the couple asked for their assistance in clearing out Billy's home. They quite openly discussed their growing feelings for each other and their plans to eventually marry. Jake demanded to know what Gemma had put in their water.

Gemma also partnered with Jake on their preschool project and in spending time with Alexa, who loved being with Jake.

"I like our garden," she repeatedly proclaimed. "I 'specially like eatin' garden stuff."

She'd already helped pick beans several times and was vigilant about checking the pea plants, eager to pinch off the fat green pods and feast. But it was the flowers that gave Alexa the most joy.

Early this morning Gemma had suggested they take a bouquet to the graveyard to place by her mother's headstone.

"My mom would like these red ones," Alexa said as she laid them down. As she sat crouched on the grass, she touched the cold, hard stone and tears rolled down her face. "I can't hardly 'member Mommy no more."

That was the one worry Gemma couldn't fix. She'd repeatedly tried to connect with Alexa's social worker with no success. In her last call, she'd left a message suggesting a visit to The Haven might be in order in a desperate ploy to help the little girl.

Today, after breakfast, Alexa's social worker, Dana, had arrived. She'd spent most of the morning with Alexa who had acted as official tour guide at The Haven.

"I'm glad you came to check on her," Gemma murmured when they'd finished lunch and the little girl had raced off to water her flowers with Jake.

"Someone should have been here weeks ago," Dana apologized. "I was her original worker, but her case was given to someone else. She went off on maternity leave and Alexa's case fell between the cracks before I was reassigned."

"There's no worry about her leaving here. We'd love to have Alexa stay with us for the entire summer," she told Dana. "We all love her." They both watched Alexa working beside Jake as they removed weeds from the carrot patch.

"She does seem happy here," Dana mused. "To tell

you the truth, seeing her so at home with you and your family is a big relief. When I first had contact with her, she seemed so lost. I've been worrying that she'd feel like she didn't belong. Many kids who go through a sudden and tragic loss of a parent have a difficult time, but she seems remarkably well-adjusted."

"She's a generally happy child, though one thing keeps recurring in our conversations." Gemma leaned forward, sensing an opportunity. "Alexa is worried she's forgetting her mom. She doesn't have any pictures or personal effects. Can you help with that?"

"I know there were personal effects recovered from their apartment. Because I was in charge of her case then, I ordered everything to be placed in storage. Let me check if it's still there." Dana dialed a number and began asking questions.

More than twenty minutes passed while Gemma told herself not to appear anxious or worried. Still, a wave of relief swept over her when the call finally ended.

"I'm sorry that took so long. Apparently we still have everything in a short-term storage facility, but that will expire at the end of the month. Then everything is scheduled to be moved into something more long-term." Dana thought for a minute. "I could go through it all, if you like, see if I could find a picture of her mom. Would that help?"

"Yes." Gemma thought about it a moment longer before she asked, "Are there a lot of things? If not, maybe you could send the whole lot here. Then Alexa could go through everything herself. Perhaps that would twig old memories and maybe ease her mind." She had a hunch this was the right move. "I'll gladly pay for express shipping."

"That's very generous of you," Dana murmured.

"I believe it's very necessary. Before we held the memorial for my husband, Alexa mentioned her mom hadn't had a funeral or memorial or anything, so we included Anna in Kurt's service. Alexa loved sharing her special memories, but I think it also sparked more fears that she's forgetting something about her mom." She met Dana's gaze square on. "That's the last thing I want. No child should forget her mom, not when we can help her remember."

"You know, my superiors agreed to let Alexa come here because your sister is a well-respected foster parent, because of your aunts' reputations and because of your husband's relationship to the child." Dana looked thoughtful. "But I see now that you have the same quality as they, a focus on working for the child's benefit and not on how uncomfortable or complicated it makes your own life. Alexa is a very fortunate child."

"Actually, we're the fortunate ones." Gemma knew it was true.

"How so?"

"Alexa has made a big connection with Jake, our handyman. He's experienced great loss in his life. I believe Alexa's presence is helping him finally accept what happened." Gemma smiled. "She's also been very good for me. I can't mope or isolate myself. You don't get away with anything when Alexa's around. She says Kurt and her mom taught her about God's love and she continually reminds us of how blessed we are."

"That's sweet," Dana said, sounding distant.

"It's also true." Gemma chuckled. "Continually being reminded to take a heavenly perspective on our situations has made both Jake and me less prone to wallowing in our troubles. Because of Alexa, I'm more focused on community involvement. She helps us with that, too, and loves every minute of it."

"What kind of community involvement?" Dana wondered.

Gemma smiled at the memories of spending time with Jake.

"Delivering food hampers, working with folks who need small renovations to their homes, local projects assisting seniors, visitation." She shrugged. "Whatever's needed. Most of the time it's Jake who's doing the helping. I'm just the gofer."

"Sounds like a great way to enjoy time together." Dana's smile held speculation. "Are you two—together?"

"Jake and I have been friends since I first came to The Haven years ago." Gemma wasn't going to tell her that most evenings they met to discuss progress on their current undertaking and to decide which project to tackle next, or that *his* outreach had now become *their* partnership. It was at those times when Gemma was absolutely certain that this was where she belonged. "Alexa loves to be included. The seniors particularly love seeing her happy smile."

"Alexa has a very big heart," Dana agreed. "I'll check into that storage and find out if I'm allowed to send her things here."

"Thank you. My biggest concern is ensuring Alexa feels secure. That's why I believe that having some of her mom's things, *their* things, would really help her," Gemma murmured.

By the time Dana waved goodbye, apparently satisfied that Alexa was well cared for, it was midafternoon and Gemma had grown very thirsty. She glanced across the yard and smiled at what she saw. Wearing wide-brimmed hats to protect against the direct sun, Jake and Alexa were back in his garden. This time they were picking spinach.

Gemma walked to the kitchen, filled a thermos with iced tea and set it in a basket with three plastic glasses and a bowl of freshly cut watermelon chunks. She laid her new picnic quilt, a recent gift from Nancy, on top. Then she walked to a spot just inside the garden gate and laid out everything on the soft green grass.

"Come on, you two," she called. "Time to take a break."

"We're havin' a picnic!" Alexa, her hand firmly attached to Jake's, tugged him toward the blanket, a huge grin lighting up her sweet face. "I like picnics."

"Me, too. You do know the other kids are making ice-cream sundaes?" Gemma asked with a wink at Jake. "Don't you want to join them?"

"Nope." Alexa flopped down on one side of the blanket and speared a piece of watermelon. She popped it into her mouth and then tried to speak around it. "Me 'n' Jake," was all Gemma understood.

"Excuse me?" She could barely suppress her laughter as Alexa gulped down the juicy fruit and then repeated what she'd said.

"Me an' Jake think some of the other kids would like to plant flowers, like I did." Alexa popped another watermelon chunk into her mouth.

"Actually, I said I wonder if some of the kids who come here might like to garden, learn about where their food comes from." Jake shrugged. "Just an idea for next year."

"Who are you and what have you done with the aunties'

handyman?" Gemma demanded, shooting him a cheeky grin. "You know. The guy who insisted my three foster sisters and I had to learn how to mow lawns and weed flower beds before we could even get near your precious garden."

Jake rolled his eyes.

"Tell me how it would work," she said. Here was another chance to collaborate.

"To begin with, if you'd get my shed emptied, we could use it as a potting shed," he grumbled, inclining his head toward the building where she'd stored everything that had arrived from her Toronto apartment.

"*Your* shed?" It suddenly felt like Jake was pushing her to deal with her past, though he couldn't possibly know much she'd been procrastinating. "There must be other spaces available."

"Not ones so near the garden. It's a perfect potting shed. You have to empty it sometime, Gem. You can't leave your stuff there until winter," he said calmly.

"Why can't I?" Truthfully, Gemma would prefer to leave it there forever. She'd barely begun to shed her insecurities about Kurt. Why resurrect them now?

"Because it will get damp and that will ruin any pictures or keepsakes you have," he shot back. "Besides, a pile of stuff like that encourages mice."

"Don't you like mouses?" Alexa asked, wide-eyed.

"This handyman does not allow mice in any of the buildings he cares for," Jake explained in a pseudo-stern tone.

Gemma was glad of the interruption and of Jake's concentration on the child. It gave her a few precious moments to gather her composure. Hopefully he wouldn't realize how desperately she wanted to avoid digging through her past life.

"There's your friend David," she heard Jake say and glanced in the direction of his pointing finger. "I think he's needs a friend. Why don't you take him some of this watermelon, Alexa?"

"Okay." The little girl chose the treat and scampered away. She carefully opened the gate, let herself out and then refastened it. After she'd handed David a spear of watermelon, they began an animated conversation. Moments later David's counsellor appeared and Alexa called to say they were going with him to play soccer.

Gemma nodded and waved. "How did you remember that boy's name, Jake?"

"Before any new group arrives, Olivia texts me a file with their names and whatever personal details we know about their situation. I try to memorize as much information as I can." Jake shrugged as if that was a simple thing. "It helps me keep an eye out to see if they need something."

"Wow!" She gaped at him, mentally doing the math over how many children visited The Haven. "More of your outreaches," she said in wonder. Appreciation for his giving heart welled inside her. "You're quite a guy, Mr. Handyman."

"I'm an ordinary man who's very curious as to why you're so reluctant to deal with your stuff," he said, eyes narrowed. "You had the movers stack the boxes in there and then locked the door. To my knowledge you haven't been back. What's with that?"

Gemma thought about prevaricating, but she doubted he'd let her get away with it, so she remained silent.

"Are you avoiding something, Gem?"

Yes!

"I'll help you go through things, if you want." That was Jake. Always the giver. But he never took, never asked her to share his solitary hikes. "What's the issue?"

"I don't want to see it," she muttered.

"See what?" Jake reached over and tipped up her chin so he could look into her eyes. "Spill it."

"Proof of how bad a wife I was." There. She'd said it aloud.

"Gemma, there is no way." His eyes, bright in his tanned face, chastised her. "You loved Kurt. I saw it myself. I think maybe since the accident your brain is playing tricks with your memory. Trust me, you did love him. You have nothing to be ashamed or afraid of." He broke off speaking to purse his lips. "It's I who failed in my marriage."

"Jake." She sighed. "I keep telling you you're not to blame—"

"Yes, I am. There were many occasions when I wasn't the husband Lily needed, or the father Thomas should have had." The self-loathing in his words was painful to hear. "Thomas was a sickly baby. It's no wonder Lily was terribly run-down. But I was so focused on my business, myself and *my* career. She had to beg me to help with his bath time sometimes, or to rock him to sleep. I was always busy. I missed so much…"

Jake's voice died. He twisted his head to peer at the Rockies in the distance.

"Why don't you count the many times you've helped me?" Gemma touched his fingers with her own and reminisced. "From the first day I came here you took pains to help me adjust. You listened to me whine when I couldn't fit in at school. You helped me understand how to be a friend and not just wait for someone to befriend me. You even helped smooth things over for me when Kurt and I came to announce we'd eloped and he argued with the aunts."

"I didn't do anything special," he mumbled.

"Yes, you did, Jake. When we left here, the tension there had been was eased, because of you. All these years, no matter how left out I felt, you'd always insist that I could belong, if I wanted to." She lowered her voice. "I don't think you did that for my foster sisters. It was me you focused on, ensuring I felt like an important part of the family. I can never thank you enough for all you did for me."

"I don't want thanks."

"I know." She sighed and released his hand, hating to let go but needing all her focus to say this. "I wish that somehow I could repay even a little of what you did for me. You're very special to me, Jake."

"Big brother." He smirked and arched an eyebrow.

"No." Gemma bent her head and studied her fingernails. "A man I'm coming to care for very deeply, more than I ever expected or imagined."

"What are you saying, Gem?"

His voice demanded that she look at him, so she did, and this time she let the turmoil of uncertainty and affection and confusion reveal itself in her expression.

"I think I had a crush on you back then, Jake. I'm beginning to wonder if that's why I feel like I failed Kurt, why I couldn't be the wife he deserved." She gulped and forced out the rest. "I never thought of it like this before, never took the time to probe my brain and try to understand, I guess."

"Now you have?"

"I'm realizing that for me, Kurt was safe. The day he first rescued me at school, I told myself I belonged with him and I just kept repeating that. To question it, to even hint that I didn't—it made me feel so insecure. It scared me to death."

Silence hung between them. Jake stared at her as if she'd grown two heads, obviously stunned by what she'd said.

"Maybe the reason I didn't love Kurt enough was because I had a crush on you." She gulped before admitting, "Maybe I still do."

A thousand things spun through Jake's brain, all of them bad. He was deeply moved that Gemma had appreciated his help all those years ago, and even more touched by her belief that she could care for him. But she couldn't care. Not like that.

If she knew, if she understood how selfish he'd been, how often his total self-focus had come between him and Lily...

"Why don't you say something?" Gem murmured.

"If I helped you all that time ago, then I'm glad. But please don't let your accident or Kurt's death muddle the truth. You did love Kurt. With all your heart." He smiled, wishing he could avoid this. "Anything you think you feel for me—it's not love. You're just vulnerable right now."

Once he'd daydreamed about Gem loving him. Instead he'd witnessed her deep devotion to Kurt. Now she was alone, mourning and trying to figure out her future. He had to warn her off. Even if she did love him, which he doubted, he could do nothing about it.

Because of his vow.

"I'll always be your friend, Gem, and I'm glad we can share things." What a tame way to describe his special moments with her. "But don't make it more than it was, then or now. Especially don't feel guilty about being my friend."

"It's become more than friendship, Jake." Gemma's voice was whisper soft.

"It can't be," he said simply. He hated saying it, hated watching pain fill her face. But there was no other way. "I'm not someone anyone can love, Gemma. I can't have love in my life because I ruin it. Lily loved me once with a precious, beautiful love, and I threw it away."

"But—"

He pressed his forefinger against her lips and shook his head.

"I was blessed when God gave me Lily and then Thomas. I said I loved them. But love doesn't let selfishness and work take over and ruin everything. I messed up. Badly." He withdrew his hand, too aware of the brush of her velvet-soft skin beneath his fingertips.

"Even if that was true, and it isn't, it doesn't mean you can't ever love again," she argued.

"Yes, Gemma," Jake said firmly. "It does."

"Why?" she demanded, tears rolling down her cheeks.

"Because the day I buried my wife, I made a vow that I would never again jeopardize another woman with my so-called love. My neglect cost Lily and Thomas their lives. Taking them is how God punished me."

"God doesn't do that," she whispered, her face ravaged by tears. "God doesn't kill the people we love for our mistakes. You're wrong."

"I will keep my promise, Gem. I'm sorry." Jake rose

and walked away. He had to. It was either that or wrap Gemma in his arms and try to soothe the pain he'd caused. He wasn't going to do that because he couldn't bear to think of Gemma one day paying for his neglect.

But oh, how he wished he could accept that beautiful gift of love she'd offered him. The problem was, to do that he'd have to accept that God had let his family die. Because of his mistakes.

That acceptance wasn't going to happen. Ever.

For the next few days, Gemma avoided Jake as much as possible. When she went with him to call on two of the townsfolk who needed help, she pretended everything was fine. She even maintained the friendship image Jake had spoken of. But privately she fought an inner battle of confusion. Did she love him? How could she prove it to herself? Or him?

By dealing with her past.

On Friday morning, while Jake was in town repairing someone's flooring, and Alexa was making doughnuts with Adele, Gemma unlocked the shed and began going through the things from her past life with Kurt. Unaware of the passage of time, she opened each box and let herself savor memories tied up in the contents. So many things she'd done for and with Kurt. Surely she'd loved him?

With no answers, she began sorting what could go and what she would keep.

"Whatcha doin'?" Alexa demanded.

"Sorting. Want to help?"

"Sure." Alexa tossed her apple core across the fence to Sweetie and then began placing piles of Kurt's clothing in the boxes Gemma indicated.

Gemma had thought she wanted to be alone to do this, but Alexa's presence was a comfort. Her barrage of questions and fulsome memories about the man they'd both cared for helped revive reminiscences of the joy she'd shared with Kurt.

"He sure liked bright colors, din't he?" Alexa held up a tie-dyed orange and purple T-shirt.

"I gave that to him when we were in India." Gemma laughed at Alexa's disgusted look. "He said he wanted a purple memory."

"Ew." The little girl stuffed the shirt in a box. "Did'ja buy these, too?" She held up a pair of frayed green shorts whose better days were long gone.

"No. His mom gave him those when we came home to tell them we were married. Kurt called them his wedding present." Gemma closed her eyes, remembering how delighted he'd been that his mother had sewn something specially for him.

"How come they gots funny legs." Alexa frowned.

"Kurt tried to patch them. He didn't sew as well as his mom." Alexa's expression made Gemma laugh so hard that she doubled over.

And so it went, item after item eliciting some fond memory of the man who'd played a big part in both their lives.

"C'n I keep this?" Alexa held up a thin silver chain. "Me an' Mommy gave it to Kurt for Christmas one time."

Touched by Alexa's memory, Gemma nodded, smiling as the little girl tucked it in her pocket.

"C'n I have some pictures, too?"

"Tell you what. Miss Dana said they found the things they got from your house when your mommy died.

She's going to send them here." Gemma smoothed Alexa's glossy hair. "When they come, you and I will go through them, add these pictures, and make a special album so you'll always be able to look at them and remember both your mom and Kurt. Okay?"

"'Kay. I gotta have more pictures though. 'Cause when I go 'way, I want to remember everybody at The Haven."

The overwhelming sadness in that thought hit Gemma hard.

Where would Alexa go? With whom would she live? Would they care about her past? Would they keep Kurt and Anna's memories alive?

"Do you like it here, Alexa?" Gemma couldn't promise anything, not with her own world so unsettled. But she did want to hear the child's feelings on being at The Haven. Was she happy?

"Yeah, I really like it." Alexa's voice wobbled. "The other kids only come for a little while, 'cept the ones that live here. I don't live here so I gotta go, too, I guess, but I dunno where."

She sounded so down about it that Gemma worked hard to make her giggle and smile as they went through the rest of the items.

"You gots lots of these picture books." Alexa flopped down on the ground and opened one. "You an' Kurt are always laughing."

"We laughed a lot. I always made a book when we went to a place we'd never been before." Gemma sat down beside her and let the memories cascade as she answered Alexa's questions.

When they'd gone through the last book, they packed them all in a box.

"Are you keeping all of this stuff?" Jake asked, surprising them with his noiseless appearance.

"Hi." Gemma couldn't stop the bubble of delight from fizzing inside her. "No. Those boxes of clothes are going. So are the trinkets. These four boxes are personal things I'm keeping."

"She's got lotsa pictures." Alexa danced up and down. "Me an' Gemma are gonna make a book for me, too. An' you're gonna be in it."

"Really? I'm very honored, Miss Alexa." He ruffled her hair, shaggy now that it was growing out. When he glanced at Gemma, she caught her breath. "Was it as bad as you anticipated?"

"No." She smiled. "You were right. I needed to go through these. It's been…cathartic."

"Here's a place you went where there's snow houses," Alexa piped up, leafing through loose pictures. "Do you always gotta wear big boots in that place?"

Gemma burst out laughing at Alexa's offended expression, and to her surprise Jake joined her.

"That place is called the Arctic, Alexa," he said. "You need big boots to keep your feet warm."

"You knew I'd gone to the Arctic?" Surprise filled her that Jake knew of that trip.

"I saw all the postcards you sent the aunts, Gem. I always knew when you were on a trip." His low rumbled tone did funny things to the equilibrium she was trying so hard to maintain.

"Oh." She couldn't make herself look away from his gentle sky-blue eyes.

"Where are ya gonna send all Kurt's funny clothes?" Alexa's shrill voice broke the tension.

"Good question. I'll load what you don't want in my

truck. We could donate or dispose of it. Your choice."
Jake waited for Gemma's nod before carrying the boxes
to his waiting truck with Alexa trailing by his side.

Gemma's phone rang. It was Victoria.

"Gemmie, we're stuck. Our presenter for tonight
can't make it. Which is a pain. He's a puppeteer and
the kids were really looking forward to seeing him.
Can you step in for him?"

"I'm no puppeteer, Vic," she declined.

"No, but everyone loves your amazing stories about
fantastic places all over the world. You have pictures,
too. Couldn't you use them?" Victoria wheedled. "The
kids will be on the edge of their seats."

Gemma recalled her month-long tour of Africa. The
unique animals and people she'd discovered would certainly lend themselves to a kids' presentation.

"Okay," she agreed. "But if they all fall asleep or
take off, it's on you."

"Not gonna happen, kiddo. Mega thanks. You'll do
great."

"Who's that?" Jake asked, arms loaded with boxes
filled with her books. He grinned when she explained.
"Then I guess you'll want one out of these," he said,
glancing at the boxes of books.

"I have everything on my computer. I just need to
put it together for a slideshow. If you could hang a sheet
or something, I'd really appreciate it," she said with a
glance around. "I'll store the stuff I'm keeping in my
room."

"Okay." He set the chosen boxes in the back seat of
his truck.

Gemma's heart thudded as they rubbed shoulders on
the way to The Haven. Alexa had insisted on sitting by

the door, leaving her squeezed next to Jake. Once they arrived, Alexa lost interest in things and went to find her friend David.

Gemma followed Jake inside the house, carrying the diary she'd kept since she'd been married and her laptop. "At least if I mess this up tonight I can still go back to touring," she muttered as they climbed the stairs.

Jake paused at the top, his face alert. "You're thinking of doing that?"

"Maybe. My company called. They've had requests for me to do a small group, in-depth tour of Egypt," she explained.

"Egypt was always your favorite, wasn't it? I remember you took a lot of history courses about it." Jake set the boxes on the floor.

"The pharaohs, the pyramids, the Nile—it fascinates me." She shrugged. "I'd love to go back. But—"

"But?" He paused, studied her. "But what?"

"I'm not quite sure touring is where I belong," she told him as her brain silently begged, *Tell me not to go, Jake.*

"You'd do an amazing job," was all he said before he left to retrieve more boxes.

"Thank you," she mumbled, wishing he'd ask her to stay.

When everything she wanted was in her room, Jake led the way back downstairs where Alexa sat moping at the table because David had gone on a hike without her. Jake chucked the little girl under the chin.

"You've got more blooms on your flowerpot flowers, missy. Want to go check them out?"

"Yes! Are they giant flowers like the pictures showed?" Alexa was halfway out the door, dragging

Jake with her, when she stopped and turned. "C'mon, Gem. We gotta see my flowers."

"Right behind you." Gemma rose. She'd put her slideshow together after supper. She knew exactly the Biblical story to go with it.

When they arrived at Alexa's plant pots, the little girl looked downcast.

"What's wrong, kiddo?" Jake asked, squatting beside her.

"They're dinky flowers." Alexa glared at the blooms.

"They've only just begun to bloom," he told her as she leaned against him. "Give them time."

"They've had to work very hard to bloom, honey," Gemma added, searching for a way to make her words reach Jake, too. "We're nearly in the mountains. It's not the kind of home these flowers are used to so they have to adapt."

"What's 'dapt?" Alexa asked.

"Well, it means that it's not as warm here as where they usually grow, and that we get cooler nights, and maybe the soil isn't as good as it is in other places." Gemma risked a glance at Jake. "These flowers have to find a way to deal with all of that. But even though they have to struggle, they are still beautiful."

"Why doesn't God make 'em grow bigger?" she demanded.

"How do you know He isn't?" Gemma held Jake's gaze. "God promised He'd always be with us, no matter what happens."

"Was He with you when the earth—when Kurt died?" Alexa asked, her face thoughtful.

"Yes, honey. Just like He was with you when your

mom died. God's always with us." Gemma bit her lip as Jake rose, his face set.

"I've got chores," he said stiffly before striding away.

"Jake's sad," the little girl said with a sigh. "I singed to him yesterday and I tol' him some jokes, too, an' he's still sad. I dunno know how to make him not sad."

"Sometimes people can't do that, even though they really want to." Wasn't that the truth?

"How come?" Alexa demanded.

"Because sometimes a person has to wait until God takes the hurt away."

"So how'm I s'posed to help Jake? He's my friend." Sweet Alexa, trying to cheer up everyone.

"Sometimes the best thing we can do for people we love is to pray for them. Then we have to keep on loving them," Gemma explained.

"'Kay. Let's pray for Jake. Me first."

As this child launched into her heartfelt prayer for the man who'd befriended her, Gemma realized that the softness in her heart for Jake wasn't better or stronger or even taking the place of what she'd felt for Kurt. She *had* loved her husband. She knew that now after looking at the remnants of their life together. But it was a different love than what she felt for Jake; not better, not worse. Just different.

Kurt was Gemma's childhood love, a first love. These feelings she carried for Jake were that of an adult, colored by loss and the trials and struggles she'd weathered. She'd loved Kurt in a happy, discovering way. But her love for the man hurting in the deepest recesses of his heart because he couldn't resolve God's part in the deaths of his loved ones was cautious, not quite ready to be tested, new and a little frightening.

Despite his own pain, Jake kept willingly reaching out to help others. That was just one of many reasons why this man held her heart.

What would he do with it?

Chapter Twelve

That evening the children were already gathered around a campfire, waiting for their evening story time, when Jake arrived to hang the sheet that would be their screen.

Having finished that task, he slid onto a bench beside Alexa, reveling in her warm smile of welcome and the sweet rightness of her clambering onto his knee and looping one arm around his neck. Pain clutched his heart as old memories cascaded.

Oh, Thomas.

"I love you, Jake," Alexa whispered.

"I love you, too, sweetheart." He swallowed past the lump in his throat. "Do you like our movie screen? It works pretty well, doesn't it?" The glow of a glistening golden desert in the first light of morning blazed, waiting.

Gemma stood to one side, peering at her laptop. In her white jeans, green cotton shirt and sneakers, with her auburn hair plaited in two braids and wound around her head, she looked ready for a safari and so lovely it made his heart race.

Suddenly the low beat of drums filled the air. Jake, like the kids, stared at the screen, intrigued by flashing scenes of acacia trees, sand dunes, watering holes and herds of wild animals, obviously filmed from above by a drone or a plane.

"Welcome to Africa." Gemma inflected just the right blend of intrigue and tour guide into her speech. "This is a place where nothing is as it appears."

Everyone jumped when a huge lion roared directly into the camera. Giggles echoed around the valley.

She has them eating out of her hand, Jake thought. Then he, too, became caught up in her dialogue and visual displays.

"Some people say that Africa was the home of the garden of Eden, where God created Adam and Eve." History and geography wove together seamlessly in her presentation. "The people who live there now, the children of Africa, are like you. They want the same things you want. To love and care for their families, to have enough to eat, to run and play and laugh. To be safe."

As her pictures appeared and disappeared, Gemma's dialogue drew them deeper into the African world. She told them how these children's worlds were often torn apart and about how they had to learn to get along to live together. Jake marveled at the way she meshed pictures and stories, speaking of a young boy whose parents had died from disease, a young girl who'd lost an arm, children who didn't have enough food to eat. They were, she repeated, children just like those visiting The Haven, struggling to belong after having their lives turned upside down.

"When you think about fighting because someone calls you names, about disobeying your foster parents, about running away, think about Africa's children," Gemma murmured, holding each child's attention with her expressive voice. "Think about how God has blessed you with people who provide a home and food for you, who are doing the best they can to help you. Think about how much God loves you. And then think about how you could bless someone else, even if it's just to say something nice or do something simple like share your lunch."

"That's not much," a young boy said.

"It's a great deal," Gemma insisted. "That's how peace starts. You befriend someone and they befriend someone and soon there's no place for hurt or pain or anger among friends. You, my dear children, are God's hope for the future."

Now a video showed children sitting on the bare dirt, singing lustily, their smiles stretched wide. When they were finished and only the soft melody could still be heard, Gemma spoke again.

"When you think of Africa, remember that many of the kids you saw don't have things or money. That doesn't matter because things and money can't make you happy. Happiness comes from inside, from having God in your life, loving you, caring for you. It comes from caring for each other." She smiled, letting the words sink in before adding, "Let's each take one of these little drums and sing a song together, just like those kids did."

Alexa slid out of Jake's arms to retrieve her drum, and this time she stayed with the others as Gemma led the song in her clear soprano voice. Jake thought he'd never heard anything so lovely as the children's voices meshed with hers, lifted in worship. It was crystal clear to him that if she decided not to return to leading tours, Gemma had a definite ministry here at The Haven. The kids loved her.

So did he.

Jake sat frozen as the truth seeped from his heart into his head. He loved Gemma Andrews. Maybe he always had? Her strength, her convictions, her gentle soul and people-first attitude—they made Gemma who she was. The woman he loved.

Was it wrong to feel such love when he'd made that vow to Lily? Jake knew it was. Yet he couldn't quench his feelings. Neither could he act on them. He'd promised. So what *was* he supposed to do?

Jake wrestled with that question until all the kids had left, Alexa among them, to enjoy their evening snack. When they were alone, he stepped from the shadows and began to help Gemma clean up.

"That was wonderful." He folded the sheet thoughtfully. "You helped them see the world in a way that relates specifically to them."

"There are so many troubled kids here. I want to encourage them, to show them they aren't as poorly off as they think," she said quietly. "And that they aren't alone. It's a lesson the aunts struggled to teach me. How many times did they tell me to remember the names of God? My favorite is *Jehovah Jireh*, the God who provides."

That was the first of God's names that Jake had begun studying only a few days ago. His personal Bible study in the aunts' library was a feeble attempt at understanding God's nature, though Jake wasn't sure that was even possible. All he knew was that he couldn't go on as he had been, avoiding God and pretending to be something he wasn't.

Gemma's return to The Haven had made him see the futility of living a lie. Though he'd now studied three of God's names, understanding why God had acted as He had with Lily and Thomas was still a long way off.

"Let me carry that." Jake slipped the sheet under one arm, grasped her laptop in his left hand and reached out with his right. "It's a steep climb here and the dew makes the grass slippery. Hang on to me."

"Thanks." Her hand slid into his, comfortable, warm. Perfect. She glanced up as they walked. "This sky is every bit as beautiful as an African one."

"You miss touring," he said, understanding the soft, yearning expression.

"Sometimes. Especially when I see my pictures again." She smiled and shook her head. "But then I talk to the aunts or my sisters or spend time with the kids and I think, what could be better than this? The Haven is a true refuge. Foster kids come here defensive, hurting, needy, and slowly they're able to find hope again as they learn about God. This ministry of Aunt Tillie and Aunt Margaret's is amazing."

"It is," he agreed.

"Speaking of missing things. Do you ever yearn to be back in a greenhouse, Jake, working entirely with plants?" Gemma stopped in a shaft of moonlight, inquisitive green eyes wide in her oval face.

"I've never considered it." He did now. He *could* return to horticulture, start his own business again, but would it ever fulfill him as much as his work at The Haven and his projects in Chokecherry Hollow? Would he ever find a partner like Gemma?

"Not that I'm suggesting you should leave here,"

she said soberly, her gaze intense. "I'd miss you, Jake. You're very special to me."

Those words and the concentration of her stare reminded him of her avowal of love. He hesitated, wanting to remind her that nothing could come of that, but she chuckled before he could respond.

"Besides, you'd be terribly hard to replace."

Jake didn't laugh. In fact, he barely heard her next words because a new thought struck him. If Gemma stayed, perhaps he *should* leave. It would be much easier to keep his vow if he didn't constantly see her.

Not see Gemma every day, not hear her full-bodied laughter, not watch her teach Alexa and the other kids how to embrace the world and trust God? No!

His heart sank. What would give meaning to his days if Gemma wasn't there?

"Jake? Are you asleep?" She peered at him, her face inches away.

It took every ounce of control Jake possessed not to breach the distance between them and kiss her.

"Jake?" Her fingers tightened around his arm.

"No," he said slowly. "I'm not asleep."

"Good. No one should sleep through a star shower like this." She slid her hand free and lifted her eyes to the heavens. *"Elohim,"* she whispered. "God of power and might."

Another name of God. For a moment Jake wondered if she knew of his Bible study. But how? He'd been so careful to sneak into the library in the early morning, long before anyone else was stirring. Then he recalled that she'd once said she'd learned God's names from her aunts.

He stood beside her for a long time, savoring these

precious moments alone together, knowing he couldn't allow it to happen again.

"I do care about you, Jake." Gemma's voice pierced the silence around them as her gaze rested on him. "Maybe you think it's wrong for me to say that so soon after Kurt's death." Her green eyes were clear and focused. "It doesn't feel wrong. I know that I loved Kurt. Maybe not enough, maybe not as I should have, but I did love him."

"Like you love me?" He hated that he'd asked that question, like some needy youth who craved reassurance. Yet nothing could have stopped it because he needed to know.

Gemma shook her head slowly from left to right.

"No, I don't love you like I did Kurt."

"Because no one can replace him in your life," he rushed to say, desperate to force her to face the truth before it led to something he couldn't derail. "You're vulnerable and you have a crush on me. You even said that."

But Gemma shook her head again, and this time tears welled in her eyes. Jake clenched his fists to stop himself from embracing her.

"I said I *had* a crush once. This is different. You can ignore it. You can pretend it's a crush if you want to," she whispered. "But that won't change how I feel now. I know my heart and it says I'm in love with you."

"But Gem." Jake raked a hand through his hair, wishing he'd avoided this entire scene. He didn't want to hurt her but neither did he want her to continue with this fantasy world. "I can't," he began.

She placed her fingers over his lips.

"I know. You made a vow." She removed her hand

and tilted her head sideways. "Why did you make that vow, Jake?"

"Why?" He frowned in confusion. "I told you—"

"Yes, yes. You felt guilty after Lily's and Thomas's deaths." She nodded. "Got that. So the vow was like your atonement? A kind of self-punishment?"

"What?" He stared at her, aghast. "No! It wasn't about me."

"Well then why?" she pressed. "I mean, why vow that? Why not take flowers to Lily's grave every month or work on making your business the best it could be in honor of them?"

"My *business* is what got them killed," Jake snarled, more irritated than he'd been in years.

"No. Carbon monoxide killed your wife and child. Maybe because of a faulty detector or maybe because of a defect in the fireplace, or perhaps both." Her voice was firm. "*You* did not kill them. Nor can you take responsibility for the storm that waylaid you."

Jake couldn't say anything, couldn't argue with her because he couldn't, *would not* follow where she was leading. So he remained silent, waiting for her to finish whatever she had to say so he could leave, hide out in his cabin and pretend Gem's love was all one-sided.

"I understand you were hurting terribly. To lose your beloved family that way—" Tears glossed her eyes as she silently wept. "I'm so sorry, Jake. So very sorry. Please believe that I'm not in any way trying to diminish your loss."

He inclined his head in acceptance but he said nothing, because he dared not.

"What I don't understand is your response to their deaths. Why would you believe that never letting anyone into your life again, never allowing anyone to get close to you, to share your journey, would take away the pain?" Gemma stared at her clasped hands. "I know that blaming yourself is natural. Perhaps it even helped for a while. But to make that vow…" Suddenly her head lifted and she looked directly at him, green eyes wide. "Is your vow something God told you to do?"

"I didn't talk to God for years after their deaths," he snapped. "Except to ask why. There was never an answer so I soon stopped asking even that."

Not true. In his heart he still asked why. Maybe always would.

"So this atonement of yours," she murmured. "How does it help you or them?"

"It helps ensure that I will never risk any woman's life again, let alone a child's." Jake glared at her. "It helps me live with the guilt and the pain."

Gemma looked at him with pity though she said nothing.

"Are we done here?" he demanded. "Because I need to take this to the house and then finish up a job or two."

"I don't think your vow is helping you, Jake. I think you suppress your real feelings by rushing around here, helping everybody, looking after the townsfolk, spending time with me. I think your vow is your excuse to stay emotionally untouched and avoid all the pain that entails." She pressed her lips together but Jake knew she wasn't finished with him.

"You might as well say it all, Gem." Maybe then they could move on.

"I will. One of the names of God that I've been relying on since the earthquake is Jehovah *Rapha*, the Lord that heals. It's an amazing name." She reached out and brushed her hand against his cheek in the most tender caress. "Why don't you try talking to God the healer, Jake? Why don't you find out what He wants and expects from you? Why don't you let Him heal the load of guilt you're carrying so you can finally be free?"

Then, without another word, Gemma hurried into the darkness.

Jake stood there, her words echoing inside his head, wondering what it would be like to live without the constant cloak of culpability that had dogged him for seven long years.

"What's wrong, Gem?"

A week later Alexa's question and the soft squeeze of her hug drew Gemma from her misery.

"Are you sad 'cause Jake don't wanna be with us no more? 'Cause he don't love us no more?" The pathos in Alexa's voice smacked Gemma in the heart.

"Sweetheart, Jake loves you very much." She brushed the newly trimmed curls off the little girl's forehead.

"Then why din't he come with us on our picnic?" Alexa demanded.

"He said he's too busy today," Gemma excused though she knew it wasn't the truth.

"Jake's not busy. I heard him talking to that Mr. Billy, tellin' him he was coming for coffee 'cause he was bored." Big tears rolled down her cheeks. "I prayed an' prayed like the aunties tole me, but Jake don't like me no more. That's why he's going away."

"Jake is leaving?" Gemma's heart sank. "When?"

"I dunno." Alexa sniffed. "But I heard the aunties say he's running. I thought he liked it at The Haven. I thought he liked me. But why does he wanna go 'way if he does?"

Truth time.

"It's not you he wants to get away from, honey. It's me," she admitted. "Jake and I had a disagreement."

"You fighted?" Alexa frowned. "How come?"

"It wasn't exactly a fight." Gemma sighed, searching for the right words. "I said something he didn't like so now he's staying away from me."

"Did you talk 'bout his little boy?" Alexa asked and sighed when Gemma nodded. "He don't like it when I talk 'bout Thomas neither. This morning I seed him lookin' at a picture of a baby, maybe like Thomas. Jake was sad, so I gave him a hug. I tol' him God and me loved him and that you did, too."

"I'm sure he liked the hug, sweetie, but why did you say that about me?"

"'Cause it's true. You do love Jake. I knowed it," she said simply. "Mommy tole me you can always tell when somebody loves somebody by how they act. Jake 'n you act like you love each other."

"I do love Jake, Alexa, but he doesn't love me." Man, it hurt to say that.

"Does so." Alexa planted her hands on her hips.

"No, sweetie." Gemma knew Alexa wasn't convinced. "He told me he can't love me. I guess he's still too sad about his family dying."

"Uh-uh." The little girl stubbornly shook her head. Then she flopped down in the tall grass. She grabbed a stem to chew on. "Jake loves you lots, Gem."

I wish. But after much prayer and consultations with her aunts, Gemma had finally accepted that she didn't belong here, didn't belong with Jake. No matter how much she wished she did.

"I knowed he loves you when I seed him put our flowers in that jar on your table." Alexa nodded at her surprised look. "An' I knowed it when he moved those benches around the fire so everybody could see your pictures more better. An' when he went huntin' for that ribbon you lost outta your hair yesterday, I knowed it, too. Jake loves you lots."

"As a friend," Gemma said, nonplused by the child's observations. "That's all. Can I explain something to you, sweetie?"

She waited for Alexa's nod while searching for a way to tell this very precious child that she'd decided to leave The Haven and resume her career of traveling the world. But she couldn't bring herself to do it. Alexa might think Gemma had stopped loving her, too, and she didn't want to hurt the child.

Instead she taught the little girl a game that tired them both so much, they happily plodded back to The Haven to enjoy an afternoon snack. Alexa stuck close by her side, clinging to her hand and refusing to join the other kids, as she'd recently begun to do.

Later that night, after Gemma had finished her presentation, she tucked Alexa into bed, listened to her prayers and kissed the little girl good-night. She was sitting in the shadowed corner of the patio, staring at the stars, when she noticed Jake sneak into the house. She knew he was going to see Alexa. He did every night.

How could she leave here, leave Jake and Alexa, the two people who, along with her aunts and her sisters, were now an integral part of her world? How would Alexa manage without someone to love her, to constantly assure her that she was not alone, that she belonged?

How would Gemma face days and nights alone, always on the outside, always wishing she belonged to someone? To Jake.

"Please make Your will clear to me," she prayed silently. "If I must leave, show me how to tell Alexa so she won't be hurt. And please, be with Jake. He needs You now more than he ever has."

Gemma sat praying until long after Jake had left, long after the moon had slid across the sky to give way to the first pink rays of dawn. When she finally rose and went to her room, her heart ached no less.

I could have belonged here, with Jake, she said to herself. *Will I ever belong anywhere?*

Chapter Thirteen

As it turned out, having Sweetie the cow wasn't as bad as Jake had thought. She listened to him rant without comment or argument the entire time he cleaned her barn. Her one failure was that she had no advice to offer.

"So you think I should go? I mean, The Haven has been home for a long time. I hate to leave the aunts, especially after all they've done for me."

Sweetie swung her head from side to side.

"You don't? You know there are tons of helpers with this ministry now and any one of them could do what I do, especially feed you. The thing is—Gem's here. If I stay I know I won't be able to keep that vow. She's dug herself into my heart."

Sweetie mooed.

"Yeah. You're right. I do need to leave. I'll tell the aunts today and plan to take off on the weekend. It will be better for Gem that way."

"Who are you talkin' to, Jake?" Alexa's high-pitched voice inquired as she peeked around the barn door. "An' what's better for Gem?"

He couldn't tell her the truth. She'd blab and things

would get very uncomfortable. To divert her attention, Jake handed her an apple to feed the cow.

"Aren't you going riding today?" he asked.

"Yep. That's why I got my boots on." Alexa stuck out her foot to show him. Then she asked, "Are you still mad at Gem?"

"I was never mad at Gemma, Alexa." He smiled at the little girl who'd wiggled her way into his heart. "We just disagree on some things."

"Mommy said that if you love someone you look for ways to make you both happy," she said sagely. "You're makin' Gem sad."

"I wish I could fix that, honey, but I can't," Jake said.

"I know." She exhaled a heavy sigh. "'Cause you're sad, too. I gotta pray 'bout you both some more, I guess."

"You've been praying for Gemma and me?" he asked in surprise.

"O' course." She gave him her *Alexa* look, the one that was both stern and sweet. "Don't you?"

"I guess." Though he'd muttered some type of prayer for himself and Gemma individually many times, he'd never thought of praying for their joint concerns—as a couple.

Why don't you try talking to God again?

What he'd been doing could hardly be called praying.

"There's the whistle. I gotta go get on the bus." Alexa reached her arms up to him for a hug.

Jake bent, throat constricting as her chubby hands stretched around his neck and pulled him close. He held her tenderly, as if she was a fragile butterfly.

"See you later, honey," he managed to say while his brain drew pictures of what Thomas might have been like at this age. He wondered whether his son would have hugged his dad so tightly.

"I love you, Jake." Alexa pressed a kiss against his cheek. "Kurt tol' me we gotta make sure to say that 'cause you never know when you won't see somebody again." She eyed him with a stern look. "You're not goin' away 'fore I finish riding, are you?"

She knew he was leaving? Shocked, Jake shook his head.

"Good. 'Cause I got things I needa tell you." Alexa fluttered a hand and then raced away.

Jake sank onto a bale and tried to sort out his whirling thoughts.

Why don't you try talking to God again?

"God? Are You there?" Silly question. God was always there. "I haven't really talked to You in a long time. I've pretended to. I've yelled at You." He paused. "I've missed You. I miss them."

The tears fell and for once he let them, let the sorrow fill his heart.

"I can barely remember them," he whispered. "I have to keep looking at their pictures to remind myself. Is that love?"

"Yes, Jake, it is." Aunt Tillie sat on the bale next to him, her voice gentle and comforting. "When we love someone and they pass away, all we have left are memories. We still cherish them, of course, always will. But eventually we have to move on with our lives, into our future. Because clinging to the past stops us from experiencing all the wonder that God has planned for us."

"But I loved them," he protested.

"Of course you did, dear. And they loved you. But they're gone now. Not forgotten, just gone." She studied him with an intensity that made Jake uncomfortable. "Would Lily want you to be stuck in the past, to never experience love again? To never know the love of another child?"

"You don't understand," he muttered. "I promised."

"You promised never to love anyone again?" Tillie shook her head. "You said that out of some feeling that it could atone for them dying, Jake. Because you blame yourself for their deaths. That is very wrong of you," she said sternly.

"Wrong?" He jerked upright and stared at her. "Why?"

"Because when we're God's children, He is in charge of everything. He's God." Tillie's voice softened. "The name *Adonai* is a name for God that means Lord, Master. You don't question your lord and master."

"I guess not." Jake tried to assimilate that.

"From the little you've told Margaret and me, Lily loved God. He decided she and Thomas would be better off with Him. As our Lord, He has the right to decide what happens in our lives, even if it means taking our loved ones. But that doesn't mean He abandoned you." She folded her hands in her lap, her face placid. "I think God brought love into your life when you came to The Haven."

These aunties... They always seemed to see beneath to the root of the problem. Jake wasn't sure how to respond.

"You've loved Gemma for a long time, haven't you?" she murmured.

What was the point in denying it?

"Yes."

"Yes. And because she loved Kurt back then she was no threat to your self-imposed isolation. Now she is because she loves you, and that demands a response. Your response is to run." Tillie patted his hand as if to reassure him. "I do believe Gemmie truly loves you, Jake. It's not a reaction to all she's gone through. It's not a whim or a flight of fancy. She cares deeply about you."

"Gemma told you this?"

"She didn't have to, dear. It's written all over her face when she sees you, talks about you." The older woman's smile warmed his spirit. "Her eyes light up as brightly as a thousand stars. Her whole demeanor changes when she sees you. She plans things with you in mind. She shares your outreach to the needy in Chokecherry Hollow because she enjoys it, of course. But also because she loves being with you, working with you. Gemma loves *you*."

"She can't," Jake blurted.

"Not that you saying that alters her love one whit," Tillie reminded with a chuckle. "But why can't she?"

"Because I'm leaving The Haven." He let it hang there for a moment, surprised by how sad those words made him feel.

"I guessed that would be your reaction." Tillie sighed. "The Haven's been your home for six years. We've been very blessed to have you. You've done so much to make our lives easier, as well as many in our surrounding area. We've all come to count on you, Jake. You've been a rich and special blessing." Tillie's words were gentle, yet oddly unemotional.

"Thank you," he murmured, moved by her comments.

"If you now feel God is leading you away from here, we will miss you greatly, but we will send you forward into new experiences with our blessings and a promise to pray for you."

"I appreciate that." A hollow sensation filled his gut that Aunt Tillie didn't argue, didn't try to persuade him not to go. "I'll leave on Saturday. Can you please keep it quiet until after I've left? I don't want anyone to know."

"Because you don't want to face Gemma's tears. Or Alexa's. You think that if you pass quietly into the night, that will make it easier for them." Tillie shook her head. "It won't. It might make it easier for you, but it will only leave them with a lot of unanswered questions. Still, if that is your decision, Margaret and I will abide by it."

"Thank you." The older woman rose. So did Jake.

"We love you, Jake. We have from that first day we saw you sitting on the corner of that street in Edmonton. You were contemplating suicide, weren't you?"

He blinked. "How did you know?"

"It's a God thing." She shrugged. "May I say one more thing?"

"Of course." *Please don't talk about Gemma. It hurts too much.*

"Promise me that you'll seek God, find out if this truly is the plan He has in mind for you or if you're simply running away again, just like you did after your family's deaths."

"Hey!" Jake burst out angrily. "I didn't run away."

"Didn't you, dear?" Tillie's sage look bugged him. "I think you started running the day you chose to make that vow and I don't believe you've stopped since. But sooner or later God will have to stop your self-destruction. Because He loves you. I pray that happens before you throw away everything precious He's given you. You belong at The Haven, Jake. I hope you come to see that. We love you."

After a tender embrace, Tillie left. Sometime later the lunch bell rang, but Jake ignored it, just like he ignored the self-doubts that now filled him. Tillie was mistaken. He hadn't been wrong to make that vow to Lily. He owed it to her memory not to risk Gemma's life by loving her.

Desperate to be rid of the merry-go-round of questions, Jake focused on finishing the chores he'd left till 'sometime.' He wanted everything in order before he left. It was the least he could do for the sweet aunties.

He was almost finished repairing a section of the garden fence when the weather warning chimed on his phone. With chagrin he read about a severe storm approaching the area including The Haven. Dangerously high winds and fierce rain were predicted. Perhaps hail. He called Victoria.

"Yes, I got it. We need to gather all the kids inside The Haven. Now," she said.

"Okay, I'll do a run, chase whomever I find to the house. The riding group?" he asked, thinking of Alexa.

"They just returned." That response relieved his worry until she continued. "There's a hiking group in the valley that I can't reach. They're probably exploring the old cave. Can you take the quad and ensure they get back safely? I'll start checking off names so we know who else is still missing."

"Gemma could help me with that." Always she was there in his head, his mind, his heart.

"She's not here. I think she's looking through some stuff Alexa's social worker sent today. I'll find her. Be safe."

"You, too, Vic. See you in a bit."

Jake drove the four-wheeler toward the hiking trails. Fortunately the hiking group's leader had received the warning and was leading them home though they struggled to hurry against the now very brisk wind.

Jake loaded the three slowest kids on his quad and tailed the group until they arrived safely at The Haven. He helped gather other stragglers to safety, made sure Sweetie was sheltered securely in the barn and chased the aunts' rescue dogs, Spot and Dot, into the house.

Jake was almost finished securing the patio furniture when Alexa yelled at him through the open kitchen window. He hurried inside and locked the window.

"Honey, you can't open the windows. The wind's—"

"Gem's not here, Jake," the little girl sobbed. "We gotta go find her."

"You can't go out in this wind, Alexa. It's too dangerous. There's stuff flying all over." He tamped down his fears and bent to her level. "Tell me when you last saw her."

"When we comed back on the bus from riding, I seed her walking. She was far away. She din't hear me call her." Alexa's tears washed her white face. "I thought she'd come back but she din't. Victoria says it's a really bad storm. We gotta go find Gemma."

His heart in his throat, Jake texted Victoria. She replied she hadn't seen her sister. Jake's worry ramped up. But one peek out the window showed debris whirling crazily, ripping flowers and bushes out of the ground. He wasn't taking a child out in that.

"Jake, can you come help us close the shutters in the library? I'm so glad we had them installed inside so we could watch movies. It will keep us safe and help entertain the children." Aunt Margaret went to Alexa and took her hand. "Come on, sweetie. We'll all ask God to keep our Gemmie safe before the movie starts."

Jake helped Olivia secure the library windows so that even if the glass was broken, it would not fall inside and injure a child. When the power failed, he turned on the backup generator that he'd filled earlier. He waited while the entire group prayed for Gemma's safety. The movie started, but it seemed to take a long time for kids to settle. Jake slipped out to the kitchen to ask Adele to make some popcorn, hoping a snack might help take their minds off the storm. It did.

But as the winds whined higher outside, his worries wouldn't quiet. Where was Gemma? Had she received the warning, taken shelter? Was she safe? He needed to find her, but with the ladies and kids huddled inside The Haven, and without the sisters' husbands here to help, Jake couldn't leave. His job was to protect these vulnerable ones, even if it was the last thing he did before he left.

"We've prayed for Gemma, Jake," Margaret murmured as they sat in the kitchen, enjoying the coffee Adele had brewed on the big gas stove. "And we'll continue praying. But we need to talk." Her stern voice brooked no argument.

"About?" *Where is Gemma?*

"About your vow to Lily. Sister told me of your conversation in the barn." Margaret shook her head at him. "I first need to know one thing. Do you truly love Gemma?"

"Yes." Jake couldn't have stopped that response if he'd wanted to. "And I need to find her. Now," he said shoving away his cup. He was halfway risen when Tillie's hand pressed downward.

"God is looking after Gemma. He's looking after all of us." Tillie's tender smile expressed her supreme confidence in her Father. "Even you."

"That vow of yours, Jake. I need to say this." Margaret's frown was fierce. "It was so wrong."

"Huh?" Jake demanded. "Tillie said that, too. Why is it wrong?"

"Because it shows your lack of trust in our heavenly Father and that must wound Him terribly." Margaret leaned forward. "God loves us. We're His children. He doesn't ask us to sacrifice something so we can get back in His good graces after bad things happen. God never asked you to give up loving someone after Lily died."

"No, I made that decision," he agreed. "Because my neglect—"

"Stop that." For the first time since he'd met her, Margaret's eyes flashed with anger. "Were Lily and Thomas not God's children?" Jake nodded. "Then He was their Lord and He was in control of their lives. Not you."

"My dear boy, your vow came from a place of guilt. It wasn't something from God. Why do you think He led us to you, led you to The Haven to help us when we so badly needed help? Why do you think He laid it on your heart to get involved in our community?" Tillie held up a hand, forestalling his objections. "And don't say it's because you're no good at anything else. God gave you specific talents for a specific purpose, my boy. Nothing is random with God. He has a plan. Always."

"Giving up love doesn't help anyone, especially not you." Margaret's softened tone made her comments easier to accept. "Cherishing love and lavishing it on others helps everyone, giver and receiver. Isn't that why you've been helping folks in Chokecherry Hollow, because you feel better for doing it?"

Jake nodded as their words percolated through his brain.

"You love Gemma, don't you?" Margaret asked.

"Yes. But I'm not sure it matters anymore," he mumbled. "She's talking of leaving."

"With God it is never too late." Tillie rested her hand on his shoulder. "You understand now that your vow was your way of keeping your heart safe, don't you?"

"I'm not sure—"

"The Bible says that if we lack wisdom we should ask God and He will give it. Let's do that now."

Jake bowed his head, listening to the sisters pray for him, for Gemma, for everyone at The Haven. As he did, understanding filled his soul until at last the heavy cloak of guilt that had weighed him down for seven long years, quietly melted away.

He didn't have to worry about Lily and Thomas. They were with God. Finally he could let go of the past.

Gemma had spent the most glorious afternoon simply wandering the familiar hills and letting their peace and serenity soothe her aching soul. She finally arrived at her favorite spot, a wooded grove where she'd so often found solace as a teen. Weary in mind and body, and desperate for answers, she sat below the giant spruce and poured out her heart to God.

"Jake cares for me. I know he does." But then she recalled her uncle and how he'd embezzled the funds his own brother had left for his child. If her own blood relative couldn't love her enough to stop his greed, how could anyone else?

In that instant her old nemesis of insecurity took control. *You love The Haven but you don't belong here, not anymore—if you ever did.*

So, telling stories—was that all she was good for?

"What do You want me to do?" she prayed aloud. "I could go back to touring. I'm good at it. I'll have opportunities to talk to people about Your world. They want me back."

But was it where she *belonged*?

"If I stay here, I can be with kids, invite Alexa more often, build a closer relationship with her." *Maybe even adopt her?*

Would that make her belong?

"If I stayed I could make Your world come alive for the kids who come. Maybe help them figure out their futures." *When you can't even figure out your own?*

A crack of lightning roused Gemma from her thoughts. Suddenly aware that the sky was now black and sending a sprinkle of rain, and that the wind was blowing with fierce abandon, she hurried to find shelter in the cleft of a rocky promontory. There, protected from the elements, she leaned her back against the granite and watched the storm play out in front of her, amazed at the awesome power and strength of the elements.

The turbulence was breathtaking. It made her feel small and insignificant, a mere speck in the chaos around her. Which she was. And yet God was in control. He wasn't upset or confused or worried by the storm. He knew just how much the trees in front of her could bend and sway in the gale-force winds without breaking.

In an instant He could stop those spears of lightning and end the sheets of white hail spewing from the heavens. He knew exactly how long it would take for the barrage of frozen stones to melt and turn to rivers that gushed downward.

Gemma felt like she stood in the middle of a crazy whirlwind that was wreaking havoc, and yet it was all under God's control. Just as the earthquake had been.

Then it was over.

Gemma remained transfixed as the first colors of a rainbow snuck across the sky and spread into multicolored glistening ribbons. The arch somehow echoed the memory of a song. Her mother's song, she suddenly realized. She could almost hear that long-silenced voice crooning the words of her favorite hymn.

This is my Father's world.

Yes, He was in control of everything. Yes, He'd saved her from an earthquake and yes, He'd brought her home. Because The Haven *was* home. This *was* where Gemma belonged. Her travels had shown her the glories of her Father's world so she could share it with kids who needed to hear of His love. She wasn't giving up anything. She was stepping into a whole new challenge, one God had given her. Because He believed in her.

Yes, she loved Jake with her whole heart. She desperately wanted him to love her. But that was in God's hands, too. Just as He managed the wind and the rain, and the rainbow, so He could be trusted to manage her future. If she was not to be with Jake, then she would, with His help, learn to deal with that.

Because not only was she home at The Haven, she was at home in God.

Gemma stepped out into the sun and lifted her face to the heavens.

"I will trust in You," she said, loud and strong and firm.

Then she began walking toward The Haven.

And Jake.

Chapter Fourteen

Jake struggled without success to get Alexa to stop crying. Finally, so she wouldn't disturb the other children, he took her up to her room.

"What are all these boxes?" he asked, easing one out of the way so he could set the little girl on her bed.

"Mommy's an' my stuff. Gem was gonna help me make a book." And off she went again, crying for Gemma.

The ladies were all busy managing things downstairs. It was up to him to handle this. Jake knelt in front of Alexa and cupped her chin in his.

"Want to hear my idea?"

She sniffed and nodded.

"I think you and I should begin this book as a surprise for Gemma when she comes back." He glanced around as if he was confused and didn't know how to begin. "Do you want all this stuff in your book?"

"No, silly. Jus' pictures." She brushed away the tears with the back of her hand and then hunkered down on the carpet, peeking into each box until she came to the last one. "Mommy made this book. It's a baby book.

See. That's me." Alexa seemed to forget Gemma as she pointed out herself at varying ages.

But Jake couldn't forget. He kept glancing out the window, not wanting to think of Gem caught in the midst of that terrifying wind. He prayed desperately that she'd found a safe place to hide.

"My mommy's really pretty, isn't she?" Alexa's fingers traced a woman's face.

"She's beautiful, sweetheart. I think hers should be the first picture." Fortunately someone, probably Gemma, had left a new photograph album on the small desk by the window. Jake handed Alexa a glue stick. "You put it where you think it looks best."

Now totally involved, Alexa took the glue stick, opened the album and began gluing picture after picture, carefully placing each on a page. She asked him to print the names underneath.

"In case I forget," she said sadly.

"I don't think you'll forget, sweetheart," he reassured. "But even if you do, you can always look here and remember."

"Yeah." She chuckled at the next snapshot. "Kurt din't fly my kite good. It crashed. He was gonna gived me a new one." Her face fell. "Now he can't."

"I can. You and I will pick one out tomorrow. Okay?" Why had he tried to shelve his memories? Suddenly he wanted to retrieve the photo albums Lily had so carefully assembled. He needed to see her lovely face and Thomas's grumpy frown and remember the joy they'd brought to his world.

"Are you still sad, Jake?" Alexa leaned her head on his arm.

"Not really," he said and realized it was true. He felt

blessed that he'd been able to share their lives, even if only for such a short time. "I was just thinking about Thomas and trying to remember what he looked like."

"Don'cha got no pictures?" she demanded.

"Yes, sweetheart, I do." Jake lifted her onto his lap and hugged her.

"Where?" Alexa wasn't about to give up. "I wanna see. You seed mine."

"I have them put away in a box," he explained.

"Well, that's silly." She shook her head. "How you gonna remember 'em if you keep 'em in a box?" She released a heavy sigh. "Sometimes I think grownups are kinda dumb."

"Me, too," he agreed.

As soon as the storm was over, Jake was going to open that box and take out that family picture. Every time he looked at it, he'd remind himself of how blessed he'd been to have such a wonderful chapter in the book of his life.

That's when Jake realized that his story wasn't over. There were more pages to come in his life-album, another chapter he needed to include because he'd been blessed again by love. It didn't compete with Lily, just as Gemma's love for Kurt didn't compete with hers for him. Each was beautiful in and of itself. Jake could accept that now. It was like his rosebushes. One branch might die, but life returned on another branch, and if treated properly, it flourished and produced wonderful roses.

He could hardly wait to tell Gemma of his newly garnered understanding.

Alexa had been repeatedly dabbing the glue stick

and plopping photos onto each page. But suddenly she stopped.

"This is my 'nother fav'rite," she whispered. "See how Gem's smiling?"

"I sure do." Jake remembered the occasion as if it was yesterday. The three of them were trying to get Sweetie to go into the barn. Successive failed attempts had sent Gemma into peals of laughter. "I think it's my 'nother fav'rite, too," Jake whispered.

"'Cause you love Gem." Alexa nodded. "I knowed it a long time ago," she said wisely and patted his cheek. Then her eyes widened. "Hey, lookit, Jake. The sun's shinin'. The storm's all done."

Someone called up the stairs for them to come outside.

Jake walked with Alexa out to the lawn where they had the best vantage point of the valley and the Rockies beyond. Among children and adults, with Alexa's hand clasped in his, Jake gazed at the beautiful rainbow stretching across the sky.

Thank you, Father. Peace calmed his soul. Yet still his heart asked, *Where is Gemma?*

As Jake scanned his surroundings and absorbed the amount of damage the storm had wreaked, fear began to move in. Broken branches littered the ground, along with shingles ripped off damaged outbuilding roofs. Had she been hit by one of them? Flower pots had been sent tumbling in the wind and now lay smashed in scattered shards, with dirt oozing out. Several outbuildings would require extensive repair, including the shed that had housed Gem's belongings such a short time ago.

It didn't matter because Jake would be here to do it all, with God's help.

"I have to go hunt for Gemma now," he told Alexa.

"Nope, you don't gotta." She giggled.

"Why not?" He frowned as he followed her pointing finger. For a moment his heart sank to his toes. His garden was a mess of balled-up fencing and uprooted plants. The entire area had been decimated by the wind and the hail. The greenhouse lay a flattened ruin of shattered glass, his roses crushed.

"She's there," Alexa squealed.

That's when Jake spotted Gemma crouched beside the broken stalks of corn, her long hair tumbling over her shoulders, dirt sifting through her fingers as she examined the carnage.

Thank you, God.

"Wait here, Alexa," he said sternly. "I need to make sure the glass didn't blow around."

"'Kay. But hurry 'cause I think she's cryin'."

Jake raced toward Gemma, fighting the fear threatening to fill his soul until he remembered the aunts' words. God was in charge.

"Gem?"

"It's ruined," she sobbed, lifting her head to stare at him. Her gorgeous green eyes brimmed with tears. "All your hard work and Alexa's pretty flowers. The raspberry canes you started, the peas the kids were going to pick tomorrow and the roses—the poor roses. There's nothing left of them. I'm so sorry, Jake."

"They'll grow again, Gem. This was just a pruning." Slowly, tenderly, Jake slid his fingers under her elbow and drew her upright to hold her in front of him. "Look at the rainbow," he whispered in her ear. "Look at the promise God's given us. Not that bad things won't happen. But that He will be there with us through all of it."

She turned to face him, eyes dark with confusion. "Don't you care about the garden?"

"We can plant again, Gem. We'll clean this up, rake the soil and start over. Isn't that what life is about? Renewal." The confident words came easily to him now.

"I—I don't understand."

Her confused whisper touched his heart. Jack wrapped his arms around her and smiled, finally free to open his heart.

"I do. I was like that garden. I felt like I'd been ripped up and torn open. I was sure nothing could ever grow in my heart again." Seeing the barrenness of his life with new perspective shocked Jake. "But God the gardener has been working on me, showing me that I was wallowing in my own loss instead of depending on Him to help me get through it."

"I—I..." She gave up and simply studied him, waiting.

"I love you, Gemma. I have for a very long time, though I couldn't accept it, couldn't see it as anything but a betrayal of Lily because I'd let guilt take over my mind." He shook his head. "I was going to run away from here, try to bury my unhappiness." He smiled. "I may eventually leave, but only if you're going, too. God will have to move us together because I intend to be wherever you are, sharing His love, reaching out to other people."

"Say all of it," she murmured when he paused.

"I want to marry you, Gem. I want us to adopt Alexa because she belongs with us. I want us to make a home here or nearby, close enough that we can continue to be part of The Haven's amazing ministry, part of the community." Jake let the dream expand in his mind. "Kids need love. Everyone needs God's love. We all need to understand the power of that love to work in us and through us so we can help others."

Gemma's continued silence was nerve-racking.

"Aren't you going to say anything?" he finally demanded, exasperated.

"Darling Jake." Her hand lifted so her fingers could trace the lines of his face. "I love you so much. I love the way you put people first, the way you cherish Alexa, my family and every single kid who comes to this place. I would be honored to marry you and continue working with you. We've proven, have we not, that we are a pretty amazing partnership?"

"You're sure?" But Jake saw the truth on her face.

"Doubting me already?"

"Never." He bent his head and kissed her, trying to infuse all his hopes and dreams for their future together into that embrace. He must have succeeded, because Gemma kissed him back, fully, completely, her response more wonderful than anything he could have ever dared dream. When they finally drew apart, Jake tilted back to get a better look at her face.

"Tell me," he said simply.

"I was watching the storm from this cave, marveling at God's awesome power. Then it was over and suddenly I just knew that staying at The Haven is God's plan for me, whether or not you were here." Her arms tightened around his neck. "I love you dearly, but I had to trust you to God, my darling Jake, if I wanted to be able to give back just a small portion of what He's blessed me with."

She kissed him once more and Jake couldn't have cared less that kids and adults alike were applauding.

"I'm sorry it took me so long to figure out who's in charge in this world," he murmured, loving the silken length of her hair in his fingers.

"Time God used very well," Gem reminded. "So don't regret it. Let's embrace our future with full hearts." She touched his cheek. "We must adopt Alexa. Kurt would be so happy to see his precious little girl in our family. Together we'll make sure she always knows she's loved. As I will you, my darling Jake."

"And I you." He kissed her again. Then he took her hand and led her through the tangled mess and out the gate to where Alexa waited.

"You sure kiss a lot," the little girl charged grumpily as she clung to Gemma's legs. "Everything got ruined and you're happy 'bout it."

"No, sweetie." Jake hunkered down to her level and brushed his lips against her cheek. "We're happy because we love each other and we're getting married and we want to adopt you as our daughter." He grinned at her. "Is that okay with you?"

"So I c'n stay here forever?" Alexa's big blue eyes glanced from him to Gemma, who nodded. Alexa squealed with joy, until she noticed the garden. "But what 'bout my flowers?"

"They'll come back, sweetheart. They're perennials," he explained. "That means they keep seeding each year so new flowers can grow."

"It's just like God's promises," Gemma added. "That's what the rainbow means, that God will always love us, always be here to help us."

"I'm stayin' here." Alexa hugged herself. Then, after a last mournful look at her dying flowers, she slid her tiny hands into theirs. "C'n we 'dopt other kids? I like

Charlotte an' Benjamin best, but maybe Jordan would be a good brother. An' David's nice." She kept listing children she thought would make great siblings.

Jake grinned at Gemma.

"So this is what it's going to be like," he murmured.

"Uh-huh." Her megawatt smile lit up her face. "Isn't it wonderful?"

"Yep." He threw her a sly grin. "If we're going to adopt all these kids we'd better get married soon. Tomorrow?"

They negotiated the deal later that evening, on the patio. Without onlookers.

Chapter Fifteen

Gemma Andrews married Jake Elliot on the third Saturday in August. It was supposed to be an intimate wedding with only family and friends.

Turned out, the couple had a lot of friends.

From far and wide, folks who'd been touched by or helped by the couple's community outreach kept visiting The Haven. Each came laden with lush potted plants, cut flowers and beautiful hanging baskets that transformed the ravaged area into a gorgeous wedding venue. Even the garden looked spectacular because Gemma's sisters had transformed it by having their husbands lay artificial turf and add an airy white gazebo.

On the morning of the wedding all was ready. Among stalks of vibrant gladioli which Billy had cut fresh from Ethel's garden, rows of white chairs waited for guests, joined by satin ropes and bows in Gemma's favorite shade of blue—to match her fiancé's eyes. In front, the wedding gazebo was swathed in fluffy white tulle, with fragrant lily of the valley and ferns adding a touch of color and scent. Here the couple would say their vows.

Of course the aunts knew someone who knew someone, and a stringed quartet softly played in one corner, the lovely strains of Beethoven filling the mountain air.

When everything was ready, Jake walked down the aisle and took his place at the gazebo entrance among his soon-to-be brothers-in-law, to wait for his bride.

"Excuse me, Jake," the pastor whispered. "But is that cow with the, er, blue bow supposed to be there?"

"Yes." Jake stifled his laughter and explained. "Alexa wanted Sweetie nearby so she could watch. Don't worry. Sweetie's tied up."

"Okay then." The pastor cleared his throat as a signal to begin.

Gemma's nieces and nephews tromped down the aisle, scattering—actually throwing—rose petals. Alexa reminded Jake of Little Bo Peep as she tried to direct them, much like one would herd sheep. His soon-to-be daughter was thrilled with her fluffy blue party dress and new white shoes and she made sure everyone noticed them.

Once the children were seated on the turf on either side of the gazebo, Victoria led the walk toward Jake, followed by Adele and then Olivia. Beside their handsome husbands, the ladies looked beautifully elegant in their floaty summer-blue dresses, which were perfect, Gemma had assured him, for a casual summer wedding.

Jake could hardly wait to see her.

At a signal from the pastor, the quartet launched into the wedding song just as Gemma emerged from a nearby white tent. Aunt Tillie and Aunt Margaret walked with her on either side, their hands looped through her elbows. Their faces glowed with pride and love.

Jake caught his breath.

Gemma was stunning in a simple ankle-length white chiffon sundress that swirled and billowed around her sandaled feet in the warm summer breeze. She carried the wildflowers some of The Haven's guest children had found in the woods earlier this morning. Her long hair had been drawn off her face by a band of pearls and left to cascade down her back in a wash of auburn beauty. Sweet Gemma. She made his heart stop.

When the threesome reached Jake, the aunts passed her hand to his, their smiles beaming through the tears filling their eyes.

"We love you both," Margaret whispered.

"So does God," Tillie added.

After sweet embraces, the ladies took their seats in the front row, next to Billy and Ethel who now claimed the title of matchmakers by assuring the entire town of Chokecherry Hollow that they'd brought Gemma and Jake together.

"You're beautiful, Gem," Jake murmured for Gemma's ears alone. "I love you."

"I love you, Jake."

There, among those who'd watched them overcome doubt and heartache, the couple said their vows, promising to love each other for the rest of their lives and to serve God in whatever path He directed. They sealed their promises with a kiss that seemed far too brief to Jake, though Alexa disagreed.

"How come it always takes 'em so long for kissin', Aunt Tillie?"

The pastor cleared his throat.

"At the couple's request, I will now read the twenty-third Psalm." The pastor began the familiar words. "'The Lord is my Shepherd...'"

Jehovah Raah. Another of God's names. Gemma smiled at Jake. Together they'd follow their shepherd wherever He led.

"Fellow guests, it is my honor to present to you, Mr. and Mrs. Elliot."

Gemma and Jake walked down the aisle, hands clasped, hearts locked, ready to enjoy this day and their future. Together.

Just before they left for their honeymoon, Tillie and Margaret gathered their family together.

"Isn't it just like God to give us The Haven to use for His work and then to bring all of our dear girls home and provide husbands who are perfectly equipped to help us carry on The Haven's ministries?" Margaret said.

"It's the best legacy we could pass on," Tillie agreed tearfully.

Later, Jake and Gemma were showered with rice as he helped her into his truck.

"For we know that all things work together for good for those who are called according to His purpose," Jake recited as he drove away. "We are being made into the image of His son. I get it now. This is our haven, too. Right, Gem?"

"I've traveled all over the world, but The Haven's where I belong, my darling," she agreed. "With you."

* * * * *

If you enjoyed this story, pick up the other
Rocky Mountain Haven books.

Meant-To-Be Baby
Mistletoe Twins
Rocky Mountain Daddy

And these other stories from Lois Richer:

The Rancher's Family Wish
Her Christmas Family Wish
The Cowboy's Easter Family Wish
The Twins' Family Wish
A Dad for Her Twins
Rancher Daddy
Gift-Wrapped Family
Accidental Dad

Available now from Love Inspired!
Find more great reads at www.LoveInspired.com.

Dear Reader,

Thank you for returning to The Haven. I hope you enjoyed Gemma's and Jake's journeys to discover that God's plan is to help us become more like His son.

This was a difficult story to write. Losing that special person in your life is a heart-wrenching road to travel. There can be plenty of roadblocks to recovery when we demand explanations from God. While your heart aches with loss, your soul cries out for reasons why. Not getting them can either shut us down or drive us to overcome and move on to discover His plan. To do that, we must trust.

I'd love to hear from you. Please contact me via my website www.loisricher.com, on Facebook, at loisricher@gmail.com or at Box 639, Nipawin, Sk. Canada. S0E 1E0. I'll do my best to respond quickly.

Until we meet again, I wish you the blessing of a full heart that has not only known but given love, the joy of enriching someone's world just by having you in it and the peace that comes from accepting that whatever happens, He has it under control.

Blessings,

Lois
Richer

Get 4 FREE REWARDS!

We'll send you 2 FREE Books plus 2 FREE Mystery Gifts.

Love Inspired® books feature contemporary inspirational romances with Christian characters facing the challenges of life and love.

FREE Value Over **$20**

"There won't be another bus going that way until the day after tomorrow."

"Are you sure?" Gemma Lapp stared at the agent behind the counter in stunned disbelief.

"Of course I'm sure. I work for the bus company."

She clasped her hands together tightly, praying the tears that pricked the backs of her eyes wouldn't start flowing. She couldn't afford a motel room for two nights.

She wheeled her suitcase over to the bench. Sitting down with a sigh, she moved her suitcase in front of her so she could prop up her swollen feet. After two solid days on a bus she was ready to lie down. Anywhere.

She bit her lower lip to stop it from quivering. She could place a call to the phone shack her parents shared with their Amish neighbors to let them know she was returning and ask her father to send a car for her, but she would have to leave a message.

Any message she left would be overheard. If she gave the real reason, even Jesse Crump would know before she reached home. She couldn't bear that, although she didn't understand why his opinion mattered so much. His stoic face wouldn't reveal his thoughts, but he was sure to gloat when he learned he'd been right about her reckless ways. He had said she was looking for trouble and that she would find it sooner or later. Well, she had found it all right.

No, she wouldn't call. What she had to say was better said face-to-face. She was cowardly enough to delay as long as possible.

She didn't know how she was going to find the courage to tell her mother and father that she was six months pregnant, and Robert Troyer, the man who'd promised to marry her, was long gone.

Don't miss
Shelter from the Storm *by* USA TODAY
bestselling author Patricia Davids,
available September 2019 wherever
Love Inspired® books and ebooks are sold.

www.LoveInspired.com

LIEXP0819

Love Inspired®

Discover wholesome and uplifting stories of faith, forgiveness and hope.

Join our social communities to connect with other readers who share your love!

Sign up for the Love Inspired newsletter at **LoveInspired.com** to be the first to find out about upcoming titles, special promotions and exclusive content.

CONNECT WITH US AT:

Facebook.com/groups/HarlequinConnection

 Facebook.com/LoveInspiredBooks

 Twitter.com/LoveInspiredBks

LISOCIAL2019